COMMUNICATING
IN
JAPANESE

COMMUNICATING IN JAPANESE

by
Hiroyoshi Noto

University Readers
San Diego, CA

Copyright © 2008 by Hiroyoshi Noto.
No part of this publication may be reproduced, stored in a retrieval system, or transmitted, in any form or by any means, without permission in writing from the publisher. University Readers is NOT affiliated with or endorsed by any university or institution.

First published in the United States of America in 2008 by University Readers

Cover design by Monica Hui Hekman

12 11 10 09 08   1 2 3 4 5

Printed in the United States of America

ISBN: 978-1-934269-24-4 (paper)

University Readers
800.200.3908 | www.universityreaders.com

Acknowledgments

　この教科書ができあがるまでに，次の方々から有形無形の援助，批判，励ましを受けた。記して謝意を表したい。(　)内は現在の所属機関

　　　アン・ウェーマイヤー　　　　　　（フロリダ大学，ジャクソンビル校）
　　　スーザン・グリズウォルド　　　　（カリフォルニア大学，デービス校）
　　　ウィリアム・シブリー　　　　　　（シカゴ大学）
　　　三橋真理　　　　　　　　　　　　（コロンビア大学）
　　　宇佐美まゆみ　　　　　　　　　　（ハーバード大学）

　また，かつてシカゴ大学の大学院生で，今はそれぞれの専門領域に進まれた次の方々にも感謝したい。

　　　清水　亮
　　　塩谷弥生
　　　山岡加奈子

　この教科書作成に対する勤務先の東アジア研究センターの経済的援助と，創拓社の方々の貴重な助言がなかったら，この本は形をなさなかったにちがいない。ありがとうございました。さらに，実際にこの教科書を使って，貴重なコメントをくれたかつての学生諸氏にもお礼を申し上げる。

　最後に，多くの日本語教師，言語学者にさまざまの恩恵を受けたことを記して感謝したい。

　　　　　　　　　　　　　　　　　　　　　　　　　　　　　　　　平成三年十一月

　　　　　　　　　　　　　　　　　　　　　　　　　　　　　　　　能登　博義

Table of Contents

Table of Contents

Acknowledgments ··· 5
Introduction ··· 13

List of *Hiragana* ··· 17
List of *Katakana* ··· 18
Consonants＋や, ゆ, よ (semi-vowel[y]＋a, u, o) ································· 19
The Original Chinese Characters for *Hiragana* and *Katakana* ··············· 20
Classroom Instructions ··· 21
Special Symbols and Abbreviations ·· 22

Lesson 1 ·· 1

    Functions   Introducing Oneself: name, major, hometown, school year   6-7
                    (name＋です／といいます)

    Grammar   N1 は N2 です。(N3 です。)
                    私はリーです。二年生です。

Lesson 2 ·· 9

    Functions   Identifying Persons: name, major, hometown, school year   1-1

    Grammar   Questions   N1 は…。
                               N1 は N2 ですか。
               Answering   はい。／ええ, そうです。
                               いいえ, 違います。／いえいえ。

Lesson 3 ·· 17

    Functions   Introducing People   6-7
                    Responding to Introduction   6-8

    Grammar   Negation: (N1 は)N2 じゃありません。
                  Asking and Answering Negative Questions:
                  日本人じゃありませんか。

Note

  The numbers after "Functions" correspond to those in the index. The details of each lesson should be referred to in the list on the first page of the lesson.

目次

Lesson 4 25

    Functions   Identifying Objects   1-1
                        Stating Factual Information   1-2

    Grammar   Demonstrative   これ、それ、あれ、どれ
                                        この、その、あの、どの＋Noun
                  The い-adj.
                  あの車は古いですね。
                  赤い車

Lesson 5 35

    Functions   Greeting   6-1
                        Presenting General Topics   6-4
                        今日はいい天気ですね。
                        Taking Leave   6-2
                        じゃ、また明日。

    Grammar   The な-adj.
                  嫌な天気
                  簡単じゃありませんでした。
                Negation of the い- and な-adj.
                  難しくありませんでした。
                  簡単じゃありませんでした。

Lesson 6 47

    Functions   Seeking Factual Information (Location 1)   1-3
                        Stating Factual Information (Location 1)   1-2

    Grammar   Place＋に（います、あります）
                  Contrastive「は」
                  Substituting a verbal phrase: です

Lesson 7 55

    Functions   Seeking Factual Information (Location 2)   1-3
                        Stating Factual Information (Location 2)   1-2
                        Making/Answering a Telephone Call   8-1／8-2

    Grammar   Locative nouns：上、中、下、前、後ろ、左、右
                  Particle「が」：お願いがあります。
                                きれいな女の人がいます。
                Topical particle「も」：ここにもありません。

Table of Contents

Lesson 8 65

    Functions   Expressing Likes/Dislikes   3-1

                        Stating Factual Information (Time, Days of the week, Numbers)   1-2

    Grammar   Numerals：1～9999
                        Counters：時, 分, 時間, 課, ページ
                        Time expressions＋に／0
                        The plain negative forms＋です
                            ありません   ⇨ないです
                            よくありません   ⇨よくないです
                            学生じゃありません   ⇨学生じゃないです

Lesson 9 75

    Functions   Inquiring About Intentions   2-10
                        Stating Intentions   2-9
                        Reason for Action/Non-Action   2-41

    Grammar   The Use of Verbs——"Will do"
                        Verbs of Motion：行きます, 来ます, 帰ります, でかけます
                        Interrogative word＋か／も…ない
                        Conjunctional particle「から」：S1 から (S2)
                        Kinship terms：父(ちち) vs. お父(とう)さん

Lesson 10 89

    Functions   Stating Factual Information (Habitual/Past Actions)   1-2
                        Seeking Factual Information (Habitual/Past Actions)   1-3

    Grammar   The Use of Verbs——Habitual/Past Actions
                        Adverbs of Frequency
                        Adverbs used with Negative Forms
                        Adverbial use of Adjectives

Lesson 11 103

    Functions   Stating Factual Information (Numbers)   1-2
                        Seeking Factual Information (Numbers)   1-3
                        Expressing Congratulations   6-19
                        Stating Want/Desire   3-16
                        Expressing Need   2-17

    Grammar   Counters：才, 本, 冊, 枚, 箱, 円, 個, 匹
                        Japanese Counting：一つ, 二つ……十
                        Numbers (10,000～)
                        Days of the Month
                        Informal Talk——Talk with friend

目次

Lesson 12 119
 Functions Stating Factual Information (Schedule) 1-2
      Seeking Factual Information (Personal Background) 1-3
      Expressing Likes/Dislikes 3-1

 Grammar Noun Modification with Verbs
      Nominalizer「の」
      Plain forms: Verbs, Adjs., and です

Lesson 13 135
 Functions Requesting Permission 2-22
      Granting Permission 2-21
      Making Requests 5-3
      Apologizing 4-1

 Grammar Uses of て-form (1): with (も) いい, いる, すみません
      S＋ん(の)です

Lesson 14 151
 Functions Extending an Invitation 2-5
      Making Requests 5-3
      Sequencing Communication 7-2

 Grammar Temporal Expressions：S1＋前／時／後／〜てから＋S2
      話し＋にくい／やすい

Lesson 15 167
 Functions Focusing on a Topic 7-3
      Inquiring About a Belief/Opinion 2-34
      Expressing a Belief/Opinion 2-33

 Grammar Uses of て-form(2): with しまう, おく, いる, みる, ある
      S＋方がいい (You should〜): 書き直した方がいい
      Verb Stem＋方 (how to〜/the way of〜)

Lesson 16 183
 Functions Stating Factual Information (Describing appearance) 1-2
      Stating Intentions 2-9
      Inquiring About Intentions 2-10

 Grammar Honorific Expressions
      Noun-Modifiers with Perfect Form
      Plural Modifiers
      S (with Perfect form)＋ことがある〔Experience〕
      Verbs for "Put on/Take off"

Table of Contents

Lesson 17			 199

        Functions   Apologizing   4-1

                        Being Hospitable (Offering Food, Drinks, etc.)   6-13

                        Talking at the Dinner/Cafe/Restaurant Table   6-9

        Grammar   Causes, Reasons

                        Selective Questions

                        て-form＋もらう

Lesson 18 213

        Functions   Stating Generalization   1-5

                        Inquiring About One's Health   6-20

                        Stating Hypothesis   1-4

        Grammar   と，たら，ば

                        （もし）〜なら

Lesson 19 229

        Functions   Introducing Oneself (Formal)   6-7

                        Expressing Capability   2-15

        Grammar   Potential：Nができる

                            Potential forms of Verbs

Lesson 20 245

        Functions   Expressing Pleasure/Likes/Displeasure/Dislikes   3-1

                        Inquiring About Pleasure/Likes/Displeasure/Dislikes   3-2

                        Expressing Possibility   2-13

                        Expressing Capability/Incapability   2-15

        Grammar   Receiving s.t. from s.b.：友達に切符をもらった

                        Desiderative form：が／を＋V stem＋たい

Lesson 21 259

        Functions   Stating Factual Information (Giving and Receiving Things/Favor)   1-2

                        Expressing Certainty/Uncertainty   2-19

                        Stating Hypothesis   1-4

        Grammar   Giving and Receiving Things：あげる，くれる，もらう

                        Giving and Receiving Favors：て＋あげる，くれる，もらう

目次

Lesson 22 275

    Functions   Comparing   2-36
                    Expressing Obligation   2-20
                    Expressing Possibility/Impossibility   2-13
                    Giving Examples   2-47

    Grammar   Comparing Two Things　：〜er
                    Comparing More Than Two Things：〜est
                    S＋かもしれない
                    S＋といけない

Lesson 23 289

    Functions   Stating Factual Information (Change)   1-2
                    Comparing   2-36
                    Inquiring About a Belief/Opinion   2-34

    Grammar   なる，する
                    S みたいだ：Figurative
                                  ：Feeling, Impression
                  〜なくては＋Negative Statement

Lesson 24 307

    Functions   Reporting Information   1-6
                    Passing on Information   7-13
                    Sequencing Communication   7-2
                    Deadline   2-40

    Grammar   Quotation：Direct, Indirect
                    Embedded Questions

Lesson 25 321

    Functions   Giving Directions   5-8
                    Narrating   2-46
                    Seeking Factual Information (Price/Fare)   1-3

    Grammar   Interjection「ね」，「ですね」
                    S と S (Signifying "Discovery")

Lesson 26 333

    Functions   Reporting Information   1-6
                    Describing   2-46

    Grammar   Indicating "Hearsay"：S＋そうだ，って，という話だ，と聞いた
                  V て-form——Adverbial Use
                  Spontaneity: 見える，聞こえる

11

Table of Contents

Lesson 27			347
	Functions	Reporting Information Through the Media	7-15
		Expressing Certainty：降りそう(には見えませんが)	2-19
		Expressing a Belief/Opinion	2-33
	Grammar	降りそう(には見えませんが)	
		S＋ようだ／みたいだ／らしい	

Lesson 28			361
	Functions	Expressing Obligation	2-20
		Taking Leave/Planning to Meet Again	6-2
		Offering Help	6-15
	Grammar	Passive (Introduction)	
		〜しなければ／しないと…いけない／ならない／駄目だ	

Lesson 29			373
	Functions	Giving Examples	2-47
		Giving Orders	5-23
	Grammar	Polite Imperative：授業にちゃんと出なさい	
		：全部するように	
		Passive	
		CL たり(CL たり)する	
		S＋ように(と)言う／頼む	
		Contraction of「〜てしまう」	

Lesson 30			387
	Functions	Telephone Behavior	8-0
	Grammar	敬語	
		Use of です，ます -forms in the middle of a sentence	
		ありまして	
		おいででしたら	

Lesson 31			405
	Functions	Requesting Clarification	7-9
		Requesting Permission	2-22
	Grammar	Causative	
		Two Causative Forms: 行かせる vs. 行かす	
		Causative Passive	

Appendices
Kanji List(漢字表) 422
Japanese-English Glossary(和英索引) 427

はじめに

Introduction

INTENDED USERS AND THE NUMBER OF CLASS HOURS

This textbook is compiled for college students who will study Japanese for the first time. Course work will require approximately 140 to 180 class hours for completion, depending on how many hours students will spend on preparing and reviewing.

It is often said that Japanese is one of the most difficult languages for English speakers together with Arabic, Chinese and Korean. Studies indicate that average students of those languages take two and a half times more class hours to reach intermediate level than their counterparts studying European languages that have some similarities with English — languages such as Spanish, French, Dutch, and so forth.

There does not seem to be any special remedy that can drastically shorten the time needed to achieve this level other than studying on a daily basis.

THE GOAL: THE LEVELS IN THE FOUR SKILLS THAT ONE CAN HOPE TO ATTAIN

After studying Japanese with this textbook for a year, a student can hope to achieve the following:

[Speaking and Listening]

A student can expect to be able not only to use the memorized expressions but also to create individual expressions to cope with basic, daily situations. He/she can offer and request personal and factual information and talk about familiar topics. Switching from formal to informal speech can be achieved with reasonable ease.

[Reading and Writing]

The student should able to read and write simple memos and notices as well as compose personal letters. The student is still dependent on prepared materials and can understand grammatical and relational details of those materials. Short authentic texts can be understood with the use of a dictionary or supplements.

THE GOALS OF THE LESSONS

The most important grammatical and functional goals of each lesson are shown in the table of contents. Goals of secondary importance are shown on the first page of each lesson together with those that are most essential.

The term "functions" in this book needs some explanation. A function is the intended meaning

Introduction

of a speaker's utterance. If your roommate, for instance, asks you if it is hot outside, you may say, "It's hot." In this example, you are "stating factual information." But using the same phrase on a person who thoughtlessly opens a window of an air-conditioned room would mean something entirely different; it would essentially be a "request" not to open the window. The two sentences differ in function, and the context is responsible for the distinction. Thus, students must be conscious of contexts and functions.

The functions catalogue is given at the end of this textbook.

BASIC IDEAS OF THIS TEXTBOOK

[Accuracy and Appropriateness]

This textbook emphasizes the "communicative approach" and, thus, pays a great deal of attention to communication between people by using the following four skills: speaking, writing, listening, and reading. In other words, a student who uses this textbook is expected to recognize the language, and more importantly, to be able to use it in its appropriate context. He/she must show active participation in class; he/she should actively use the language to talk with and listen to fellow students. Sometimes classmates will be able to offer mutual aid in learning language. Using this approach, a student will be given various language excercises in Japanese so that he/she can express himself or herself with acceptable fluency.

At the same time, this book recognizes that "accuracy" is of prime importance in dealing with grammar and other rules such as appropriateness of usage. Language teachers are in general agreement that acquiring accuracy on this level is of absolute necessity for a student to improve his or her skills on the upper levels.

Nobody can deny the importance of making grammatical sentences. It is also undeniably essential, however, to learn to use these grammatically correct sentences in discussing a special topic, under particular circumstances, with a specific person. Imagine, for example, that a teacher in class asks a student, "May I ask you a question?" and the student answers, "Yes, you may." The student's answer is grammatical but not socially acceptable. The student must know the appropriate response in such cases. To sum up, the ability to make a grammatical sentence is no more than a part of the entire communicative ability, and students must pay attention to the "appropriateness of the utterances in its context."

[Drills and Exercises]

Based on this basic premise of accuracy and appropriateness, the drills presented to the students will be divided into two parts. First, there are drills used to acquire accuracy. These drills are contained in the textbook. Second, there are exercises that are to be done in class with classmates. They are not included in the textbook because the exercises should reflect real communication; in such instances it is difficult to predict the content of a speaker's utterance. In other words, there is an "**information gap**" between a speaker and a hearer; one of them has some information, which the other does not. To set up the situation where there is the "information gap," some exercises are excluded from the textbook. They can be found in the teacher's guide.

[The Role of the Textbook in Class]

As clearly seen above, this textbook may be said to be a main text or primary source of drills; however it is not the only source. Students need a different variety of drill in class after they undergo drills for accuracy at home. This means that the textbook can work on a full scale when accompanied by supplementary exercises in class.

[The Roles of the Teachers and Students]

The roles of the teachers and students in this method of learning differ from the those of traditional roles. The teacher facilitates the learning of students, and the students are responsible for their own work.

[Cultural Aspects]

The cultural aspects of the Japanese language are downplayed in this textbook. Studying cultural elements of a language becomes increasingly productive in the level when students can manipulate appropriate words and expressions. Thus, at the beginner's level, it is most fruitful to concentrate on the basic language skills and cultural elements that are found in sections of the main texts and drills. In principle, therefore, the situations related to culture in this textbook are limited to those that students are likely to encounter in their daily life. Students may meet Japanese businessmen or students living in their community with whom they may wish to talk in Japanese. Although there are some exceptions, this is the basic premise of the situations that are set up in this textbook.

[*Kanji* (Chinese Characters)]

A special note is in the order of presentation of *kanji*, Chinese Characters, in this textbook. The reader should be aware that this work contains more *kanji* than any other published textbook available to the English speaker.

Kanji is frequently referred to as the big obstacle that makes learning Japanese overwhelmingly difficult for the students and eventually leads them to forgo their studies.

If students of Japanese intend to read Japanese newspapers, academic papers, and magazines, they must take three or four years to thoroughly learn about two thousand characters. They must know one thousand for recognition and another thousand for writing. To learn this many *kanji*, students must necessarily foster a systematic and effective learning routine. In the second or intermediate level, after accumulating the knowledge of *kanji* in the elementary level, students will not find it burdensome to study them in a systematic fashion.

Beginning students must be acquainted with some *kanji* at the elementary level so that they may use them with great facility in the future. There are about three hundred and fifty in this textbook for writing and two hundred and eighty words for recognition. The underlying idea for the decision to introduce *kanji* at this early stage is that if one cannot avoid a difficult task, one had better start as soon as possible to overcome it rather than postpone it to a later time.

Memorizing eighty percent of *kanji* correctly should be considered satisfactory.

Introduction

[Spiral Way of Presentation]

The grammar points and functions are presented several times in various lessons as much as space would allow. It is designed so the students can learn the essentials thoroughly and retain what they have so far learned. *Kanji* characters are also presented in a similar fashion. They are, initially, introduced for recognition and then for writing.

[Index]

At the end of this textbook, there are three kinds of lists: Japanese English Glossary, Kanji List and the Functions Index. The first two will be useful for students daily studying and the Function Index helps students review when they are through with the whole textbook.

TO THE INSTRUCTORS

There is a "Teacher's Guide" to supplement this textbook. Its main function is to present some of the hints for communicative drills and other essential points for instruction.

People who would like to know about tapes should contact the author directly at the following address:

Hiroyoshi Noto
1050 E. 59th St., Chicago, Illinois 60637 U.S.A.
Tel. 312-702-5805
Fax. 312-702-9861

[五十音図(List of *Hiragana*)]

	W	R	Y	M	H	N	T	S	K	
ん	わ	ら	や	ま	は	な	た	さ	か	あ	A
		り		み	ひ	に	ち	し	き	い	I
		る	ゆ	む	ふ	ぬ	つ	す	く	う	U
		れ		め	へ	ね	て	せ	け	え	E
	を	ろ	よ	も	ほ	の	と	そ	こ	お	O

[Letters with two dots or a circle]

P	B		D	Z	G	
ぱ	ば		だ	ざ	が	A
ぴ	び		(ぢ)	じ	ぎ	I
ぷ	ぶ		(づ)	ず	ぐ	U
ぺ	べ		で	ぜ	げ	E
ぽ	ぼ		ど	ぞ	ご	O

[五十音図 (List of *Katakana*)]

	W	R	Y	M	H	N	T	S	K	
ン	ワ	ラ	ヤ	マ	ハ	ナ	タ	サ	カ	ア	A
	リ		ミ	ヒ	ニ	チ	シ	キ	イ	I
		ル	ユ	ム	フ	ヌ	ツ	ス	ク	ウ	U
	レ		メ	ヘ	ネ	テ	セ	ケ	エ	E
	ヲ	ロ	ヨ	モ	ホ	ノ	ト	ソ	コ	オ	O

[Letters with two dots or a circle]

P	B	D	Z	G	
パ	バ	ダ	ザ	ガ	A
ピ	ビ	(ヂ)	ジ	ギ	I
プ	ブ	(ヅ)	ズ	グ	U
ペ	ベ	デ	ゼ	ゲ	E
ポ	ボ	ド	ゾ	ゴ	O

子音＋や，ゅ，ょ (半母音 [y]＋a, u, o)

[Consonants＋や，ゅ，ょ (semi-vowel [y]＋a, u, o)]

[ひらがな]

	き	し	ち	に	ひ	み	り
	ぎ	じ	(ぢ)		び		

や	きゃ	しゃ	ちゃ	にゃ	ひゃ	みゃ	りゃ
	ぎゃ	じゃ	(ぢゃ)		びゃ		

ゆ	きゅ	しゅ	ちゅ	にゅ	ひゅ	みゅ	りゅ
	ぎゅ	じゅ	(ぢゅ)		びゅ		

よ	きょ	しょ	ちょ	にょ	ひょ	みょ	りょ
	ぎょ	じょ	(ぢょ)		びょ		

[カタカナ]

	キ	シ	チ	ニ	ヒ	ミ	リ
	ギ	ジ	(ヂ)		ビ		

ヤ	キャ	シャ	チャ	ニャ	ヒャ	ミャ	リャ
	ギャ	ジャ	(ヂャ)		ビャ		

ユ	キュ	シュ	チュ	ニュ	ヒュ	ミュ	リュ
	ギュ	ジュ	(ヂュ)		ビュ		

ヨ	キョ	ショ	チョ	ニョ	ヒョ	ミョ	リョ
	ギョ	ジョ	(ヂョ)		ビョ		

ひらがな・かたかなの字源

[The Original Chinese Characters for *Hiragana* and *Katakana*]

	W	R	Y	M	H	N	T	S	K	
ん 无	わ 和	ら 良	や 也	ま 末	は 波	な 奈	た 太	さ 左	か 加	あ 安	A
		り 利		み 美	ひ 比	に 仁	ち 知	し 之	き 幾	い 以	I
		る 留	ゆ 由	む 武	ふ 不	ぬ 奴	つ 川	す 寸	く 久	う 宇	U
		れ 礼		め 女	へ 部	ね 祢	て 天	せ 世	け 計	え 衣	E
	を 遠	ろ 呂	よ 与	も 毛	ほ 保	の 乃	と 止	そ 曽	こ 己	お 於	O

	W	R	Y	M	H	N	T	S	K	
ン (レ)	ワ 和	ラ 良	ヤ 也	マ 万	ハ 八	ナ 奈	タ 多	サ 散	カ 加	ア 阿	A
		リ 利		ミ 三	ヒ 比	ニ 二	チ 千	シ 之	キ 幾	イ 伊	I
		ル 流	ユ 由	ム 牟	フ 不	ヌ 奴	ツ 川	ス 須	ク 久	ウ 宇	U
		レ 礼		メ 女	ヘ 部	ネ 祢	テ 天	セ 世	ケ 介	エ 江	E
	ヲ 乎	ロ 呂	ヨ 与	モ 毛	ホ 保	ノ 乃	ト 止	ソ 曽	コ 己	オ 於	O

[Classroom Instructions]

The following English expressions on the right are the translations of the Japanese classroom expressions on the left that will be used frequently in class. These translations are just for your convenience and the details will be explained later as they appear in the textbook. These are basically for classroom use and some expressions such as もう一度, 言ってください may be inappropriate outside the class.

1. もう一度
2. みんなで
3. 日本語で ┐ 言って ┐
4. もっと大きい声で │ 読んで │ ください。
5. もっとはっきり │ 話して ┘
6. もっと速く
7. 教科書を見ないで
8. 会話を ┐ 聞いて ┐ ください。
9. Aさんに ┘
10. これを見て
11. ちょっと待って ┐ ください。
12. 静かにして ┘
13. 教科書を見ないで ┐
14. 英語で話さないで │ ください。
15. 教えないで ┘
16. よくできました。
17. よくなりました。
18. そうです。
19. そうですか。
20. 正しいですか, 正しくありませんか。
21. どうですか。
22. 違います。
23. Aさん, どうぞ。
24. Aさん, Bさんになってください。
25. 授業を始めましょう。
26. 授業を終わりましょう。

1. Again
2. All together
3. In Japanese ┐ say ┐
4. Louder │ read │ Please
5. More clearly │ speak ┘
6. Faster
7. Without looking at the textbook
8. Listen to the conversation.
9. Ask Mr. / Ms. / Mrs. A.
10. Please look at this.
11. Please wait a minute.
12. Please be quiet.
13. Please don't look at the textbook.
14. Please don't speak in English.
15. Please don't tell others.
16. Well done!
17. You have much improved.
18. That's right.
19. Is that right?
20. Is it correct or not?
21. How is it?
22. You are wrong.
23. Mr./Ms./Mrs. A, please.
    (or A san, go ahead.)
24. A san, please take the role of B.
    (or A san, become B.)
25. Let's start class.
26. Let's finish class.

[Special Symbols and Abbreviations]

N	noun
N1	the first noun
N2	the second noun
NP	noun phrase
V	verb
v.i.	intransitive verb
v.t.	transitive verb
Ⅰ	Group I verb
Ⅱ	Group II verb
Ⅲ	Group III verb
VP	verbal phrase
adj.	adjective
い-adj.	い-adjective
な-adj.	な-adjective
adv.	adverb
Pred.	predicate
CL	clause
CL1	the first clause
CL2	the second clause
S	sentence
S1	the first sentence
S2	the second sentence
L.	Lesson
Affirm.	affirmative
Neg.	negative
Pl.	plain (form)
Imperf.	imperfect
Perf.	perfect
dic.f.	dictionary form
lit.	literally
s.b.	somebody
s.t.	something
⬆	honorific （尊敬語）
⬇	humble （謙譲語）
P	polite （丁寧語）

[ ] ……… indicates that this part is rephrased. In the translation of dialogues, this indicates the sounds of agreement(あいづち).

( ) ……… indicates that this part can be omitted. When it is used in the translation of dialogues, the expressions in the parentheses are supplementary to make the translation easier to understand.

／ ……… indicates that the two (or more) expressions are interchangeable.

一課

内容表

文法	N1 は N2 です。N3 です。 My name is ～. Possessive particle　の Topical particle　は て-form of copula で	私(わたし)はリーです。二年生(にねんせい)です。 私は～です。／～といいます。 大学院(だいがくいん)の学生(がくせい) 私は／専門(せんもん)は／出身(しゅっしん)は 専門は人類学(じんるいがく)で，大学院の学生です。
機能	Introducing Oneself　　　　　　6-7 　name, major 　school year/grade, hometown	

(N stands for noun.)

Note

| 一課(いっか) | Lesson 1 | 表(ひょう) | List | 機能(きのう) | Function |
| 内容(ないよう) | Content | 文法(ぶんぽう) | Grammar | | |

Lesson 1

会話 (かいわ)

1

A： 私はリーです。　　　　　　　　　　(As for me,) I am Lee.
　　二年生です。　　　　　　　　　　　(I am) a sophomore.
　　出身はイリノイ州です。　　　　　　(I am) from (the state of) Illinois.

2

B： 私はロングです。　　　　　　　　　(As for me,) I am Long.
　　ロー・スクールの学生です。　　　　(I am) a law school student.
　　出身はジョージア州です。　　　　　(I am) from Georgia.

3

C： 私は林といいます。　　　　　　　　(As for me,) I am Hayashi.
　　専門は人類学で、大学院の学生です。　My major is anthropology and I am a
　　出身は東京です。　　　　　　　　　graduate student. (I am) from Tokyo.

単語表 (たんごひょう)

会話(かいわ)	dialogue, conversation	州(しゅう)	state
単語表(たんごひょう)	word list	**2**	
関連語句(かんれんごく)	related phrases	学生(がくせい)	student
練習(れんしゅう)	drills, practice	**3**	
1		専門(せんもん)	major, speciality
私(わたし)	I, me	人類学(じんるいがく)	anthropology
二年生(にねんせい)	sophomore	大学院(だいがくいん)	graduate school
出身(しゅっしん)	one's native place/hometown		

一課

関連語句 (かんれんごく)

一年生(いちねんせい) freshman	四年生(よねんせい) senior
三年生(さんねんせい) junior	ビジネス・スクール business school
東アジア研究(ひがしアジアけんきゅう)	East Asian Studies
専門(せんもん)はありません。	I don't have a major.
わかりました。	I understand./I see.
ありがとうございました。	Thank you (for what you have done).

Names of Subjects

文学 (ぶんがく)	literature	社会学(しゃかいがく)	sociology
歴史学(れきしがく)	history	経済学(けいざいがく)	economics
政治学(せいじがく)	political science	言語学(げんごがく)	linguistics
美術史(びじゅつし)	art history	経営学(けいえいがく)	management
法律学(ほうりつがく)	law	哲学 (てつがく)	philosophy

文法 (ぶんぽう)

● **N1 は N2 です**　　1-1

This indicates that N1 (the first noun) is equivalent to N2 (the second noun). The function of *wa* is to present the topic of the sentence or the paragraph. Once the topic is established with *wa*, it normally remains unrepeated unless special circumstances necessitate its recurrence.

Take sentence A, for example. Both Lee *desu* and *ninensei desu* are explanations of the topic I in the first sentence. In other words, *watashi* is the topic of these sentences. Unlike subjects in English, *watashi wa* should not be repeated in every sentence.

Grammatically は is called a "topical particle" and is pronounced *wa* (not *ha* in this use).

Desu is called a "copula" or a linking word, but more importantly, this indicates some politeness or formality.

Note the small number 1-1 after the headline indicates the section in the dialogue or conversation where the pattern appears; in this case, it is found in the first line of the first section.

● **N1 の N2 (ロー・スクールの学生)**　　2-2

の is also a particle. The basic meaning is that N2 belongs to N1, or that N2 is of N1.

　私の専門 (my major)　　大学院の学生 (graduate student)

Lesson 1

● **Name** と いいます　　3-1

This expression can also be used to introduce yourself. It is slightly more formal than (*Watashi wa*) Name *desu*.

● で (て-form of copula)　　3-2

You may have noticed that all the sentences in the first two monologues of this lesson end with *desu*. This repetition does not pose any grammatical problem, but if you want to avoid it for stylistic reasons, an alternative is to replace *desu* with an expression like *to iimasu* after your name. Another way to reduce the continued use of *desu* is to use *de* in the following way:

私 はロー・スクールの学生です。二年生です。
⇨ 私 はロー・スクールの学生で，二年生です。

The underlined で in the second sentence is the て-form of *desu*.

One of its important functions is to combine two sentences into one in the meaning of "and." The sentence above can be translated as "I am a law school student and a second year student." In other words, "I am a second year law student."

[About the Characters]

Three writing systems are used in this lesson: *kanji*, *hiragana*, and *katakana*. It is quite normal in Japanese to use these sets of letters as shown in the monologues. As we shall see however, there are particular rules and methods which govern their usage within a sentence.

Kanji, which means Chinese characters, were invented and developed by the Chinese. According to some studies, the oldest *kanji*, inscribed on oracle bones, date back to the 13th or 14th century B.C. The number of *kanji* contained in the biggest *kanji* dictionary is about 50,000, more than ninety percent of which are not used on a daily basis in Japan and even in China. In studying Japanese, if you have a thorough knowledge of 2,000 characters, you will have no problem reading newspapers and most academic material. *Kanji* was first introduced to Japan around the fifth century; *hiragana* and *katakana* were created from *kanji*.

Hiragana characters came about from the cursive form of certain *kanji*, and *katakana* were produced by taking a particular part of a whole *kanji* character. *Kanji*, in contemporary Japanese, are used to write most nouns and unchangeable parts of words; *hiragana* are used for the changeable parts.

The use of *katakana* is limited to writing loan words from the West and to serving as "italics" in Japanese.

[ふりがな]

In the text in this lesson, small *hiragana* are placed above the *kanji*. They are *furigana* and show the readings of the corresponding *kanji*. They are ordinarily not used in papers and academic writings and you need not use them in your writing. The *furigana* are used here to help you familiarize yourselves with the readings of *kanji*.

[Reading of *kanji* in Japanese]

For those who know Chinese or Korean, many of the *kanji* in this lesson may sound similar to the readings of the same characters in those respective languages. The exception here is 林 (はやし). This is because in Japanese, there are at least two ways of reading *kanji*: 訓読み(くんよ) (Japanese reading) and 音読み(おんよ) (Chinese reading). 林 here is read in the Japanese reading, while all the other Chinese characters in this lesson are read in the Chinese reading. Scholars report that three quarters of *kanji* compounds in Japanese are pronounced in the Chinese reading.

Please be aware that knowledge of Chinese or Korean may give some students a clue to the readings of some *kanji*; but it is no more than a mere clue. Sometimes the reading can be entirely different from that of modern Chinese or Korean because the Chinese readings in Japanese were adopted from the pronunciations used during different periods of time in different areas in China.

For example.

行く	(いく)	to go
行う	(おこなう)	to do, act

⟶ 訓読み

行	(こう)
	(ぎょう)
	(あん)

⟶ 音読み

[Accents in Japanese]

The Japanese accent differs from the English "stress accent." It is called "pitch accent," and differentiates homonyms by its relative pitch, as illustrated below.

For example, both "chopsticks" and "bridge" are written as はし in *hiragana*.

In the case of "chopsticks," the は is pronounced higher than the し, while "bridge" consists of low は and high し.

はし (chopsticks) は/し ; はし (bridge) は\し

On the word lists in this textbook, the accents are shown in the following way:

¯はし (chopsticks)   は¯し (bridge)   はし¯ (a tip, edge)

The accent for "chopsticks" indicates that the sound falls in pitch after は and, in "bridge," it falls after し. The third はし above indicates that whatever sound follows し is pronounced at the same pitch as し.

The accent pattern is socially accepted and is regarded as part of the language. It is used in broadcasts all over the country and can be understood by almost all Japanese.

The accents shown in the word lists are based on the Tokyo dialect which is the core of "Standard Japanese." It is, therefore, important to know the basic rules of the "Tokyo Accent."

1. The first and second syllables are always different in pitch:

    Correct ○/○ ○\○   Wrong ○—○ ○—○

2. There is always only one high pitch in a word, never more than one, although that pitch may have more than one syllable.

Lesson 1

Correct

Wrong

[The length of Japanese syllables]

Each *kana* (Japanese phonetic character) makes a syllable with the exception of smaller や, ゆ and よ, which are considered to be components of one syllable. For example, しゅ is considered one syllable. *Kana* such as the small つ and ん, however, stand as one syllable. To illustrate, ねん has two syllables.

Each Japanese syllable should be given equal time. In order to accomplish this, it is important to avoid English stress accents.

[Unvoiced vowels]

When the vowels *i* and *u* come between two unvoiced consonants (*k*, *s*, *t*, *h*, *p*), they become unvoiced vowels, that are pronounced like a whisper without using the vocal cords. The vowel *u* of く in がくせい, for example, must be voiceless because it is placed between *k* and *s*. Also, *i* in *Hayashi* becomes unvoiced in the sentence 林といいます since the sound comes between two unvoiced consonants. In a sentence with a falling intonation ending in です or ます, the *u* in す becomes unvoiced.

練習 (れんしゅう)

練習(れんしゅう)　1	N1 は N2 です

Practice how to tell who you are and what you are, as shown in the examples.

　　例(example)　リー　　⇨私はリーです。　（Lee　　⇨I am Lee.）
　　　　　　　　一年生　⇨私は一年生です。(freshman　⇨I am a freshman.)

　　1．レーガン　2．カーター　3．フォード　4．ニクソン　5．ブッシュ　　　　(names)
　　6．一年生　　7．二年生　　8．三年生　　9．四年生　　10．大学院の学生　(titles)

練習(れんしゅう)　2	N1 は S1. S2.

Put each of the two items together as shown in the example.

　　例　リー, 一年生　(Lee, first year student)
　　　　　⇨私はリーです。一年生です。(I am Lee. I am a first year student.)

Use the cues in 練習1.

練習(れんしゅう)　3	N の N

Practice using the possessive particle.

例　ビジネス・スクール (business school)
　　⇨ 私はビジネス・スクールの学生です。(I am a business school student.)

1．ロー・スクール　　　　2．大学院　　　　　3．人類学
4．政治学(せいじがく)　　5．歴史学(れきしがく)　　6．美術史(びじゅつし)

練習(れんしゅう)　4	わたしの N

Practice again with the particle の in a different context by using the words 専門 and 出身.

例　ビジネス　　⇨ 私の専門はビジネスです。
　　(business　　⇨ My major is business.)
　　ジョージア州　⇨ 私の出身はジョージア州です。
　　(Georgia　　⇨ My hometown is Georgia.)

1．法律学(ほうりつがく)　2．イリノイ州　3．ワシントン州　4．人類学
5．経済学(けいざいがく)　6．テキサス州　7．ノースダコタ州　8．歴史学

練習(れんしゅう)　5	Identifying oneself

Practice identifying yourself in a way other than by using 〜です.

例　リー　⇨ 私はリーといいます。(Lee　⇨ I am Lee.)

1．レーガン　2．カーター　3．フォード　4．ニクソン　5．ブッシュ　(names)

練習(れんしゅう)　6	S で S

Practice combining two sentences by means of で, as shown in the example.

例　私はシカゴ大学の学生です。　(I am a student of the University of Chicago.)
　　二年生です。　　　　　　　　(I am a second year student.)
　　⇨ 私はシカゴ大学の学生で，二年生です。
　　　(I am a second year student of the University of Chicago.)

1．私はシカゴ大学の学生です。三年生です。
2．私はビジネス・スクールの学生です。一年生です。
3．私は政治学の学生です。四年生です。
4．私は大学院の学生です。専門は人類学です。
5．私は二年生です。出身はニューメキシコ州です。
6．私は大学院の人類学の学生です。出身はインディアナ州です。

Lesson 1

| 練習(れんしゅう) 7 | Confirming |

This is an exercise in learning how to confirm what someone said by repeating the uttered expression with a falling intonation. Please pay special attention to the intonation, since a rising intonation indicates that you are asking again what the speaker has said. Also notice that the suffix "*san*" is absolutely essential when you repeat the person's name.

例　私はリーです。　⇨リーさんですか。(You are Lee san!)
　　出身は東京です。⇨東京ですか。　　(You are from Tokyo!)

1．私はロングです。　2．ロー・スクールの学生です。　3．出身はシカゴです。
4．私は林です。　　　5．専門は人類学です。　　　　　6．大学院の学生です。

| 練習(れんしゅう) 8 | Describing another person |

If you substitute わたし with other topics, you can describe these topics. Please describe the following person as in the example.

例　ダンさん
　　三年生
　　しゃかいがく
　　社会学
　　ニュージャージー
　⇨ダンさんは三年生で，専門は社会学です。出身はニュージャージー州です。
　　(Dunn san is a junior, and her major is sociology. She is from New Jersey.)

1．キムさん
　　大学院の学生
　　経済学
　　ソウル

2．林
　　東京
　　四年生
　　社会学

3．ロング
　　ビジネス
　　フロリダ州
　　ビジネス・スクールの二年生

二課

内容表

文法	Questions: N1 は…。 　　　　　N1 は N2 ですか。 Two kinds of「か」 Three kinds of intonations Honorific / Polite prefix Instrumental particle (by means of)		お名前は…。／出身は？ ダンさんは大学院の学生ですか。 私ですか。↗ そうですか。↘ flat　　お名前は…。→ rising　私ですか。↗ falling　そうですか。↘ お(名前) (英語)で
機能	Identifying Persons; name, major, hometown, school year Starting Conversation Refocusing Communication Expressing Failure to Understand Expressing Understanding Expressing Agreement 　and Disagreement Requesting Translation Expressing Thanks Responding to Thanks Terminating Conversation	1-1 6-3 7-4 2-3 2-3 2-1 7-9 6-17 6-18 6-5	 失礼ですが， 私ですか。 はっ？ 何年生ですか。 どこですか。 何ですか。 ニューヨークですか。 ああ，そうですか。 わかりました。 はい。／ええ，そうです。 いいえ，違います。／いえいえ。 〜は英語で何といいますか。 どうもありがとうございました。 いいえ，どういたしまして。 どうもありがとうございました。

Lesson 2

会話 (かいわ)

A：失礼ですが、お名前は…。	Excuse me, but (what is) your name?
B：私ですか。	(You mean) me?
A：はい。	Yes.
B：ダンです。	(My name is) Dunn.
A：ダンさんは大学院の学生ですか。	Are you a graduate student, Dunn san?
B：いいえ、違います。三年生です。	No, I am not. I am a junior.
A：はっ？ 何年生ですか。	Pardon? Which year?
三年生ですか。	A junior?
B：ええ、そうです。	Yes, that's right.
A：出身は？	Where are you from?
B：ニューアークです。	From Newark.
A：はっ？ どこですか。	Pardon? Where is it?
ニューヨークですか。	New York?
B：いえいえ。ニューアークです。	No. Newark.
A：ああ、そうですか。わかりました。	Oh, is that so? Now I've understood.
専門は何ですか。	(What is) your major?
B：人類学です。	(It is) anthropology.
A：はっ？ 何ですか。	What is it?
B：人類学です。	Anthropology.
A：人類学は英語で何といいますか。	How do you say *jinruigaku* in English?
B：anthropology です。	(It is) anthropology.
A：ああ、そうですか。わかりました。	Oh, I see. (Now) I understand.
どうもありがとうございました。	Thank you very much.
B：いいえ、どういたしまして。	You are welcome.

単語表（たんごひょう）

失礼(しつれい)ですが	Excuse me, but ~	何(なん)といいますか	What do you call ~? How do you say ~?
名前(なまえ)	name	英語(えいご)	English language
いいえ，違(ちが)います	No, that's not right.	何(なん)ですか	What (is it)?
はい，そうです	Yes, that's right.		
どこですか	Where is it?		

関連語句（かんれんごく）

大学(だいがく)	college, university	社会学(しゃかいがく)	sociology
仕事(しごと)	work, job	政治学(せいじがく)	political science
日本語(にほんご)	Japanese language	会社(かいしゃ)	company
いいえ,どういたしまして	You are welcome.		

文法（ぶんぽう）

● 私ですか　　2

As in English, you can say "Me?" in Japanese: *Watashi?* (without the *wa* in *watashi wa*) It can be used in more or less the same situations as its English counterpart. But when *desu ka* is deleted, politeness disappears.

In other words, the です is used as an indicator of "politeness" which is necessary when you talk to someone older than or unfamiliar to you.

With friends you can do without *desu ka*, but you must use it with strangers or remote acquaintances. This rule applies to all uses of です.

Friendliness is generally revealed more slowly in Japanese than in English. So, do not rush to delete "ですか."

● はい，ええ　　3, 9

These words show the speaker's agreement with the question or with the statement addressed to him/her. The difference between the two, for present purposes, is that *hai* sounds more formal than "*ee*."

● ええ，そうです／いいえ，違います　　6, 9

The first phrase is used to indicate that what has been said is correct. If it is incorrect, say いいえ，違います.

Lesson 2

● ダンさんは大学院の学生ですか　　5

As explained in the first lesson, the particle は presents the topic of a sentence or a paragraph. Students of Japanese may think that the subject or topic is dispensable in a sentence. This is only true when the topic is clearly understood by both the speaker and hearer. When the topic changes as shown in the dialogue, from one thing (お名前) to another (ダンさん), it must be mentioned.

Out of context this sentence could be ambiguous. It could mean either of the following:
1. Dunn san, are you a graduate student?
2. Is Dunn san a graduate student?

The ambiguity disappears if you take the context into account.

[Three basic intonations in Japanese]

In this lesson, you will find three basic intonations;

　　Flat　　　→　(as in お名前は。)
　　Rising　　↗　(as in 私ですか。)
　　Falling　　↘　(as in ダンです。)

The rising and falling intonations are more commonly found than the flat one. Using the flat intonation usually solicits the rest of the sentence from the hearer. Consequently, it sounds gentle but sometimes may not convey the speaker's intention very clearly.

A rising intonation indicates that the speaker demands a response from the hearer. As a hearer, you are expected to respond. On the contrary, a falling intonation implies an end to a response; it signifies that the speaker has reached an understanding of something, or has given the solicited information.

　　そうですか。↗　Is that so? / Do you really think so? / I wonder if it is so.
　　そうですか。↘　Is that so! / I see.

These intonation patterns are slightly different from those in English in that the rise and fall take place abruptly in the final syllable while, in English, the intonations rise or fall more gradually.

ことばの使い方 (ことばのつかいかた)

● 失礼ですが　　1

This phrase indicates that the question following it may be intrusive or too personal to the hearer. When you want to ask somebody about his or her marital status, age, nationality, etc., use this expression. It is not used in asking directions or requesting impersonal information.

● お名前は… 1

"お" is a prefix which is attached to some nouns to show respect for the addressee, the person you are talking about, or the situation in which you are talking. This is, therefore, indispensable when meeting someone for the first time. You cannot use this honorific prefix to refer to yourself.

In Japanese, particularly in polite Japanese, choice of words depends on whether you are talking about yourself or about another person. The above prefix represents an important aspect of the language.

● はっ？ 7

This expression indicates that the speaker did not catch or understand what was just said. When you are unable to hear well, this expression is very useful.

This っ usually occurs before an unvoiced consonant, and is recognised as a space without a sound (except before *s* or *sh*). In this example, the っ stop can be made if you halt the stream of air suddenly by closing your throat as you do before clearing your throat.

● (英語)で 20

The particle で means "by means of." Like English prepositions, particles have more than one meaning.

● ああ, そうですか 22

When you come to understand something, use this expression to confirm that comprehension with yourself. *Ka,* as a sentence-final particle, has two important functions. One, as seen in *Watashi desu ka*, is to ask a question. The other, as illustrated by this example, is to indicate that the speaker has reached an understanding or he has been surprised by what he has heard. The difference between the two usages is very well distinguished by their respective intonations.

練習 (れんしゅう)

練習(れんしゅう) 1   失礼ですが／Intonation

Ask the questions as shown in the examples. Pay special attention to the flat intonation.

例　お名前　⇨失礼ですが, お名前は…。
　　(name　⇨ Excuse me, but what is your name?)
　　出身　　⇨失礼ですが, 出身は…。
　　(hometown　⇨ Excuse me, but where are you from?)

1．大学　　2．お名前　　3．お仕事　　4．会社　　5．専門　　6．出身

Lesson 2

練習(れんしゅう)　2　　　　　Refocusing on topics

Respond to the questions in the following way.

例　失礼ですが，お名前は…。　⇨　名前ですか。
　　　(Excuse me, but what is your name ...?　⇨　My name?)

1．大学　　2．専門　　3．出身　　4．会社　　5．お仕事　　6．お名前

練習(れんしゅう)　3　　　　　Requesting translation

Make a question as shown in the example.

例　人類学　⇨　人類学は英語で何といいますか。
　　　(*jinruigaku*　⇨　How do you say *jinruigaku* in English?)

1．社会学(しゃかいがく)　2．仕事　3．政治学(せいじがく)　4．大学　5．一年生(いちねんせい)　6．四年生(よねんせい)

練習(れんしゅう)　4　　　　　Requesting translation

Form a question as shown in the example. You take A's role.

例　anthropology
　　　⇨　A：anthropologyは日本語(にほんご)で何といいますか。
　　　　　B：人類学です。
　　　　　A：ああ，そうですか。わかりました。どうもありがとうございました。
　　　　　B：いいえ，どういたしまして。

1．economics　2．sociology　3．junior　4．sophomore　5．senior　6．major

---
練習(れんしゅう)　5　　　　　Expressing failure to understand

Ask a question to clarify what the speaker said using an interrogative word that corresponds to the part you could not hear clearly.

例　私の出身は東京(とうきょう)です。⇨　はっ？　どこですか。
　　　(I am from Tokyo.　⇨　Pardon? Where are you from?)

1．林(はやし)さんは二年生(にねんせい)です。　　　　2．林さんの専門は社会学です。
3．林さんの出身はニューヨークです。　　4．ダンさんの専門は英語です。
5．ダンさんは四年生です。　　　　　　　6．ダンさんの出身はテキサスです。

| 練習(れんしゅう) 6 | Expressing agreement / disagreement |

Look at the picture below and answer the questions as shown in the example.

例　リーさん　　　大学院の学生／ボストン／政治学

① リーさんは四年生ですか。⇨いいえ，違います。
   (Lee san, are you a senior?　⇨ No, I'm not.)
② 出身はボストンですか。⇨はい，そうです。
   (Are you from Boston?　⇨ Yes, I am.)
③ 専門は社会学ですか。⇨いいえ，違います。
   (Is your major sociology?　⇨ No, it's not.)

１．リンさん　　　三年生
　　　　　　　　　シカゴ
　　　　　　　　　人類学

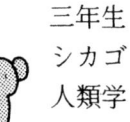

２．林さん　　　　四年生
　　　　　　　　　ワシントン
　　　　　　　　　英語

| 練習(れんしゅう) 7 | Expressing agreement / disagreement |

This time, give the information that the questioner might need, as in the example.

例　リーさん　　　大学院の学生／ボストン／政治学
① リーさんは四年生ですか。⇨いいえ，大学院の学生です。
② 出身はボストンですか。⇨はい，ボストンです。
③ 専門は社会学ですか。⇨いいえ，政治学です。

Use the cues in　練習6．

三課

内容表

文法	Negation: (N1 は) N2 じゃありません。		(私の国は)中国じゃありません。
	Asking and Answering Negative Questions		日本人じゃありませんか。
			ええ、日本人じゃありません。
			いいえ、日本人です。
	Honorific / Polite Prefix「御〜」		御紹介します。
	Sentence final「か」: exclamation		日本人じゃありませんか。
機能	Starting Conversation	6-3	御紹介します。
			あのう〜。
	Introducing People	6-7	Aさん、こちらはBさんです。
	Responding to Introduction	6-8	はじめまして、どうぞよろしく。
			こちらこそ、どうぞよろしく。
	Identifying Persons	1-1	何とおっしゃいますか。
	Seeking Factual Information	1-3	お国はどちらですか。
	Apologizing	4-1	失礼しました。
	Expressing Corrections	5-10	中国じゃありません。韓国です。

会話 (かいわ)

A：	リーさん。[はい。]	Mr. Lee! [Yes.]
	御紹介します。	I (would like to) introduce (Tanaka san).
	こちらは田中さんです。	This is Tanaka san.
B：	はっ？ 何とおっしゃいますか。	Pardon? What is the name?
A：	田中さんです。	Tanaka san.
C：	田中です。	(My name is) Tanaka.
	はじめまして、どうぞよろしく。	How do you do?
B：	リーです。	(My name is) Lee.
	こちらこそ、どうぞよろしく。	How do you do?
C：	リーさんですね。[ええ、そうです。]	Your name is Lee san, right? [Right.]
	あのう失礼ですが、リーさんのお国はどちらですか。	May I ask you which country you are from?
	中国ですか。	Is it China?
B：	いいえ、中国じゃありません。	No, it isn't China.
	韓国です。	It is Korea.
C：	韓国ですか。	Oh, Korea, I see.
B：	田中さんは、日本人ですか。	Are you Japanese, Tanaka san?
C：	いいえ、日本人じゃありません。	No, I am not.
B：	ああ、そうですか。失礼しました。	Oh, is that right! I am sorry.
	日本人じゃありませんか。	You are not Japanese?!
C：	ええ、ハワイ出身の日系アメリカ人で、三世です。	That's right. I am a third generation Japanese American, from Hawaii.

単語表 (たんごひょう)

御紹介(ごしょうかい)	introduction	どちら	どこ (formal)
御紹介します	introduce	中国(ちゅうごく)	China
こちら	this person (formal)	韓国(かんこく)	Korea
田中(たなか)さん	Mr. / Miss / Mrs. Tanaka	日本人(にほんじん)	Japanese
(と)おっしゃいます	〜といいます (formal)	日系(にっけい)アメリカ人(じん)	Japanese American
お国(くに)	(your, his) country	三世(さんせい)	third generation

関連語句 (かんれんごく)

Countries	Nationalities	Languages
日本(にほん／にっぽん)	日本人(にほん／にっぽんじん)	日本語(にほんご)
中国(ちゅうごく)	中国人(ちゅうごくじん)	中国語(ちゅうごくご)
韓国(かんこく)	韓国人(かんこくじん)	韓国語(かんこくご)
アメリカ／米国(べいこく)	アメリカ人(じん)／米国人(べいこくじん)	英語(えいご)
イギリス／英国(えいこく) (Britain)	イギリス人(じん)／英国人(えいこくじん) (British)	
ロシア	ロシア人(じん)	ロシア語(ご)

Note 1 The above is a list of countries and their corresponding nationalities and languages; note that there are irregularities which make some of them very different from their English equivalents.

Note 2 There are two names each for the United States and Britain. Since the *kanji* titles are shorter than the *katakana*, they are most often used in writing.

Note 3 The accent patterns of the nationalities and languages are mostly regular. The first syllable in a word describing a person's nationality, "〜人" is low; this is followed by a high pitch which continues through the syllable which precedes 人. The only exception is にほんじん.

　　ちゅうごくじん　　アメリカじん　　タイじん (Thai)

Exception: にほんじん

In the words for languages, there are no exceptions. All of them become flat.

　　ちゅうごくご　　えいご　　タイご

Lesson 3

Note 4　The above country list appears here again with the correct accent symbols:

にほん

かんこく　　ちゅうごく　　ロシア

アメリカ(べいこく)　　イギリス(えいこく)

Here are some more countries:

タイ　　　　ドイツ (Germany)　　スイス　　　　　インド

フランス　　イタリア　　　　　エジプト　　　　ベトナム

スペイン　　オーストラリア　　ニュージーランド

文法 (ぶんぽう)

One of the grammatical objectives of this lesson is learning how to make a negative pattern from "N1 は N2 です." The negative sentence is made by changing "です" into "じゃ(では)ありません."

The form in the parentheses, では, is the written equivalent of じゃ and is used in newspaper articles, academic publications, and other formal writings. では is also used in formal speech. For the time being, let us simply use "じゃ."

Affirmative	N1 は N2 です	リンさんは学生です。
Interrogative	N1 は N2 ですか	リンさんは学生ですか。
Negative	N1 は N2 じゃありません	リンさんは学生じゃありません。

Note:　In future lessons, we will learn the negative patterns of "N は adj. です." To avoid confusion later, remember that in the negative pattern that we are studying here, there is a noun preceding です.

● 御(紹介)　　2

This 御 before a noun has the same function as お in お名前 in L. 2. 御 usually precedes a noun which has a Chinese reading; お, on the other hand, is placed before a noun which has a Japanese reading.

御専門(ごせんもん)　　御出身(ごしゅっしん)

お国(おくに)　　お名前(おなまえ)　　お仕事(おしごと)

● 日本人じゃありませんか　　20

In L. 2, we learned that there are two variants of the sentence-final particle か: one with a rising intonation indicates a question, and the other with a falling intonation expresses affirmation or surprise.

20

The か in this sentence certainly belongs to the latter, and shows the speaker's surprise.

[Asking and answering negative questions]

The basic rule to remember in answering "Yes-No" questions in Japanese is that, if the proposition is correct, say はい or ええ, and repeat the proposition. Otherwise say いいえ and add the correct proposition.

リンさんは学生です か ⇨ ┌はい，(リンさんは)学生です。
                    └いいえ，(リンさんは)学生じゃありません。

リンさんは学生じゃありません か ⇨ ┌はい，(リンさんは)学生じゃありません。
                              └いいえ，(リンさんは)学生です。

ことばの使い方 (ことばのつかいかた)

● (リー)さん　　1

San is attached to both first and last names, regardless of sex or marital status. The most common way of addressing people in Japanese is to use the last name plus *san*. Using a first name is limited to addressing family members or childhood friends.

● (何と)おっしゃいますか　　4

This is a polite way of asking someone's name. The verb おっしゃいます is used to refer to someone you don't know well, or someone older or higher in position than you. Like お in お名前 or *san* attached to a person's name, this verb cannot be used to refer to yourself. In that case, use 〜といいます for the time being to talk about yourself.

● (リーさんです)ね　　10

ね is a sentence-final particle which indicates that the speaker is asking for the hearer's agreement, or is giving the speaker's consent. This can also be accompanied by either a falling or rising intonation. This particle indicates that the speaker is almost certain about the proposition. か does not have such an implication.

● はじめまして　　7

This can be roughly translated as: "(I am honored to meet you) for the first time." This phrase alone can be used in greeting someone for the first time. Or, it can be used in combination with the phrase which follows it. Never forget to tell the person your name.

● どうぞよろしく　　7

Literally, this phrase means: "Treat me favorably." "どうぞよろしく" is a shortened form of "どうぞよろしくおねがいします." The long form is more formal and may be used more often in the business world.

● こちらこそ　　9

This greeting literally means: "It is I who should say so."

Lesson 3

● あのう　11

This expression is used here to draw the attention of the hearer or to give time to the hearer to prepare for the answer. If you do not say this, the sentence may sound abrupt and, consequently, impolite. In short, this phrase may be a device which makes the speaker sound reserved and polite.

● （お国は）どちらですか　12

どちら is the polite equivalent of どこ.

　　出身はどちらですか。(Where are you from?)
　　会社(かいしゃ)はどちらですか。(Which company are you working for?)
　　　　　　　　　　　　　(Which company do you belong to?)
　　大学(だいがく)はどちらですか。(Which university are you attending?)

● 失礼しました　19

Use this phrase when you have committed a slight breach of etiquette. It comes in handy when you want to apologize for being late for an appointment.

練習 (れんしゅう)

練習(れんしゅう)　1	Introducing people

Introduce the second person to the first as shown in the example.

　例　リーさん，田中さん
　　　⇨リーさん，こちらは田中さんです。
　　　　(Lee san, this is Tanaka san.)

1．ロングさん，リンさん　　　　　　2．田中さん，リーさん
3．リンさん，リーさん　　　　　　　4．林(はやし)さん，田中さん

練習(れんしゅう)　2	Asking personal questions

Ask the questions politely.

　例　お国，中国　⇨あのう失礼ですが，リーさんのお国は中国ですか。
　　　　(May I ask you, Lee san, are you from China?)

1．お国，イギリス　　2．御出身(とうきょう)，東京　　3．御専門(ぶんがく)，文学
4．御出身，ハワイ　　5．お国，韓国　　　　　　　　6．御専門，社会学(しゃかいがく)

練習(れんしゅう) 3　　Expressing correction

Answer in the following way.

例　あのう失礼ですが、リーさんのお国は中国ですか。　（アメリカ）
　⇨いいえ、中国じゃありません。アメリカです。
　(No, I am not from China. I am from the United States.)

1．あのう失礼ですが、リーさんの御専門は人類学ですか。　（政治学）
2．あのう失礼ですが、リーさんの御出身は中国ですか。　（韓国）
3．あのう失礼ですが、田中さんは日本人ですか。　（アメリカ人）
4．あのう失礼ですが、田中さんは四年生ですか。　（大学院の学生）

練習(れんしゅう) 4　　Apologizing

Ask the question and, if you are wrong, apologize. Take the role of A.

例　A：あのう失礼ですが、キムさんのお国は中国ですか。（アメリカ）
　　B：いいえ、中国じゃありません。アメリカです。
　　A：そうですか。失礼しました。(Is that so? I am sorry.)
　　B：いいえ。　　　　　　　(It's alright.)

1．あのう失礼ですが、リーさんの御専門は人類学ですか。　（政治学）
2．あのう失礼ですが、リーさんの御出身は中国ですか。　（韓国）
3．あのう失礼ですが、田中さんは日本人ですか。　（アメリカ人）
4．あのう失礼ですが、田中さんは四年生ですか。　（大学院の学生）
5．あのう失礼ですが、ロングさんのお名前はジョン・ロングですか。（ボブ・ロング）

練習(れんしゅう) 5　　Expressing confirmation

Confirm what you have heard as shown in the example. Take the role of B.

例　A：私は中国出身です。　　　(I am from China.)
　　B：わかりました。中国ですね。(I see. You are from China.)
　　A：はい、そうです。　　　　(That's right.)

1．こちらは田中さんです。　　　　2．こちらはダンさんとおっしゃいます。
3．リーさんのお国は韓国です。　　4．田中さんは日系アメリカ人です。
5．ダンさんは大学院の学生です。　6．田中さんはハワイ出身です。

四課

内容表

文法	Demonstrative(こ，そ，あ，ど)		これ，それ，あれ，どれ この／その／あの／どの＋Noun
	The い-adj.		高(たか)い，古(ふる)い，赤(あか)い，汚(きたな)い，いい
	1) as a predicate		あの車(くるま)は古いですね。 (That car is old, isn't it?)
	2) as a noun-modifier		あの赤い車ですよ。 (That red car over there.)
	〜でしょう (I guess 〜.)		高いでしょう。
	Sentence-final particle「よ」		違(ちが)いますよ。
	Conjunctional particle「が」		S1 が S2（汚いですがいいです）
機能	Identifying Objects	1-1	これは何(なん)ですか。 この器械(きかい)は何といいますか。
	Stating Factual Information	1-2	それはワード・プロセッサーですよ。
	Commenting on a Topic / Subject	7-11	よくわかりませんが，
	Inquiring About Certainty	2-19	〜でしょう。(高いでしょう。)
	Admitting	2-4	ええ，まあ。
	Seeking Factual Information 　(Price)	1-3	いくらですか。
	Inquiring About Denial	2-27	どうしてわかりますか。

Lesson 4

会話 (かいわ)

1

A：先生、これは何ですか。 Sensei, what is this?
B：どれですか。 Which one (do you mean)?
A：これです。 (I mean) this.
B：ああ、それですか。 Oh, that (is what you mean).
A：よくわかりませんが、コンピューターですか。 I don't know for sure, but is this a computer?
B：いいえ、違いますよ。 No, that's not correct.
A：タイプライターじゃありませんね。 This isn't a typewriter, is it?
B：ええ。それは日本語のワード・プロセッサーですよ。 That's right. (No, it isn't.) It's a Japanese word processor.
A：高いでしょうね。 I guess it is expensive.
B：ええ、まあ。 Yes, sort of.
A：いくらですか。 How much is it?
B：忘れました。 I have forgotten.

2

A：この器械は何といいますか、先生。 What do you call this machine, Sensei?
B：その器械はプリンターですよ。 That machine is a printer.

3

A：あの車はずいぶん古いですね。　　That car is terribly old, isn't it?

B：どの車ですか。　　Which car?

A：あの赤い車ですよ。　　That red car over there.

B：そんなに古くありませんよ。　　Not as old as you may think.

A：どうしてわかりますか。　　Why do you know that (How can you tell)?

B：あの車は私のです。　　That car over there is mine.

A：あら，失礼しました。　　Oh, I am sorry. (I was rude.)

B：いいえ。あの車はちょっと汚いですが，かなりいいですよ。　　No. (It's OK.) That car is a bit dirty, but is pretty good.

単語表 (たんごひょう)

1

先生(せんせい)	☞ことばの使い方
これ	this one
何(なん，なに)	what
どれ	which one
それ	that one
よく	well
わかりません	I don't know.
コンピューター	computer
タイプライター	typewriter
日本語(にほんご)	Japanese language
ワード・プロセッサー	word processor
高(たか)い	expensive
まあ	sort of
いくらですか	How much is it?

2

| 器械(きかい) | machine |
| プリンター | printer |

3

あの	that
車(くるま)	car
ずいぶん	extremely, quite
古(ふる)い	old
どの＋N	which ～

Lesson 4

赤(あか)い	red	あら	oh (in feminine speech)
そんなに	as you say, as you think	ちょっと	a little
どうして	why, how	汚(きたな)い	dirty, messy
わかります(わかる)	understand, know	かなり	comparatively, pretty, quite
私(わたし)の	mine	いい	good, nice

関連語句 (かんれんごく)

本(ほん)	book	自転車(じてんしゃ)	bicycle
誰(だれ)	who	誰(だれ)の	whose
かばん	satchel, briefcase	ノート	notebook
席(せき)	seat, place to sit down	ケーキ	(Western style) cake
新(あたら)しい	new	ひどい	terrible
安(やす)い	inexpensive, cheap	ほんとうに	really, truly

文法 (ぶんぽう)

● **Demonstratives**

In English, there are two kinds of demonstratives: this vs. that (these vs. those). In Japanese, three kinds of demonstratives are used. If the speaker talks about something closer to himself than to the hearer, he uses これ or この, while things nearer to the hearer are referred to in terms of それ or その. To mention things located away from both of them, あれ or あの is used. See the illustration below.

When you want to know which one (of more than three things), use どれ or どの.

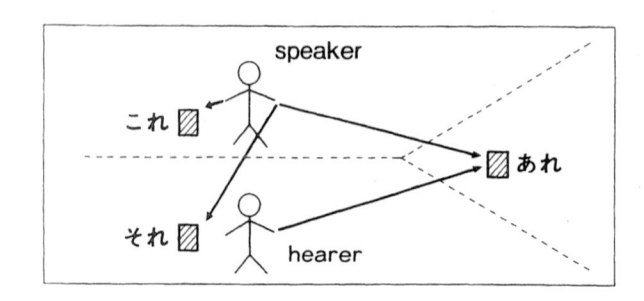

The difference between これ and この: これ can be used independently, while この is always used in combination with a noun.

Compare these two sentences from the dialogue:

これは何ですか。 (What is this?)
この器械(きかい)は何といいますか。 (What do you call this machine?)

As you can see, これ, それ, あれ, どれ are independent, and are not followed by nouns. この, その, あの, どの, however, need nouns. The English "this" can work both as an independent demonstrative pronoun and as a noun modifier. But in Japanese, the これ series has the former function and the この series has the latter.

〔い-adjectives〕

In dialogue ②, several adjectives are used. These adjectives are called い-adjectives because of their forms as noun modifiers. The other kind of adjective, which will appear in the next lesson, is called a な-adjective.

1. あの車は古(ふる)いです。 (That car is old.)
2. あの赤(あか)い車です。 (It's that red car.)
3. 古くありません。 ((That car is) not old.)
4. あの車は汚(きたな)いです。 (That car is dirty.)
5. あの車はいいですよ。 (That car is good.)

All the underlined words are adjectives used in the present tense; all except number 3 are affirmative, and numbers 1, 4, and 5 are used as predicates.

From these facts, we can conclude as follows:

1. All adjectives in the present affirmative (**the dictionary form** of an adjective) end with い. (See 1, 2, 4, 5)
2. The dictionary form is used as the predicate in the structure "N1 *wa* adj. *desu*" (See 1, 4, 5), and it also functions as a noun modifier. (See 2)
3. The present negative form is made by replacing い with く, and then adding ありません.

   古いです ⇨ 古くありません   (It is old. ⇨ It is not old.)
   いいです ⇨ よくありません   (It is good. ⇨ It is not good.)

Note 1　In the last phrase above (いいです), it should be noted that the first い is changed to よ; this, however, is the only irregularity of the い-adjs.

Note 2　There are lists of い-adj. and な-adj. in the next lesson.

● よくわかりませんが　　1-5

This expression is used to indicate that you are not very confident of what you are going to say. This can also be used to show modesty.

A：林(はやし)さん、リーさんは中国出身(ちゅうごくしゅっしん)ですか。
　　(Hayashi san, is Lee san from China?)
B：よくわかりませんが、韓国(かんこく)でしょう。
　　(I am not sure but I guess he is from Korea.)

Lesson 4

● （高い）でしょう　　1-11

The presumptive form of ～です is ～でしょう and it signifies the presumption or conjecture of the speaker.

  この本は私のです。　　(This book is mine)
  この本は私のでしょう。(I guess this book is mine.)
  シカゴは寒いです。　　(It is cold in Chicago.)
  シカゴは寒いでしょう。(It is cold in Chicago, I suppose.)

ことばの使い方 (ことばのつかいかた)

● 先生　　1-1

This term of respect is used to refer to such professionals as school teachers, professors, medical doctors, lawyers, politicians, artists, and anyone who is respected for his or her skill. You can add the last name before the word 先生, as in 田中先生. Do not put the words in the English order; in Japanese, the title follows the name.

In Japanese, addressing a person by his/her title is considered respectful. A company employee calls the president "社長" (president), and even at home a younger brother calls his elder siblings "おにいさん" (elder brother) or "おねえさん" (elder sister). Similarly, 先生 is a term of respect, and, therefore, should not be used to refer to yourself or your family-member.

● （違います）よ　　1-7

The sentence final particle よ indicates that the preceding proposition is the speaker's opinion or confident assertion. Do not use it too frequently as you may sound over-confident. Unlike か and like ね, this is ordinarily not used in written Japanese.

● ええ，まあ　　1-12

This is a convenient answer which is handy when you want to be elusive, that is, when you neither want to give a straightforward, detailed answer, nor negate something flatly. This expression indicates that you generally admit to what was said, but do not want to go into the details.

  A：林さん，あの人はガールフレンドですか。
   (Is she your girlfriend, Hayashi san?)
  B：ええ，まあ。(Sort of.)

● いくらですか　　1-13

This phrase means, "How much is it?" If you want to know the price of a specific item, put the word or phrase plus は before いくらですか.

  この本はいくらですか。(How much is this book?)

● どうして　　3-5

This interrogative word is used at the head of the sentence to ask a reason. To answer a どうして question at this point, use an ordinary sentence.

● 私のです　　3-6

In the dialogue, the original sentence is あの車は私のです. Here, 私の means 私の車. When N2 in the pattern "N1 *no* N2" (L. 1, p. 3) is clearly understood, it can be omitted.

● あら　　3-7

This is used only by women to express slight surprise. A similar masculine expression is あっ. In speaking Japanese, men and women adopt slightly different ways of speaking, especially in colloquial, conversational usage. But the difference lies in the rather peripheral parts of the language, such as exclamations (as seen in this example), sentence final particles, and word selection. Generally, women tend to speak more politely than men.

● (汚いです)が　　3-9

が here is a conjunctional particle like the English "but," which links together two sentences. In most cases, two sentences are contrasted with each other as illustrated by this sentence.

In this construction "S1 が S2." (S stands for a sentence), S2 is more important than the first sentence.

There are times, however, as in "失礼ですが," when が links two sentences loosely to indicate that even though the first sentence is completed, a second is to follow.

[Abbreviation of loan words]

Because of the Japanese phonetic system in which a vowel follows a consonant most of the time, a loan word tends to be felt too long for daily use by many Japanese people. As a result, they occasionally make words shorter as illustrated below;

　　ワード・プロセッサー　　　⇨ワープロ
　　パーソナル・コンピューター　⇨パソコン
　　タイプライター　　　　　　　⇨タイプ

練習 (れんしゅう)

練習(れんしゅう)　1	こ／そ／あ／どれ

Look at the picture and ask questions as shown in the example. Be careful in choosing from こ, そ, and あ. Take the role of A.

例　A：リンさん、これは何ですか。
　　B：どれですか。
　　A：これです。
　　B：ああ、それはワード・プロセッサーです。

Lesson 4

1.　　　　　　　　　　2.

3.　　　　　　　　　　4.

| 練習(れんしゅう)　2 | Omission of a noun |

Make a sentence as shown in the example.

例　この車，私　⇨　この車は私のです。(This car is mine.)

1．その本，リーさん　　2．あのかばん，リンさん　　3．この車，誰
4．あの自転車，林さん　5．この本，田中先生　　　　6．そのノート，誰

| 練習(れんしゅう)　3 | Omission of a noun |

Change the sentence as shown in the example.

例　私の車は，この古い車です。⇨私のは，この古いのです。(Mine is this old one.)
　　この古い車は，私の車です。⇨この古いのは私のです。(This old one is mine.)

1．リーさんの本は，この新しい本です。
2．この汚い自転車は，林さんの自転車です。
3．先生の車は，あの赤い車です。
4．この高いタイプライターは，リンさんのタイプライターです。
5．あの安いコンピューターは，私のコンピューターです。
6．この赤いノートは，ロングさんのノートです。

練習(れんしゅう) 4　　　これ vs. この

Make a sentence as shown in the example.

例　車, どれ　⇨ リーさんの車はどれですか。(Lee san, which is your car?)
　　本, この　⇨ リーさんの本はこの本ですか。(Lee san, is this your book?)

1．ケーキ, どの　　　　2．かばん, あの　　　　3．ノート, それ
4．コンピューター, これ　5．自転車, その　　　　6．器械, どれ

練習(れんしゅう) 5　　　これ vs. この／Identifying objects

Substitute the nouns as shown in the example.

例　その本は何といいますか。(What is the title of that book?)
　　（その車）⇨ その車は何といいますか。(What is that car called?)
　　（それ）　⇨ それは何といいますか。(What is it called?)

1．この器械　　　2．あれ　　　　　3．このコンピューター
4．これ　　　　　5．そのケーキ　　6．それ

練習(れんしゅう) 6　　　Identifying objects

Answer as shown in the example.

例　その本は何といいますか。(What is the title of the book?)
　　（日本語）⇨ この本は『日本語』といいます。(This book is called "Nihongo".)

1．その器械は何といいますか。　（プリンター）
2．そのかばんは何といいますか。（バックパック）
3．そのケーキは何といいますか。（チーズケーキ）
4．その器械は何といいますか。　（コンピューター）
5．その車は何といいますか。　　（キャデラック）

練習(れんしゅう) 7　　　い-adj. as a predicate and as a noun-modifier

Answer as shown in the example.

例　あの車は古いですね。⇨ ええ, 古いですね。ほんとうに古い車ですね。
　　(That car is old, isn't it?　⇨ Yes, it is old. It is really an old car.)

1．このタイプライターはいいですね。　2．この本は新しいですね。
3．そのノートは古いですね。　　　　　4．林さんのかばんは新しいですね。
5．リーさんの自転車はひどいですね。　6．田中さんの車は古いですね。

Lesson 4

練習(れんしゅう)　8　　　　　　　～でしょう

Answer as shown in the example.

例　あの車は古いですか。⇨よくわかりませんが，古いでしょう。

(Is that car old?　⇨ I am not sure but I suppose it is a little old.)

1．これはいいタイプライターですか。　2．この本はいいですか。
3．そのノートは古いですか。　　　　　4．林さんのかばんは安いかばんですか。
5．リーさんの自転車は高いですか。　　6．田中さんの車はあれですか。

練習(れんしゅう)　9　　　　　　Negative form of an い-adj./antonyms

Answer as shown in the example.

例　林さんの車は古いですか。

(Is Hayashi san's car old?/ Hayashi san, is your car old?)

⇨いいえ，古くありませんよ。かなり新しいですよ。

(It is not old. It is quite new.)

1．林さんの本は古いですか。　　　　2．ロングさんのかばんは新しいですか。
3．ダンさんの自転車はいいですか。　4．リーさんのコンピューターは高いですか。
5．田中さんのノートは新しいですか。6．この器械は安いですか。

練習(れんしゅう)　10　　　　　　S1　が　S2

Make a sentence as shown in the example.

例　新しい，いい　⇨私のタイプライターは新しくありませんがいいですよ。

(My typewriter is not new, but it's good.)

1．古い，汚い　　2．いい，新しい　　3．古い，ひどい　　4．新しい，いい

五課

内容表

文法	The な-adj.		嫌(いや)な天気 簡単(かんたん)じゃありませんでした。 大変(たいへん)でした
	て-form of adjectives …… (and)		暖(あたた)かくて、いい日(ひ)
	Perfect vs. Imperfect forms Affirmative vs. Negative （な-adj., Noun, い-adj.）		See the lists in 文法(ぶんぽう)
	Demonstrative 　こう, そう, ああ, どう 　ここ, そこ, あそこ, どこ		こう (like this, in this manner) ここ (here, this part, this place)
機能	Greeting	6-1	おはようございます etc.
	Presenting General Topics	6-4	Speaking of the weather
	Taking Leave	6-2	じゃ、また明日(あした)。 失礼(しつれい)します。
	Changing a Topic	7-12	ところで
	Inquiring About an Opinion	2-34	宿題(しゅくだい)はどうでしたか。
	Extending an Invitation	2-5	始(はじ)めましょう。 終(お)わりましょう。
	Expressing Sympathy	3-15	大変でしたね。
	Starting Conversation	6-3	すみませんが。
	Explaining How Something Works	1-9	こうですよ。
	Making Requests	5-3	見(み)てください。 見(み)せてください。

会話 (かいわ)

1

A：おはようございます。　　　　　　　　Good morning.

B：おはようございます。　　　　　　　　Good morning.

A：今日はいい天気ですね。　　　　　　　(It's a) nice day today.

B：本当に暖かくていい日ですね。　　　　(It's) really a warm and nice day.

A：昨日は寒くて，嫌な天気でしたね。　　It was cold and unpleasant yesterday.

B：ええ，ひどい天気でした。　　　　　　Yes, it was terrible weather.

A：ところで宿題はどうでしたか。　　　　By the way, how was the homework?
　　簡単でしたか。　　　　　　　　　　　Was it simple?

B：いいえ，簡単じゃありませんでした。　No, it wasn't simple.

A：難しかったですか。　　　　　　　　　Was it difficult?

B：難しくありませんでしたが，二時間　　It was not difficult, but it took (me) about
　　ぐらいかかりました。　　　　　　　　two hours.

A：そうですか。大変でしたね。　　　　　Is that right? It was a lot of work, wasn't it?
　　あ，もう時間ですね。[はい。]　　　　Oh, it's time already. [Yes.]
　　じゃ，始めましょうか。[はい。]　　　Then, let's start, shall we? [Yes.]

2

A：じゃ，今日はこれで終わりましょ　　　Then, let's stop with this (what we have
　　う。[はい。]　　　　　　　　　　　　done). [Yes.]
　　じゃ，また明日。　　　　　　　　　　Well, (see you) again tomorrow!

B：失礼します。　　　　　　　　　　　　Goodbye, (sir / ma'am).

3

A：山田さん，すみませんが，この字を見　Excuse me Yamada san but would you take
　　てください。[はい。]　　　　　　　　a look at this character? [Yes.]

この字は、正しいですか。	Is this character correct?
B：ちょっと見せてください。［はい。］	Show me for a second. [Here it is.]
ああ、少しおかしいですね。	Oh, it is a little strange.
A：おかしいところはどこですか。	Which part is it that is strange?
B：ここです。ここは、こうですよ。	It's here. This part should be like this.
A：ああ、こうですか。わかりました。	Oh, like this! I understand.

単語表（たんごひょう）

1

おはようございます	Good morning.
今日（きょう）	today
暖（あたた）かい	(pleasantly) warm
天気（てんき）	weather
日（ひ）	day
昨日（きのう）	yesterday
寒（さむ）い	cold
嫌（いや）な	unpleasant
〜でした	past form of です
ところで	by the way
宿題（しゅくだい）	homework
〜はどうでしたか	How was 〜?
簡単（かんたん）な	simple
難（むずか）しい	difficult
二時間（にじかん）	two hours
ぐらい、くらい	about
かかりました	past form of かかります（←かかる）, took
大変（たいへん）な	needs a lot of work, hard, difficult, terrible
もう	already
時間（じかん）です	It is time (to do 〜.)
始（はじ）めます	begin

2

終（お）わります	end, finish
また	again
明日（あした）	tomorrow
失礼（しつれい）します	goodbye sir/ma'am

3

山田（やまだ）	a surname
すみませんが	Excuse me, but/ sorry to bother you
字（じ）	character, letter
（〜を）見（み）てください	Please look at 〜.
正（ただ）しい	correct, right
ちょっと	for a moment
ああ	oh, ah
少（すこ）し	a little
おかしい	strange, funny, absurd
ところ	part, place
ここ	here, this part
こうです	like this, this way

Lesson 5

関連語句（かんれんごく）

おいしい	tasty, delicious	まずい	(as for food) terrible, tasteless
やさしい	easy	コーヒー	coffee
暑(あつ)い	hot	大学(だいがく)	college, university
涼(すず)しい	cool		

文法（ぶんぽう）

● な-ADJECTIVE

In Japanese, there are two kinds of adjectives. Because of their formal characteristics as noun modifiers, they are called い-adjectives, and な-adjectives. The adjectives in L. 4, such as いい, 古い, 赤い, 汚い, and ひどい are all い-adjs. which modify nouns in these forms, whereas な-adjs. take な to modify nouns.

な-adj.＋Noun	い-adj.＋Noun
嫌(いや)な天気(てんき)	いい天気
簡単(かんたん)な宿題(しゅくだい)	難(むずか)しい宿題
大変(たいへん)な仕事(しごと)	やさしい仕事

Just like い-adjs., な-adjs. can be used as predicates in a phrase like in "N は な-adj. です." In this case, as well as in their negative forms, な-adjs. act like nouns.

　この宿題は簡単です。　　　　　　　(This homework is simple.)
　田中さんの仕事は大変です。　　　　 (Tanaka san's job is demanding.)
　この宿題は簡単じゃありません。　　 (This homework is not simple.)
　田中さんの仕事は大変じゃありません。(Tanaka san's job is not demanding.)

● PAST TENSE

The past tense forms of "N／な-adj. ＋です" and い-adj. ＋です are shown as follows:

1. N／な-adj. ＋です (N stands for a noun or a noun phrase such as いい天気 as a whole.)

　〔Affirmative〕　です ⇨ でした

　　昨日(きのう)はいい天気でした。(The weather was good yesterday.)
　　宿題は簡単でした。　(The homework was simple.)

Note that, in the first example, いい天気 as a whole functions as a noun phrase and いい does not have anything to do with the past tense.

　〔Negative〕　じゃありません ⇨ ＋でした

38

昨日はいい天気じゃありませんでした。(The weather was not good yesterday.)
宿題は簡単じゃありませんでした。　　(The homework was not simple.)

	Present	Past
Affirm.	学生／簡単です	学生／簡単でした
Neg.	学生／簡単じゃありません	学生／簡単じゃありませんでした

2．い-adj. ＋です

〔Affirmative〕 (寒)いです ⇨ (寒)かったです。

昨日は寒かったです。　　(It was cold yesterday.)
宿題は難しかったです。(The homework was difficult.)

〔Negative〕⇨ (寒)くありません ⇨ ＋でした

昨日は寒くありませんでした。　　(It was not cold yesterday.)
宿題は難しくありませんでした。(The homework was not difficult.)

	Present	Past
Affirm.	寒いです	寒かったです
Neg.	寒くありません (寒くないです)	寒くありませんでした (寒くなかったです)

The handling of い-adjs. is more complicated than that of nouns and な-adjs. because there are three different forms.

They are:

　　　　　＋　い　　→　です　　　　　(present affirm.)
　寒　＋　かった　→　です　　　　　(past affirm.)
　　　　　＋　く　　→　ありません (present neg.) ＋でした (past neg.)

● "て-form"

In L. 1 (p. 4), the て-form of the copula です was introduced. This grammatical device enables us to connect two sentences. The て-form, therefore, is equivalent in function to the English conjunction "and."

　　私は大学院の学生です。専門は人類学です。
　　　⇨私は大学院の学生で，専門は人類学です。
　　　　(I am a graduate student, and my major is anthropology.)
　　リーさんは一年生です。ダンさんは二年生です。
　　　⇨リーさんは一年生で，ダンさんは二年生です。
　　　　(Lee san is a first year student, and Dunn san is a second year student.)

In the above example, the て-form of the copula is used with nouns. The same form can be used with な-adjs.

　　宿題は簡単です。やさしいです。
　　　⇨宿題は簡単で，やさしいです。(The homework is simple and easy.)

Then, how is the "て-form" of い-adjs. made? Unlike nouns and な-adjs., い-adjs. have their own "て-forms." Follow these two steps to create the "て-form" of い-adjs.: First, take

Lesson 5

the く-form of the adjective (this is the form used in negating these adjectives). Then add て to this く-form.

> 今日は暖かいです。いい天気です。
> ⇨今日は暖かくて，いい天気です。(It is warm and fine today.)

A sentence in the dialogue reads as follows:

> 昨日は寒くて，嫌な天気でした。

If you paraphrase this sentence into two, you will get the sentences below.

> 昨日は寒かったです。嫌な天気でした。

This example illustrates the lack of tense-marker in the "て-form" itself. The tense of the "て-form" is determined by the tense of the predicate. If the predicate shows the present tense, then the "て-form" signifies the present tense in accordance with it. The same is true of the past tense. This is presumably why some scholars call the "て-form" a gerund. But the "て-form" is more widely used in spoken Japanese than its English counterpart.

● こう，そう，ああ，どう

This is another series of こ，そ，あ，ど：

こうです	like this / in this way	/ as I do
そうです	like that / in that way	/ as you do
ああです	like that over there	/ as he/she does
どうですか	like what / how	

A：これは，どう食べますか。(How shall I eat this?)
B：見てください。こうです。(Look at me. Like this.)

● ここ，そこ，あそこ，どこ

This series indicates places:

ここ	here	/ this part
そこ	there	/ that part
あそこ	over there	/ the part over there
どこ	where	/ which part

ことばの使い方 (ことばのつかいかた)

● おはよ(早)うございます　　1-1

This is a common greeting used in the morning. Since it literally means "It is early" it should not be used late in the morning. When this phrase cannot be used, people adopt various expressions appropriate for each situation. Speaking about the weather, asking where the addressee is going, and asking if he/she is busy (おいそがしいですか。) are very ordinary tactics used to avoid possible awkward feelings and uncomfortable silences.

Other greetings are:

<u>こんにちは</u>。　　　(Good afternoon.)

<u>こんばんは</u>。　　　(Good evening.)

おやすみなさい。(Good night.)

As with similar expressions in English, こんにちは and こんばんは are not used with members of your family or in-group. Also avoid these greetings with your superiors as they sound slightly casual. For this purpose, mentioning the weather would work.

● 天気　　1-3

This word can be modified by such adjectives as いい, 嫌な, and ひどい. It is not right to say 暑い天気 or 寒い天気. To talk about hot or cold weather, simply say 今日は暑いです or 昨日は寒かったです.

● 暖かい　　1-4

In Japanese, 暖かい refers to pleasant, warm temperatures in winter and spring. It cannot be used to describe summer climates. The word 涼しい means the cool, comfortable temperatures in summer and fall.

● ところで　　1-7

This conjunction is used as a signal to indicate that the speaker is changing the topic of conversation, or that he/she is introducing a new topic.

● (宿題は)どうでしたか　　1-7

As explained on the previous page, this is an expression used to ask the opinion of the addressee after he/she has tried something.

　　このケーキはどうでしたか。　　　(How was this cake?)
　　昨日のコンサートはどうでしたか。(How was yesterday's concert?)

● 二時間　　1-11

The word 時間 means "hour(s)." The numbers from one to ten that can be used with 時間 are as follows:

1．いち(一)　2．に(二)　3．さん(三)　4．よ(四)　5．ご(五)
6．ろく(六)　7．なな／しち(七)　8．はち(八)　9．く(九)　10．じゅう(十)

As for the accent, it is always ○(○)じかん.

● (二時間)ぐらい　　1-12

ぐらい expresses an approximation, and is attached to numbers and amounts. くらい is a variant of ぐらい.

● (大変でした)ね　　1-13

ね here has an important function of conveying the speaker's sympathy and empathy. Without it, the statement is flat, and the speaker's empathy is not communicated.

● じゃ　　1-15

This short expression means, "If the situation is like this, then ...." In the dialogue, *Sensei*, taking a look at his watch, noticed that it was time to start class. In another example from the dialogue, he realized that time was up and, therefore, he had to say goodbye.

Lesson 5

● じゃ，またあした　　2-3

In Japanese, at least three kinds of greetings are used when parting. This is the most popular one among friends. The final part "あした" is interchangeable with such time expressions as "来週"(next week), "来月"(next month), and so forth. The teacher in the dialogue greets his class by using terms ordinarily exchanged among friends, to show his feeling of closeness to the students. The students respond with a greeting appropriate for addressing superiors, 失礼します. It can be used on a variety of occasions, for example, on entering someone's room, or when passing in front of somebody.

The third greeting is さようなら(さよなら) which cannot be used with superiors. There are people who say that さよなら sounds too strong and pathetic, as if you were parting forever. There are many others, however, who use it in a very casual way.

● すみませんが　　3-1

This phrase indicates that the speaker is about to ask somebody to do something. It is helpful, for example, when you approach a stranger for directions to a certain location, or perhaps, to ask the time.

Don't confuse this phrase with 失礼ですが which sets up the preface for asking personal questions.

You may put あのう in front of this expression. In an ordinary conversation, many people may pronounce this phrase す<u>い</u>ませんが.

練習(れんしゅう)

練習(れんしゅう)　1	Greetings

Return the greetings, as in the example.

例　おはようございます。⇨おはようございます。(Good morning.)

1．こんにちは。　2．こんばんは。　3．おやすみなさい。　4．おはようございます。
5．いい天気ですね。　6．暑いですね。　7．寒いですね。　8．暖かいですね。

練習(れんしゅう)　2	Negative forms of　い／な-adj.

Answer in the negative, as shown in the examples.

例　暑いですか。(Is it hot?)
　　　⇨いいえ，暑くありませんよ。(No, it isn't hot.)
　　大変ですか。(Is it hard?)
　　　⇨いいえ，大変じゃありませんよ。(No, it isn't hard.)

1．寒いですか。　2．簡単ですか。　3．難しいですか。　4．嫌ですか。
5．暖かいですか。　6．大変ですか。　7．ひどいですか。　8．簡単ですか。

| 練習(れんしゅう) 3 | Negative forms |

Answer in the negative, as shown in the example.

例　この仕事は，嫌ですか。⇨いいえ，嫌じゃありません。
　　(Is this job unpleasant?　⇨ No, it isn't unpleasant.)

1．この宿題は大変ですか。　2．この仕事は簡単ですか。　3．林さんは一年生ですか。
4．この車はいいですか。　　5．この仕事は嫌ですか。　　6．明日はいい天気ですか。

| 練習(れんしゅう) 4 | Negative, antonyms |

Answer as shown in the example.

例　このコーヒーはおいしいですか。⇨いいえ，おいしくありません。まずいです。
　　(Is this coffee tasty?　⇨ No, it isn't. It's awful.)

1．日本語は簡単ですか。　　　　2．田中さんの車は新しいですか。
3．きょうの宿題は大変ですか。　4．ワード・プロセッサーは難しいですか。
5．明日はいい天気ですか。　　　6．この字はおかしいですか。

| 練習(れんしゅう) 5 | Past |

Answer as shown in the example.

例　(暑い)⇨A：昨日は暑かったですね。
　　　　　B：ええ，昨日は暑かったですが，今日は暑くありませんね。
　　　　　　(A：It was hot yesterday, wasn't it?)
　　　　　　(B：Yes, it was hot yesterday, but it isn't today.)

1．暖かい　　2．暑い　　3．涼しい　　　　4．寒い
5．いい天気　6．嫌な天気　7．ひどい天気

| 練習(れんしゅう) 6 | Past negative |

Answer as shown in the example.

例　(昨日の宿題，やさしい)
　　⇨A：昨日の宿題はどうでしたか。やさしかったですか。
　　　B：いいえ，やさしくありませんでした。
　　　　(A：How was yesterday's homework? Was it easy?)
　　　　(B：No, it wasn't easy.)

1．このケーキ，おいしい　　　　2．このタイプライター，いい
3．日本語の宿題，大変　　　　　4．この器械，難しい
5．この仕事，簡単　　　　　　　6．この車，いい

Lesson 5

練習(れんしゅう) 7　　　　Noun modification with い／な-adj.

Answer as shown in the example.

例　この宿題はやさしいですね。⇨ええ、やさしい宿題ですね。
　　(This homework is easy, isn't it?　⇨ Yes, it's easy homework.)

1．このケーキ，おいしい　　2．このタイプライター，いい　　3．この宿題，大変
4．この器械，難しい　　　　5．この仕事，簡単　　　　　　　6．この車，いい
7．この大学，ほんとうにいい　8．このコーヒー，おいしい

練習(れんしゅう) 8　　　　て-form of い-adj.

Answer as shown in the example.

例　暑い，嫌　⇨今日は暑くて嫌な天気ですね。
　　　　　　(Today the weather is hot and unpleasant, isn't it?)

1．暖かい，いい　　　2．暑い，ひどい　　　3．寒い，大変
4．寒い，ひどい　　　5．涼しい，いい　　　6．暑い，嫌

練習(れんしゅう) 9　　　　て-form of い-adj.

Answer as shown in the example.

例　ケーキ，おいしい，簡単　⇨このケーキはおいしくて簡単です。
　　　　　　　　　　　　　　(This cake is tasty and easy to make.)

1．コーヒー，おいしい，安い　　　　2．この車，簡単，いい
3．ケーキ，高い，まずい　　　　　　4．器械，やさしい，簡単

練習(れんしゅう) 10　　　　S1 が S2

Answer as shown in the example.

例　この器械，やさしくありません，いい
　　⇨この器械はやさしくありませんが、いいですよ。
　　　(This machine is not easy to operate, but it's good.)

1．このタイプライター，簡単じゃありません，いい
2．インスタント・コーヒー，おいしくありません，簡単
3．今日の宿題，難しくありません，大変
4．この車，新しくありません，いい
5．今日，暖かくありません，いい天気

練習(れんしゅう) 11	すみませんが

Substitute as shown in the example.

例 （正しい）
山田さん，すみませんが，この字を見てください。この字は正しいですか。

(Yamada san, sorry to bother you, but please take a look at this character. Is it correct?)

1．おかしい　　　　　　　2．いい
3．違います　　　　　　　4．ひどい
5．正しい　　　　　　　　6．正しくありません
7．おかしくありません　　8．ひどくありません

練習(れんしゅう) 12	見てください vs. 見せてください

Say the following in Japanese.

例　Look at this character.　⇨この字を見てください。
　　Show me that character.　⇨その字を見せてください。

1．Show me your Japanese book.　　2．Look at my new car.
3．Look at my homework.　　　　　4．Show me your homework.

六課

内容表

文法	Location (Animate / Inanimate) Demonstrative (Places) Place＋に(います, あります) Contrastive「は」 Substituting a verbal phrase: です		Place＋に(います／あります) ここ，そこ，あそこ，どこ 読売新聞(よみうりしんぶん)はありませんが，朝日新聞(あさひしんぶん)はあります。 あそこです。 どこですか。
機能	Seeking Factual Information 　(Location 1) Stating Factual Information 　(Location 1) Expressing Thanks Responding to Thanks Identifying Objects Expressing Uncertainty Taking Leave	1-3 1-2 6-17 6-18 1-1 2-19 6-2	リーさん，いますか。 新聞はどこにありますか。 あそこです。 あそこにいますよ。 どうもありがとうございました。 どうも。 いいえ(どういたしまして)。 何(なん)という新聞ですか。 多分(たぶん)(書庫(しょこ)ですよ)。 じゃ，ちょっと。

Lesson 6

会話 (かいわ)

1

A： すみませんが、新聞はどこにありますか。 　　Excuse me but where are the newspapers?

B： 日本語の新聞ですか。[はい。] 　　(You mean) Japanese newspapers? [Yes.]
あそこです。 　　Over there.

A： はい、わかりました。 　　Yes, I see.
あのう、読売新聞はありますか。 　　Ummm, do you have the *Yomiuri*?

B： はっ？　何という新聞ですか。 　　What? What's the name of the paper?

A： 読売新聞です。 　　(It is) the *Yomiuri*.

B： 読売新聞はありませんが、朝日新聞はありますよ。 　　We don't have the *Yomiuri*, but we have the *Asahi*.

A： そうですか。どうもありがとうございました。 　　Really? Thank you very much.

B： いいえ。 　　Not at all.

2

C： あのう、すみませんが…。 　　Excuse me ...

B： はい、何ですか。 　　Yes, what is it?

C： リーさん、いますか。 　　Is Mr. Lee here?

B： 多分、書庫ですよ。 　　He is probably in the stacks.

C： そうですか。じゃ、ちょっと。 　　Really? Then, excuse me.

(C sees B come back from the stacks)

B： いませんでしたか。 　　Wasn't he there?

C： ええ、いませんでした。 　　Right (No). He wasn't there.

B： おかしいですね。あ、あそこにいますよ。 　　Strange! Oh there he is.

C：どこですか。　　　　　　　　　　　Where?
B：新聞のところにいますよ。　　　　　By the newspaper rack.
C：ああ，いますね。どうも。　　　　　Oh yes, he is. Thank you.
B：いえいえ。　　　　　　　　　　　　You are welcome.

単語表 (たんごひょう)

1

新聞(しんぶん)	newspaper
あそこ	over there
朝日新聞(あさひしんぶん)	The *Asahi*
読売新聞(よみうりしんぶん)	The *Yomiuri*

2

書庫(しょこ)	stacks
雑誌(ざっし)	magazine
多分(たぶん)	probably
ところ	place

関連語句 (かんれんごく)

人(ひと)	person	図書館(としょかん)	library
駅(えき)	railway station	建物(たてもの)	building
言語学(げんごがく)	linguistics	スーパーマーケット	supermarket
参考書(さんこうしょ)	reference books	台所(だいどころ)	kitchen
お手洗(てあら)い	toilet, bathroom	家(うち)	house, home
居間(いま)	living room	食堂(しょくどう)	dining room
書斎(しょさい)	study room	玄関(げんかん)	entrance to a building or a house

例のように練習しなさい。　Practice as (shown in the) example.

Lesson 6

文法 (ぶんぽう)

● **N1 は N2 (place) にあります／います**　　1-1

This pattern is used to indicate the location of someone or something. The choice of the verb います or あります is determined by whether the topic N1 is animate or inanimate. An animate topic takes います, and an inanimate one takes あります. (For other uses, see P. 68, 127, 128)

　　リーさんは書庫にいます。(Lee san is in the stacks.)
　　その本は書庫にあります。(That book is in the stacks.)

The particle に indicates the location of the topic. The conjugation of verbs is done in the following way:

	Present	Past
Affirm.	あります／います	ありました／いました
Neg.	ありません／いません	Present neg.＋でした

● **（あそこ）です**　　1-4

From the context, we can determine that the above sentence is equivalent to あそこにあります. This example illustrates the third function of です. (For the first two functions, see P. 3, P. 11—ですか.)

In the dialogue, the person who asked the question just wanted to know where the newspapers were, so the respondent could have provided the sought information by simply saying "あそこ". However, such an answer would have been impolite. That the verb can be dropped means that it is not very important in this sentence. In Japanese, when a verb is of secondary or tertiary importance, the verb, together with the preceding particle, can be replaced by です.

This function of です can often be seen in the answers to the questions with interrogative words (where, why, who, what, when, how) in which the most important information is, of course, signified by the interrogative words.

　　1．A：新聞はどこにありますか。(Where is the newspaper?)
　　　 B：あそこです。　　　　　(It is over there.)
　　2．A：何を食べますか。　　　(What will you eat?)
　　　 B：ハンバーガーです。　　(I'll eat a hamburger.)

But, occasionally, です is used in questions as a replacement for a verb.

　　リーさんはどこですか。(Where is Lee san?)
　　田中さんの家はどこですか。
　　　(Where is your house, Tanaka san? / Where is Tanaka san's house?)

In the last example, です sounds more natural than にあります.

● **The contrastive は**　　1-9

The two nouns in the pattern "N1 は Pred(icate), N2 は Pred.," are placed in contrast to each other. Even without second "N2 は" this contrastive nuance is retained. See 文法「机の上にはありません。」 in the next lesson.

　　林さんはいますが、リーさんはいません。(Hayashi san is here, but not Lee san.)

六課

ことばの使い方 (ことばのつかいかた)

● すみませんが　　1-1　☞P. 42

● 何という（新聞ですか）　　1-7
This is roughly equal to この新聞は何といいますか in its function. Both are used to ask names and titles.
　　1．A：あの人は何という人ですか。　　（What is that person's name?）
　　　　B：山田さんという人です。　　（That person is Yamada san.）
　　2．A：その本は何という本ですか。　　（What's the title of that book?）
　　　　B：『日本の新聞』という本です。　　（Its title is *Nihon no Shinbun*.）

● 読売新聞　　1-6
よみうりしんぶん is one of the three major newspapers in Japan. The other two are: 朝日新聞 and 毎日新聞.

● はい，何ですか　　2-2
はい indicates that the speaker understood what the previous speaker said. In this case, ええ cannot be used.

● いいえ／いえいえ　　1-13, 2-13
These words are used in response to a person's thanks or apology. Their formal equivalent is いいえ，どういたしまして．

● リーさん　いますか　　2-3
In conversation, particularly among friends, some particles are often omitted. In this example, "は" is dropped. Do keep in mind, however, that you cannot omit particles randomly.

● 新聞のところ（にいます）　　2-11
The particle に indicates the location of people and objects. Like 新聞 here, there are many nouns, however, which do not express a sense of location. In such a case, adding 〜のところ (lit. "the place of the newspaper") will enable you to use the noun to express location.
　　1．A：その本，どこにありましたか。
　　　　　（Where was that book? / Where did you find the book?）
　　　　B：辞書のところにありましたよ。（It was where the dictionaries are.）
　　2．A：紙はどこにありますか。　　（Where is the paper?）
　　　　B：先生のところにありますよ。　（It is where the teacher is.）

● じゃ，ちょっと　　2-5
This is an informal equivalent of the expression じゃ，ちょっと失礼します．ちょっと, in this context, means "for a second."

Lesson 6

練習（れんしゅう）

練習（れんしゅう）　1	あのう，すみませんが／Place＋にあります

例のように練習しなさい。

例　あのう，すみませんが，新聞はどこにありますか。（雑誌）
　　　(Excuse me, but where are the newspapers?)
　　⇨あのう，すみませんが，雑誌はどこにありますか。
　　　(Excuse me, but where are the magazines?)

1．日本語の本　　　　2．言語学の本　　　　3．英語の雑誌
4．図書館　　　　　　5．駅　　　　　　　　6．スーパーマーケット

練習（れんしゅう）　2	〜という N

例　新聞，シカゴ・トリビューン
　　⇨A：これは何という新聞ですか。
　　　　B：シカゴ・トリビューンという新聞ですよ。
　　　　(A：What is the name of this paper?)
　　　　(B：It is the *Chicago Tribune*.)

1．雑誌，タイム　　　　　　　　　2．図書館，スタイン図書館
3．コンピューター，アップルⅡ　　4．ケーキ，チーズケーキ
5．器械，プリンター　　　　　　　6．車，BMW

練習（れんしゅう）　3	N1 は，N2 は

例　タイム，ライフ
　　⇨A：タイムはありますか。
　　　　B：タイムはありませんが，ライフはありますよ。
　　　　(A：Do you have *Time* magazine here?)
　　　　(B：I don't have *Time* but I have *Life*.)

1．コーヒー，コーラ　　　　　　　　2．自転車，車
3．コンピューター，ワード・プロセッサー　　4．新聞，雑誌
5．中国語の本，韓国語の本　　　　　6．読売新聞，朝日新聞

練習(れんしゅう)　4	います vs. あります

例　あのう，すみませんが，リーさんいますか。(Excuse me, is Lee san there?)
　　（言語学の本）⇨あのう，すみませんが，言語学の本ありますか。
　　　　　　　　　(Excuse me, is there a book on linguistics?)

1．田中さん　　　　　2．コーヒー　　　　　3．今日の新聞
4．ダンさん　　　　　5．日本語の雑誌　　　6．コーラ

練習(れんしゅう)　5	Past vs. Present

Carry on the dialogue as shown in the example. Take the role of A.

例　リーさん　A：リーさん，いませんでしたか。(Wasn't Lee san there?)
　　　　　　　B：ええ，いませんでした。　　(No, he wasn't.)
　　　　　　　A：あ，あそこにいますよ。　　(Oh, he's over there.)
　　　　　　　B：ああ，いますね。　　　　　(Yes, he certainly is.)

1．田中さん　　　　　2．コーヒー　　　　　3．今日の新聞
4．ダンさん　　　　　5．日本語の雑誌　　　6．コーラ

練習(れんしゅう)　6	N1 は, N2 は／Neg. vs. Affirm.

例　日本語の本，ここにありますか。(Are Japanese books here?)
　　（あそこ）⇨ここにはありませんが，あそこにありますよ。
　　　　　　　(They aren't here but they're there.)

1．林さん，ここにいますか。　　　　　　　（図書館）
2．図書館，この建物にありますか。　　　　（あの建物）
3．ダンさん，食堂にいましたか。　　　　　（お手洗い）
4．私の本，ここにありましたか。　　　　　（あそこ）
5．スーパーマーケットはあそこにありますか。（そこ）

練習(れんしゅう)　7	です replacing verbal phrases

例　日本語の本，どこにありますか。(Where are the Japanese books?)
　　（あそこ）⇨日本語の本は，あそこですよ。(The Japanese books are over there.)

1．林さん，どこにいますか。　　　　　　　（図書館）
2．図書館，この建物にありますか。　　　　（あの建物）
3．ダンさん，どこにいますか。　　　　　　（お手洗い）
4．リーさんの家，どこですか。　　　　　　（ニューヨーク）
5．スーパーマーケットはどこにありますか。（そこ）

七課

内容表

文法	Locative nouns ＋います／あります		上, 中, 下, 前, 後ろ, 左, 右
	Omission of the final particle か		どうしました(か)？
	Modifying a noun with two adjs.		黄色い大きい封筒
	Contrastive「は」		机の上にはありませんね。
	Verb て-form＋くれませんか		ひきだしの中を見てくれませんか。
	Topical particle「も」		ここにもありません。
	Using the plain form for the speaker's monologue		困ったなあ。
	Perfect form indicating discovery		ああ, よかった。
	Interrogative words＋でしょう		いすの下にありました。
	Particle が used to introduce a noun as an agent or subject		どうでしょう。 お願いがあります。 きれいな女の人がいます。
機能	Seeking Factual Information	1-3	上, 中, 下, 前, 後ろ, 左, 右
	Stating Factual Information (Location 2)	1-2	
	Making / Answering a Telephone Call	8-2	もしもし, 〜さんですか。
		8-1	はい。
	Expressing Concern	6-21	どうしました？
	Expressing Agreement	2-1	いいですよ。
	Making Requests	5-3	〜て＋くれませんか。
	Expressing Relief	3-35	ああ, よかった。
	Admitting	2-4	さあ, どうでしょう。
	Expressing Fear / Worry	3-6	困ったなあ。

Lesson 7

会話 (かいわ)

1 [電話での会話]

A：もしもし，石井さんですか。	Hello, (is this) Ishii san?
B：はい。ああ，スナイダーさん。	Yes. Oh, Sneider san?
どうしました？	What's the matter?
A：ちょっと，お願いがありますが。	I have a favor to ask of you.
B：ええ，いいですよ。何ですか。	Fine. What is it?
A：机の上に封筒がありますか。	Is there an envelope on the desk?
B：何色ですか。	What color is it?
A：黄色い大きい封筒ですが…。	It's a big yellow envelope.
B：机の上にはありませんね。	It isn't there (on the desk).
A：じゃ，ひきだしの中を見てくれませんか。	Then, won't you take a look inside the drawers?
B：ここにもありませんよ。	It's not here, either.
A：そうですか。困ったなあ。	Really? Oh, dear!
B：ああ，これですね。	Oh, this must be the one.
いすの下にありましたよ。	Here it is under the chair.
A：そうですか。ああ，よかった。	Really? I am relieved.

2

A：あ，一番前に木村さんがいますよ。	Oh, Kimura san is in the front row.
B：彼の右にきれいな女の人がいますよ。	A beautiful girl is on his right.
A：ガールフレンドですか。	Is she his girlfriend?
B：さあ，どうでしょう。わかりません。	Well, I'm not sure. I don't know.
A：木村さんの後ろの人は誰ですか。	Who is the person behind Kimura san?
B：ジョンソン先生でしょう。	I guess it's Johnson Sensei.
A：違うでしょう。	I don't think it's him.

B：あ，シュルツ先生ですね。　　　　　　Oh, it's Shultz Sensei.
A：そうですね。あ，もう時間ですね。　　That's right. Oh, it's time, now.
B：ええ，始まりますね。　　　　　　　　Yes. It's going to start.

単語表 (たんごひょう)

1

電話(でんわ)	telephone
石井(いしい)	a surname
お願(ねが)い	request, favor
机(つくえ)	desk
封筒(ふうとう)	envelope
何色(なにいろ)	what color
黄色(きいろ)い	yellow
大(おお)きい	big, large
ひきだし	drawer
中(なか)	in, inside
見(み)て	⇨見る look, see
困(こま)った	⇨困る be in trouble
いす	chair
下(した)	under, below

2

前(まえ)	in front of, before
木村(きむら)	a surname
右(みぎ)	right
きれいな	beautiful, pretty
女の人(おんなのひと)	woman
後(うし)ろ	behind, in back of
誰(だれ)	who
始(はじ)まります	⇨始まる begin, start

関連語句 (かんれんごく)

左(ひだり)	left	たばこ	cigarettes
灰皿(はいざら)	ashtray	ノート	notebook
えんぴつ	pencil	ボールペン	ball-point pen
男(おとこ)	man, male	財布(さいふ)	wallet, pocket book

Lesson 7

文法 (ぶんぽう)

● **N1 が Predicate**　　1-4

が is used to introduce a previously unmentioned noun (as an agent or as a subject of a sentence). It cannot be used when you want to form a contrast with other nouns. See the sentences from the dialogue:

1. お願いがありますが。⇨ (お願いというのは) 何ですか。
2. 封筒がありますか。　⇨ (封筒は) どこにありますか。
3. 木村さんがいますよ。⇨ (木村さんは) どこにいますか。
4. 女の人がいますよ。　⇨ (女の人は) どこにいますか。

The above left sentences are the first remark about the agent or subject (the word before が). The portions in parentheses would normally be deleted but should it be necessary to repeat them later, は must be used, since it would no longer be the initial mention of the agent or subject.

● 黄色い大きい(封筒)　　1-8

Modification of a noun with two adjectives is possible in two ways;

1. Using the adjectives in the form given in the word lists.
    黄色い大きい封筒　(big, yellow envelope)
    簡単な安い辞書　(simple, inexpensive dictionary)
2. Using the て-form
    黄色くて大きい封筒
    簡単で安い辞書

● 机の上にはありません　　1-9

The basic function of は is to present a topic. Topics are not strictly limited to nouns. As illustrated in this sentence, a phrase like 机の上に can be a topic as well. In this example, the speaker states that the envelope is not located "on the desk," but leaves open the possibility that it may be "in" or, perhaps, "under" the desk.

This contrastive meaning is derived from the basic function of は and is often found in sentences giving negative answers.

● 上, 中, 下, 前, 後ろ, 右, 左

In Japanese, these words are classified as nouns that signify location. You can, therefore, link them with other nouns by using の, as in 机の上. Like other nouns, these phrases can function as a topic or subject.

　　机の上が汚いですね。　　(The surface of the desk is dusty.)
　　机の上の私の本を見てください。(Look at my book on the desk.)

● ひきだしの中を見てくれませんか　　1-10

The を here is a particle that works as an "object marker." In English, in most cases, an object is indicated by the word order (as in "John loves Mary").

In Japanese, particles play an important role in making the object; word order can often be changed around in Japanese conversation.

● ここにもありませんよ　　　1-12

This も means "either," "too," or "also," depending on whether the sentence which contains も is in the affirmative or the negative. Note the following dialogues:

1. A：私は学生です。　　　　　　（I am a student.）
   B：私も学生です。　　　　　　（I am a student, too.）
2. A：私は学生じゃありません。（I am not a student.）
   B：私も学生じゃありません。（I am not a student, either.）

When the second proposition is in accordance with the first one, も can be used regardless of whether it is positive or negative.

ことばの使い方 (ことばのつかいかた)

● もしもし　　　1-1

もしもし, like "hello," is a phrase a caller first uses in a telephone conversation to make sure that he/she has not reached a wrong number. It is quite common, however, for the receiver of a call to identify his/her household immediately after picking up the phone.

もしもし is also used to draw the attention of a stranger when you see him/her drop or forget something.

● どうしました (**Omission of the sentence-final** か)　　　1-3

This question does not have the sentence-final particle か. It is quite commonly dropped in informal conversation, but the intonation still holds the rising tone. The final す in です, ます with falling intonation is pronounced as if there were no vowel after *s* (i. e. *u* becomes unvoiced). With a rising intonation, however, "*u*" becomes voiced so that the intonation can be heard clearly.

● どうしました　　　1-3

When you notice that something urgent has come up for a person, or that something is wrong, use this expression to ask what is the matter.

● 見てくれませんか　　　1-10

The て-form of a verb plus くれませんか means "Won't you do ～ for me?" The more polite equivalent is the て-form plus くださいませんか, which is polite enough to be used in addressing a superior.

● いいですよ　　　1-5

When you accept a request, you can say いいですよ, or simply はい.

● (困った) なあ　　　1-13

This is a male expression addressed to the speaker himself. Women would say 困ったわ in the same situation.

● 困った, よかった　　　1-13, 1-16

You will notice that these phrases do not end in です or ます. These sentence forms (without です or ます) are called the **plain forms**, and are commonly used among close

Lesson 7

friends. But, as a rule of thumb, this form should be avoided for the time being; the above two sentences are exceptions. 困った is one of the few verbal past forms that we have encountered. In Japanese, verbs are better understood in terms of "perfect" and "imperfect," rather than "past" and "present." When です and でした (which we have been studying from early on in the textbook) are preceded by nouns or the past form of adjectives, it is, in most cases, safe to say that they represent the "past" tense. However, 困った, above, is an exception. With verbs in the た-form, you should not automatically assume that they are in the "past" tense; rather, think of them as representing the "perfect" tense. 困った, above, does not mean "I was in trouble"; it means "I have gotten into trouble," and, as a result, "I am in trouble." The interpretation of ありました, which follows, can also be easily understood if you consider the sentence in terms of "perfect" or "imperfect." Think of it to mean "I have found it!" rather than as a "past" or "present" form.

● ありました　　　1-15

This phrase should express excitement about something you have found. Notice that the perfect tense form is used.

● 一番(いちばん)　　　2-1

一番, when attached to adjectives, represents the superlative case. Examples are: 一番大きい, 一番小(ちい)さい, 一番いい, 一番きれいな.

It is also used with some nouns which signify location such as 前, 後ろ, 右, 左, 上, 中, and 下.

● 彼, 彼女　　　2-2

These words are said to have been created as translations of the third person singular pronouns of European languages; they have been used mainly in written Japanese. These days, however, young people use them with increasing frequency in the spoken language. Some people from a generation or two before theirs tend to frown upon this usage in conversation. Thus, you are advised not to use them with such sensitive elderly persons. Use あの人 or their names instead.

● さあ　　　2-4

さあ is used when you cannot respond immediately to a question because you do not know the answer or cannot think of what to say. This expression is usually followed by どうでしょう or わかりません.

● どうでしょう　　　2-4

どうでしょう, "I am not sure," is used when you are unsure about whether the answer to a question is "yes" or "no." If a question contains an interrogative word (what, when, etc.), then どう cannot be used; instead of どう use the interrogative word plus でしょう. Note the examples below.

　　　1．A：あの人は誰(だれ)ですか。(Who is that person?)
　　　　 B：さあ誰でしょう。　(Well, who could it be?)
　　　2．A：これは何ですか。　(What could it be?)
　　　　 B：何でしょう。　　　(I don't know what it is.)

● （ジョンソン先生）でしょう　　　2-6

でしょう is the presumptive form of the copula です, and is usually translated as "I

60

guess" or "probably." By using this phrase, you indicate a supposition which you believe is probably correct, but about which you are not absolutely certain. The でしょう in the next sentence in the dialogue, 違うでしょう serves the same function.

The degree of the certainty varies as follows:

  ジョンソン先生ですよ。   (100% certain)
  多分，ジョンソン先生ですよ。 (95%?)
  ジョンソン先生でしょう。 (90%?)
  多分，ジョンソン先生でしょう。(80%?)

練習 (れんしゅう)

練習(れんしゅう) 1　　　　Nouns expressing location

例　on ⇨ A：机の上に封筒がありますか。(Is there an envelope on the desk?)

1. in　2. under　3. in front of　4. behind　5. left side　6. right side　7. on

練習(れんしゅう) 2　　　　じゃ，…てくれませんか

You should take A's role.

例　机の上，ひきだしの中
  A：机の上に財布(wallet)がありますか。
  B：机の上にはありませんね。(It's not on the desk.)
  A：じゃ，ひきだしの中を見てくれませんか。
   (Then, won't you take a look inside the drawer?)

1．かばんの中，ポケットの中　　　　2．机の上，テレビの上
3．本の下，ノートの下　　　　　　　4．テレビの前，テレビの後ろ
5．コンピューターの右，プリンターの左　6．かばんの上，かばんの下

練習(れんしゅう) 3　　　　Nのところ

Take the role of A.

例　書庫，新聞のところ
  A：田中さん，書庫にいましたか。(Was Tanaka san in the stacks?)
  B：書庫にはいませんでした。(He wasn't in the stacks.)
  A：じゃ，すみませんが新聞のところを見てくれませんか。
   (Then won't you take a look by the newspapers?)

Lesson 7

1．あそこ，そこ　　　　　　　　　　2．図書館(としょかん)，林(はやし)さんのところ
3．雑誌(ざっし)のところ，コーヒーのところ　　4．家(いえ)，図書館
5．テレビのところ，ワープロのところ　　6．食堂(しょくどう)，テレビのところ

練習(れんしゅう)　4　　　　　　　も，は，が

Take the role of A.

例　（ダンさん，リーさん，ロングさん）ジョンソンさん
　　　A：ダンさん，いますか。(Is Dunn san there?)
　　　B：はい，います。(Yes, he is.)
　　　A：リーさんもいますか。(Is Lee san also there?)
　　　B：はい，リーさんもいます。(Yes, Lee san is also here.)
　　　A：ジョンソンさんもいますか。(Is Johnson san also there?)
　　　B：いいえ，ジョンソンさんはいません。ロングさんがいます。
　　　　　(No, Johnson san is not here. Long san is here.)

1．(山田(やまだ)さん，石井(いしい)さん，木村(きむら)さん)田中(たなか)さん
2．(たばこ，灰皿(はいざら)，マッチ)ライター
3．(本，ノート，えんぴつ)ボールペン
4．(女の学生，男の学生，図書館の人)先生
5．(テレビ，ステレオ，自転車(じてんしゃ))車(くるま)
6．(ジョンソンさん，ロングさん，リーさん)ダンさん

練習(れんしゅう)　5　　　　　　Talking to yourself

Take the role of A.

例1　石井さん，人
　　　A：ここに石井さんという人がいますか。
　　　B：ええ，いますよ。
　　　A：そうですか。ああ，よかった。
　　　　　(A：Is there a person here named Ishii san?)
　　　　　(B：Yes, there is.)
　　　　　(A：Is that so? Oh, I'm relieved. / I'm glad.)

例2　GMW，車
　　　A：ここにGMWという車がありますか。
　　　B：いいえ，ありません。
　　　A：そうですか。困ったなあ／困ったわ。
　　　　　(A：Is there a car here called a GMW?)
　　　　　(B：No, there isn't.)
　　　　　(A：Is that so? I'm in trouble.)

1．林さん，女の人　　2．日本語の文法，本　　3．スタイン・ホール，建物
4．田中さん，男の学生　5．ジョンソン先生，女の先生　6．GMW，車

練習（れんしゅう）　6　　　　　　Nouns for locations

Look at the illustration below and answer the questions as shown in the example. Take the role of A.

例　石井さん
　　A：あっ，石井さんがいますよ。
　　B：どこにいますか。
　　A：佐藤さんの右にいます。
　　　　（A：Oh, Ishii san is there.）
　　　　（B：Where?）
　　　　（A：To the right of Sato san.）

1．ダンさん　　　　　2．田中さん
3．リーさん　　　　　4．石井さん
5．佐藤さん

練習（れんしゅう）　7　　　　　　Reservation

例1　あしたはいい天気ですか。 ⇨ さあ，どうでしょう。
　　（Will the weather tomorrow be good?　⇨ Well, I am not sure.）
例2　あの人は誰ですか。　　⇨ さあ，誰でしょう。
　　（Who is that person?　⇨ Well, I wonder who it is.）

1．この器械は何ですか。　　　2．財布はテレビの上にありますか。
3．林さんの家は，どこですか。　4．先生の車は何色ですか。
5．木村さんの家は大きいですか。　6．あの人は誰ですか。

練習（れんしゅう）　8　　　　　　〜は誰ですか

Take the role of A.

例　右⇨　A：佐藤さんの右の人は誰ですか。
　　　　　　（Who is the person to Sato san's right?）
　　　　　B：石井さんです。
　　　　　　（It's Ishii san.）

1．前　　2．左　　3．後ろ　　4．右

八課

内容表

文法	Numerals: 1～9999 Another use of あります Days of the week		お知らせがあります。 月/火/水/木/金/土/日＋曜日 何曜日
	The plain negative forms＋です 　ありません 　よくありません 　学生じゃありません	⇨ ⇨ ⇨	ないです よくないです 学生じゃないです
	Counters:		～時, ～分, ～時間, ～課, ～ページ
	"Time expressions＋に／０" Replacing the predicate with です		月曜日に／明日 何曜日ですか。(試験をしますか) 八時半からです。(始めます)
	"From ～ through(to) ..."		～から…まで
機能	Expressing Likes/Dislikes	3-1	いいですね/嫌ですね
	Stating Factual Information	1-2	(Time, Days of the week, Numbers)
	Seeking Factual Information	1-3	
	Stating Intentions	2-9	明日, 試験をします。
	Expressing Failure to Understand	2-3	何曜日ですか。
	Expressing Resignation	3-36	しかたありませんね。
	Encouraging One to Perform	5-11	がんばってください。

Lesson 8

会話 (かいわ)

A：ええ，みなさん，お知らせがあります。	Well, class, I have something to tell you.
B：何ですか。	What is it?
C：いい知らせですか。	(Is it) good news?
A：さあ，あまりよくないでしょう。	Well, I think it's not so good.
来週の月曜日に試験をします。	Next Monday, we'll have an examination.
B：試験ですか。	An exam!
C：嫌ですねえ。	(That's) awful.
B：先生，すみません，何曜日ですか。	Excuse me Sensei, on what day (will it be)?
A：月曜日ですよ。	On Monday.
C：何時から始めますか。	From what time shall we start?
A：八時半からです。	From eight-thirty.
B：何分ぐらいですか。	About how long (will it take)?
A：一時間ぐらいかかります。	It will take roughly an hour.
C：何課から何課までですか。	From which lesson to which?
A：一課から五課までです。	From lesson one to lesson five.
B：先生，試験は何ページですか。	Sensei, how many pages is the exam?
A：四ページぐらいでしょう。	I think it will be about four pages.
B：長くて大変ですね。	That's long and such a lot of work.
C：しかたありませんね。	(There's) no choice. (It can't be helped.)
B：ええ。	Right.
A：それから，試験はこの教室でします。	And the exam will be in this classroom.
B, C：はい，わかりました。	I understand.
A：じゃ，がんばってください。	Then, keep at it.
今日は，これで終わります。	We'll end here for today.
B, C：はい。じゃ，失礼します。	Yes. Goodbye sir.
A：はい，また明日。	Yes, see you tomorrow.

単語表(たんごひょう)

みなさん	☞ことばの使い方	八時半(はちじはん)	8:30
お知(し)らせ	notice, news, announcement	何分(なんぷん)	how many minutes
あまり…ない	not very	何課(なんか)	which lesson
よくない	plain form of よくありません	AからBまで	from A to (through) B
来週(らいしゅう)	next week	何(なん)ページ	how many pages
月曜日(げつようび)	Monday	長(なが)い	long, lengthy
試験(しけん)	examination	しかたありません	☞ことばの使い方
何曜日(なにようび)	what day of the week	それから	and then, after that
何時(なんじ)	what time	教室(きょうしつ)	classroom
始(はじ)めます	⇨始める begin (v.t.)	がんばって	☞ことばの使い方

関連語句(かんれんごく)

	last	this	next
Day	昨日(きのう)	今日(きょう)	明日(あした)
Week	先週(せんしゅう)	今週(こんしゅう)	来週(らいしゅう)
Month	先月(せんげつ)	今月(こんげつ)	来月(らいげつ)
Year	去年(きょねん)	今年(ことし)	来年(らいねん)

小(ちい)さい	small	短(みじか)い	short
きれい(な)	clean, beautiful	今(いま)	now, this moment

Lesson 8

文法 (ぶんぽう)

● あります　　1

In the previous lesson, あります was used to indicate the location of objects. It is also used to express whether or not one has possessions. When appropriate, the "possessor" is followed by the particle は.

1. A：石井さん、時間がありますか。(Do you have time, Ishii san?)
   B：ええ、ありますよ。　　　　(Yes, I do.)
2. 私は車がありません。　　　　　(I don't have a car.)

● よくない (Plain negative forms)　　5

This is the plain negative form of the adjective いい. よくない means the same as よくありません. However, these two forms differ in their function and level of politeness within a sentence. よくない can modify nouns, and can also function as a predicate. When です follows it, the phrase represents a high level of politeness, while used alone, it indicates a lesser degree of politeness. よくありません can only be used in the predicate position, and in the polite form. Adjectives have two kind of negative forms as shown below.

いい	⇨よくありません／よくない	——い-adj.
寒い	⇨寒くありません／寒くない	
簡単な	⇨簡単じゃありません／簡単じゃない	——な-adj./Noun
学生です	⇨学生じゃありません／学生じゃない	
あります	⇨仕事がありません／仕事がない	——Verb (Only this verb)

In short, this form is made by substituting ありません with ない (です).

To make perfect forms of these negative forms with ない, change ない to なかった and add です as a politeness marker.

● The Verb Tense in Japanese

Japanese verbs do not have a special form for the future tense. Instead, the future is indicated by the use of temporal expressions like 来週の月曜日, or by adopting expressions of uncertainty like でしょう. Generally, Japanese verbs in the so-called "present tense" form do not simply indicate the present; they show that an action is incomplete.

In English, time is basically divided into three parts: past, present, and future. In Japanese, there are only two categories of time: perfect (complete) and imperfect (incomplete). The phrase 試験をします is imperfect—meaning that the action of giving an exam is not over yet. The phrase, therefore, should be interpreted as belonging either to the present or the future.

● (月曜日)に　　6

This particle indicates a point in time when something takes place. There are two groups of words which express time: those which are followed by に and those which are not.

The followings are examples of the two groups of nouns which describe time. The expressions in the first group, which are not followed by に, are set in the context of when they are used; they are relative time expressions which do not specify time objectively and, thus, cannot be used for historical description. On the contrary, the second group, which is accompanied by に, shows absolute time. When the two types of time expressions are combined, as in 1914年の今日, the final expression determines whether or not the phrase takes に.

WITHOUT に		WITH に	
今 (いま)	now	月曜日 (げつようび)	(days of the week)
さっき	a little while ago	十日 (とおか)	(days of the month)
昨日 (きのう)	yesterday	八時 (はちじ)	(time)
今日 (きょう)	today	十一月 (じゅういちがつ)	(month)
明日 (あした)	tomorrow	1946年 (ねん)	(year)
先週 (せんしゅう)	last week		
今週 (こんしゅう)	this week		
来週 (らいしゅう)	next week		

● 何曜日ですか　9

The following two dialogues are from the text.

1．A：来週の月曜日に試験をします。　　2．A：何時から始めますか。
　　B：何曜日(に)ですか。　　　　　　　　　B：八時半からです。

In the sentences spoken by B in both dialogues, です is used to replace the predicate: in the first example, です is used instead of 試験をします and in the second instead of 始めます. Please note that B's question in the first dialogue no longer has the particle に, while in the second, から remains in place.

When です is used to replace predicates, some particles will be deleted and some other particles will be retained. To understand this rule, see L. 11 文法「文房具です」.

● **NUMERALS**

Numbers in Japanese:

1から10まで									
一	二	三	四	五	六	七	八	九	十
いち	に	さん	よん / し	ご	ろく	なな / しち	はち	きゅう / く	じゅう

11から19まで
十(じゅう)＋いち，に，さん……

20から90まで
に，さん，よん……＋十(じゅう)
For 四十，七十，and 九十 use よん，なな，きゅう

Lesson 8

100から900まで
100 ひゃく(百)　200 に・ひゃく……900 きゅう・ひゃく
Exceptions:　300 さん・びゃく
600 ろっ・ぴゃく　　800 はっ・ぴゃく

1000から9000まで
1000 せん(千)　2000 に・せん……9000 きゅう・せん
Exception:　3000 さん・ぜん

Between numbers 1 and 10, you may have noticed that 4, 7, and 9 have two readings; the correct choice is usually determined by the counter expressions which follow the words. "Seven o'clock" is definitely しちじ, for example, but "seven books" is ななさつ. (さつ is a counter for books.)

● **Telling Time**

To ask "What time is it?" say 「何時(なんじ)ですか。」. To tell time, first say the hour and then the minute. For example, 2:46 is 二時四十六分(にじよんじゅうろっぷん). Another way, as in English, to say 2:46 is 三時十四分前(さんじじゅうよんぷんまえ) (14 minutes before three). If you want to emphasize the fact that it is "past" the hour, the word すぎ is used, as in 三時五分すぎ (5 minutes past three).

As seen in the dialogue, 半(はん) is used to mean thirty minutes, but it is quite appropriate to say 三十分(さんじっぷん). There is no special word to express a quarter of an hour.

To say the hour, use the upper reading for the numerals.
The following are exceptions:
　　4 o'clock　よじ　　7 o'clock　しちじ　　9 o'clock　くじ
As for the accent pattern, all but 三時 and 十時 are pronounced as:
　　○時　(e.g. いちじ　にじ　……じゅうにじ)
　　Exceptions:　三時　さんじ　　十時　じゅうじ
To give "minutes," use 分(ふん, ぷん).

ぷん	一分(いっぷん)　三分(さんぷん)　四分(よんぷん)　六分(ろっぷん)
	八分(はっぷん)　十分(じっぷん／じゅっぷん)　　　何分(なんぷん)
ふん	二分(にふん)　五分(ごふん)　七分(ななふん)
	九分(きゅうふん)

The accent patterns for the first group with ぷん, and the second group with ふん are:
　　○○ぷん　　(○)○ふん　(e.g. にふん　ななふん)
　　Exception:　九分　きゅうふん

Note that 十 and its compounds (numbers ending in 十, such as 三十) are pronounced じっ or じゅっ when they are used together with counters such as this.

● ～から～まで　　15

The particles から and まで are often used together to show the starting and terminating points in time and space.
　　ニューヨークから東京(とうきょう)まで何時間かかりますか。

(How many hours does it take from New York to Tokyo?)

今日は九時から五時まで図書館にいます。
(Today I will be at the library from nine to five.)

● 教室でします　22

で is a particle which signifies a place where an action takes place. Do not confuse this with the particle に which indicates the location of an animate or inanimate object.

私は図書館 {で} 勉強します。 (I study at the library.)
　　　　　 {に} います。　　 (I am at the library.)

ことばの使い方 (ことばのつかいかた)

● みなさん　1

You can probably guess from the presence of さん in this word, that it has a polite nuance. In this lesson, the teacher politely used the word to mean "everybody" in the class. This word, therefore, cannot be used to mean "everyone in my family" or "everyone in the world". In these cases, use みんな.

● 試験をします　6

This expression implies that the speaker is the one who will give the examination. 試験があります is an appropriate phrase for the students to use.

● **DAYS OF THE WEEK**

月曜日	げつようび (Monday)	金曜日	きんようび	(Friday)
火曜日	かようび (Tuesday)	土曜日	どようび	(Saturday)
水曜日	すいようび (Wednesday)	日曜日	にちようび	(Sunday)
木曜日	もくようび (Thursday)	何曜日	なに／なんようび	(What day of the week)

Note 1　These words are often pronounced without the final び in conversation.
Note 2　The accent is ○○ようび.

● 嫌ですねえ　8

When the speaker hears bad news, as in this example, he/she can use this expression to mean, "I don't like it." or "It's terrible." If the news is tragic, this is not the correct expression to use. On the contrary, if you hear some good news, you can say いいですねえ.

The ねえ at the end works like an exclamation point. Normally, it is accompanied by a falling intonation.

1．A：あっ，ごきぶりがいますよ。(Oh, there's a cockroach!)
　　B：えっ。嫌ですねえ。　　　(Oh, no.)
2．A：土曜日にパーティーをしましょう。(Let's have a party on Saturday.)
　　B：いいですねえ。　　　　　(It's a good idea.)

Lesson 8

● しかたありません　20

This phrase is used by a speaker to express that there is no solution or alternative to the situation he/she is in at the moment. Literally, しかた means "way of doing something" or "how to do something." Thus it means, "There's no other solution" or "It can't be helped." As we can see in the text, が is often dropped in conversation.

● がんばってください　24

While しかたがありません is a rather pessimistic expression, がんばって represents the opposite mentality: "never give up, keep at it." You can use this expression to encourage a person who is preparing for a serious endeavor or trial, such as an interview for a job, an examination, or a first date that he/she has been dying to go out on. The English equivalent in usage, though not in meaning, may be "good luck."

The "て-form" of the verb with ください represents a request. Among friends, ください may be dropped to create an informal feeling.

   A：今日、試験があります。　　　　(I have an examination today.)
   B：そうですか。じゃ、がんばって。　(Really? Then, keep at it!)
   A：ええ、がんばります。　　　　　　(Yes. I will.)

練習 (れんしゅう)

練習(れんしゅう)　1	Possession

例　(タイプライター)
　　大木さん、タイプライターがありますか。(Oki san, do you have a typewriter?)

1. 仕事　　2. 専門　　3. 時間　　4. お金　　5. 試験　　6. ステレオ

練習(れんしゅう)　2	Plain neg. of adjs.／あまり…ない

例　今日は寒いですか。(Is it cold today?)
　　⇨あまり寒くないでしょう。(I guess it isn't very cold.)

1. 明日の試験は難しいですか。　　2. この本はいいですか。
3. 黄色い封筒は大きいですか。　　4. 中国語はやさしいですか。
5. この机は古いですか。　　　　　6. あの人のアパートは汚いですか。

練習(れんしゅう) 3　　　　Plain neg.

例　試験は嫌ですか。(Do you hate exams?)
　　⇨いいえ，嫌じゃないですよ。(No, I don't find them terrible.)
　今日は寒いですか。(Is it cold today?)
　　⇨いいえ，寒くないですよ。(No, it isn't.)

1．あの人はこの大学の学生ですか。　2．明日はいい天気ですか。
3．ダンさんの自転車は赤いですか。　4．リーさんの仕事は簡単ですか。
5．この器械は新しいですか。　　　　6．石井さんの専門は人類学ですか。

練習(れんしゅう) 4　　　　Days of the week

Take the role of B.

例　(月曜日)　A：今日は何曜日ですか。(What day of the week is it today?)
　　　　　　　B：月曜日ですよ。　　　(It's Monday.)
　　　　　　　A：じゃあ，昨日は…。　(Then yesterday it was ......)
　　　　　　　B：日曜日ですよ。　　　(Sunday.)

1．水曜日　2．金曜日　3．火曜日　4．土曜日　5．木曜日　6．日曜日　7．月曜日

練習(れんしゅう) 5　　　　Time words＋に／0

例　今，試験をしましょう。(Let's have an exam now.)
　　(三時) (3 o'clock)⇨三時に試験をしましょう。(Let's have an exam at three.)

1．月曜日　　　　2．今日　　　　3．明日　　　　4．来週の水曜日
5．今日の六時　　6．今　　　　　7．今週　　　　8．今週の金曜日

練習(れんしゅう) 6　　　　～から～まで

例　二時間かかります。(It takes two hours.)
　　(うち，大学) (home, university)⇨うちから大学まで二時間かかります。
　　　　　　　　　　　　　　　　　(It takes two hours from my home to the university.)

1．わかりません。　　（十ページ，十二ページ）　2．汚いですね。　　（そこ，ここ）
3．暖かいでしょう。　（明日，金曜日）　　　　　4．図書館にいます。（九時，五時）
5．四時間かかります。（ここ，ニューヨーク）　　6．ここにいます。　（三時，七時）

Lesson 8

練習(れんしゅう)　7　　　　　　Confirming what is said

例　月曜日に試験をします。⇨すみません。何曜日ですか。
　　　(On Monday we'll have an exam.　⇨ Pardon me, but what day of the week is it?)

1．八時半から試験をします。　　　2．試験は一時間ぐらいかかります。
3．試験は一課から五課までです。　4．試験は四ページです。
5．試験はこの教室でします。　　　6．試験は九時半に終わります。

練習(れんしゅう)　8　　　　　　Likes / Dislikes

Respond with either one of the two expressions as shown in the example.

例　試験は長いです。⇨嫌ですねえ。(The exam is long. That's terrible.)
　　試験は簡単です。⇨いいですねえ。(The exam is easy. That's great.)

1．今日はひどい天気ですよ。　　2．明日は土曜日ですね。
3．日本語の試験は大変ですよ。　4．今週，パーティーをしましょう。
5．試験は簡単でしたよ。　　　　6．明日は月曜日ですね。

練習(れんしゅう)　9　　　　　　Antonyms

例　今日は寒いですか。(Is it cold today?)
　　⇨あまり暖かくないですが，寒くないですよ。
　　　(It's not very warm but it isn't cold.)

1．明日の試験は難しいですか。
2．今日の宿題は長いですか。　　（短い）
3．黄色い封筒は大きいですか。　（小さい）
4．中国語はやさしいですか。
5．この机は古いですか。
6．あの人のアパートは汚いですか。（きれいな）

九課

内容表

文法	The Use of Verbs——"Will do"		どうします？
	Interrogative word＋か／も…ない		何か (something)／何も…ない (nothing)
	The position of a particle		どこかへ／どこへも
	Conjunctional Particle「から」		お金がありませんから(行きません。)
	Verbs of Motion		行きます, 来ます, 帰ります, でかけます
	来ます vs. 行きます		
	Particles used with "Motion Verbs" to show the destination「へ, に」		どこへ行きますか。親戚の家に行きます。
	Nouns derived from い-adjs.		遠く, 近く, 多く
	Topical particle「も」		父も母も来ます。
	Kinship terms		両親, 父, 母 vs. 御両親, お父さん, お母さん
	～でしょう (Conjecture) vs. ～ましょう (Volitional)		楽しいでしょう。行きましょう。
	Sと思います		楽しいと思います。
	S1 し，(それに)S2		若い人も来ますし，それに知っている人も来ますから。
	N (を)します Nは漢語／loan word		お邪魔します。／テニスをします。
機能	Inquiring About Intentions	2-10	感謝祭の休みに，吉田さんはどうします？
	Stating Intentions	2-9	私はここにいます。
	Reason for Action/Non-Action	2-41	お金がありませんから。(休みましょうよ。)多くの学生は授業に出ませんよ。
	Rejecting a Fact/Situation	2-38	そんなことありませんよ。
	Requesting Clarification	7-9	N1ってN2のことですか。
	Expressing Certainty	2-19	きっと～でしょう。～と思います。
	Offering Invitations	5-6	私の家へ来ませんか。
	Accepting Invitations	5-7	お邪魔します。
	Extending an Invitation	2-5	(授業を)休みましょう。

会話 (かいわ)

1

A：感謝祭の休みに、吉田さんはどうしますか？

B：感謝祭の休みですか。私はここにいます。

A：どこへも行きませんか。

B：ええ。お金も時間もありませんから。

マクドナルドさんは家へ帰りますか。

A：家って両親の所ですか。[ええ。] いいえ、帰りません。親戚の家に行きます。

B：遠くですか。

A：いえいえ。この近くですよ。

B：お父さんやお母さんは？

A：父も母も来ます。[そうですか。] 家族はみんなこの家に集まります。

B：きっと、賑やかで楽しいでしょうね。

A：ええ。きっと、楽しいと思います。

What will you do during the Thanksgiving holidays, Yoshida san?

The Thanksgiving holidays? I'll be here.

You aren't going anywhere?

Right. Because I don't have the money or the time.

Are you going home, McDonald san?

Home? You mean my parents' place? [Yes.] No, I won't go. I am going to my relatives' house.

Is it far?

No. It's close by.

(How about) your father and mother?

Both of them will come. [Really.] All of my family will come to this house.

It will most probably be lively and a lot of fun.

I think it sure will.

2

C：吉田さん、感謝祭に私の家へ来ませんか。

B：ありがとうございます。でも、悪いですよ。

Yoshida san, won't you come to my house for the Thanksgiving holidays?

Thank you. But it will inconvenience you.

C：そんなこと，ありませんよ。若い人もたくさん来ますし，それに吉田さんが知っている人も来ますから。

No, it won't. Many young people are coming, and people you know are also coming.

B：そうですか。それじゃ，お邪魔します。でも，本当(ほんとう)にいいですか。

It that right? Well, then I will go. But are you sure it's OK?

C：もちろんですよ。水曜日(すいようび)の午後(ごご)でかけます。

Of course! We'll go Wednesday afternoon.

B：水曜日の午後の授業はどうします？

What shall we do about classes on Wednesday afternoon?

C：休みましょうよ。多くの学生は授業に出ませんよ。［そうですか。］

Let's skip them. Most students won't attend classes. [Really?]

単語表（たんごひょう）

1

感謝祭(かんしゃさい)	Thanksgiving
休(やす)み	holiday, vacation
吉田(よしだ)	a surname
どこへも…ない	☞文法
お金(かね)	money, cash
Nって	☞ことばの使い方
両親(りょうしん)	parents
帰(かえ)る	go back, return
親戚(しんせき)	relatives
遠(とお)く	(place) far from here
近(ちか)く	(place) near, close
賑(にぎ)やか(な)	lively
楽(たの)しい	enjoyable, cheerful
Sと思(おも)います	☞文法
お父(とう)さん	☞関連語句
家族(かぞく)	family
みんな	everyone, all
集(あつ)まる	gather
きっと…でしょう	☞ことばの使い方

2

でも	but
悪(わる)い	causing trouble, bad
そんなことありませんよ	☞ことばの使い方
若(わか)い	young
たくさん	many
吉田さんが知っている人	☞ことばの使い方
(に)お邪魔(じゃま)する	visit (lit. interrupt)
もちろん	of course, needless to say

Lesson 9

でかけます	go out	休(やす)みます	☞ことばの使い方
午後(ごご)	afternoon	多(おお)くの N	many of N, most
授業(じゅぎょう)	class	(Nに)出(で)ます	attend N

関連語句(かんれんごく)

[KINSHIP TERMS]

Family-members of others	Your own family	Core meaning
御両親(ごりょうしん)	両親(りょうしん)	parents
御家族(ごかぞく)	家族(かぞく)	family
御兄弟(ごきょうだい)	兄弟(きょうだい)	siblings
: お父(とう)さん	父(ちち)	father
: お母(かあ)さん	母(はは)	mother
: お兄(にい)さん	兄(あに)	elder brother
: お姉(ねえ)さん	姉(あね)	elder sister
弟(おとうと)さん	弟(おとうと)	younger brother
妹(いもうと)さん	妹(いもうと)	younger sister

Note 1　Please note the words in the first column preceded by a colon. These are used to address the members in your family who are older than you. Younger brothers and sisters are called by their names. In Japanese, people older than and superior to the speaker are addressed by their titles or their kinship terms. When addressing those who are your subordinates, or who are younger than you, use their given names.

[Four seasons]

春(はる) spring　夏(なつ) summer　秋(あき) fall, autumn　冬(ふゆ) winter

Note 2　By adding 休み, you can create words for seasonal vacations——for example, 夏休み, "summer vacation."

週末(しゅうまつ)	weekend	アルバイト	part-time job
クリスマス	Christmas	テレビ	television

文法 (ぶんぽう)

● **Interrogatives＋か／も**　　1-5

Interrogatives	＋か	＋も…ない
何(なに) what	何か something	何も…ない nothing
誰(だれ) who	誰か somebody	誰も…ない nobody
どこ where	どこか somewhere	どこも…ない nowhere
いつ when	いつか sometime	いつも always

The words on the chart above are used as follows:

1. A：何か食べましたか。　　(Did you eat anything?)
   B：いいえ，何も食べません。(No, nothing.)
2. A：誰か来ましたか。　　(Did anybody come?)
   B：いいえ，誰も来ませんよ。(No, nobody came.)

In conversation, が, は, and を are quite often omitted, as can be seen in the examples above, while other particles are not omitted, as shown in the examples which follow. The particles cannot be omitted below, because without them, the meaning of the sentences cannot be properly conveyed.

Note the position of the particles in the sentences below.

3. A：誰かに知らせましたか。　　(Did you tell anybody?)
   B：誰にも知らせません。　　(No, I have not told anybody.)
4. A：どこへも行きませんか。　　(Aren't you going anywhere?)
   B：どこかへ行きますよ。　　(Yes, I am going somewhere.)
5. A：シカゴのどこかにありますか。(Is it somewhere in Chicago?)
   B：どこにもありませんよ。　　(No, nowhere in Chicago.)

● **S1 から S2**　　1-6, 2-7

から is a conjunctive particle whose function is to connect two sentences. It gives a reason or cause for an occurrence or situation.

Basically it is used in the following pattern: (S stands for "sentence")

> S1 から S2。　(Because S1, S2. / As S1, S2. / Since S1, S2.)

1. お金(かね)がありませんから，家(うち)にいます。
   (Because I don't have money, I will stay home.)
2. 私は一年生(いちねんせい)ですから，専門(せんもん)はありません。
   (As I am a freshman, I don't have a major.)
3. いい天気(てんき)ですから，テニスをしませんか。
   (Since the weather is nice, shall we play tennis?)

The examples above are all put in the order of S1 and S2, but in actual conversation, depending on which of the two sentences is more important to answer the posed question, the order of the sentence may change to "S2, S1 から."

1. A：明日(あした)はどうしますか。(What will you do about tomorrow?)

Lesson 9

　　　　B：家にいます。お金がありませんから。
　　　　　　　(I'll stay home, since I don't have money.)
　　2．A：専門は？(What's your major?)
　　　　B：ありません。一年生ですから。(I don't have one, since I'm a freshman.)

In these examples, S2 contains the requested information and S1 is added on only as supplementary information.

On the contrary, if the speaker feels that S1 is the sought-for information and that S2 is self-evident, he/she can simply say: S1＋から. If S2 is not as obvious as the speaker believed it to be, there is room for misunderstanding; but most of the time, other clues can be found in a conversation to determine the speaker's intention.

● へ／に　　　1-5, 1-7, 2-1

PLACE＋ { へ / に } ＋MOTION VERBS　　| 来ます　行きます |
　　　　　　　　　　　　　　　　　　　| 帰ります　でかけます　etc. |

Like the English preposition "to," these particles へ and に indicate the destination of a movement. へ can be replaced by に but not vice versa. へ is used only with motion verbs, while に has many other functions.

でかけます belongs to this group of motion verbs. Unlike the other verbs in the group which are preceded by a word specifying a destination＋へ／に, でかけます is normally used alone. Hence, 学校へでかけます does not sound correct.

● 遠く，近く，多く　　　1-11, 1-12, 2-13

These are derived from the adjectives 遠い，近い and 多い; in the く-form they function as nouns. Note that these are the only adjectives with this usage.

　　1．A：吉田さんの家は大学から近いですか。　　(adj.)
　　　　B：いいえ，近くありません。　　(adj.)
　　　　　　(A：Yoshida san, is your home close to/from the university?)
　　　　　　(B：No, it's not close.)
　　2．A：吉田さんの家は大学の近くですか。　　(noun)
　　　　B：いいえ，近くじゃありません。　　(noun)

● N1 や N2　　　1-13
　　（お父さん）や（お母さん）　☞p.94

● N1 も N2 も　　　1-6

This means "both N1 and N2" or "neither N1 nor N2," depending on whether the sentence is affirmative or negative.

　　日本語も中国語もわかります。(I understand both Japanese and Chinese.)
　　私は中国語も日本語もわかりません。(I don't understand either Japanese or Chinese.)

In the above examples, if you want to say that you can understand one of the languages, but not the other, you would not use も, but rather the contrastive particle は：

　　日本語はわかりますが，中国語はわかりません。
　　　(I understand Japanese but not Chinese.)
　　日本語はわかりませんが，中国語はわかります。
　　　(I don't understand Japanese but I understand Chinese.)

も functions not only as a "topic marker" (like は) but also as an "object marker" (like を) in the sense already explained.

私はテニスもピンポンもしますよ。(I play both tennis and pingpong.)

● S と思います　　　1-17

This pattern will be studied later in L. 14. と is a quotational particle that indicates the end of a quotation of what a person says or what he/she thinks. The words which precede this particle と cannot end in です or ます.

● S1 し，（それに）S2　　　2-6

し is a conjunctive particle which connects related sentences. The English equivalent of this phrase is "S1 and besides, S2" or "S1, moreover, S2."

S1 and S2 must be of a similar nature; if S1 is something positive S2 has to be something positive, too. If S1 is of a negative nature, S2 has to be negative. The sentence here ends with the ます-form, but it most commonly takes the plain-ending form. それに means "besides" or "moreover," and it has an emphatic function in the phrase.

● 休みましょう (Volitional form)　　　2-13

The volitional form of a verb invites the hearer to do something together with the speaker. The English equivalent is "Let's do～." There is a restriction on the nature of the verbs which can be used in this pattern: the verbs have to indicate a controllable action. 始めます, 行きます, います are examples of controllable action, and they can be used in the volitional form. On the other hand, 始まります and あります are verbs which do not indicate control, and thus, cannot be used in this form.

Don't confuse this with the sentence expressing conjecture "S でしょう."

ことばの使い方 (ことばのつかいかた)

● どうします　　　1-1

This expression means "What will you do?" or "What shall we do?" どうしました, which we studied in L. 7, is the perfect form of this phrase. どうしました means "What did you do?", "What have you done?", "What happened?" or "What is the matter?"

● 来ます／行きます　　　1-14

来ます means "to come." It is used only when the actor in a sentence is going to the location of the speaker, or will be there at the time when the action takes place.

行きます means "to go." It specifically means that the actor in the sentence is going to a place where neither he/she nor the speaker is situated at the time of the utterance.

1．吉田：明日，学校へ行きますか。
　　ダン：ええ，行きます。

　　　(Yoshida: Are you going to school tomorrow?)
　　　(Dunn:　 Yes, I'll go.)

学校

吉田
ダン

Lesson 9

    2．吉田：明日，学校へ来ますか。
       ダン：ええ，行きます。
          (Yoshida: Will you come to school tomorrow?)
          (Dunn: Yes, I'll come.)
                (See the explanation below.)
    3．吉田：明日，学校へ来ますか。
       ダン：ええ，来ます。
          (Yoshida: Will you come to school tomorrow?)
          (Dunn: Yes, I'll come.)

  The second example above illustrates the difference between "come" and 来ます. In English, if someone calls you, you would respond, "I'm coming." And when you accept an invitation over the phone, you would say "I will come." In Japanese, however, 行きます is the only correct response in these cases.

● きっと(楽しいでしょう)   1-17

  This word indicates conjecture, but it is highly positive. The speaker has almost no doubt about what he/she is saying.
       A：田中さんは，来ますか。   (Will Tanaka san come?)
       B：あの人は，きっと来ますよ。 (He will most probably come.)

● って／て   1-8

  って／て are the colloquial equivalents of というのは ("the one called～, what you call～") in this context, and are used to confirm the meaning of an ambiguous word. In the dialogue, 家 can be either the home of the hearer or that of his/her parents. The expression was used to clarify what exactly the speaker meant.
  て follows ん；って is otherwise used.
       A：ジョンさんから，お電話がありました。
       B：ジョンて，ジョン・トーマスですか。
         (A：There was a telephone call from John san.)
         (B：When you say John, do you mean John Thomas?)

● 悪いですよ   2-3

  Literally, this means "It's bad." The phrase, however, is used to turn down an offer which the hearer feels would be an imposition or an inconvenience to the speaker.

● そんなことありませんよ   2-5

  This represents a vigorous denial of the statement which preceded this phrase. It is often used in the following situation: the basic meaning of this expression is that what was said is far from the truth.
    1．When somebody says something absolutely incorrect:
       学生：先生，明日は休みですか。(Sensei, is tomorrow a holiday?)
       先生：そんなことありませんよ。(No, it isn't!)
    2．When you receive compliments:
       A：発音がいいですね。   (Your pronunciation is good.)
       B：いいえ，そんなことありませんよ。(No, not really.)
    3．To give encouragement to someone who is pessimistic or negative:
       A：私は頭が悪いから…。 (Because I am dumb...)

B：そんなことありませんよ。(No, you aren't.)

● 吉田さんが知っている人　　2-6

In Japanese, all modifying phrases are put before the word to be modified. Verbal phrases are no exceptions. In the example, 吉田さんが知っている modifies 人 and, as a whole, this phrase means "people (whom) Yoshida san knows." There are no relative pronouns used in Japanese to modify nouns with verbal phrases. Plain forms are used instead. Knowing no plain forms in Japanese is, therefore, the same as knowing no relative pronouns in English. We will begin studying this form in L. 12.

● お邪魔します　　2-8

The literal meaning of this phrase is "I will disturb you" or "I will interrupt," but it is actually used as a humble expression meaning "to visit someone." It is also used as a greeting at the point of entering a person's house or office. The basic idea underlying this phrase is that you feel badly that your visit may be an inconvenience.

　　1．(ノックの音)　　　　(knocking on the door)
　　　A：はい，どうぞ。　　(Yes, come in.)
　　　B：お邪魔します。　　(Sorry to interrupt.)
　　2．A：明日家に来てください。(Please come to my home tomorrow.)
　　　B：はい。何時にお邪魔しましょうか。
　　　　　　　　　　　　　(Alright. Around what time should I come?)

● kango (漢語) ＋します　　2-8

Like お邪魔＋する, many kango (Chinese words) are combined with する and used as verbs. Some Western loan words are also used in the same way.

Here are some examples:

勉強	study		to study
仕事	work		to work
旅行	travel		to travel
結婚	marriage	＋します	to get married
テニス　(を)	tennis		to play tennis
ソフトボール(を)	softball		to play softball
アルバイト　(を)	part-time job		to work part-time

Note 1　In the case of Western loan words, を is generally used between the noun and します.

Note 2　Look at the first two examples below. These sentences are both grammatical and natural but the third sentence is ungrammatical because it violates the rule which prohibits the use of two object markers in one sentence.

　　1．日本語を　　勉強します
　　　　noun　　　　verb
　　2．日本語の勉強を　　します
　　　　noun (phrase)　　verb
　　3．×日本語を　勉強を　します

Lesson 9

- 午後　　2-10

This word can be divided into two parts: 午 means "noon" and 後 means "after." The opposite word is 午前 which means "before noon." These words precede time expressions, in 午前三時 or 午後二時; they are normally avoided, however, when it is clear that the speaker means sometime "in the morning" or "in the afternoon."

- 家に来ませんか (Invitation/Offering something)　　2-1

The negative question form is used in making invitations and offers. Affirmative question forms do not function well as invitations/offers; they sound like mere questions. To accept the offer, use はい and to decline, give a reason.

- 授業　　2-12

This word can be used with various verbal phrases as you can see below. Pay special attention to the particles used in these phrases.

授業があります　⇨今日，日本語の授業があります。
　　　　　　　　　(There is a Japanese class today.)
授業に出ます　　⇨今日，日本語の授業に出ますか。
　　　　　　　　　(Will you attend Japanese class today?)
授業を休みます　⇨今日，日本語の授業を休みました。
　　　　　　　　　(I skipped Japanese class today.)

練習 (れんしゅう)

練習(れんしゅう)　1	Time words＋に／0, どうしますか

例　感謝祭の休みに，吉田さんはどうしますか。
　　(What will you do, Yoshida san, during the Thanksgiving holidays?)
　冬休み　⇨冬休みに吉田さんはどうしますか。
　　(What will you do, Yoshida san, during the winter holidays?)
　今　　　⇨今，吉田さんはどうしますか。
　　(What will you do now, Yoshida san?)

1. 今晩　　2. 明日　　3. 夏休み　　4. 今日の午後　　5. 週末
6. 明日の朝　7. 来月　　8. 春休み　　9. クリスマスの休み

練習(れんしゅう)　2	Verb　(Future)

例　感謝祭の休みにダンさんはどうしますか。(シカゴにいます。)
　　(What will you do, Dunn san, during the Thanksgiving holidays?)
　　⇨感謝祭の休みですか。私はシカゴにいます。
　　　(Thanksgiving holidays? I will be in Chicago.)

1．クリスマスの休みにダンさんはどうしますか。（仕事をします。）
2．今週の土曜日にダンさんはどうしますか。（親戚の家へ行きます。）
3．春休みにダンさんはどうしますか。（両親の所へ帰ります。）
4．夏休みにダンさんはどうしますか。（日本へ行きます。）
5．明日，ダンさんはどうしますか。（テニスをします。）
6．来年，ダンさんはどうしますか。（日本で勉強します。）

練習（れんしゅう）　3	Interrogative＋か

例　家に誰がいますか。(Who is at home?)
　　　⇨よくわかりませんが，誰かいます。(I don't know for sure but there is somebody.)

1．土曜日に何をしますか。　　　　　2．お母さんはどこへ行きますか。
3．机の下に何がありますか。　　　　4．ダンさんはどこにいますか。
5．教室に誰がいますか。　　　　　　6．私の日本語の本はどこにありますか。

練習（れんしゅう）　4	Interrogative＋も＋neg.

例1　Q：そこに何かありますか。　　　(Is there something there?)
　　　A：何もありませんよ。　　　　　(No, there's nothing.)
　2　Q：林先生はどこにいますか。　　(Where is Hayashi sensei?)
　　　A：どこにもいませんよ。　　　　(She is nowhere.)

1．今日，家に誰か来ますか。　　　　2．どこへ行きますか。
3．今日の午後，何をしますか。　　　4．林先生はどこにいますか。
5．今，教室に誰かいますか。　　　　6．机の上に何かありますか。

練習（れんしゅう）　5	S1からS2／Turning down an invitation

例　日曜日に家へ来ませんか。(Won't you come to my house on Sunday?)
　　（宿題）⇨ありがとうございます。でも，宿題がありますから。
　　　(Thank you. But, since I have homework (I can't).)
　　今日，レストランへ行きませんか。(Won't you come to a restaurant with me today?)
　　（お金）⇨ありがとうございます。でも，お金がありませんから。
　　　(Thank you. But, since I don't have the money (I can't).)

1．今日，バーへ行きませんか。　　　　　　　　　　（アルバイト）
2．感謝祭の休みにニューヨークに行きませんか。　　（時間）
3．今週の週末，旅行に行きませんか。　　　　　　　（仕事）
4．日曜日に林さんの家に行きませんか。　　　　　　（試験）

Lesson 9

5．今日の午後，家に来ませんか。　　　　　　（宿題）
6．金曜日(きんようび)にパーティーをしませんか。　（お金）

練習(れんしゅう)　6　　　　　来ます／行きます

You should take the role of 田中.

例　[ダン][田中][林]　　ダン：明日，林さんの家に行きませんか。（はい）
　　　　　　　　　　　田中：はい，行きます。

1．[ダン][田中]　　ダン：明日，家に来ませんか。（ええ）
　　　　　　　　田中：

2．[ダン／田中][学校]　　ダン：明日，学校に来ますか。（はい）
　　　　　　　　　　　田中：

3．[ダン][田中]　　ダン：明日パーティーをしますから，来ませんか。（はい）
　　　　　　　　田中：

4．[ダン／田中][学校]　　ダン：来週，学校へ行きますか。（はい）
　　　　　　　　　　　田中：

練習(れんしゅう)　7　　　　　Confirm the meaning of words

例　感謝祭の休みに家へ帰りますか。(Will you go home for Thanksgiving holidays?)
　　（両親の所）⇨家って両親の所ですか。
　　　　　　　　(When you say home, do you mean my parents' place?)

1．クリスマスに家にいますか。　　　　（私のアパート）
2．土曜日に家に来ませんか。　　　　　（今週の土曜日）
3．明日，仕事がありますか。　　　　　（アルバイト）
4．春休みにワシントンに行きませんか。（ワシントン州(しゅう)）
5．リンさんの家はこの近くですか。　　（シカゴ）
6．スミスさんが来ましたよ。　　　　　（ジョン・スミス）

練習（れんしゅう） 8　　「も」

例　○　○
　　父　母　（来ます）　⇨父も母も来ます。
　　　　　　　　　　　　　(My father and mother are both coming.)
　　×　○
　　兄　姉　（行きます）　⇨兄は行きませんが，姉は行きます。
　　×　×
　　両親　兄弟（でかけます）⇨両親も兄弟もでかけません。

1．×　　×　　　　　　　　2．○　　○　　　　　　3．○　　×
　　車，自転車(あります)　　　お金，仕事(あります)　　弟，妹 (います)
4．×　　○　　　　　　　　5．○　　○　　　　　　6．×　×
　　吉田さん，林さん(来ます)　家族，親戚(集まります)　　父，母(います)

練習（れんしゅう） 9　　Conjecture

例　この車はいい車ですか。(Is this car good?)
　　　（多分）(probably)　⇨ええ，多分いい車でしょうね。
　　　　　　　　　　　　　(It's probably a good car, I guess.)

1．林さんは若いですか。　　　　　　　　（きっと）
2．この仕事はやさしいですか。　　　　　（多分）
3．明日は暑いですか。　　　　　　　　　（多分）
4．金曜日の試験は簡単ですか。　　　　　（きっと）
5．あの人はこの大学の学生じゃないですか。（多分）
6．明日は寒くないですか。　　　　　　　（きっと）

練習（れんしゅう） 10　　Volitional

例　今日，先生の家にお邪魔しませんか。(Let's visit Sensei's house today, shall we?)
　　　⇨ええ，お邪魔しましょう。　　　(Yes, let's do so.)

1．クリスマスの休みにスキーに行きませんか。
2．今週の土曜日に日本語の勉強をしませんか。
3．今日の午後の授業を休みませんか。
4．夏休みに私の家の近くでアルバイトをしませんか。
5．今日は天気がいいですから，ソフトボールをしませんか。
6．今日は天気が悪いですから，家でテレビを見ませんか。

Lesson 9

練習(れんしゅう) 11	Kinship terms

例　father　⇨お父さんはお元気ですか。(Is your father well?)

1．family　　2．mother　　　　3．younger sister　　4．elder brother
5．parents　 6．elder sister　　7．younger brother

練習(れんしゅう) 12	Kinship terms

例　お父さんはお元気ですか。　(Is your father well?)
　　⇨父ですか。元気です。　　(Father? He is fine.)

1．お母さんはお元気ですか。　　　2．御家族はお元気ですか。
3．弟さんはお元気ですか。　　　　4．お兄(にい)さんはお元気ですか。
5．御兄弟はお元気ですか。　　　　6．お姉(ねえ)さんはお元気ですか。

十課

内容表

文法	The Use of Verbs——Habitual Actions / Past Actions	普通, 何時頃起きますか。 電話しました。
	Adverbs of Frequency	いつも, 普通, だいたい, よく, ときどき あまり, ほとんど, 全然
	Adverbs used with Negative Forms	あまり, ほとんど, 全然…ない
	Adverbial use of Adjectives	い-adj. 早い ⇨ 早く な-adj. 簡単な ⇨ 簡単に
	Verb て-form……"and" (introduction)	八時半に始まって, 二時頃終わります。
	Nの後(に)／前(に)	授業の後, すぐ家へ帰りますか。
	そ-series that refers to what was mentioned	その時間
	Particle「や」"N1, N2, and so on"	新聞や雑誌
	Particle「に」—Purpose	ジョギングに行きました。
	Particle「で」—Cause	ジョギングで疲れた
	Particle「でも」—Representative	何か用事でも？
	Quantity noun (its position in a sentence and its relation to the particle.)	何回ぐらいしますか。 十時間ぐらい寝ました。
	Conjunction meaning "therefore"	だから／ですから
機能	Stating Factual Information　1-2 Seeking Factual Information　1-3 　Habitual Actions 　Past Actions Expressions to Use When One is Unable to Respond　7-14 Reason for Action/Non-Action　2-41 Expressing Happiness/Enthusiasm　3-20 Sequencing Communication　7-2 　Nの前／後(に)	普通, 何時頃起きますか。 電話しました。 そうですね…。 (十時間ぐらい寝ました。)だから 元気いっぱいですよ。 授業の後

Lesson 10

会話 (かいわ)

1

A：中村さんは普通何時頃起きますか。

B：そうですね…。大体七時半頃ですね。

A：毎朝、朝御飯を食べますか。

B：はい、いつも食べます。

A：授業は何時から何時までですか。

B：日によって違いますが、大体八時半に始まって、二時頃終わります。

A：授業の後、すぐ家へ帰りますか。

B：いいえ。六時頃まで図書館で勉強します。

A：晩御飯は自分で作りますか。

B：あまり作りませんが、時々は自分で料理します。

A：新聞や雑誌はよく読みますか。

B：ほとんど読みませんね。

A：テレビは見ますか。

B：全然見ません。ありませんから。

Nakamura san, what time do you usually get up?

Well, let's see. Most of the time, (I get up) around seven-thirty.

Do you have breakfast every morning?

Yes, I always do.

From what time to what time do you have classes?

It depends on the day, but generally from eight-thirty to about two.

Do you go home right away after classes?

No. I study at the library until six or so.

Do you cook dinner yourself?

Not very often. But sometimes I cook.

Do you often read newspapers and magazines?

I hardly read them at all.

Do you watch TV?

Not at all, because I don't have one.

2

A：昨日の晩、八時頃電話しましたが…。

I called you last night at around eight but ....

B：ああ、失礼しました。その時間にジョギングに行きましたから。 — Oh, sorry. At that time I was gone jogging.

A：十一時頃にも、電話しましたけど。 — I also called at eleven (but ...).

B：ジョギングで疲れましたから、早く寝ました。何か用事でも？ — I went to bed early since I got tired from jogging. What did you want?

A：いいえ。中村さんは、この頃、よく運動しますね。週に何回ぐらいしますか。 — Nothing in particular. Nakamura san, you've been exercising a lot lately, haven't you? About how many times a week do you exercise?

B：三回ぐらいですね。運動はいいですよ。昨日は十時間ぐらい寝ましたよ。だから今日は元気いっぱいですよ。 — About three times. Exercise is really good, you know. Last night I slept for about ten hours. So, I am full of energy today.

単語表 (たんごひょう)

1

中村(なかむら)	a surname
普通(ふつう)	usually, normally
(何時)頃(ごろ)	about (what time)
起(お)きる	get up
そうですね…	☞ことばの使い方
大体(だいたい)	most of the time
朝御飯(あさごはん)	breakfast (lit. morning meal)
いつも	always
食(た)べる	eat
日(ひ)によって	☞ことばの使い方
違(ちが)う	differ
Nの後(あと)	after N
すぐ	right away, soon
勉強(べんきょう)する	study
時々(ときどき)	sometimes
料理(りょうり)する	cook
よく	often, well
ほとんど〜ない	hardly
全然(ぜんぜん)〜ない	not〜at all

2

晩(ばん)	evening
電話(でんわ)する	phone, call
疲(つか)れる	get tired
早(はや)く	☞文法
寝(ね)る	go to bed, sleep
用事(ようじ)	errand, business
この頃(このごろ)	lately
運動(うんどう)する	exercise
週(しゅう)に	per week

Lesson 10

晩御飯(ばんごはん)	dinner, supper	何回(なんかい)	how many times
自分(じぶん)で	☞ことばの使い方	だから	☞ことばの使い方
作(つく)る	make, cook	元気(げんき)いっぱい	full of energy

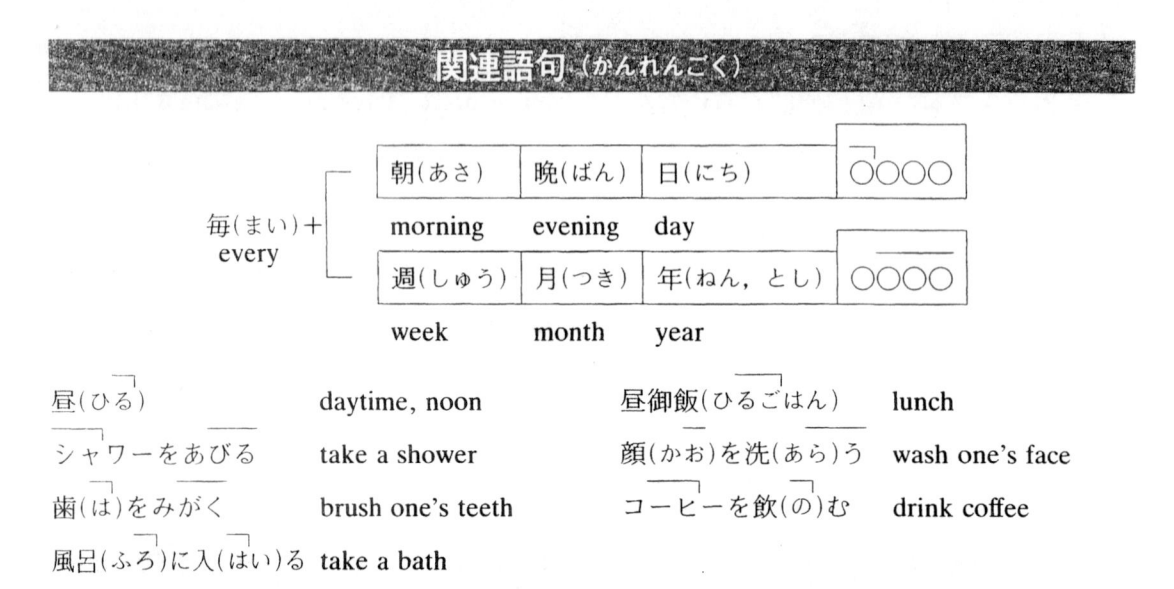

関連語句(かんれんごく)

毎(まい)+ every

朝(あさ)	晩(ばん)	日(にち)	○○○○
morning	evening	day	
週(しゅう)	月(つき)	年(ねん, とし)	○○○○
week	month	year	

昼(ひる)	daytime, noon	昼御飯(ひるごはん)	lunch
シャワーをあびる	take a shower	顔(かお)を洗(あら)う	wash one's face
歯(は)をみがく	brush one's teeth	コーヒーを飲(の)む	drink coffee
風呂(ふろ)に入(はい)る	take a bath		

文法(ぶんぽう)

● VERBS

In Japanese, as in English, there are two types of verbs: intransitive (v.i.) and transitive (v.t.) verbs. Transitive verbs require an object to which action, feeling, or thought is directed. In Japanese, を follows the object of a transitive verb. This を is called an "object marker." Although を does not always function as an "object marker," let us simply say for the time being that verbs which take を are transitive and the rest (which do not take を) are intransitive.

In English, you cannot really master verbs until you learn the prepositions which are used with them. The same can be said for Japanese particles. You should learn which particles are combined with each verb in order to effectively use the verbs.

The verb forms are shown in the diagram below:

	Imperfect (present)	Perfect (past)
Affirm.	～ます	～ました
Neg.	～ません	～ませんでした

92

Most of the sentences in the dialogue in this lesson are given in the imperfect tense. This tense basically shows that the action described by the verb is not yet complete. In this lesson, however, as we can see from the dialogue, the imperfect tense is used to indicate habitual action. In a different context this tense is used to describe things that will happen in the future as shown in the sentence such as 明日、学校へ行きますか.

● **CONTRASTIVE は**　☞ L.7「机の上にはありません」

The most basic function of は is to mark a topic; however, just as は can be used to mark the phrase 机の上に as a topic in the sentence "机の上には封筒はありませんよ." は can also be used to set off the object of a verb as the topic of a sentence.

Compare the two sentences:
1. 私はビールを飲みません。
2. 私はビールは飲みません。

Both sentences mean: "I don't drink beer." The sentence with を has no particular connotation, whereas the sentence with は indicates that, while the speaker does not drink beer, he/she may drink something other than beer.

In sentence 2, it is clear that the speaker does not drink beer, but what he/she may drink is left unclear. To resolve the mystery the missing information must be provided in the sentence pattern "N1 は〜, N2 は〜" in the following way:

3. 私はビールは飲みませんが、ワインは飲みます。
   (I don't drink beer, but I do drink wine.)
4. 田中さんは行きますが、私は行きません。
   (Tanaka san will go, but I won't.)
5. 普通は六時間ぐらい寝ますが、週末は十時間ぐらいです。
   (Ordinarily I sleep about six hours, but on weekends I sleep about ten hours.)

● **ADVERBS**

In this lesson we have several adverbs which indicate the frequency of an occurrence. If they were organized, from high to low, in the order of the frequency they signify, they would be as follows:

いつも＞普通＞大体＞よく＞ときどき＞あまり＞ほとんど＞全然

Note 1　Some of these adverbs have other meanings as well.
Note 2　The underlined adverbs are always followed by a negative predicate.

● 始まって　　1-8

This て-form of 始まる is used in the meaning of "and." The て-form of verbs have some irregularities. This form will be explained in L.13.

● 授業の後(に)　　1-9

The opposite expression is 授業の前(に). に in these examples functions in the same way as the に of "a point in time" such as in the phrase 三時に.

● 図書館で　　1-10

As already seen in L.8(教室でします), when で follows a word which designates a place, it indicates a location where an action takes place. It is important to distinguish this で from に which signifies where something exists or is located.

93

Lesson 10

	に	います, あります	location
PLACE+	で	勉強します, 寝ます, 食べます	action
	へ/に	来ます, 行きます, 帰ります	motion

● 新聞や雑誌　　　1-14

In Japanese, there are two particles, や and と, which, like the English "and," are used to list multiple nouns; however, while "and" in English can connect sentences as well as simple nouns, や and と are used in Japanese only to connect nouns. The difference between や and と is that や indicates the existence of other items not specifically mentioned: "A, B, and so on," while と simply connects two things: A と B means "A and B."

ビールやウィスキー　　　　　　　　　　(beer, whisky, and so on.)
　　　　　　　　　を飲みました。 (I drank
ビールとウィスキー　　　　　　　　　　　beer and whisky.)

● その時間に　　　2-2

こ, そ, あ, ど are used to refer to not only visible things, but also to words or phrases that have been with previous mentioned. In the dialogue, A san mentioned "eight o'clock," and B san refers to the time as "その時間." The そ-series is the most common way of referring to a word that has been previously mentioned. The こ-series is used for this purpose, but there is a slight difference in nuance or tone. It can be used if the speaker wishes to refer to the topic as if it were in his/her presence. An example of this can be seen in the following sentence from L.9:

家族は, みんなこの家に集まります。

For the use of the あ-series, see p.157「それまで」.

● ジョギングに行きました　　　2-2

In this sentence, ジョギング indicates the purpose of the verb. The particle に, when used with "motion verbs," expresses the purpose as well as location or destination.

デパートに　買い物に　行きませんか。
[location]　[purpose]　　　(Won't you go shopping to the department store?)

● ジョギングで疲れた　　　2-5

で indicates the cause of the condition indicated by the verb which follows it. So far the following uses of で have been introduced:

英語で何といいますか。　　(Indicating "a means," or "an instrument")
図書館で勉強します。　　　(Indicating "the place where an action takes place")
病気で授業を休みました。 (Cause "because of illness")

● 早く寝ました　　　2-5

The origin of 早く is "早い" an い-adj.; it functions as an adverb. The following describes how adverbs are made from the two kinds of adjectives:

い-adj.	～い ⇨ ～く

　　　大きい ⇨ 大きく
　　　安い　 ⇨ 安く　　　　　Exception: いい ⇨ よく

な -adj.	〜な ⇨ 〜に
	簡単な ⇨ 簡単に
	きれいな ⇨ きれいに

● 十時間ぐらい（寝ました）**(Quantity noun)**　　2-11

A numeral and counter (such as 時間) combine to make a quantity noun. Pay special attention to its position in relation to the predicate and the particle: it is usually placed immediately before the predicate and after the particle.

　　ジョギングを三回しました。(I jogged three times.)
　　勉強を二時間しました。　　(I studied for two hours.)

　Wrong:　ジョギング三回をしました。／勉強二時間をしました。

ことばの使い方 (ことばのつかいかた)

● 何か用事でも　　2-6

でも is a particle which shows one item as a representative of a number of closely related things. "〜でも" can be translated as "things like〜." This particle indicates that the speaker is talking about one choice from a large variety of possibilities, and gives the hearer a chance to select what he/she wants.

　　コーヒーでも飲みませんか。　(Shall we have coffee or something?)
　　土曜日にでも家に来ませんか。(Won't you come to my house, say, on Saturday?)

● 頃（ころ／ごろ）　　1-1, 1-2

This word is used with expressions of time. It indicates the approximate time of day. It cannot be used with 時間. Use くらい／ぐらい with 時間.

　　毎日，七時頃起きます。(I get up at about seven o'clock every day.)
　　毎日，七時間ぐらい勉強します。(I study about seven hours every day.)

● そうですねえ…　　1-2

This expression is a "filler" used to indicate that the speaker is searching for or thinking about a proper answer. Be aware of the flat intonation.

● 日によって　　1-6

Literally, this means "depending on the day."

　　ことば (language, words) は，国によって違います。
　　　(Languages differ from country to country.)
　　英語の発音は出身によって違いますね。
　　　(English pronunciation varies, depending on where the speaker is from.)

● 違います　　1-7

We have encountered this phrase in "いいえ，違います。" 違う is a verb which means that "something is different" or "something differs."

Lesson 10

● S が／けど　　2-1

This が is the same as the が which appears in "S1 が S2." The sentence in the dialogue could have been "電話しましたが，いませんでしたね，" but the speaker avoided adding the latter part so that the hearer would have a chance to complete the sentence. Without が or けど, the sentence sounds as if the speaker is criticizing or accusing the hearer. One of the most important functions of が is to prevent a sentence from sounding harsh or too direct.

けど is a colloquial variant of が.

A：もしもし，中村さんでしょうか。
B：はい，中村ですが。
　　(A：Hello, is this the Nakamura residence?)
　　(B：Yes, it is.(What can I do for you?))

● 自分で　　1-12

Like the English reflexive pronoun, 自分 refers to the actor (the person who does the action described by the verb in the sentence). Together with で, this phrase means "by oneself" or "on one's own."

この料理は林さんが自分で作りましたか。
　　(Did you cook this dish (by) yourself, Hayashi san?)

● (週)に　　2-8

This に means "per" as in a ratio, frequency, or the number of times per (day, week, month, etc.).

私の父は，年(or 一年)に，三回ぐらいヨーロッパに仕事で行きます。
　　(My father goes to Europe on business about three times a year.)
石井さんの弟さんは，日(or 一日)に五回ぐらい御飯を食べます。
　　(Ishii san's brother has about five meals a day.)
日本語のクラスでは，三週間に一回，試験があります。
　　(In Japanese class, we have an examination once every three weeks.)

● だから　　2-12

This conjunctive から shows a cause and effect relationship between S1 and S2 in the sentence pattern "S1. だから S2." It is like the function of から in "S1 から S2." While から is attached to a sentence, だから is used independently at the beginning of a sentence. We have seen that ～です can substitute a verbal phrase; similarly, だ of だから, which is the plain form of です, replaces the sentence which precedes it. ですから is usually used in sentences with です，ます endings for stylistic reason.

私は，テレビがありませんから，全然見ません。
　　(Since I don't have a TV, I don't watch it at all.)
　　⇨私は，テレビがありません。だから，全然見ません。
　　(I don't have a TV; therefore, I don't watch it at all.)

96

[動詞(どうし)]

The list below shows the representative form of each verb group.

In Japanese, there are three kinds of verbs; they are classified according to their forms. For now, let us call them: **GROUPS I, II,** and **III.** Group III consists of two irregular verbs while Groups I and II have many verbs.

	ます-form	意味(いみ)	Dictionary form	て-form
I	言います	say, call	言う	言って
	行きます	go	行く	行って
	話します	speak	話す	話して
	待ちます	wait	待つ	待って
	死にます	die	死ぬ	死んで
	読みます	read	読む	読んで
	作ります	make, cook	作る	作って
	泳ぎます	swim	泳ぐ	泳いで
	遊びます	play	遊ぶ	遊んで
II	始めます	begin	始める	始めて
	起きます	get up	起きる	起きて
III	します	do	する	して
	来ます	come	来る	来て

[ます-form]

a. As you have already learned, this form is used in polite or formal conversation.

b. The part preceding ます is called the "stem" or "pre-ます form." In most cases, the stem ends in an "*i*" sound, as in Group I and III. Group II verbs end in "*e*" and "*i*.": 始めます, 寝ます, 食べます.

c. The ます-form is used to combine various verbs to form compound meanings.

　　　　食べ(ます)＋始めます　⇨ start eating
　　　　話し(ます)＋終わります　⇨ finish talking

[Dictionary form]

a. This is used as the basic verb form in written Japanese and in informal conversation among friends.

b. As the name indicates, all verbs are listed in this form in dictionaries.

c. This form is used when modifying nouns as we have seen in: 吉田さんが知っている人 (the person Yoshida san knows).

d. All dictionary forms end in an "*u*" sound. Verbs in Groups II and III end in る. Group I verbs end in く, す, つ, ぬ, む, る, ぐ, ぶ, or, as in いう and ちがう, in a single "*u*."

e. しぬ is the only verb in modern Japanese which ends in ぬ.

Lesson 10

練習(れんしゅう)

練習(れんしゅう)　1	V. neg./affirm.

例　行きますか (Will you go?)　（ええ）　⇨ええ, 行きます。　(Yes, I'll go.)
　　行きますか (Will you go?)　（いいえ）⇨いいえ, 行きません。(No, I won't go.)

1．起きますか　（ええ）　　2．食べますか(いいえ)　　3．始まりますか(はい)
4．終わりますか(はい)　　　5．帰りますか(いいえ)　　6．勉強しますか(いいえ)
7．作りますか　（はい）　　8．読みますか（ええ）　　9．料理しますか(いいえ)
10．見ますか　　（いいえ）　11．走りますか(はい)　　12．入りますか　（いいえ）
　　　　　　　　　　　　　　　　はし　　　　　　　　　　　はい
13．寝ますか　　（いいえ）

練習(れんしゅう)　2	V. dic. f. ⇨ます

例　起きる (Will you get up?)　（ええ）　⇨ええ, 起きます。(Yes, I'll get up.)

1．行く　　（いいえ）　　2．食べる(ええ)　　　3．始まる　（いいえ）
4．終わる(ええ)　　　　　5．帰る　（いいえ）　6．勉強する(はい)
7．作る　（いいえ）　　　8．読む　（はい）　　9．料理する(いいえ)
10．見る　（ええ）　　　　11．走る　（いいえ）　12．入る　　（はい）
13．寝る　（いいえ）

練習(れんしゅう)　3	Object-marker を

例　朝御飯　⇨朝御飯を食べますか。(Will you eat breakfast?)

1．テレビ　　　　　2．新聞や雑誌　　　3．運動
4．お風呂　　　　　5．昼御飯　　　　　6．料理

練習(れんしゅう)　4	Habitual action/〜時

例　get up　⇨中村さんは普通何時頃起きますか。
　　　　　　(What time do you usually get up, Nakamura san?)

1．have breakfast　　　　2．come to the university　　3．have lunch
4．go to the library　　　5．go home　　　　　　　　　6．cook dinner
7．read the newspaper　　8．take a bath　　　　　　　　9．go to bed

十課

| 練習(れんしゅう) 5 | Habitual action/〜時間 |

例　sleep　⇨中村さんは普通何時間ぐらい寝ますか。
　　　　　　(How many hours do you usually sleep, Nakamura san?)

1．have classes　　　2．stay at school　　　3．study in the library
4．watch TV　　　　5．exercise　　　　　　6．run
7．sleep　　　　　　8．read the newspaper　9．study
10．stay at home

| 練習(れんしゅう) 6 | Adverbs of frequency |

例　always　⇨私はいつも朝御飯を作ります。(I always prepare breakfast.)

1．usually　　　　　2．most of the time　　3．often
4．sometimes　　　　5．not very often　　　6．hardly
7．not at all　　　　8．always　　　　　　　9．often

| 練習(れんしゅう) 7 | まで |

例　sleep　⇨中村さんは，普通何時まで寝ますか。
　　　　　　(Until what time do you usually sleep, Nakamura san?)

1．have classes　　　2．stay at school　　　3．study in the library
4．watch TV　　　　5．exercise　　　　　　6．stay at home
7．sleep　　　　　　8．read the newspaper　9．study

| 練習(れんしゅう) 8 | Verb, tense |

例　昨日学校へ行きましたか。　⇨いいえ，昨日は行きませんでしたが，今日は行きます。
　　(Did you go to school yesterday?　⇨ I didn't yesterday but I will today.)

1．先週パーティーをしましたか。　　2．先月，試験がありましたか。
3．去年，日本へ行きましたか。　　　4．昨日，宿題がありましたか。
5．先週，友達が来ましたか。　　　　6．去年，大学院に入りましたか。

Lesson 10

練習(れんしゅう)　9　　　　　Place＋で/に

例　佐藤さんはよく図書館にいます。(Sato san is often in the library.)
　　　（勉強します）⇨佐藤さんはよく図書館で勉強します。
　　　　　　　　　　　　(Sato san often studies in the library.)

1．行きます　　　　2．新聞を読みます　　　3．寝ます
4．います　　　　　5．雑誌を読みます　　　6．来ます

練習(れんしゅう)　10　　　　　Times per ～

例　月，映画(movie)
　⇨中村さんは月に何回ぐらい映画を見ますか。
　　　(How many times a month do you see a movie, Nakamura san?)

1．週，ジョギング　　2．日，アイスクリーム　　3．年，御両親の所
4．日，コーヒー　　　5．週，運動　　　　　　　6．年，カリフォルニアに行く

練習(れんしゅう)　11　　　　　Nの前に，Nの後

例　朝御飯の前に歯をみがきますか。(Do you brush your teeth before breakfast?)
　⇨いいえ，朝御飯の後，みがきます。(No, I brush them after breakfast.)

1．勉強の後，テレビを見ますか。
2．勉強の後，コーヒーを飲みますか。
3．ジョギングの前に何かしますか。
4．お風呂の前にビールを飲みますか。
5．日本語の授業の後，何か食べますか。
6．日本語の授業の前に図書館で勉強しますか。

練習(れんしゅう)　12　　　　　と vs. や

例　何を食べましたか。(アイスクリーム，ケーキ，バナナ)
　⇨アイスクリームやケーキを食べました。
　　　(I ate ice cream, cake, and other things.)
　　誰が来ましたか。(中村さん，林さん)
　⇨中村さんと林さんが来ました。(Nakamura san and Hayashi san came.)

1．何を作りましたか。　　　　（すし，てんぷら）
2．昨日何を勉強しましたか。　（日本語，中国語，英語）
3．誰が料理をしましたか。　　（私，ダンさん，ロングさん）
4．何で疲れましたか。　　　　（勉強，アルバイト，用事）

5．何という新聞を読みますか。（朝日新聞，読売新聞）
6．今そこに誰がいますか。　　（田中さん，山田さん，石井さん）

練習(れんしゅう)　13　　　ですから

例　私は一年生ですから，専門はありません。
　　(Since I am a freshman, I don't have a major.)
　　⇨私は一年生です。ですから，専門はありません。
　　(I'm a freshman. Therefore, I don't have a major.)

1．今日は天気がよくないですから，家にいます。
2．今日は暖かいですから，ジョギングに行きます。
3．昨日は勉強で疲れましたから，早く寝ました。
4．今，林さんに電話しましたから，すぐ来ます。
5．昨日よく寝ましたから，今日は元気いっぱいですよ。
6．レストランの昼御飯は高いですから，自分で作ります。

練習(れんしゅう)　14　　　その

例　昨日，日本語の先生の家へ行きました。
　　(Yesterday I went to the Japanese teacher's house.)
　　⇨ Where is "the house?"
　　⇨その家はどこですか。

1．いい本を読みましたよ。　　　　　　　　⇨What book is "the book?"⇨
2．昨日おいしいケーキを食べました。　　　⇨Where did you eat "the cake?"⇨
3．昨日新しい料理を作りました。　　　　　⇨Was "the dish" tasty?⇨
4．家の近くのスーパーマーケットに行きました。⇨Was "the supermarket" good?⇨
5．三時頃でかけました。　　　　　　　　　⇨I called you at "the time."⇨
6．昨日女の人が来ましたよ。　　　　　　　⇨What was her name? (Use 何という人)⇨

十一課

内容表

文法	Counters		才(歳), 本, 冊, 枚, 箱, 円, 個, 匹
	Days of the Month		一日 …………… 三十一日
	Japanese Counting		一つ, 二つ ………… 十
	Numbers (10,000 ～)		万, 億, 兆
	"I want N." (Object-marker が)		(私は)タイプライターが欲しいです。
	"N1 needs N2." (Object-marker が)		(私は)きゅうりが要ります。
	"May I have N?" / "Please give me …."		卵を二つ下さい。
	Informal Talk (Limited to expressions related to〜です)		ライアンさんは, 何才?
機能	Stating Factual Information	1-2	本, 冊, 枚, 箱, 円, 個, 匹
	Seeking Factual Information (Numbers, Days of the Month)	1-3	
	Expressing Congratulations	6-19	お誕生日, おめでとうございます。
	Listing	2-48	鉛筆を十二本と…を一台買いました。
	Stating Want/Desire	3-16	Nが欲しいです
	Expressing Need	2-17	Nが要ります
	Making Requests	5-3	卵を二つ下さい。 大きいのを一つお願いします。
	Avoiding Commitments	5-21	猫はどうも…。

103

Lesson 11

会話(かいわ)

1

A：ライアンさんは，何才(なんさい)？
B：十九才(じゅうきゅうさい)です。
A：十九才！　若(わか)いねえ。ライアンさんの誕生日(たんじょうび)は何月何日(なんがつなんにち)？
B：今日(きょう)です。
A：十一月二十三日(じゅういちがつにじゅうさんにち)！［はい。］お誕生日，おめでとう。
B：ありがとうございます。

2

A：何(なに)を買(か)いましたか。
B：文房具(ぶんぼうぐ)ですよ。そこの文房具屋(ぶんぼうぐや)で，今日は色々安(いろいろやす)く売(う)っていますよ。
A：随分(ずいぶん)，たくさん買いましたね。
B：ええ。鉛筆(えんぴつ)を十二本(じゅうにほん)と、ノートを六冊(ろくさつ)と、カードを二百枚(にひゃくまい)と、消(け)しゴムを三(みっ)つと、クリップを二箱(ふたはこ)買いました。ああ、そうそう、それからタイプライターを一台(いちだい)買いました。
A：タイプライターは，私も欲(ほ)しいですが、いくらでした？
B：値段(ねだん)ですか。四万円(よんまんえん)ぐらいでした。

3

A：卵(たまご)は何個(なんこ)要(い)りますか。
B：二(ふた)つ下(くだ)さい。
A：じゃがいもは，いくつ…。
B：大(おお)きいのを一つお願(ねが)いします。
A：はい。きゅうりは一本(いっぽん)要りますか。
B：一本は要らないでしょう。

104

1

A：Ryan san, how old are you?

B：I am nineteen years old.

A：Nineteen years old! You are young. What month and what day (i.e. when) is your birthday?

B：It's today.

A：November 23rd! [Yes.] Happy birthday to you.

B：Thank you.

2

A：What did you buy?

B：Some stationery items. They have various things on sale today at that stationery store.

A：You've bought quite a lot, haven't you?

B：Yes. I bought 12 pencils, 6 notebooks, 200 cards, 3 erasers, and 2 boxes of clips. Oh yes, and I bought a typewriter.

A：I want a typewriter, too; how much was it?

B：The price? It was about 40,000 yen.

3

A：How many eggs do you need?

B：Please give me two.

A：How about potatoes?

B：Please give me one large one.

A：O.K. Do you need one cucumber?

B：I don't think I'll need (a whole) one.

Lesson 11

4

A：伊藤さん，猫の子は要りませんか。

B：猫の子ですか。

A：三匹も生まれて困りました。

B：家には犬が二匹いますから，猫はどうも…。

単語表（たんごひょう）

1

何才(なんさい)／いくつ	how old
誕生日(たんじょうび)	birthday
何月(なんがつ)	what month
何日(なんにち)	what day
十一月(じゅういちがつ)	November
二十三日(にじゅうさんにち)	23rd

2

買(か)う	buy
文房具(ぶんぼうぐ)	stationery
文房具屋(ぶんぼうぐや)	stationery shop
色々(いろいろ)	in wide variety
安(やす)く	cheaply, inexpensively
売(う)る	sell
売(う)っている	be selling
たくさん	in large quantity
鉛筆(えんぴつ)	pencil
本(ほん，ぼん，ぽん)	a counter
冊(さつ)	a counter
カード	card
枚(まい)	a counter
消(け)しゴム	eraser

三(みっ)つ	three
二箱(ふたはこ)	two boxes (packets)
それから	and, in addition
台(だい)	a counter
欲(ほ)しい	want
値段(ねだん)	price
四万円(よんまんえん)	forty thousand yen

3

卵(たまご)	egg
いくつ	how many
じゃがいも	potato
お願(ねが)いします	please
きゅうり	cucumber
要(い)る	need
(要らない)でしょう	I suppose (it isn't necessary.)

4

猫(ねこ)	cat
猫の子(ねこのこ)	kitten
匹(ひき，びき)	a counter
生(う)まれる	be born
犬(いぬ)	dog

4

A：Ito san, would you care to have a kitten?

B：A kitten?

A：(My cat) had three, and I don't know what to do.

B：I have two dogs at home, so I don't really think a cat would be ....

関連語句（かんれんごく）

飲み物(のみもの)	drinks	りんご	apple
たばこ	cigarette	使(つか)う	use
サラリー	salary	人口(じんこう)	population
映画館(えいがかん)	movie theater	紙(かみ)	paper

Lesson 11

文法 (ぶんぽう)

● **COUNTERS**

In Japanese, "counters" are used as suffixes to numerals to express the quantity of things. The combination of a numeral and a counter creates a quantity noun. The choice of a counter is determined by the shape or nature of a thing.

Some counters we have already learned are: 時(じ), 時間(じかん), 課(か), ページ, and 分. Here are some more counters:

Counter	Things to be counted	Examples
才(さい)	age	十八才(じゅうはっさい) (eighteen)
月(がつ)	month of the year	十二月(じゅうにがつ) (December)
週間(しゅうかん)	weeks (duration)	十週間(じ(ゅ)っしゅうかん) (ten weeks)
か月(げつ)	months (duration)	三か月 (three months)
年(ねん)／年間(ねんかん)	years (duration)	四年(よねん) (four years)
本(ほん)	narrow, long things	pen, pencil, bottle, pin, belt, tie, tree, umbrella
枚(まい)	thin, flat things	paper, plate, record, coin, shirt, board, photos
冊(さつ)	things shaped like a book	book, magazine, notebook, dictionary
杯(はい)	things in cups, bowls	tea, coffee, rice, water
匹(ひき)	small animals, insects, fish	
人(にん)	people	
個(こ)	relatively small objects	marble, candy, fruit
一つ(ひと)／二つ(ふた)…	relatively small objects, abstract things	marble, candy, fruits class, subject, homework
回(かい), 度(ど)	time	二回, 二度 (twice)
円(えん)	Japanese monetary unit	千円 (¥1000)
番(ばん)	order	一番 (No.1)
パーセント	percent	百パーセント (100%)
箱(はこ)	things in a box, packet	一箱(ひとはこ) (one box)

The following counters below have been put into sub-groups according to their phonetic characteristics:

A: Counters which undergo no phonetic change:

Note that the numbers shown in the left column are basic ones and only the numbers that differ from them are given in the right columns.

		枚　台　度 番　マイル ドル($)	ページ パーセント キロ	課　回 か月 個	時 時間 年	円	才　週 週間 冊
1	いち			いっ			いっ
2	に						
3	さん						
4	よん				よ		
5	ご						
6	ろく			ろっ			
7	なな				しち		
8	はち						はっ
9	きゅう				く		
10	じゅう		じ(ゅ)っ				じ(ゅ)っ
?				なん			

B: Counters which undergo phonetic change:

	本　匹　杯	分
1	いっぽん　　P	いっぷん
2	にほん	にふん
3	さんぼん　　B	P さんぷん
4	よんほん	P よんぷん
5	ごほん	ごふん
6	ろっぽん　　P	ろっぷん
7	ななほん	ななふん
8	はっぽん　　P	はっぷん
9	きゅうほん	きゅうふん
10	じっぽん　　P じゅっぽん	じっぷん じゅっぷん
?	なんぼん　　B	P なんぷん

Lesson 11

In L.8, we learned to count using the Chinese reading. There are two counting methods: Chinese and Japanese readings. All the counters we have so far encountered are used with the Chinese reading numerals. There are, however, a small number of counters which are combined with a different series of Japanese numerals, ひとつ, ふたつ..., up to ten.

Things counted	ひとつ, ふたつ small objects abstract things	日 (にち) number of days	日 (ひ) date	箱 (はこ) 月 (つき)
1	ひとつ	いちにち	ついたち	ひと
2	ふたつ	ふつか		ふた
3	みっつ	みっか		み
4	よっつ	よっか		
5	いつつ	いつか		
6	むっつ	むいか		
7	ななつ	なのか		
8	やっつ	ようか		
9	ここのつ	ここのか		
10	とお	とおか		
?	いくつ	なんにち		

Note 1　Numerals over ten in this series are given the Chinese reading.

Note 2　For dates and numbers of days higher than ten, the counter is changed from か(日)to にち(日), as in じゅういちにち(十一日), じゅうににち(十二日)……さんじゅうにち(三十日). The readings change, although the characters remain the same. The exceptions are 十四日(じゅうよっか), 二十日(はつか), and 二十四日(にじゅうよっか).

Note 3　In the case of 箱(はこ) and 月(つき), numerals larger than three take Chinese numerals. To say "How many," use いくつ for boxes and 何か月(げつ) for months.

Note 4　Use *kanji* to write these numeric words. The words were written here in *hiragana* so that the phonetic changes could be easily observed.

● 文房具です　　2-2

In dialogue ②, there is the following "question and answer":

　　A：何を買いましたか。
　　B：文房具ですよ。

As we have studied in L.6 (P.50「あそこです」), です can be a substitute for a verb in the context in which the verb is not the main concern. When です takes the place of a verb, sometimes you can delete a particle and sometimes not. Usually が, は, を and に are omitted and other particles stay. へ and で can either remain or be left out without affecting the meaning. Study the list on the next page.

Noun	+particle+Verb	⇨	Noun	+(particle)+です
だれ	が 来ましたか。	⇨	林さん	です。
何	を 作りますか。	⇨	チーズケーキ	ですよ。
リーさん	は どこにいますか。	⇨	その教室(きょうしつ)	です。
どこ	へ 行きますか。	⇨	日本	(へ) です。
何	で 行きますか。	⇨	車(くるま)	(で) です。
いつ	から 行きますか。	⇨	来週	から です。
いつ	まで 日本にいますか。	⇨	九月の終(お)わり	まで です。
ガールフレンド	も 行きますか。	⇨	ええ,ガールフレンド	も です。

● 欲しい　2-7

This is an adjective, unlike English "to want." It takes が to describe the object that is desired. This can be used to refer to the speaker's desire or to ask about the hearer's desire, if he is close friend of yours; but it is never used with a third person. The Japanese consider it impossible to talk about the feelings and desires of a third person as if they are one's own. An exception: mothers use this form to talk about young children. Moreover, asking direct questions about a person's feelings or desire is considered rude. So it is advisable to limit the use of this expression to yourself.

For the time being, use 欲しい in only the following pattern;

> 私(わたし)は N が欲しいです。(I want a N.)

1．私は新しい車が欲しいです。(I want a new car.)
2．私はいい友達(ともだち)が欲しいです。(I want a good friend.)
3．私は,お金は欲しくありませんが,もう少し時間が欲しいです。
　　(I don't want money, but I want a little more time.)

● 要ります　3-1

> N1 は　N2 が　要ります

In this pattern, N1 is an agent or an event in need of N2 and N2 is the object of what N1 needs. Sometimes it appears in the variant pattern; "N1 <u>に</u>は N2 が要ります".

1．私は,飲み物は何も要りません。
　　(I need nothing to drink.)
2．誕生日にはケーキが要りますね。
　　(A cake is necessary on a birthday.)
3．パスポートには,写真(しゃしん)が要りますよ。
　　(A photo is needed on a passport.)

● 下さい　3-2

This is a polite imperative form which is used to request something from someone. It means "I would like ..." or "Please give me ..." You can use this expression at a store, for example, to buy something, at a restaurant with a waiter to make your order, or to anyone in general to request something.

In most cases, お願(ねが)いします is interchangeable.

The pattern of this expression is: > N を　下さい

Lesson 11

And if you want to indicate the quantity of N, insert a numeral and counter immediately before 下さい.

1. すみません。この本を一冊下さい。
   (Excuse me. Please give me a copy of this book.)
2. すみませんが、塩を下さい。(May I have salt, please?)

● 三匹も　　4-3

も after a quantity noun indicates that the number is either unusually large (in the affirmative) or small (in the negative).

1. この教室には、学生が五十人もいます。
   (There are as many as fifty students in this classroom.)
2. その映画館には、人が五十人もいませんでした。
   (There were not even fifty people in that movie theater.)

ことばの使い方 (ことばのつかいかた)

● **Informal talk**

In the first dialogue, A san does not use です, ます endings in his utterances, while B san uses them. As these endings are "politeness-markers," we can see that A san is speaking to B san casually and informally. The loss of "politeness markers" indicates that A san is a man who is older than B san, and at the same time, he knows B san quite well. B san is younger than A san, and as younger people are expected in Japanese society to speak politely to their seniors, B san speaks in a polite style. This is quite commonly found in daily conversation. Age difference is a much more important factor in Japan than in English-speaking societies as a method to determine speech style.

There are variations in casual talk: A san would say "若いわねえ," instead of "若いねえ," if A san were a woman.

In conversations among friends of the same age, people talk like A san: in plain-form endings instead of です, ます. Here is a chart which roughly shows how です endings are changed to the informal casual style.

	男	女	
です	(だ)	0	
ですか ↗ / ↘	(か)	0 ↗ / ↘	
N／な-adj.＋ですよ／ね	〜だよ／ね	〜だわよ／だわね	〜ね／よ
い-adj.＋ですよ／ね	〜よ／ね	〜わよ／わね	

Note 1　だ and か in the parentheses indicate that they can be used, but using them would make the speech sound rough. だ is a plain-form of です.

Note 2　わ, which appears often in female speech, indicates that:
   a. the previous part is her opinion or judgment.

b. the speaker is surprised or slightly moved.

Note 3　This list is not detailed one.

● 十九才 (**Telling a person's age**)　　1-2

A person's age is expressed by using a numeral and the counter 才; however, 才 is often omitted. The irregular form for "twenty years old" is はたち (二十才). Although にじっさい is correct, はたち has been traditionally preferred.

　　はたち and にじっさい in *kanji* are both written 二十才.

　　いくつ "how many," also means "how old," and is used to ask a person's age.

The more polite form おいくつ is used in questions concerning a person who is your senior or someone you do not know well.

● 何月何日　　1-3

This is used to ask about a day of the month. いつ, "when" also be used to get the same information. If you want to know just the year, month, or date, use 何年, 何月, or 何日.

Make sure that the order of your response is arranged in the order of the largest to the smallest unit.

　　ジョージ・ワシントンの誕生日は1732年2月22日ですか。
　　(Is George Washington's birthday on February 22, 1732?)

● おめでとう(ございます)　　1-5

　　This is a commonly used greeting to congratulate someone on such happy occasions as New Year's Day, a wedding, or a birthday. If someone offers this greeting, respond by saying ありがとうございます, except on New Years Day when everybody simply says おめでとうございます. It is appropriate to say simply おめでとう to your close friends in all of the above situations.

● 随分　　2-3

This is an adverb that intensifies the degree of some state or action. This has so much emotional overtone that it is not used in ordinary writings.

This adverb indicates that the speaker is impressed or surprised by the degree of the topic in question.

　　1．A：昨日は八時に寝ました。　　(I went to bed at eight last night.)
　　　　B：随分早く寝ましたね。　　(You went to bed so early!)
　　2．A：今日は授業が五つあります。大変ですよ。
　　　　　(I have five classes today. It is terrible.)
　　　　B：随分たくさんありますね。
　　　　　(So many classes!)

● ああ，そうそう　　2-5

This expression indicates that what has just been said or heard reminds you directly or indirectly of something related to it.

　　A：さっき伊藤さんに会いましたよ。
　　　(I saw Ito san a little while ago.)
　　B：そうですか。ああ，そうそう，私も会いました。
　　　(Oh, did you? Oh yes, I saw him, too.)

Lesson 11

● それから　　2-5

それから has two meanings: 1) "in addition" or "and"; 2) "and then" or "after."

1. 英語の辞書と、それから日本語の辞書を買いました。
   (I bought an English dictionary and a Japanese one.)
2. 東京に三日いました。それから、京都へ行きました。
   (I stayed in Tokyo for three days and then I went to Kyoto.)

● 四万円　　2-8

The Western system of counting goes by 3—one thousand (1,000), 1 million (1,000,000), 1 billion (1,000,000,000) and so on. In writing numbers, Japanese banks and businesses will use the Western method, placing the commas after every three digits. The *names*, however, change every four digits, following the old Chinese system. It is simplest to understand numerals over ten thousand if you separate them every four digits.

1234	⇨せん・にひゃく・さんじゅう・よん
1234, 0000	⇨せん・にひゃく・さんじゅう・よん＋万
1234, 0000, 0000	⇨せん・にひゃく・さんじゅう・よん＋億
One million	⇨百万（ひゃく・まん）
One billion（アメリカ）	⇨十億（じゅう・おく）
One trillion（アメリカ）	⇨一兆（いっ・ちょう）

The next four digits after 億 is 兆（ちょう）.

● 大きいの　　3-4　☞P. 31「私のです」

● 猫はどうも　　4-4

どうも is a phrase which indirectly expresses a warning that a disagreeable statement will follow, and that you feel badly about it. どうも by itself is used quite often, and means どうもありがとうございます、どうもすみません in daily conversation. Etymologically, they had a negative meaning.

1. A：わかりましたか。　　　　　(Do you understand?)
   B：まだ、どうも(わかりません。)　(Not quite.)
2. A：チーズ、どうですか。　　　(How about having some cheese?)
   B：私、チーズはどうも。　　　(Sorry, I can't eat cheese.)
   　　　　　　　　　　　　　　　(Sorry, I don't like cheese.)

十一課

練習 (れんしゅう)

練習(れんしゅう)　1　　　　Counters

例　鉛筆を買いました。(I bought pensils.)
　　　（12）⇨鉛筆を十二本買いました。(I bought twelve pencils.)

1．昨日，本を読みました。（5）　　　2．ピザを食べました。（2）
3．大学院の学生が来ました。（4）　　4．ビールを飲みました。（1）
5．旅行をしました。（3）　　　　　　6．犬の子が生まれました。（3）

練習(れんしゅう)　2　　　　いくら

例　この鉛筆はいくらですか。(How much is this pencil?)
　　　⇨この鉛筆は一本いくらですか。(How much is one pencil?)

1．このりんごはいくらですか。　　　2．このシャツはいくらですか。
3．このカードはいくらですか。　　　4．このコーラはいくらですか。
5．このノートはいくらですか。　　　6．このタバコはいくらですか。

練習(れんしゅう)　3　　　　です　Substituting verbals

例　誰が来ますか。(Who is coming?)
　　　（伊藤さん）⇨伊藤さんです。(Ito is.)
　　どこから来ますか。(Where is he coming from?)
　　　（大学）⇨大学からです。(From college.)

1．何を食べますか。　　（ハンバーガー）　2．どこで食べますか。　（ここ）
3．どこへ行きますか。　（日本）　　　　　4．何で行きますか。　　（車）
5．猫はどこにいますか。（ここ）　　　　　6．何時から始まりますか。（八時）
7．何時に終わりますか。（九時）　　　　　8．何時までしますか。　（十時）

練習(れんしゅう)　4　　　　N が欲しい／N が要る

例　テープ・レコーダーが欲しいです。
　　　（1）⇨テープ・レコーダーが一台欲しいです。(I want a tape recorder.)

1．紙(paper)が欲しいです。（7）　　2．レモンが要ります。（3）
3．お金が要ります。（1000）　　　　4．猫が欲しいです。（1）

Lesson 11

5．トマトが欲しいです。（3） 6．たばこをお願いします。（1）

| 練習(れんしゅう)　5 | Interrogatives ＋ counters |

例　学生が来ました。 ⇨学生は何人来ましたか。(How many students came?)

1．伊藤さんの誕生日です。 2．シャツを買いました。
3．猫の子が生まれました。 4．卵が要ります。
5．じゃがいもを使(つか)います。 6．コーラを飲みます。

| 練習(れんしゅう)　6 | N と，それから N |

例　買います(ノート，消しゴム)
　　　⇨ノートを一冊と，それから消しゴムを一つ買います。
　　　(I will buy a notebook and an eraser.)

1．買いました(きゅうり，トマト) 2．要ります(タイプライター，紙)
3．お願いします(ビール，コーラ) 4．家にいます(猫，犬)
5．食べました(チョコレート，ケーキ) 6．今週(こんしゅう)読みました(英語の本，日本語の本)

| 練習(れんしゅう)　7 | Readings of numerals |

例　伊藤さん，1974／11／23
　　　⇨伊藤さんの誕生日は1974年11月23日です。
　　　(Ito san's birthday is on November 23, 1974.)

1．父，1950／8／17 2．母(はは)，1952／12／20
3．兄(あに)，1972／4／10 4．姉(あね)，1973／10／19
5．妹(いもうと)，1983／1／1 6．弟(おとうと)，1984／2／29

| 練習(れんしゅう)　8 | Perfect tense |

例　今年，ライアンさんは，十九才です。(去年)
　　　(Ryan san is nineteen years old this year.)
　　　⇨去年，ライアンさんは十八才でした。
　　　(Ryan san was eighteen years old last year.)

1．今日，文房具を安く売っています。(昨日)
2．今週，休みが欲しいです。　　　　(先週)
3．今月，お金がたくさん要ります。　(先月)
4．今年，新しい車が欲しいです。　　(去年)

5．明日，猫の子が生まれます。　　　（昨日）
6．今日，文房具が安いです。　　　　（昨日）
7．今日，金曜日です。　　　　　　　（昨日）

練習(れんしゅう)　9	Days of the month

例　今日は二十三日です。（昨日）(It is the 23rd today.)
　　⇨昨日は二十二日でした。(It was the 22nd yesterday.)

1．明日は五日です。　　（今日）　　2．今日は九日です。　　（明日）
3．昨日は十三日でした。（明日）　　4．明日は二十一日です。（今日）
5．今日は二日です。　　（昨日）　　6．昨日は六日でした。　（明日）

練習(れんしゅう)　10	下さい

例　大きいの，二つ　⇨大きいのを二つ下さい。(Give me two big ones.)

1．赤いの，三個　　　2．きれいなの，二本　　3．林さんの，二枚
4．この消しゴム，二個　5．そのノート，六冊　　6．あのカード，二百枚

練習(れんしゅう)　11	お願いします

Use お願いします with the cues above.

練習(れんしゅう)　12	Readings of numerals

Read the sentences below.
1．リーさんのサラリーは一年に70,000ドルです。
2．林さんのサラリーは一か月500,000円です。
3．アメリカの人口(population)は，240,000,000人です。
4．中国の人口は1,200,000,000人です。
5．東京の人口は12,000,000人です。
6．このワープロの値段は300,000円でした。

十二課

内容表

文法	Noun Modification with Verbs		試験_{しけん}がある日_ひ
	Plain forms: Verbs, Adjs., and です		See 文法
	Nominalizer「の」		漢字_{かんじ}を勉強_{べんきょう}するの(はおもしろい)
	Counting "People"		一人_{ひとり}, 二人_{ふたり}, 三人_{さんにん}
	「ある」(To have)		御兄弟_{ごきょうだい}はありますか。
	Particle しか…(ない)		六日_{むいか}しかない
	Adverbs――Intensifier		とても, 大変_{たいへん}
機能	Stating Factual Information (Schedule)	1-2	See 会話 ①
	Seeking Factual Information (Personal Background) (Directions)	1-3	See 会話 ② 東_{ひがし}／西_{にし}／南_{みなみ}／北_{きた}
	Expressing Likes/Dislikes	3-1	N (NP) が　おもしろい ｜ つまらない 　　　　　楽_{たの}しい ｜ 退屈_{たいくつ}だ 　　　　　好_すきだ ｜ 嫌_{きら}いだ

Lesson 12

会話 (かいわ)

1

女子学生：日本語の学期末試験がある日は，いつ？

男子学生：十二日じゃない？

女子学生：それじゃ，試験が終わる最後の日ね。じゃ，あと六日しかないわね。

男子学生：うん，そうだね。

女子学生：試験が始まるのは八時？

男子学生：うん。始まるのは八時で，終わるのは十時。

2

A：佐藤さんが生まれた所はどこですか。

B：私が生まれたのは東京です。

A：育った所も東京ですか。

B：いいえ。育ったのは京都です。

A：今，御両親が住んでいるのは？

B：両親ですか。横浜です。

A：横浜という所はどこにありますか。

B：東京の南です。

A：御兄弟はありますか。

B：兄が一人と，姉が二人あります。

3

A：漢字を勉強するのはどう？　おもしろい？

B：ええ。漢字の練習は少しつまらないけど，意味を調べるのはとても楽しいわ。

A：何度も漢英辞典を引くのは退屈じゃない？

B：ええ，少しも退屈じゃないわ。私は辞書を読むのが好きだから。

1

Female student : On which day is it that we will have the Japanese final examination?

Male student : Probably the 12th.

Female student : Then it's the last day of finals (week), isn't it? Well then, it's only six days away.

Male student : Yes, that's right.

Female student : Will the exam begin at 8 o'clock?

Male student : Yes, it will begin at 8 and end at 10.

2

A : Sato san, where were you born?

B : I was born in Tokyo.

A : Were you raised in Tokyo as well?

B : No, I was raised in Kyoto.

A : Where do your parents live now?

B : My parents? In Yokohama.

A : Where is Yokohama (located)?

B : To the south of Tokyo.

A : Do you have any brothers and sisters?

B : I have one older brother and two older sisters.

3

A : How is studying *kanji*? Is it interesting?

B : Yes. Practicing *kanji* is a little boring, but looking up the meanings is a lot of fun.

A : Isn't it boring to look up (*kanji*) over and over again (in) the Chinese-English character dictionary?

B : No, it's not a bit boring, since I like to read the dictionary.

Lesson 12

単語表 (たんごひょう)

1

女子学生(じょしがくせい)	female student
男子学生(だんしがくせい)	male student
学期(がっき)	school term
～末(まつ)	end of ～
(Place で)ある	be held
いつ	when
最後(さいご)	last
日(ひ)	day
あと六日(むいか)	six more days
しか…ない	only, just
うん	☞ことばの使い方 Informal talk

2

生(う)まれる	be born
所(ところ)	place
育(そだ)つ	grow, be raised
住(す)んでいる	to live (somewhere)
横浜(よこはま)	Yokohama
南(みなみ)	south
ある	have
一人(ひとり)	one (person)
二人(ふたり)	two (persons)

3

おもしろい	interesting
練習(れんしゅう)	practice, exercise
少(すこ)し	a little
つまらない	uninteresting
意味(いみ)	meaning
調(しら)べる	check, investigate
とても	very (much)
楽(たの)しい	enjoyable, cheerful
何度(なんど)も	many times
辞典(じてん)	dictionary
漢英辞典(かんえいじてん)	Chinese-English Dictionary
(辞典を)引(ひ)く	consult a dictionary
退屈(たいくつ)な	boring, monotonous
少(すこ)しも…ない	not ... at all
辞書(じしょ)	dictionary
好(す)きだ	to like

関連語句 (かんれんごく)

便利(べんり)な	convenient
乗り物(のりもの)	transportation
百(ひゃく)ドル	100 dollars
(Nと)話(はな)す	talk with ～
ちっとも…ない	not ... at all
東(ひがし)	east
北(きた)	north
好(す)きな	favorite
結婚式(けっこんしき)	wedding
奈良(なら)	Nara (old capital)
(Nと)遊(あそ)ぶ	have fun with
ちょっと	a little
西(にし)	west

十二課

文法 (ぶんぽう)

● **Modification of nouns**

In previous lessons we learned how to modify a noun with two kinds of adjectives (い／な -adj.), with a noun plus の (i.e. 私の本), and some special demonstratives such as この (本).

In this lesson, we will learn the modification of a noun with a sentence which has verbs, adjectives, and nouns with or without a subject or an agent. The expressions we will learn here are comparable to the English relative pronouns and relative adverbs.

Let us first learn the "plain forms" rather than the polite forms, because it is this form that is used in the modification of nouns.

〔い-adj.〕

	Affirmative	Negative
Present	寒いです	寒くありません／ないです
	寒い	寒くない
Past	寒かったです	寒くありませんでした
	寒かった	寒くなかった

These forms may look familiar to you, as you have already seen them in L.5. The forms in the lower column enclosed in thick lines are the "plain forms" of い-adj., represented here by 寒い.

When modifying a noun, you should keep the noun-modifier in the same position in Japanese, right in front of the noun, regardless of the modifiers.

天気がよくない 日は，家で本を読みます。
Modifier　　　Noun

On <u>days</u> <u>when the weather isn't good</u>, I read books at home.
　　Noun　　　　Modifier

〔な-adj. ／ nouns＋です〕

	Affirmative	Negative
Present	学生です	学生じゃありません
	便利です	便利じゃありません
	学生だ／(学生の)／(学生な)	学生じゃない
	便利だ／(便利な)	便利じゃない
Past	学生でした	学生じゃありませんでした
	便利でした	便利じゃありませんでした
	学生だった	学生じゃなかった
	便利だった	便利じゃなかった

Lesson 12

In this list the only difference between the な-adjs. and the noun lies in the present affirmative which has more than one form. The uses of these forms will be explained in more detail in later lessons. For the time being, remember that the second present affirmative form must be used to modify a noun.

1. 今年十八才の 学生は, 佐藤さんです。
　　Modifier　　　Noun

The student who is eighteen this year is Sato san.
　Noun　　　　Modifier

2. タクシーは 私が好きな 乗り物ではありません。
　　　　　　　Modifier　　Noun

A taxi is not a vehicle that I like.
　　　　　　Noun　　Modifier

〔Verbs〕

	Affirmative	Negative
Present	行きます	行きません
	行く	行かない
Past	行きました	行きませんでした
	行った	行かなかった

The plain forms of verbs cannot be as easily formed as those of the い-adjs., な-adjs., and nouns, all of which we have already learned. To handle these forms properly, you must know the various phases of a verb. Before we go into detail, see p.97 動詞(どうし).

〔Explanation of the diagram on the next page〕

Base: The unchanged portion of the verb, usually written in *kanji* or *kanji* + *hiragana*. An exception is 来る; the reading of the base 来る changes according to the verb form. In the case of 始まる and 始める, even though their bases are はじま and はじめ respectively, a part of their base is written in *hiragana* so that the distinction may become clear.

1. In order to manipulate these forms, you should first of all memorize two irregular verbs: 来る and する (and the latter's compounds, such as 失礼する and 勉強する, which can be handled with knowledge of する).

2. Verbs with dictionary forms that do not end in る are members of Group I. Those that end in る, for the most part, are called Group II verbs. The only exception up to now is 帰る, 作る, 売る, 知る, 終わる and 要る. There are more verbs in Group I, however, which end in る; and distinguishing them from Group II verbs may present some difficulty. To make such a distinction, you must know at least one of the following:
    1. the plain negative form of the verb
    2. the group to which the verb belongs

Take いる for instance. This verb has two possibilities (リーさんがいる, 卵が要る): it is either a Group I or Group II verb. If its plain negative form is いらない, then you can easily tell that this verb is a member of Group I, since all Group I verbs have "-a" before ない. (The only exception is ある which simply has ない rather than あらない as a plain negative form in modern Japanese.)

If you know that a verb belongs to Group I, then you can find its correct plain negative form and, consequently, its other forms as well.

	Base	Plain neg. (―ない)	Stem (―ます)	Dic. form ―N / ―。	て-form
I	行 (い) 引 (ひ)	か	き	く	って (exception) いて
	話 (はな)(speak) 返 (かえ)(return)	さ	し	す	して
	立 (た)(stand) 育 (そだ)	た	ち	つ	って
	死 (し)(die)	な	に	ぬ	んで
	読 (よ) 住 (す)	ま	み	む	んで
	終 (お)わ 始 (はじ)ま	ら	り	る	って
	言 (い) 違 (ちが) 使 (つか) 買 (か)	わ	い	う	って
	泳 (およ)(swim)	が	ぎ	ぐ	いで
	遊 (あそ)(play) 飛 (と)(fly)	ば	び	ぶ	んで
II	見 (み) 起 (お)き 食 (た)べ 寝 (ね)	―	―	る	て
III	(来)	こ	き	くる	きて
	(す)	し	し	する	して

[Reading the Diagram]

To make the plain negative form (pre-*nai* form) of 行く, for example, add か to its base (い). If you add き, you will get its pre-*masu* or stem form, and adding く makes the dictionary form.

You may have noticed that the three letters in the above example are members of the "か-line" in the diagram of the 50 letters of the syllabary from the beginning of the course. The letters appear in the syllabic order. In fact, you will see in the course of studying that Group I verbs such as 行く conjugate like: か, き, く, け, こ, and a verb like 話す will be さ, し, す, せ, そ. Because of this characteristic, Group I verbs are called *Godan doshi* (five level verbs), whereas Group II verbs are called *Ichidan doshi* (one level verbs) since they do not have levels of conjugation, and it takes place in one level (い／え-level).

If the dictionary form, therefore, of a Group I verb has く at its end, its plain negative form has か because the conjugation follows the か-line.

If you only know the ます-form of a verb, and want to find its dictionary form, there are two ways to figure out the correct answer:

1) substitute the vowel before ます with the "-*u*" form from the same line of conjugation, or...
2) simply add る. If the verb belongs to Group I you can get the correct dictionary form by following 1).

If 1) does not work, following 2) will provide you with the correct form.

● 試験が終わる　最後の日　　1-3

The dictionary form and the comma in this example indicate that 試験が終わる modifies the word 日 but not 最後. In other words, 日 is modified by two phrases 最後の and 試験が終わる, and the modifying phrases are put next to each other because of restrictions placed on the writing system. The important thing here is that when you see a plain form in the middle of a sentence, you should think about what it modifies. Usually the modified noun follows the modifier, but as seen in this example, it may not be directly juxtaposed.

● 試験が終わる日　　1-3

In a noun-modifying phrase, the subject or the agent has to be followed by either が or の.
　　私は本を買いました。(I bought a book.)
　　　⇨これは，私が／の買った本です。(This is a book that I bought.)

● 試験が始まるのは　　1-5

We have learned one use of の as a substitute of a noun.
　　あの車は私のです。(L.4) (That car is mine.)
　　大きいのを一つお願いします。(L.11) (One big one, please.)

In the first example, 私の means 私の車 and in the second example, it is 大きいじゃがいも. That is to say, の is used as a substitute for a noun to avoid repetition. In the dialogue in this lesson, 試験が始まるの is the same as 試験が始まる時間, and の in this sentence is used in the same way as the の above. Later in this section, another use for の will be introduced.

● **Counting People**　　2-10

A special counter is needed to count people. Use 人(にん) for numbers larger than two and with 何 (as in 何人(なんにん)). For expressing "one person" and "two persons" respectively, use 一人(ひとり)

and 二人(ふたり).

- **Plain Perfect (Past)** ……生まれた／育った   2-1, 3

To form the plain perfect of verbs, start with て-form and simply replace the て with た and the で with だ.(☞P.145)

- 御兄弟はありますか   2-9

This may sound strange to you after studying the distinction between the animate いる and the inanimate ある in terms of animate and inanimate objects. (☞L.6) When something animate is conceived, however, in a static and/or abstract way, regardless of the time, place, situation in which it exists, rather than as something dynamic, it can take ある. On the contrary, inanimate things can take いる when they are thought in terms of their mobility, they can take いる instead of ある.

 かわいい金魚(きんぎょ)，あります。
  (We have lovely gold fish.——Advertisement at a pet shop)
 かわいい金魚(きんぎょ)がいますね。
  (Here are some lovely gold fish.)
 家の前にある車は林(はやし)さんのです。
  (The car that is in front of this house is Hayashi san's.)
 林さんの家の前にパトカーがいますが，どうしたんでしょうね。
  (A police car is in front of the Hayashi's. What has happened?)

When you talk about closely-related people, such as your in-groups, you can use ある. This ある can be replaced by いる.

 私(に)は，兄弟が三人あります。(I have three siblings.)
 あの人(に)は，友達(ともだち)が何人もあります。(He has many friends.)

- 勉強するのは(おもしろい)   3-1

This の is different from the の on the previous page. It is not a substitute for a concrete noun. Its function is to nominalize a phrase (i.e. to make the verbal phrase a noun as a whole.) の is attached to plain forms of speech.

 漢字を勉強するのはおもしろいですよ。(It is fun to study *kanji*.)
 Verbal phrase＋の ⇨ Noun phrase
 アメリカで車がないのは大変です。(Having no car in America is terrible.)
 Adj. phrase＋の ⇨ Noun phrase

- とても **(Intensifier)**   3-2

とても is used to intensify the meaning of an adjective in the meaning of "very." Some other words can be used in a similar way:

 大変 ⇨今日は大変寒いですね。(It's very cold today.)
 ひどく ⇨昨日(きのう)は，運動(うんどう)の後(あと)，ひどく疲(つか)れました。
  (I got terribly tired yesterday after exercise.)

Of these three, とても is most widely used in conversation. ひどく sounds as though the speaker feels he got extraordinarily or unusually tired.

Lesson 12

ことばの使い方 (ことばのつかいかた)

● **Informal talk**
うん is an informal word to show agreement just like はい and ええ. The opposite is ううん. Both men and women can use these but they seem to convey a lighter degree of formality for women than for men. Hence many women still use ええ and いいえ in conversations while men may use うん and ううん.
けど is an informal equivalent of が as in "S1 が S2."

● 試験がある日　　　1-1
ある in this phrase means "to be held." Used in this capacity, ある takes で to express location of action.
　明日, 中村(なかむら)さんの家でパーティーがありますが, 行きますか。
　　(Tomorrow a party will be held at Nakamura san's. Will you go?)

● あと(六日)　　　1-3
あと before a quantitative expression means "another ～" or "～ more." It shows that something reaches an end or goal at the designated number.
　試験はあと五分(ごふん)で終わりですよ。
　　(The exam will be over in another five minutes.)
　私(わたし)の誕生日(たんじょうび)まであと一週間(いっしゅうかん)です。
　　(There's one more week left before my birthday.)

● しか…ない　　　1-3
This pattern, always used with the negative ない, means that the quantity mentioned is not satisfactory, or is too small. If there is no quantity noun, the speaker is emphasizing the fact that there is nothing or nobody else besides the referent.
　今日の授業には学生は十人しか来ませんでした。
　　(Only ten students came to class today.)
　今日の授業には佐藤(さとう)さんしか来ませんでした。
　　(Only Sato san ... and nobody else ... came to class today.)

● 横浜という所　　　2-7
As already seen in L.6, "～という N" means "an N called～," or "an N titled～." This should not be used to refer to nouns well-known to everybody. For the speaker in the dialogue, Yokohama apparently does not sound familiar. That is why this expression —— rather than just Yokohama —— is used.

● 東京の南　　　2-8
The four directions in Japanese are:

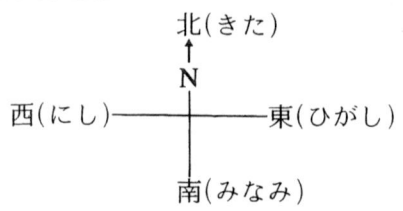

```
          北(きた)
            ↑
            N
西(にし)─────┼─────東(ひがし)
            │
          南(みなみ)
```

東京の南 can be interpreted in two ways as shown in the following diagram.

●　東京　　　　　　　　　　東京
↓
○　(south of Tokyo)　　　◎　(southern Tokyo)

● 何度も　　　3-3

In L. 9, we learned the pattern, "interrogative word"＋か／も. In this section we will learn: "Interrogative words for quantity"＋か／も.

Interrogative	Int.＋か	Int.＋も＋affirm.	Int.＋も…ない
何度(回)	several times	more than a few times	not many times
何人	several people	more than a few people	not many people
何枚	several sheets	more than a few sheets	not many sheets

　　私は東京には何度か行きました。
　　　　(I went to Tokyo several times.)
　　そのパーティーに学生が何人も来ました。
　　　　(Many students came to the party.)
　　カメラを買いましたが，写真はまだ何枚も撮っていません。
　　　　(I bought a camera but I have not taken many pictures yet.)

● 少しも　　　3-4

This is always followed by a negative and has the same meaning as 全然…ない "not at all." Be careful not to confuse this with 少し which means "a little." The meaning of も is like "even."

not at all	a little
全然………ない	
少しも………ない	少し
ちっとも……ない	ちょっと

Lesson 12

練習(れんしゅう)

練習(れんしゅう) 1　　　　　の substituting a noun

例　授業が終わる日はいつですか。　⇨授業が終わるのは四日です。

12月 4日	金	授業が終わる
7日	月	日本語の試験
12日	土	家へ帰る
13日	日	クリスマスの買(か)い物(もの)
14日	月	デパートでアルバイトを始(はじ)める
19日	土	姉(あね)の結婚式(けっこんしき)に出(で)る
24日	木	十時(じゅうじ)までアルバイトをする
25日	金	自分(じぶん)で日本語(にほんご)の勉強を始める
1月 3日	日	シカゴに帰(かえ)る
4日	月	冬学期(ふゆがっき)が始まる

1．日本語の試験がある日は何曜日ですか。
2．家へ帰る日は何日ですか。
3．お姉さんの結婚式に行く日はいつですか。
4．冬学期が始まる日は何月何日ですか。
5．アルバイトをする所はどこですか。
6．自分で日本語の勉強を始める日は何日からですか。

練習(れんしゅう) 2　　　　　の substituting a noun

例　日本語の試験があるのはどこですか。
　　⇨試験がある所ですか。103教室(きょうしつ)ですよ。

日本語の試験	
12月 7日(水)	9：30～11：30
教室	103教室
試験する課(か)	一課～十二課

1．試験があるのは何曜日ですか。　　2．試験するのは何課からですか。
3．試験が始まるのは何時ですか。　　4．試験があるのは何日ですか。
5．試験があるのはどの教室ですか。　6．試験が終わるのは何時ですか。

練習(れんしゅう) 3　　　　Place＋に／で

例　東京，生まれる　⇨私は東京で生まれました。(I was born in Tokyo.)
　　横浜，住む　　　⇨私は横浜に住んでいました。(I lived in Yokohama.)

1．京都，育つ　　2．大学，日本語を勉強する　　3．ワシントン，生まれる
4．ボストン，育つ　5．シカゴ，住んでいる　　　6．大学，言語学(げんごがく)を勉強する

練習(れんしゅう) 4　　　　の substituting a noun

NOTE: The plain past form of する is した (2, 6)

例　東京，生まれる　⇨私が生まれたのは東京です。
　　　　　　　　　　(The place where I was born is Tokyo.)
　　横浜，住んでいる　⇨私が住んでいたのは横浜です。
　　　　　　　　　　　(The place where I lived is Yokohama.)

1．京都，育つ　　2．大学，日本語を勉強する　　3．ワシントン，生まれる
4．ボストン，育つ　5．シカゴ，住んでいる　　　6．大学，言語学を勉強する

練習(れんしゅう) 5　　　　しか〜ない

例　学生が二人(ふたり)来ます。(Two students will come.)
　　⇨学生が二人しか来ません。(Only two students will come.)

1．お金が百ドルあります。　　2．試験が一つあります。
3．友達が二人います。　　　　4．誕生日まで三日あります。
5．一つわかりました。　　　　6．ビールを一本飲みました。

練習(れんしゅう) 6　　　　〜という N

例　横浜，所　　　⇨横浜という所はどこにありますか。
　　　　　　　　　(Where is this place called Yokohama [located]?)
　　佐藤先生，先生　⇨佐藤先生という先生はどこにいますか。
　　　　　　　　　　(Where is this teacher named Prof. Sato?)

1．スタイン図書館(としょかん)，図書館　　2．佐藤さん，男の学生
3．ライアンさん，女の学生　　　　　　　4．タイム，雑誌(ざっし)
5．石井(いしい)さん，大学院(だいがくいん)の学生　6．東京大学，大学
7．奈良(なら)，所

Lesson 12

練習(れんしゅう) 7	Possession

例　私は兄(あに)が一人あります。(I have one older brother.)
　　　(younger sister)　⇨私は妹(いもうと)が一人あります。(I have one younger sister.)

1．younger brother　　2．two　　3．elder sister　　4．three
5．one elder sister and two elder brothers
6．two younger brothers and three younger sisters
7．three elder brothers and one younger brother

練習(れんしゅう) 8	Nominalizer の

例　おもしろい　　⇨漢字を勉強するのは，おもしろいです。
　　　　　　　　　(It's fun to study *kanji*.)
　　自分(じぶん)で料理(りょうり)をする　⇨自分で料理をするのはおもしろいです。
　　　　　　　　　(It's fun to cook by myself.)

1．楽しい　　2．佐藤さんと話す　　3．つまらない　　4．猫(ねこ)の子(こ)と遊(あそ)ぶ
5．退屈だ　　6．辞書を引く　　7．おもしろい　　8．漢字の意味を調べる

練習(れんしゅう) 9	Perf. vs. Imperf.

例　おもしろい
　　　⇨漢字を勉強するのは，前はおもしろかったですが，今はおもしろくありません。
　　　(In the past, it was fun to study *kanji*, but now it's not.)
　　自分で料理をする
　　　⇨自分で料理をするのは，前はおもしろかったですが，今はおもしろくありません。
　　　(In the past, it was fun to cook by myself, but now it's not.)

1．楽しい　　2．佐藤さんと話す　　3．つまらない　　4．猫の子と遊ぶ
5．退屈だ　　6．辞書を引く　　7．おもしろい　　8．漢字の意味を調べる

練習(れんしゅう) 10	少し，少しも etc.

例　漢字を勉強するのは退屈だ。
　　(少し)　⇨漢字を勉強するのは少し退屈です。
　　　　　　(It's a little tedious to study *kanji*.)
　　(少しも)⇨漢字を勉強するのは，少しも退屈じゃありません。
　　　　　　(It's not a bit tedious to study *kanji*.)

1．おもしろい　　2．全然　　3．自分で料理をする　　4．少し
5．ちっとも　　6．ちょっと　　7．少しも　　8．つまらない

練習(れんしゅう) 11	N(NP) が好きです

例　コーヒー　⇨私は，コーヒーが好きです。(I like coffee.)
　　日曜日(にちようび)の朝(あさ)，コーヒーを飲(の)む　⇨私は日曜日の朝コーヒーを飲むのが好きです。
　　　　　　　　　　　　　　　　　　　(I like to drink coffee on Sunday mornings.)

1．漢字の勉強　　　2．漢字を勉強する　　　3．料理　　　4．料理をする
5．犬(いぬ)　　　　6．犬と遊ぶ　　　　　　7．運動(うんどう)　8．運動する

練習(れんしゅう) 12	Perf. vs. Imperf.

例　コーヒー，好きだ
　　⇨私は，前はコーヒーが好きでしたが，今はあまり好きじゃありません。
　　　　　(In the past I liked coffee, but now I don't like it very much.)
　　新しいタイプライター，欲しい
　　⇨私は，前は新しいタイプライターが欲しかったですが，今はあまり欲しくありません。
　　　　　(In the past I wanted a new typewriter, but now I don't want it as much.)

1．授業，退屈だ　　　2．猫，好きだ　　　　　　3．仕事(しごと)，つまらない
4．アルバイト，いる　5．私の育った所，好きだ　6．テレビを見る，おもしろい
7．誕生日，楽しい

練習(れんしゅう) 13	Neg. question

例　これは好きじゃありませんか。(Don't you like this?)
　　（ええ）　⇨ええ，好きじゃありません。(No, I don't like it.)

1．つまらなくありませんか。　　　　　　　　（いいえ）
2．この本はおもしろくありませんか。　　　　（ええ）
3．この旅行(りょこう)(trip)は退屈じゃありませんか。（ええ）
4．好きじゃありませんでしたか。　　　　　　（いいえ）
5．つまらなくありませんでしたか。　　　　　（いいえ）
6．この映画(えいが)(movie)は，つまらなくありませんか。（ええ）

十三課

内容表

文法	Uses of て-form (1) 　1) て＋(も)いい 　2) て＋いる 　3) て＋すみません 　4) て＋ください 　　～ないでください 　5) て＋Verbal phrase S＋ん(の)です V. Stem＋に＋motion verb V. Stem＋ながら Plain perfect form of Verbs S＋みたい(です) (Introduction) て＋来る (Toward the speaker)	お邪魔してもいいですか。 佐藤さんを待っている。 (その窓は)こわれていて… 遅れてすみません。 来てください。 開けないでください。 気を付けて歩いて来てね。 何をしているの。 遊びに行く。 雪を見ながらお酒を飲みましょう。 書いていた，積もった，買った It seems S. 歩いて来てね。
機能	Requesting Permission　　　　2-22 Granting Permission　　　　　2-21 Making Requests　　　　　　5-3 　1) Affirmative 　2) Negative Apologizing　　　　　　　　　4-1 Expressing Forgiveness　　　　4-2 Starting Conversation　　　　　6-3 Making a Telephone call　　　　8-2 Ending a Telephone Conversation　8-9 Expressing a Belief / Opinion　　2-33	お邪魔して(も)いいですか。 どうぞ(いらしてください)。 来てください。 開けないでください。 遅れてすみません。 いいえ。 もしもし もしもし，森さん，今晩は。 五分くらいで行く。 じゃ，気を付けて歩いて来てね。 S＋みたい(だ)

Lesson 13

会話 (かいわ)

1

A：お邪魔してもいいですか。

B：ええ，どうぞ。

A：何をしているんですか。

B：佐藤さんを待っているんですよ。

A：さっき食堂で誰かと話していましたよ。

B：ああ，来ました。来ました。

C：どうも遅れてすみません。

B：いいえ。

2

A：暑いですね，この部屋は。この窓を開けてもいいですか。

B：すみません。今ちょっと開けないでください。紙が飛びますから。

C：あ，もしもし，開きませんよ，その窓は。

A：こわれているんですか。

C：ええ，こわれていて動きません。

3

A：もしもし，森さん。今晩は。

B：ああ，秋山さん，今晩は。

A：今，何をしているの。

B：友達に手紙を書いていたのよ。秋山さんは？

A：僕は雪の降っているのを窓から見ていたんだけど。

B：よく降るわね。もう，かなり積もっているでしょう。

A：本当に，よく降るねえ。もう三十センチぐらい積もったみたい。あ，そうだ。これから遊びに行ってもいい？

1

A：May I join you? (Lit. May I interrupt you?)

B：Yes, certainly.

A：What are you doing?

B：I'm waiting for Sato san.

A：A while ago he was speaking to someone in the dining room.

B：Oh, here he is. He's here.

C：I'm sorry I'm late.

B：That's O.K.

2

A：It's hot in this room, isn't it? May I open this window?

B：I'm sorry. Please don't open it just now. The papers will blow around.

C：Oh, excuse me. That window doesn't open.

A：Is it broken?

C：Yes. It's broken and won't budge.

3

A：Hello, Mori san. Good evening.

B：Well, Akiyama san, good evening.

A：What are you doing now?

B：I was writing a letter to my friend. How about you, Akiyama san?

A：I was watching the falling snow from my window.

B：It's really coming down. There must be quite an accumulation by now.

A：It really is. It seems that it accumulated about 30 centimeters. Oh, by the way, may I come and visit you now?

B：ええ，どうぞいらしてください。

A：この間，買ったお酒を持って行くよ。雪を見ながら，お酒でも飲みましょう。五分くらいで行く。

B：はい。じゃ，気を付けて歩いて来てね。

単語表（たんごひょう）

Note that some verbs in these lists have Roman numeral Ⅲ in their translations. This number means that they are group II verbs.

1

どうぞ	☞ことばの使い方
佐藤（さとう）	a surname
（〜を）待（ま）つ	wait
食堂（しょくどう）	dining room / hall
（〜と）話（はな）す	talk to / with, speak
遅（おく）れる	be late (for) Ⅲ

2

暑（あつ）い	hot
部屋（へや）	room
窓（まど）	window
（〜を）開（あ）ける	to open (v.t.) Ⅲ
紙（かみ）	paper
（〜が）飛（と）ぶ	fly
もしもし	☞P. 59
（〜が）開（あ）く	to open (v.i.)
（〜が）こわれる	get broken Ⅲ
（〜が）動（うご）く	move

3

森（もり）	a surname
秋山（あきやま）	a surname
友達（ともだち）	friend
手紙（てがみ）	a letter
僕（ぼく，ぼく）	☞P. 160
（〜を）書（か）く	write
雪（ゆき）	snow
（〜が）降（ふ）る	fall (snow, rain)
もう	already
かなり	pretty (much), quite
（〜が）積（つ）もる	pile, accumulate
センチ	centimeter
みたい	☞文法
これから	from now
遊（あそ）ぶ	have fun / play
いらして	☞ことばの使い方
この間（あいだ）	the other day
（〜を）買（か）う	buy
お酒（さけ）	alcoholic drink, *sake*
持（も）って行（い）く	take 〜 (and go)
（〜に）気（き）を付（つ）ける	pay attention to, be careful about Ⅲ
歩（ある）く	walk

B： Certainly, please come by.

A： I will take along some *sake* that I bought the other day. Let's drink while we watch the snow. I'll be there in about five minutes.

B： Well then, please walk carefully.

関連語句 (かんれんごく)

晴(は)れる	to clear up (v.i.) Ⅱ	曇(くも)る	become cloudy (v.i.)
雨(あめ)	rain	やむ	stop (rain or snow) (v.i.)
忘(わす)れる	forget (v.t.) Ⅱ	返(かえ)す	return (v.t.)
たばこ	cigarette	すう	smoke, inhale (v.t.)
調(しら)べる	investigate (v.t.) Ⅱ	閉(し)める	close, shut (v.t.) Ⅱ
夜遅(よるおそ)く	late at night	電気(でんき)	light, electricity
つく	turn on (v.i.)		

Lesson 13

文法 (ぶんぽう)

● て-form

As you will see later, this verb form is so commonly used that, without mastering the way to create it and to combine it with others, you will find it difficult to express yourself well. The correct use of plain verb forms (L. 12) and the て-forms (in this lesson) are crucial in order to advance to higher levels of Japanese.

〔How to make the て-form〕

To make this form, you must know the dictionary form of the verb and the group to which it belongs. If a verb is a member of either Group II or III, add て to the stem (pre-*masu* form). The Group I verbs will cause the most difficulty in the beginning. The て-form of Group I verbs is determined by its dictionary form ending.

〔て-form of Group I Verbs〕

Ending	Examples	Meaning	Add to base	て-form
—く	書く(かく) 引く(ひく)	write check (a dic.)	—いて	書いて 引いて
—ぐ	泳ぐ(およぐ) 研ぐ(とぐ)	swim sharpen	—いで	泳いで 研いで
—す	話す(はなす) 返す(かえす)	speak return	—して	話して 返して
—つ	立つ(たつ) 育つ(そだつ)	stand grow	—って	立って 育って
—る	終わる(おわる) 始まる(はじまる)	end start	—って	終わって 始まって
—う	言う(いう) 買う(かう)	say buy	—って	言って 買って
—ぬ	死ぬ(しぬ)	die	—んで	死んで
—む	読む(よむ) 住む(すむ)	read live	—んで	読んで 住んで
—ぶ	遊ぶ(あそぶ) 飛ぶ(とぶ)	have fun fly	—んで	遊んで 飛んで

〔て-form of Groups II, III〕

Group	Examples	Meaning	Add to base	て-form
II	起きる(おきる) 見る　(みる)	get up see	ー て	起きて 見て
	食べる(たべる) 寝る(ねる)	eat sleep		食べて 寝て
III	来る(くる) する	come do		来て(きて) して

Exception: 行く ⇨ 行って(×行いて)

〔Usages of the て-form〕

The patterns with the て-form in this lesson are listed below. Following this list is a detailed explanation.

	Pattern	Meaning	例
1	て(も)+いい	Permission	入(はい)って(も)いいですか。 May I come in?
2	て+いる	Continuation of Action Continuation of State	テレビを見ています。 (I am) watching TV. このテレビはこわれています。 This TV set is broken.
3	て+すみません	Apology	朝(あさ)早(はや)く電話(でんわ)をしてすみません。 Sorry to call you so early.
4	て+ください	Request	三時にここへ来てください。 Please come here at three.
5	ないで+ください	Negative request	これを食(た)べないでくださいね。 Please don't eat this.
6	て+verb	☞Explanation 6 below	晩御飯(ばんごはん)を食べて、すぐ行きます。 I'll eat dinner and go right away. 歩(ある)いて行きますよ。 I'll go on foot.

● 1. て(も)+いいです　　1-1

When this is used in an interrogative sentence, the speaker is asking for permission and, in the affirmative, is giving permission. The meaning of も is somewhat similar to "even." If you feel you are asking for something extreme or outrageous, も should be used.

1. A：先生(せんせい)、辞書(じしょ)を引(ひ)いてもいいですか。　　(May I consult a dictionary?)
　　B：試験(しけん)ですから、辞書は引かないでください。 (Please don't. This is a test!)

Lesson 13

  2．A：これ，食べていいですか。 (May I eat this?)
    B：もう少し，待っていてください。(Please wait a while longer.)

● 2．て＋いる 1-3

  The function of this pattern is to indicate the continuation of either an action (in this case, it is the same as the English "progressive": be＋〜ing) or a state resulting from an action, which may be translated into English as: "be＋adj. or past participle" as shown in the examples.

  The interpretation depends on the nature of a verb; if a verb signifies either motion (行く，来る，帰る, etc.) or change which occurs instantly or in a short period of time (most of these verbs are intransitive verbs), then this construction shows the "continuation of a state." On the other hand, if a verb indicates an action that can be continued, then it indicates "be＋ing," a continuous action.

  1．今日は朝から雪が降っています。
    (It has been snowing since morning today.)
  2．さっきまで，雨が降っていましたが，今は晴れていますよ。
    (It was raining till a little while ago, but it is clear now.)
  3．佐藤さんは部屋で御飯を食べています。
    (Sato san is having a meal in his room.)
  4．佐藤さんの部屋に電気がついています。
    (A light is on in Sato san's room.)
  5．秋山さんが来ています。
    (Akiyama san has come ...... Akiyama san is here.)
  6．森さんは今，学校に行っていますよ。
    (Mori san is now at school.)

Other uses of て＋いる：
  To describe an occupation——兄は大学院へ行っています。
            (My brother attends graduate school.)
         あの人はギターを教えています。
            (That person is teaching guitar.)

Note: Such verbs as 知る and 住む are usually used in the て-form.
    あの人を知っていますか。いいえ，知りません。
      (Do you know that person? No, I don't know him.)
    前は東京に住んでいましたが，今は東京には，住んでいません。
      (I used to live in Tokyo, but now I don't live there.)

● 3．て＋すみません 1-7
  昨日電話するのを忘れて，すみませんでした。
    (I'm sorry about forgetting to call you yesterday.)
  長い間本を返さないで，すみませんでした。
    (Sorry for not returning the book for a long time.)
  夜遅く電話してすみませんが，先生いらっしゃいますか。
    (I am sorry to call late at night, but is Sensei at home?)

十三課

● 4. て＋ください　　3-9

This is a polite imperative form; however, it is very close to a "request." To increase the degree of politeness, add ませんか and make it a question. A less polite equivalent of て＋ください ませんか is て＋くれませんか, which we have studied in L. 5 and 7. Among friends or in a family situation, the て-form by itself is often used.

　　ちょっと来て。　　　　　　　（Please come here for a second.）
　　悪いけど，窓，開けないで。（Sorry, but please don't open the window.）

● 5. ないで＋ください　　2-2

This is the negative counterpart to the above pattern. The form 〜ないで is called the negative て-form and it is made by adding で to the plain negative form of a verb.
　Both くださいませんか and くれませんか are used to soften the tone.

　　すみませんが，この部屋ではたばこをすわないでください。
　　　（Excuse me, but please don't smoke cigarettes in this room.）
　　このタイプライターはこわれていますから，使わないでくださいね。
　　　（Don't use this typewriter because it is broken.）
　　明日は遅れないでください。（Don't be late tomorrow.）

● 6. て＋VP　　3-12

When the て-form precedes a verbal phrase, two interpretations are possible. As we have seen in a very early lesson, one of the functions of the て-form is to connect phrases. It means "and."

　　私は大学院の学生で，専門は人類学です。
　　　（I am a graduate student and my major is anthropology.）

This is the て-form of です, and the meaning can be found in all て-forms.

The other function of the て-form is to modify a final verb or predicate as an adverbial phrase. It signifies how the action or state in the final verb is carried out or comes into being.

　　自転車に乗って来ました。（I came here, riding on a bicycle — on my bike.）
　　辞書を引いて調べました。（I looked it up by consulting a dictionary.）
　　このことは，佐藤さんに電話をして聞いてください。
　　　（Please call Sato san and ask about this matter.）

A complicated example of this て-form use can be found in Dialogue 3.

　　〔（気を付けて）歩いて〕来て。
　　　（Please come walking, paying attention — walk carefully when you come.）

In this sentence, 気を付けて modifies 歩く; it means that the walking should be done carefully. 気を付けて歩いて as a whole modifies the final 来て（ください）. Whenever you come across a て-form, pay special attention to see if it is connecting two sentences or modifying the final verb.

● んです　　1-3

Orthographically, this should be のです, however, in spoken Japanese it is pronounced んです. Use のです in writing and んです in speech.

Plain forms (see L. 12 文法) must precede this phrase.

　The only exception: when the plain form is だ, it is replaced by な.

　　× 学生だんです⇒学生なんです。／× 便利だんです⇒便利なんです。

Lesson 13

In the affirmative form, this expression functions to give an explanation for what you have said or done. When used in questions, it signifies that the speaker wants to receive further information or explanation.

1. A：わかりませんか。
   B：はい。

2. A：わからないんですか。
   B：はい。昨日勉強しませんでした。

In the first example, A is confirming whether or not B has understood, whereas in the second dialogue A wants not only to confirm it but also to receive an explanation as to why B has not understood. It is not appropriate to simply answer "yes" or "no" in the latter case. You must give a further explanation.

● 来ました   1-6

This perfect tense form is the same as the phrase ありました used when one discovers or notices something (L. 7). In this context, 来ました has a "present perfect" and not a "past" meaning.

● 積もっているでしょう   3-6

We have already studied でしょう used with a noun (P. 60「ジョンソン先生でしょう」) and with an い-adj. (P. 30「高いでしょう」). In this example, でしょう can also take a verb in the plain form. A sentence with this use of でしょう expresses the same meaning as in the previous cases: "I guess" or "I presume." As a simple rule of thumb, we can say that whatever comes before でしょう is in plain forms. The only exception is だ which must be deleted before でしょう. Both でしょう and だ are derivatives of です, and two such derivatives cannot be repeated consecutively.

● 遊びに行く   3-8

Verb Stem＋に＋Motion Verb; This pattern describes the purpose of the motion verb.

スミスさんは，四月から日本語を勉強しに，東京へ行きます。
(Smith san will go to Tokyo to study Japanese from April.)
ちょっと昼御飯を食べに，家に帰ります。
(I am going back home for a while to have lunch.)
太郎さん，卵を買いにスーパーまで行ってきてくれない？
(Taro san, won't you please go to the supermarket to buy eggs for me?)

Note that these stems can be replaced by "Noun＋に" as in the sentence「ジョギングに行きました」(P. 94). The sentences above can be:

日本語の勉強に行きます。
食事に帰ります。
買い物に行ってきてくれない？

● 雪を見ながらお酒を飲む   3-10

V. stem＋ながら＋V: This form is used to describe two concurrent actions by one person. The final verb is given more importance than the verb before ながら. The concurrency will not necessarily be exact, as seen in the second example.

1. 御飯を食べながら，新聞は読まないで。
   (Don't read the newspaper while eating.)

２．あの人はアルバイトをしながら、大学へ行っています。
　　　　(He is going to college while working part-time.)
　　３．私はシャワーをあびながら、歌を歌うのが好きです。
　　　　(I like singing songs while taking a shower.)

● **The Plain Perfect Form of Verbs**　　3-10

The plain form is used 1) to modify nouns and 2) as ordinary sentence endings in conversations among friends. The forms are as follows:

	Affirm.	Neg.
Imperf.	書く	書かない
Perf.	書いた	書かなかった

If you know either the plain negative form of a verb or the group to which it belongs, you can make the plain affirmative form. Once you have the plain negative form, you can get its past negative form. The plain past affirmative can be made by changing the て-form ending to た.

　　書く　　⇨　書いて　⇨　書いた
　　泳ぐ　　⇨　泳いで　⇨　泳いだ
　　食べる　⇨　食べて　⇨　食べた
　　来る　　⇨　来て　　⇨　来た
　　する　　⇨　して　　⇨　した

This form indicates the perfect tense (completion of an action) rather than the past tense. This will be explained in L. 14.

● 積もったみたい　　3-7

みたい is attached to the plain ending forms of sentences. The sentence means: "It seems that S." As in the case of でしょう, だ is deleted when it comes at the end of a sentence and precedes みたい. (For details, see L. 23「ハワイみたいです」.)

● お酒を持って行く　　3-10

持って行く means "to go somewhere carrying something." Because of the difference between Japanese motion verbs 来る, 行く and their English counterparts, this phrase may be slightly confusing. To see the difference, review 来ます／行きます on P. 81.

The object of 持って行く has to be something you can carry. People and animals cannot be such an object. Use 連れて行く in this case. As for 連れて行く, see L. 21「連れて行く」in「ことばの使い方」.

　　Ａ：コーヒー、持って来てくれない？　(Will you please bring some coffee?)
　　Ｂ：コーヒー？　今、持って行くわ。　(Coffee? I will bring it right away.)

Lesson 13

ことばの使い方（ことばのつかいかた）

● **Informal talk**

	男	女
S＋のです(か)	の	
S＋のですよ／ね	んだよ／ね	んだわ ／ のよ／のね
V ます(か)	dic. f.(＋わ—女)	
V ますよ／ね	dic. f.＋よ／ね	dic. f.＋わよ／わね

● どうぞ　　1-2

This expression indicates that the speaker allows, encourages, or requests someone to do something. In 「ええ，どうぞ」 in the first dialogue, it signifies that the speaker is sanctioning an action or state, while in 「どうぞよろしく」 the expression is used as a request. In the third dialogue, 「どうぞいらしてください」 is an example of encouragement. どうぞ will be most commonly heard when someone is offering something to you.

1． A：お邪魔します。〔Entering a room.〕
　　B：どうぞ。　　〔Inviting the person in.〕
2． A：すみません。これを見せてください。〔Asking a clerk to show him/her something.〕
　　B：こちらですか。どうぞ。　　　　〔Showing it.〕

● もう　　3-6

The function of this adverb is to indicate that an action, state or event has reached or exceeded a certain point or level assumed by the speaker. The sentence in the dialogue, もうかなり積もっている, means that the snow has fallen to such an extent that it has reached or passed the level one can call かなり.

The opposite is まだ which indicates that an action, state or event has not yet reached a certain assumed level.

1． A：秋山さん，まだ教室にいますか。(Is Akiyama san still in the classroom?)
　　B：もう帰りましたよ。　　　　(He has already gone home.)
2． A：秋山さん，まだ教室にいますか。(Is Akiyama san still in the classroom?)
　　B：もう，いませんよ。　　　　(He is no longer there.)
3． A：宿題，まだ終わりませんか。　(Haven't you finished your homework yet?)
　　B：もう，終わりました。　　　(I have already finished it.)

もう＋affirmative	⇨ already	まだ＋affirmative	⇨ still
もう＋negative	⇨ no longer	まだ＋negative	⇨ not yet

● あ, そうだ　　3-7

In the course of a conversation, when you suddenly get an idea which has some direct or indirect association with what you have been talking about, this expression can be used. Sometimes you may hear あ，そうそう, its variant form.

A：昨日の宿題，大変だったね。(Yesterday's homework was hard, wasn't it?)
B：宿題？　あっ，そうだ，宿題があったんだ。
(Homework? Oh, my! There was homework!)

● いらして　　　3-9

This is the て-form いらっしゃる that is equivalent in meaning to いる，来る，行く; however it is far more polite than 来る，行く，いる. Since this is a polite form (敬語), you cannot use it to refer to yourself. This verb theoretically belongs to Group I. This was the case in classical Japanese, but in modern Japanese there are some irregularities.

base	plain neg. (—ない)	stem (—ます)	dic. form	て-form
いらっしゃ	ら	い	る	って いらして

The irregularities can be seen in the stem and the て-form. In the case of the stem, it has い, instead of the expected り. This change occurs only in a couple of verbs besides いらっしゃる: i.e. おっしゃる (polite form of 言う) and ござる (as seen in おはようございます).

● 五分くらいで　　　3-10

A temporal expression plus で indicates the time necessary to complete an action. This can be translated as "within" or "in."

A：食事，あと何分くらいかかるの。
(How many more minutes will it take to prepare the meal?)
B：十分くらいで，できますよ。(It'll be ready in ten minutes or so.)

練習 (れんしゅう)

練習(れんしゅう)　1　　　　　S＋んです

例　何をする　⇨何をしているんですか。(What are you doing?)

1．誰を待つ　2．誰と話す　3．何を食べる　4．何を読む
5．何を見る　6．誰が話す　7．誰が待つ　8．誰が来る

練習(れんしゅう)　2　　　　　S＋んです

例　このアパートは便利ですか。(Is this apartment convenient?)
　　⇨このアパートは便利なんですか。
　　森さんは来ますか。(Will Mori san come?)
　　⇨森さんは来るんですか。

Lesson 13

1．あの人はこの大学の学生ですか。　2．アルバイトをしながら勉強していますか。
3．秋山さんは授業に来ていますか。　4．宿題は簡単ですか。
5．今日は，誰の誕生日ですか。　6．佐藤さんは何才ですか。

練習(れんしゅう)　3　　　　　～ていません

例　雪は降っていますか。(Is it snowing?)
　　　⇨いいえ，降っていませんよ。(No, it's not.)

1．雨はやんでいますか。　　　2．秋山さんは来ていますか。
3．晴れていますか。　　　　　4．曇っていますか。
5．何かしていますか。　　　　6．テレビを見ていますか。

練習(れんしゅう)　4　　　　　Selective Q.

例　雪が降る，やむ　⇨雪は降っていますか，やんでいますか。
　　　　　　　(Is it snowing or not? / Is it snowing, or has it stopped?)
　　このドアがこわれる，こわれない
　　　⇨このドアはこわれていますか，こわれていませんか。
　　　(Is this door broken or not?)

1．田中さんが来る，来ない　　　2．窓が開く，閉まる
3．雪が積もる，積もらない　　　4．森さんがいらっしゃる，いらっしゃらない
5．雪がやむ，やまない　　　　　6．秋山さんが行く，行かない
7．晴れる，曇る　　　　　　　　8．何かする，何もしない

練習(れんしゅう)　5　　　　　～てもいい

例　お邪魔する　⇨お邪魔してもいいですか。(May I come over and visit?)

1．ここで待っている　2．食堂へ行く　3．少し遅れる　4．窓を開ける
5．窓を閉める　　6．この新聞を読む　7．お酒を飲む　8．遊びに行く

練習(れんしゅう)　6　　　　　～ないでください

例　窓を開ける　⇨すみませんが，窓を開けないでください。
　　　　　(Excuse me, but please don't open the window.)

1．ドアを閉める　2．たばこをすう　3．このお酒を飲む　4．教室で寝る
5．遠くへ行く　　6．ひきだしの中を見る　7．英語で話す　8．その雑誌を読む

練習(れんしゅう)　7	S＋のを見る／待つ

例　雪が降っている，見る　⇨雪の降っているのを見ています。
　　　　　　　　　　　　　　(I am watching the falling snow.)
　　佐藤さんが来る，待つ　⇨佐藤さんの来るのを待っています。
　　　　　　　　　　　　　　(I am waiting for Sato san to come.)

1．雨が降っている，見る　2．雨がやむ，待つ　3．先生の話が終わる，待つ
4．森さんが走る，見る　5．授業が終わる，待つ　6．佐藤さんが勉強する，見る

練習(れんしゅう)　8	V (stem)＋に行く

例　ピザを食べる　⇨ピザを食べに行きませんか。
　　　　　　　　　(Let's go to eat some pizza. / Won't you go to eat some pizza?)

1．映画を見る　2．文房具を買う　3．それを調べる　4．コーヒーを飲む
5．遊ぶ　　　　6．試験の勉強をする　7．日本語の練習をする

練習(れんしゅう)　9	V (stem)＋に行く

例　ハンバーガーを食べる，マクドナルド
　　⇨ハンバーガーを食べに，マクドナルドへ行きませんか。
　　　(Let's go to the McDonald's to eat some hamburgers.)

1．テレビを見る，私の家　　　　2．文房具を買う，そこの文房具屋
3．それを調べる，図書館　　　　4．コーヒーを飲む，私の部屋
5．遊ぶ，町　　　　　　　　　　6．試験の勉強をする，図書館
7．日本語の練習をする，ラボ　　8．冬の買い物をする，デパート

練習(れんしゅう)　10	て＋来てください

例　気を付ける　⇨気を付けて来てくださいね。
　　　　　　　　(Please be careful when you come.)
　　この本を読む　⇨この本を読んで来てください。
　　　　　　　　　(Please come after you've read this book.)

1．歩く　　　　2．走る　　　　3．卵を買う　　4．お酒を持つ
5．よく勉強する　6．漢字を練習する　7．辞書を持つ　8．窓を閉める
9．御飯を食べる

Lesson 13

練習(れんしゅう)　11　　　　　て＋すみません

例　遅れる　⇨遅れてすみません。　　(I'm sorry I'm late.)
　　遅れた　⇨遅れてすみませんでした。(I'm sorry I was late.)

1．朝早く電話をする　　2．夜遅く電話をした　　3．教室で寝る
4．宿題を忘れた　　　　5．遅れて来る　　　　　6．遅れて行った

練習(れんしゅう)　12　　　　　～ないで＋すみません

例　電話をしない　　　　⇨電話をしないですみません。
　　　　　　　　　　　　　(I'm sorry not to call.)
　　電話をしなかった　　⇨電話をしないですみませんでした。
　　　　　　　　　　　　　(I'm sorry not to have called.)

1．勉強しない　　　　　2．テープを聞かなかった　　3．漢字の練習をしない
4．宿題を持って来ない　5．八時に電話しなかった　　6．日曜日に遊びに行かない

練習(れんしゅう)　13　　　　　Plain perfect

例　書く，手紙　⇨これは，私が書いた手紙です。(This is a letter I wrote.)

1．作る，料理　2．読む，雑誌　3．買う，辞書　4．生まれる，所
5．育つ，所　　6．勉強する，学校　7．着る，着物　8．乗る，自転車

練習(れんしゅう)　14　　　　　ながら

例　ビールを飲む，話す　⇨ビールを飲みながら，話しましょうよ。
　　　　　　　　　　　　(Let's talk over beer. / Let's talk while we drink beer.)

1．コーヒーを飲む，テレビを見る　　2．歩く，話をする
3．雪を見る，お酒を飲む　　　　　　4．日本語の練習をする，歩く
5．朝御飯を食べる，新聞を読む　　　6．車で行く，話す

練習(れんしゅう)　15　　　　　時間＋で

例　五分，行きます　⇨五分くらいで行きますよ。(I'll come in about 5 minutes.)

1．一時間，宿題が終わる　2．十分，映画が始まる　3．五分，図書館に行く
4．二日，試験が終わる　　5．三日，試験が始まる　6．一月，両親が遊びに来る

十四課

内容表

文法	Temporal Expressions		S1＋前／時／後／〜てから＋S2
	Sと思う		I think S.
	S1 ので S2		Since S1, S2. Because S1, S2.
	時間＋「で」		In / Within 〜
	Sでしょう		I guess S. Probably S.
	Plain volitional：行こう		Let's 〜.
	Sつもりだ		Frame of mind / Intention
	「を」出る（家を出る）		From / out of / through
	Difference between「そ」と「あ」		それまで
	まで		ここまで
	話し＋にくい／やすい		Hard/Easy to talk to
	こと		Nominalizer
	「が」と「は」in relation to two predicates		家内が帰ってきてから行きます。
機能	Inquiring About Remembering	2-12	知っていますか。
	Expressing Uncertainty	2-19	三時でしょう。
			遅れるだろうと思います。
	Extending an Invitation / Offer	2-5	行かない
	Making Requests	5-3	家を出る時，電話くれない？
	Expressing Agreement	2-1	ああ，いいね。
	Reason for Action / Non-Action	2-41	三時だから，遅れます。
			買い物に行っているので
	Sequencing Communication	7-2	S1＋前に，後，〜てから，時＋S2
	Inquiring About Intentions	2-10	何を見に行くつもり（ですか）。
	Expressions to Use When One is Unable to Answer	7-14	そうね。
	Requesting Clarification	7-9	〜って何ですか。
	Expressing Possibility	2-13	来られますか(Introduction)。

Lesson 14

会話 (かいわ)

1

A：今日の講演が始まる時間を知っていますか。

B：三時でしょう。

A：そうですか。それじゃ，講演の始まる少し前に行きましょうか。

B：僕は授業の終わるのが三時だから，少し遅れます。

A：そうですか。

B：ええ，十分ぐらい遅れるだろうと思います。

2

A：今夜，映画を見に行かない？

B：ああ，いいね。行こう。何を見に行くつもり？

A：大学でやる映画よ。

B：ああ，そう。それじゃ，竹井さんが家を出る時，電話くれない？ それまで宿題をしているから。

A：うん。じゃ，そうね，七時半頃電話するわ。

3

A：松田さん，ちょっとお願いがあるんですが。

B：何ですか。

A：ちょっと電話じゃ話しにくいことなんですよ。

B：何ですか，電話じゃ話しにくい話って。

A：会った時に話しますよ。すみませんが，ここまで来てくれませんか。

B：じゃ，家内が今，買い物に行っているので，帰ってきてから，行きます。

A：何分ぐらいで，来られますか。

B：三十分で行きますよ。

A：すみませんが，お願いします。

B：はい，わかりました。

1

A：Do you know what time the lecture begins today?

B：At 3 o'clock, I think.

A：I see. Well then, shall we go shortly before the lecture begins?

B：Since my class ends at 3 o'clock, I'll be a little late.

A：I see.

B：Yes, I think I'll probably be about 10 minutes late.

2

A：Would you like to go to see a movie tonight?

B：Yes, that sounds good. Let's go. What do you intend to see?

A：The movie they're showing at school.

B：Oh, I see. Well then, Takei san, give me a call when you leave your house. I'll be doing my homework until then.

A：Alright. Then, let's see, I'll call you around seven-thirty.

3

A：Matsuda san, I have a favor to ask of you.

B：What is it?

A：It's something I find a little difficult to talk about over the phone.

B：What is it that you find so difficult to talk about on the phone?

A：I'll tell you when I see you. I'm sorry to trouble you but won't you come over here?

B：My wife is out shopping now, so I will come over after she returns.

A：How soon can you come?

B：I'll be over in 30 minutes.

A：I'm sorry for the inconvenience.

B：It's alright.

Lesson 14

単語表 (たんごひょう)

①		くれる	give me / us Ⅲ
講演(こうえん)	public lecture	それまで	until then
僕(ぼく，ぼく)	☞ことばの使い方	③	
遅(おく)れるだろう	☞文法	松田(まつだ)	a surname
②		話(はな)しにくい	difficult to talk to / about
今夜(こんや)	tonight	こと	things, matters
映画(えいが，えいが)	movie	(〜に／と)会(あ)う	see
やる	する	ここまで	as far as this place
竹井(たけい)	a surname	家内(かない)	(my) wife
(〜を)出(で)る	get out of, leave Ⅲ	買い物(かいもの)	shopping
電話(でんわ)	telephone, call	来(こ)られる	potential of 来る Ⅲ

関連語句 (かんれんごく)

子供(こども)	child(ren)	(Nが)上手(じょうず)だ	be good at 〜
高校(こうこう)	high school	(〜を)卒業(そつぎょう)する	graduate
近道(ちかみち)	short-cut	(〜を)通(とお)る	go through, pass
電車(でんしゃ)	electric train	言葉(ことば)	word, language
町(まち)	town, city	(お)箸(はし)	chopsticks
変(へん)な	strange, absurd	静(しず)かな	quiet, still
食事(しょくじ)	meal, dinner	遅(おそ)くまで	until late
(御)主人(しゅじん)	husband	夫(おっと)	husband (neutral)
奥(おく)さん	wife	妻(つま)	wife (neutral)
アパート	apartment	手紙(てがみ)を出(だ)す	mail a letter
困(こま)ったこと	problem	歌(うた)を歌(うた)う	sing a song
乗り物(のりもの)	transportation	飛行機(ひこうき)	airplane
(〜に)乗(の)る	ride, get on	コップ	glass
水(みず)	water		

文法（ぶんぽう）

● 三時でしょう　　1-2

While 三時です shows that the speaker does not have any doubt about the time, 三時でしょう indicates that he/she is not certain. He/She is quite sure, but not one hundred percent. This basically expresses an uncertainty felt by the speaker.

　　　A：あの人は、この大学の先生でしょうか。
　　　　　(Could that person be a professor at this college?)
　　　B：ええ、そうでしょう。
　　　　　(Yes, probably.)

As a matter of fact, any kind of sentence can be put before でしょう as long as the ending is a plain form. The only exception is だ, which has to be deleted before でしょう. This is because both endings are derived from です.

　　　三時には来ません。
　　　　⇨三時には来ないでしょう。(Probably he will not come at three.)
　　　　　　　　　　　　　　　　(I guess he won't come at three.)
　明日は寒いです。
　　　　⇨明日は寒いでしょう。(It will probably be cold tomorrow.)
　去年、佐藤さんは、日本にいました。
　　　　⇨去年、佐藤さんは日本にいたでしょう。(I guess Sato san was in Japan last year.)

To summarize, the forms that can precede でしょう are:

	Verb	い-Adj.	な-Adj.	Noun
Imperfect	行く	寒い	0 (だ)	
Perfect	行った	寒かった	だった	

Note: Even though this list does not include negative forms, plain negative forms can be used.

The form でしょう can also precede と思います in its plain form だろう to express probability or uncertainty.

　　　田中さんは三時に来るだろうと思います。
　　　　(I think Tanaka san will probably come at three.)
　cf.　田中さんは三時に来ると思います。
　　　　(I think Tanaka san will come at three.)

● S＋と思います　　1-6

The "S" stands for a sentence and と is a quotational particle which marks the end of the content of a thought or a person's speech. The sentence before と ends in a plain form unless the sentence is a direct quotation.

　　1．秋山さんは、今日、授業を休むと思います。
　　　　(I think Akiyama san will be absent from class today.)
　　2．私は、その本は前に読んだと思いました。
　　　　(I thought I read / had read that book before.)

Lesson 14

3．その日，田中さんは病気(びょうき)だったと思います。
　　　(I think Tanaka san was ill on that day.)

Do not interpret Japanese sentences in terms of the English "tense agreement" in complex sentences. The Japanese past tense is more like a perfect tense and the present tense is an imperfect tense. See the examples below:

　行くと思います。　　(I think he goes/will go.)
　行ったと思います。　(I think he went/has gone.)
　行くと思いました。　(I thought he went/would go.)
　行ったと思いました。(I thought he had gone.)

● 行こう　　2-2

If you change 〜ます to 〜ましょう, you get the volitional form that means "Let's 〜" as explained in L. 5. By adding か to the end of this, you can get a sentence "Let's 〜, shall we?" Although か is used, this pattern expresses confirmation rather than a question. The intonation, therefore, is a falling intonation.

Another function of this pattern will be discussed in the next lesson.

　1．A：映画を見に行きましょうか。(Let's go to see a movie, shall we?)
　　　B：ええ，行きましょう。　　　(Yes, let's go.)

Do not confuse this with でしょう, which is usually used to refer to the third person.

　2．結婚(けっこん)するでしょう。(I imagine he will marry.)
　3．結婚しましょう。　(Let's get married.)

The plain volitional form is shown below.

Group I	会う ⇨ 会おう	書く ⇨ 書こう	話す ⇨ 話そう
	立(た)つ ⇨ 立とう	死(し)ぬ ⇨ 死のう	飲む ⇨ 飲もう
II	食べる ⇨ 食べよう	起(お)きる ⇨ 起きよう	寝(ね)る ⇨ 寝よう
III	来(く)る ⇨ 来(こ)よう	する ⇨ しよう	

● **Temporal expressions**　　2-4

The words 時(とき)，前(まえ)，後(あと) are nouns but are quite often used like conjunctions in Japanese. What you must do, therefore, to make sentences with these conjunctive expressions is basically the same as noun-modification.

There are some restrictions on the forms which can precede these words.

plain form＋時	食べる時,	食べた時,	食べない時,	食べなかった時
dic. form of V＋前(に)	食べる前,	×	×	×
perfect form＋後	×	食べた後	×	×

　1．家を出る時，電話します。　(I will call you when I leave home.)
　2．家を出た時，電話します。　(I will call you when I have left home.)
　3．家を出る前に，電話します。(I will call you before I leave home.)
　4．家を出た後，電話します。　(I will call you after I leave home.)

Notice the difference between sentences 1 and 2. The first sentence, which has an imperfect verb, is similar to the third sentence, while the second sentence shares common elements with the fourth.

As these are nouns, expressions such as the following are possible:

子供の時 (in one's childhood / when one was a child)

あの人は、アメリカへ来る前から、英語が上手でした。
(That person had been good at English before he came to the States.)

● 宿題をしているから　　　2-4

This から is grammatically the same as から in "S1 から S2" in L.9 (P.79), which shows a cause and effect relationship. When S2 is a request, order, or judgment of the speaker, S1 is the reason or justification for S2. Sometimes there is no longer a clear "cause and effect" relationship, and it may be best not to translate から into English, as shown in the second example.

1．いい本だから、一度読んでください。
(It's a good book, so please read it once.)

2．僕はここで待っているから、ひとりで行ってきてくださいよ。
(Please go by yourself. I will wait here for you.)

● つもり（です）　　　2-2

This noun, つもり, indicates a "frame of mind" or "intention" and follows plain forms.

1．今夜は勉強するつもりです。
(My frame of mind is such that I will study tonight.)
(I intend to study tonight.)

2．今夜は勉強しないつもりです。
(My frame of mind is such that I will not study tonight.)

Study the following examples to understand the negation of this use of "frame of mind."

1．私はヨーロッパへ行くつもりはありません。中国へ行くつもりですから。
(I have no intention of going to Europe. I intend to go to China.)

2．私は今年はヨーロッパへ行かないつもりです。去年、行きましたから。
(My frame of mind is such that I will not go to Europe this year because I went last year.)

● 家を出る　　　2-4

We have learned about を as an object-marker used with transitive verbs. It can also be used with intransitive verbs to mean two things: in the examples following 1, を means "from" or "out of"; in 2, it means "through."

1．私はいつも十分でお風呂を出ます。
(I always get out of the bath in ten minutes.)

妹は、来年高校を卒業します。
(My sister will graduate from high school next year.)

2．近道を通りましょう。
(Let's go through the short-cut. / Let's take the short-cut.)

● それまで　　　2-4

This means "until then." In the sentence in the dialogue それまで can be safely translated as "until you call me." When you want to refer to what has been said, use the そ-series: それ、その、そこ, etc. When the speaker uses the あ-series, he/she feels it necessary to emphasize that the referent is an item of shared knowledge with the hearer. In the dialogue below, B at first used その人 to refer to Tanaka, but he changed その to あの when he realized that

Tanaka was someone known to both the speaker and the hearer.

>A：昨日、田中さんに会いましたよ。　　（I saw Tanaka san yesterday.）
>B：その人、私の知っている人ですか。　　（Is he somebody I know?）
>A：田中一郎ですよ。　　（Tanaka Ichiro.）
>B：ああ、あの人ですか。知っています。（Oh, that guy! I know him.）

● 電話じゃ　　　3-3

In the same way that では in ではありません is pronounced じゃ, the instrumental で＋contrastive は is changed to じゃ in the spoken language.

>電車じゃ時間がかかりますよ。(It takes a long time by train.)

● 話しにくい　　　3-3

V stem＋にくい means "difficult to V / hard to V." The difficulty expressed in this pattern can be either psychological or physical. The opposite is **V stem＋やすい**.

Note that に in the last three examples indicates that 私 is a criterion of judgment or standard of valuation that can be translated as "for 〜."

>1．この言葉は、とても言いにくいです。
>　　（This word is very difficult to pronounce.）
>2．あの人は話しにくい人ですね。
>　　（He is difficult to talk to.）
>3．この町は、私にはとても住みやすい所です。
>　　（This town is very comfortable for me to live in.）
>4．お箸は、私には使いやすいですよ。
>　　（Chopsticks, for me, are easy to use.）
>5．この雑誌は、子供にはよくありませんね。
>　　（This magazine is not good for children.）

● 話しにくいこと　　　3-3

こと, in this situation, means "something," or "what someone says, hears, feels, understands, and so on." It is used to refer to abstract things.

>1．私はわからないことがある時は、松田さんに聞きます。
>　　（When I have something I can't understand, I ask Matsuda san.）
>2．昨日、竹井さんが変なことを言っていましたね。
>　　（Takei san was saying something strange yesterday, wasn't he?）
>3．私の言うことをよく聞いてくださいね。
>　　（Please listen carefully to what I am going to say.）

● 家内が買い物に行っているので　　　3-6

ので is used in the pattern "S1 ので S2." It can be considered to be the て-form of "のです," but it is now used in the meaning "because" or "since" as if it were one conjunctive particle. The forms of the words that precede it are identical to those that come before のです. です／だ, therefore, has to be changed to な.

>ここは、静かなので、好きです。
>　（I like this place because it is quiet.）
>私の専門は日本語なので、日本語の本をかなりたくさん読みます。
>　（As my major is Japanese, I read a lot of Japanese books.）

The difference between から and ので is that, while から expresses a strong logical relationship between S1 and S2, ので offers an explanation. Hence ので is used more often than から in formal situations in which the excessively logical tone of から might give the impression that the hearer is being lectured at by the speaker. On the other hand, から is preferred when a clear logicality must be conveyed in the orders, requests or judgments from the speaker to friends or juniors. ので is often used to refer to two events, situations or actions that have actually occurred.

● て＋から   3-6

This pattern combines two sentences and means "after finishing S1, S2." Don't confuse this から with から for reasons. The から introduced here follows only the て-form but the から in "S1 から S2." does not.

今夜は，友達と映画を見てから，食事をしてきました。
　　(After seeing a movie with my friend tonight, I had dinner and returned.)
松田さんが来てから，行きましょう。(Let's go after Matsuda san comes.)
松田さんが来たから，行きましょう。(Now Matsuda san has comes, let's go.)

ことばの使い方 (ことばのつかいかた)

● **Informal Talk**

We must now learn the difference between male and female speech in the area of sentence-final particles. Here, we will study よ, ね and わ.

		Pl. forms of V / い-adj.	です，ます	な-adj. / N＋だ
わ	男	×	×	×
	女	行くわ／寒いわ	行きますわ／寒いですわ 学生ですわ／静かですわ	学生だわ／静かだわ
よ	男	行くよ／寒いよ	行きますよ／寒いですよ	学生だよ／静かだよ
	女	×(Except わ＋よ)	学生ですよ／静かですよ	学生(だわ)よ／静か(だわ)よ
ね	男	行くね／寒いね	行きますね／寒いですね	学生だね／静かだね
	女	×(Except わ＋ね)	学生ですね／静かですね	学生ね／静かね 学生(だわ)ね／静か(だわ)ね

Note 1　よ or ね cannot directly follow plain forms in female speech. The following sentences, all in male speech, can be changed to female speech by adding わ to the place before ね or よ.

```
―――――――男の言葉―――――――
学生だね       わからないよ       寒いよ
学生だったね   わからなかったよ   寒かったよ
```

Lesson 14

Note 2　The rules above are based on "socially accepted female speech." You will hear the forms that are considered unacceptable here used in casual situations, especially among young women.
In formal situations, however, they are rare.

Note 3　わ is sentence-final particle used in conversation only be women. It is used:
1　Like よ, when the speaker wants to be assertive. (It sounds more gentle than よ.)
　　私はアイスクリームにするわ。(I have decided to have ice cream.)
2　To express slight surprise, like なあ.
　　困ったわ。お財布忘れてきたらしいの。
　　(Oh no! I think I forget my wallet.)

〔Showing two agents in the pattern "S1, S2."〕

In this lesson, there are many patterns which use S1 and S2. 前, 時, 後 and て＋から (although, in the case of てから, it is not quite accurate to call S1 and S2 sentences) all take two sentences. S1, in these patterns, presents the "condition" in which S2 takes place. If these sentences have different agents, the first agent in S1 must be marked by either が or の just like the agents in a noun-modifying clause, because, in Japanese, 前, 時, 後 are nouns. The exception is てから; it is not a noun and only takes が.

In general, the rule is that が must mark the first agent in the pattern "S1, S2" in which S1 and S2 have different agents. This rule applies to other sentences representing "conditions." If the word that connects S1 and S2 is a noun, such as 前, 時, 後, then の can be used.

If the agents in S1 and S2 are identical, it is usually put at the beginning of the sentence and is marked by は.

　　父が晩御飯を食べる時，母はビールを飲みます。
　　(When my father eats dinner, my mother drinks beer.)
　　父は晩御飯を食べる時，ビールを飲みます。
　　(When my father has dinner, he drinks beer.)

● 僕　　1-4

This is a first person singular pronoun like "私," but its use is strictly restricted to men in casual situations. There is no corresponding pronoun for women. "わたし" covers a wider range in the case of women. (☞P.393「わたくし」)

● ここまで　　3-5

まで basically shows a limit or end of a sphere in the temporal or spatial sense. In the sentence in the dialogue, the speaker could have said ここへ来てください, but the apologetic tone that ここ is far from where the speaker is (and that he feels he is inconveniencing the hearer) would have disappeared.

　　試験の前の日は，夜遅くまで勉強します。
　　(I study till late at night on the days before an exam.)
　　ちょっと東京まで行って来ます。
　　(I am going as far as Tokyo and will be back soon.)

● 家内　　3-6

This is a term used for one's own wife, and 奥さん is used to refer to other people's wives. For husbands, 主人 refers to one's own, while 御主人 refers to somebody else's. The literal meaning of 家内 is "a person inside a house," and 奥さん, "the person in the rear." 主人 means a "main person" or a "master." Even though these words seem chauvinistic, they are still in use today.

Note 1　In Japanese, these kinship terms can be used as proper nouns.
　　　　もしもし。あ，松田さんの奥さんですか。御主人いらっしゃいますか。
　　　　(Hello, Oh, Mrs. Matsuda? Is Mr. Matsuda at home?)

Note 2　The words with a neutral reference are used to refer to husbands and wives in general.

Note 3　There are some young women who avoid 主人 because of its chauvinistic meaning when it is written in *kanji* and use 夫 or his given name or surname.

	One's own	Other's	Neutral Reference
wife	家内	奥さん	妻 (つま)
hus.	主人	御主人	夫 (おっと)

● 来られます　　3-7

This is the potential form of 来る, which we will study later. One thing which we must keep in mind is that the conjugation of this potential form no longer follows the original form of 来る. It conjugates as a Group II verb. See L. 19 文法 for more details.

　　　　来る Group III　⇨　来られる (dic. form) Group II
　　　　　　　　　　　　　来られない
　　　　　　　　　　　　　来られて

練習 (れんしゅう)

練習(れんしゅう)　1	Sでしょう

例　三時頃です。⇨三時頃でしょう。(It's probably around three o'clock.)
　　彼は来ます。⇨彼は来るでしょう。(He'll probably come.)
　　このアパートは静かです。⇨このアパートは静かでしょう。
　　　　　　　　　　　　　　(This apartment is probably quiet.)

1．佐藤さんはすぐ来ます。　　　　2．佐藤さんは来ません。
3．佐藤さんは昨日，来ませんでした。　4．明日は雪が降ります。
5．昨日は雪が降って寒かったです。　6．明日は曇りです。
7．昨日は曇りでした。　　　　　　8．佐藤さんは昨日，来ました。

Lesson 14

| 練習(れんしゅう) 2 | S だろうと思う |

例　三時頃です。⇨三時頃だろうと思います。(I think it's probably three o'clock.)
　　彼は来ます。⇨彼は来るだろうと思います。(I think he'll probably come.)
　　このアパートは静かです。⇨このアパートは静かだろうと思います。
　　　　　　　　　　　　　　　(I think this apartment is probably quiet.)

1．佐藤さんはすぐ来ます。　　　　2．佐藤さんは来ません。
3．佐藤さんは昨日，来ませんでした。　4．明日は雪が降ります。
5．昨日は雪が降って寒かったです。　6．明日は曇りです。
7．昨日は曇りでした。　　　　　　8．佐藤さんは昨日，来ました。

| 練習(れんしゅう) 3 | Noun-modification |

例　The time when the lecture will begin
　　⇨講演が始まる時間を知っていますか。
　　　(Do you know the time when the lecture will begin?)

1．The place where the lecture will be held
2．The person who will give the lecture
3．The time when the lecture will end
4．The day when Takei san will come back
5．The place where Matsuda san is
6．The time when the movie will start

| 練習(れんしゅう) 4 | V stem に＋行く／来る |

例　映画を見る　⇨映画を見に行きましょう。(Let's go to see a movie.)

1．テレビを見る　　2．レコードを買う　3．佐藤さんに電話する
4．松田さんにお願いする　5．お酒を飲む　6．食事をする

| 練習(れんしゅう) 5 | つもり(です) |

夏休みのスケジュール
行く所　　　　日本
行く日　　　　六月二十四日
帰(かえ)って来る日　九月三十日
乗(の)り物(もの)　　飛行機(ひこうき)
　　　　　　　エコノミー
日本で買(か)う物　カメラ
日本で会(あ)う人　佐藤さん

左の表を見て，例のように答えなさい。
(Study the list on the left and answer as in the example.)

例　夏休みは，どうしますか。仕事(しごと)をしますか。
　　(How will you spend the summer vacation? Will you work?)
　　⇨いいえ。旅行(りょこう)するつもりです。
　　　(No. I intend to travel.)

1．どこへ行くんですか。 2．いつ行くんですか。
3．何か月ぐらい日本にいるんですか。 4．何日に帰って来るんですか。
5．何に乗って行くんですか。 6．日本で何か買いますか。
7．日本で誰かに会いますか。

練習(れんしゅう) 6　　　　　後，前に

例　母に話した後，父に話します。(I will talk to my father after I talk to my mother.)
　　⇨父に話す前に，母に話します。(I will talk to my mother before I talk to my father.)

1．電話をした後，手紙を出します。 2．晩御飯を作った後，ケーキを作ります。
3．買い物をした後，家へ帰ります。 4．映画を見た後，友達に会います。
5．友達と話した後，先生と話します。 6．漢字の練習をした後，テープを聞きます。

練習(れんしゅう) 7　　　　　後⇨てから

例　母に話した後，父に話します。(I will talk to my father after I talk to my mother.)
　　⇨母に話してから，父に話します。

(I will talk to my father after I talk to my mother.)

1．電話をした後，手紙を出します。 2．晩御飯を作った後，ケーキを作ります。
3．買い物をした後，家へ帰ります。 4．映画を見た後，友達に会います。
5．友達と話した後，先生と話します。 6．漢字の練習をした後，テープを聞きます。

練習(れんしゅう) 8　　　　　て⇨後

例　母に話して，父に話しました。(I talked to my mother and [then] to my father.)
　　⇨母に話した後，父に話しました。

(After I talked to my mother, I talked to my father.)

1．電話をして，手紙を出しました。 2．晩御飯を作って，ケーキを作りました。
3．買い物をして，家へ帰りました。 4．映画を見て，友達に会いました。
5．友達と話して，先生と話しました。 6．漢字の練習をして，テープを聞きました。

練習(れんしゅう) 9　　　　　S＋時　(Imperf.)

例　水を飲む，コップを使う　⇨水を飲む時，コップを使います。
　　　　　　　　　　　　(When I drink water, I use a glass.)

1．車に乗る，ドアを開ける 2．料理を作る，料理の本を見る
3．漢字を調べる，辞書を使う 4．レコードを聞く，窓を閉める
5．ジョギングをする，ウォークマンを聞く 6．寝る，辞書を読む

Lesson 14

| 練習(れんしゅう) 10 | S＋時 (perf.) |

例　朝，起きる，コーヒーを飲む
　　　⇨私は，朝，起きた時，コーヒーを飲みます。
　　　　(When I wake up in the morning, I drink coffee.)

1．遅くまで勉強する，ワインを少し飲む　　2．朝早く起きる，ジョギングをする
3．竹井さんに会う，本を返す　　　　　　　4．いい本を読む，メモを書く
5．わからないことがある，あの人に聞く　　6．困ったことがある，母に話す

| 練習(れんしゅう) 11 | V (stem)＋にくい |

例　竹井さんの字，読む　⇨竹井さんの字は読みにくいです。
　　　　(It's difficult to read Takei san's writing.)

1．この漢字，書く　　　　2．佐藤さんの日本語，わかる　　3．この辞書，使う
4．このベッド，寝る　　　5．この自転車，乗る　　　　　　6．あの人，話す

| 練習(れんしゅう) 12 | V (stem)＋やすい |

例　竹井さんの字，読む　⇨竹井さんの字は読みやすいです。
　　　　(It's easy to read Takei san's writing.)

1．この漢字，書く　　　　2．佐藤さんの日本語，わかる　　3．この辞書，使う
4．このベッド，寝る　　　5．この自転車，乗る　　　　　　6．あの人，話す

| 練習(れんしゅう) 13 | SのでS |

例　昨日よく勉強しました，授業が楽しいです
　　　⇨昨日よく勉強したので，授業が楽しいです。
　　　　(Since I studied well yesterday, the class is enjoyable.)

1．試験が近いです，毎日大変です
2．この部屋は静かです，勉強しやすいです
3．私はお金が要ります，仕事をします
4．今日は休みです，家にいます
5．私は時間が欲しいです，アルバイトはしません
6．今晩友達が来ます，早く帰ります

十四課

練習(れんしゅう)　14	〜てもいい

例　この窓を開ける　⇨すみませんが，この窓を開けてもいいですか。
　　　　　　　　　　(Excuse me, but may I open this window?)

1．ちょっとお邪魔する　　　　　　2．今晩，林さんの家に遊びに行く
3．明日の授業に少し遅れる　　　　4．今，ここで宿題をする
5．この仕事を明日までにお願いする　6．ここで新聞を読んでいる
7．ここで友達を待っている　　　　8．ちょっと買い物をして来る

練習(れんしゅう)　15	Plain volitional

例　食事をしようよ。⇨食事をしましょうよ。(Let's have dinner.)
　　近道を通って行こうね。⇨近道を通って行きましょうね。(Let's take a short-cut.)

1．林さんに手紙を出そうよ。　　　2．タクシーに乗って行こうね。
3．お箸を使おうね。　　　　　　　4．静かに話そうよ。
5．コップを洗おうね。　　　　　　6．三時頃，家を出ようよ。

十五課

内容表

文法	Uses of て-form (2) て＋Verb （しまう，おく，いる，みる，ある）		
	お＋stem＋する (Humble Expression)		お返しする
	S＋じゃないですか (Strong Assertion)		いいじゃないですか。
	～過ぎる ("Too ～")		簡単過ぎる。
	S＋方がいい (Affirm. Perfect) 　　　　　　(Neg. Imperfect)		書き直した方がいい
	Verb Stem＋方 (how to ～, the way of ～)		辞書を引く⇨辞書の引き方
	～ましょう(か) (Should/Shall I)		調べてみましょうか。
	S＋ところです(た，る，ている)		(Have just done, be about to, in the process of)
	か Showing a Choice (A or B)		上野さんか誰か
機能	Focusing on a Topic	7-3	～のことなんですが。
	Inquiring About an Opinion	2-34	どう思いますか。 (簡単過ぎない)でしょうか。
	Inquiring About Ease	2-32	簡単過ぎないでしょうか。
	Expressing a Belief/Opinion	2-33	
	Pointing Out Exceptions	2-49	ただ
	Inquiring About Advice	5-5	S＋方がいいでしょうか。
	Inquiring About Remembering	2-12	覚えている／忘れてしまう
	Expressing Fear / Worry	3-6	Nに困る
	Offering to Do Something	2-8	調べてみましょうか。
	Expressing Impossibility	2-13	どうしてもわからないんですよ。

Lesson 15

会話 (かいわ)

1

A：加藤さん，この前お願いしたリポートのことなんですが…。
B：はい，読んでおきましたよ。はい，お返しします。
A：これ，どう思いますか。
B：とてもいいじゃないですか。
A：そうでしょうか。簡単過ぎないでしょうか。
B：はっきりしていて，わかりやすいですよ。ただ，ここには，問題があると思います。
A：ここですか。ここは，私も困ってしまったんですよ。書き直した方がいいですね。
B：そうした方がいいですね。

2

A：リースさん，この漢字の読み方を覚えてる？
B：どれ？[これなのよ。]ああ，前に習った漢字だね。でも，忘れちゃったなあ。
A：そう。漢字にはいつも困っちゃうわ。
B：辞書を持ってるから，調べてみようか。
A：じゃ，悪いけど，調べてみてくれる？　私は辞書の引き方が，まだわかんないの。
B：ああ，この字だね。
A：うん，そうそう。

1

A：Kato san, it's about the paper I asked you (to read) the other day.

B：Yes, I have read it. Here, I'll return it to you.

A：What do you think about this?

B：It's very good!

A：Do you think so? Isn't it too simplistic?

B：It's clear and easy to understand. However, I think there's a problem here.

A：Here? I had trouble here. It would be better to rewrite it, wouldn't it?

B：Yes, it would be better to do that.

2

A：Reese san, do you remember the reading of this character?

B：Which one? [This one.] Oh, it's a character we learned before. But I've forgotten it.

A：Really? I always find characters to be a problem.

B：I have a dictionary, so shall I look it up?

A：Yes, I don't want to trouble you, but please look it up. I still don't know how to use a dictionary.

B：Oh, it's this character, isn't it?

A：Yes, that's it.

Lesson 15

3

A：明日の宿題，もうやってありますか。

B：ええ，今終わったところです。二時間もかかってしまいました。

A：僕は今やっているところなんですが，わかりにくいところが二つ三つあるんですよ。

B：どこですか。

A：これなんですが。この問題がどうしてもわからないんですよ。

B：私もですよ。上野さんか誰かに聞いてみましょうか。

A：そうしましょう。

単語表 (たんごひょう)

1

加藤(かとう)	a surname
この前(まえ)	the other day
お願(ねが)いする	ask, request
リポート／レポート	report, paper
どう思(おも)いますか	☞ことばの使い方
とても	very
簡単過(かんたんす)ぎる	too simplistic
はっきりしている	clear
ただ	except
問題(もんだい)	a problem
書き直す(かきなおす)	rewrite

2

読み方(よみかた)	how to read
覚(おぼ)えてる	remember ☞Informal talk
前(まえ)に	before
習う(ならう)	learn
でも	but
忘(わす)れちゃった	☞Informal talk
まだ…ない	not yet

3

終(お)わったところだ	☞文法
二つ三つ(ふたつみっつ)	two or three of ～
どうしても	by any / all means
聞(き)く	ask, listen

3

A: Have you already done the homework for tomorrow?

B: Yes, I just finished it. It took me two hours!

A: I'm doing it now, but there are two or three parts which I find difficult to understand.

B: Where are they?

A: Here. I can't understand this question by any means.

B: It's the same for me. Shall we try and ask Ueno san or someone?

A: Yes, let's.

関連語句 (かんれんごく)

会議(かいぎ)	meeting, conference	服(ふく)	clothes
セーター	sweater	着(き)る	put on, wear Ⅱ
持(も)つ	hold, carry	遅(おそ)い	late, not on time
寂(さび)しい	lonely	教科書(きょうかしょ)	textbook
病気(びょうき)	illness, sickness	掃除(そうじ)する	clean
奨学金(しょうがくきん)	scholarship	貸(か)す	lend
運転(うんてん)する	drive	生け花(いけばな)	flower arrangement
教(おし)える	teach Ⅱ		

Lesson 15

文法 (ぶんぽう)

● て-form＋おく（読んでおきました）　1-2

The literal meaning of おく is "to put or place something," and the basic meaning of this pattern is "to do something in advance."

1．明日、会議がありますから、これを読んでおいてください。
  (We will have a meeting tomorrow, so please read this in advance.)
2．昨日、よく勉強しておいたので、今日の試験は難しくなかった。
  (As I studied well yesterday, today's exam was not difficult.)
3．明日デパートへ行って、春の服を買っておくつもりなんですが、一緒に行きませんか。
  (I intend to go to a department store tomorrow to buy clothing for spring. Won't you come with me?)

● て-form＋しまう（困ってしまった、忘れちゃった）　1-7

The literal meaning of しまう is "to complete something" and the whole pattern means "to do completely or perfectly." Apart from its basic meaning, as you may notice from the sentences in the dialogue, this pattern is often used when you have come up against an undesirable circumstance or a situation you regret. て＋しまう and て＋しまった are often contracted into ちゃう, ちゃった in conversation. (☞P.380)

1．宿題は、一時間で全部やってしまいました。
  (I completely finished my homework in an hour.)
2．あの人の名前を忘れてしまいました。(I forgot his name!)

● て-form＋みる（調べてみましょうか、聞いてみましょう）　2-4

The literal meaning of this pattern is "to do something and see how it is."

1．このセーターはとてもいいですね。ちょっと着てみてもいいですか。
  (This sweater is very nice. May I try it on?)
2．わからないことは、何でも、上野さんに聞いてみた方がいいですよ。
  (You should ask Ueno san about whatever you don't understand.)

● お返しします　1-2

お＋stem＋する: This pattern indicates that the speaker (or someone closer to him) does something for a listener whom he does not know well or who is his superior (in age, social position, etc.). Note that the action must involve a listener who is unfamiliar or superior to the speaker.

1．この本、お返しします。
  (I'll return this book. — the book must belong to a superior or to someone the speaker does not know well —)
2．先生、それ、お持ちしましょうか。
  (Sensei, shall I carry that? — "that" must belong to the Sensei —)

● とてもいいじゃないですか（じゃありませんか）　1-4

S＋じゃないですか: This pattern is used when you make a strong assertion, accuse, encourage, or scold a listener. The S ends with a plain form; the ending だ, however, is an ex-

172

ception. Because じゃない is derived from です, だ must be deleted in this pattern. In less polite conversation among friends, this pattern may be shortened to S＋じゃない. Note that there is a falling intonation in this sentence pattern.

どうしたんですか。遅いじゃありませんか。
(What happened? You are late!)
何ですか, これは。全然わからないじゃないですか。
(What is this? It's absolutely impossible to understand!)
どうして, あの人が嫌いなの。とてもいい人じゃない。
(Why do you hate that person? He is a nice person.)

● 簡単過ぎる　　　1-5
V stem (行き)　　⇨行き過ぎる (go too far)
い-adj. (寒)　＋過ぎる　⇨寒過ぎる　(too cold)
な-adj. (静か)　　⇨静か過ぎる (too quiet)

This pattern indicates that something goes beyond the limit of what is considered acceptable, and, as a result, it is not desirable anymore.

As in **V stem＋にくい／やすい**, note that に appears after an agent. This に indicates a criterion of judgment or a standard of valuation. See example 2.

1. A：この部屋は, 静かでいいですね。
   B：いいえ。静か過ぎて寂しいですよ。
   (A：This room is nice because it is quiet.)
   (B：It is so quiet I feel lonely.)
2. A：この日本語の教科書は, 私には少し難し過ぎます。
   B：そうですか。私には少しやさし過ぎると思います。
   (A：This Japanese textbook is a little too difficult for me.)
   (B：Is that right? For me, it's a little too easy, I think.)

● 書き直した方がいい　　　1-7

S＋方がいい: This is a pattern used in giving advice. When a verb is used in S in the affirmative, it is usually in the plain perfect form. If S is negative, only the negative imperfect form is used.

講演は三時からですから, 早く行った方がいいですよ。
(Since the lecture starts at three, you should go soon.)
病気の時は, あまり食べない方がいいですよ。
(When you are ill, you should not eat very much.)

● 漢字の読み方　　　2-1

Note the examples below to see how this form is constructed:

料理を作る　　⇨料理の作り方　　(how to cook, way of cooking)
日本料理を食べる⇨日本料理の食べ方　(how to eat Japanese dishes)
リポートを書く　⇨リポートの書き方　(how to write a paper, way of writing a paper)

● 調べてみようか　　　2-4

In the previous lesson we learned that the pattern **V stem＋ましょう** or its plain volitional form means "Let's ～." In this sentence, the same pattern means "Shall I/we ～?" The con-

Lesson 15

text is the only clue to making a distinction between the two meanings.

● て-form＋ある　　　3-1

In L. 13, we learned て-form＋いる; when a verb is either a "motion verb" or a "verb of change," the pattern indicates the continuing result of an action. We also learned that the verbs of motion and change are all intransitive verbs. Then how is it possible to express the same idea — the continuing result of an action — with a transitive verb? This is our topic of study now. Study the following examples:

	V.i. て＋いる	V.t. て＋ある
1	窓が開いています。 (The window is open.)	窓が開けてあります。 (The window is (kept) open.)
2	電気がついています。 (The light is on.)	電気がつけてあります。 (The light is (kept) on.)
3	ドアが閉まっています。 (The door is closed.)	ドアが閉めてあります。 (The door is (kept) closed.)
4	………………	宿題がしてあります。 (Homework is done.)

The difference between the two is that **V.t.** て＋ある indicates the result of somebody's intentional action, while **V.i.** て＋いる does not portray that nuance; results expressed in the **V.i.** て＋いる pattern may be naturally caused. Sometimes て＋ある sounds very similar to て＋おく. See below:

1. 今日友達が来るので、部屋を掃除しておきました。
   (I cleaned my room since my friend is coming today.)
2. 今日、友達が来るので、部屋が掃除してあります。
   (The room is cleaned since my friend is coming today.)

Note that the first example concerns "what the speaker did today," and the second describes the condition of the room. In other words, て＋ある is used to describe "how things are," "what the state of things is." Pay attention to the particle が, which in real conversation, may be omitted (as in the dialogue) or replaced by は.

● S＋ところです　　　3-3

Depending on the verbal ending of the sentence, this pattern has three different meanings:

1. Plain perfect　　　私は今、晩御飯を食べたところです。
   (I have just had dinner.)
2. て＋いる　　　　私は今、晩御飯を食べているところです。
   (I am in the middle of having dinner.)
3. Plain imperfect　　私は今、晩御飯を食べるところです。
   (I am just about to have dinner.)

● 上野さんか誰か　　　3-6

か between two expressions means "either ～ or ～." You will occasionally see a second か following the second expression.

今日か明日(か)，映画に行きませんか。
(Shall we go to see a movie, either today or tomorrow?)
その問題は，田中さんか加藤さんに聞いた方がいいですよ。
(You should ask Tanaka san or Kato san about that problem.)

ことばの使い方 (ことばのつかいかた)

● **Nのことなんですが**　1-1
Nのことなんですが is a phrase introducing the topic about which you will talk. This makes it easier for the listener to mentally prepare himself or herself for the discussion. Nのこと means "matters concerning N."

　　A：先生，奨学金のことなんですが，お願いがあります。
　　　　(Sensei, I have a favor to ask of you concerning a scholarship.)
　　B：はい，どんなことですか。
　　　　(Yes. What is it?)

● **はい，お返しします**　1-2
When you are handing something to somebody, はい is often used.

　　A：すみません。ちょっとボールペンを貸してください。
　　B：はい，どうぞ。
　　　　(A：Excuse me, but please lend me a ball-point pen.)
　　　　(B：Here you are.)

● **どう思いますか**　1-3
〔N(を)〕どう思いますか is used to solicit the opinion of others about N. The noun can be dropped if what is being discussed is clear. It is quite common in conversation to omit を.

　　この辞書，どう思いますか，先生。
　　(What do you think of this dictionary, Sensei?)
　　加藤さん，あの映画をどう思いましたか。
　　(Kato san, what did you think of the movie?)

● **そうでしょうか／簡単過ぎないでしょうか**　1-5
Compared to です，でしょう sounds slightly more humble because with でしょう you reserve some uncertainty. This ending is effective when you want to state your opinion without sounding over-confident.

● **はっきりしている**　1-6
はっきり is originally an adverb meaning "clearly." As a noun modifier it takes した or している, and as a predicate, it takes している. In this group of adverbs, there are words like ぼんやり (vaguely), のんびり (in a relaxed way), which end in り.

　　もっとはっきり話してください。
　　(Please speak more clearly.)
　　この問題は，あまりはっきりしていないので，とても答えにくいです。

Lesson 15

(This question is not very clear and, therefore, hard to answer.)

そのことは，私ははっきりしたことは知りません。

(I don't know the details about that.)

● ただ　　1-6

This is a conjunction which connects a sentence of "general opinion or impression" with a sentence that shows a partially opposite opinion.

あの映画はとてもよかったと思います。ただ，長過ぎます。

(I think that the movie was really good, except that it was too long.)

● 書き直す　　1-7

直す by itself means "to correct" and with a verb stem standing before it, it means "to do ～ again to improve it."

リースさん，そこを読み直してください。(Read that part again, Reese san.)

これは，きたな過ぎますから，もう一度書き直した方がいいですね。

(You should write this again because it is too messy.)

● Informal Talk

Some phonetic changes take place in casual talk. Here are examples:

て＋おく ⇨ とく	書いておく ⇨ 書いとく 読んでおく ⇨ 読んどく	
て＋しまう⇨ちゃう	書いてしまう⇨ 書いちゃう　～てしまった⇨ ～ちゃった 読んでしまう⇨ 読んじゃう　～でしまった⇨ ～じゃった	
て＋いる ⇨ てる て＋いた ⇨ てた	書いている ⇨ 書いてる　読んでいる⇨ 読んでる 書いていた ⇨ 書いてた　読んでいた⇨ 読んでた	

Note that these forms are used in casual conversation and not in writing.

● 覚えて(い)る　　2-1

This is, needless to say, the て-form of 覚える. 覚える means "memorize" and 覚えている literally means "in the state of having been memorized." In normal English it means "keep in mind" or "remember."

1．漢字を覚えるのは大変ですか。(Is it hard to memorize *kanji*?)

2．あの人の顔は覚えているんですが，名前は覚えていないんですよ。

(I remember that person's face but I don't remember his name.)

● 習う　　2-2

This word means "to learn a skill from somebody."

1．私は車の運転を習っています。

(I have been learning to drive a car.)

2．加藤さんは生け花を習っています。

(Kato san is learning flower arrangement.)

○　日本語を習う／ピアノを習う

×　人類学を習う

十五課

● （忘れちゃった）なあ　　2-2

なあ was introduced in the phrase 困ったなあ in L. 7. This functions like an exclamation point and indicates that the whole sentence expresses the strong feeling of the speaker. This can be used when you do not have an audience; this is the primary difference between なあ and ねえ (ねえ needs an audience).

なあ is also more casual than ねえ. For women, わ is recommended as a substitute.

あの新しいコンピューター，欲しいなあ。
　　(I really want to have that new computer. ... I wish I had that ～.)
この問題，難しいなあ。(How tough this question is!)

● わかんない　　2-5

This is a very casual way of saying わからない and is not suitable for writing.

In general, らりるれろ can be changed to ん before な in informal conversation. This is, however, just for recognition but not recommended for your use.

● 漢字にはいつも困ります　　2-3

This can be translated "*kanji* is always a problem." The cause of the problem are marked by に.

1．この車には本当に困りますよ。朝はいつもエンジンがかからないんですよ。
　　(This car is really a pain in the neck. Every morning, the engine does not start.)
2．あの人には困りますね。いつも遅れて来るんですから。
　　(He is a problem. He's always late.)

● 二つ三つ　　3-3

To cite an approximate number of things, you can put two numerals as shown here. Any two numbers can be placed in this way. The only exception is the combination of 9 and 10, which may be mistaken for the number 90.

1．私は，東京に八，九年住んでいました。
　　(I lived in Tokyo for eight or nine years.)
2．昨日の講演には，学生と先生が五，六十人来ました。
　　(Fifty or sixty students and professors came to the lecture yesterday.)
3．加藤さんの奥さんは四十七，八才だと思いますが，とても若いですよ。
　　(I guess Mrs. Kato is forty-seven or eight but she is/looks young.)

● どうしても　　3-5

どうしても means "by all means," or "definitely."

私はどうしても漢字が覚えられないんです。本当に困ってしまいます。
　　(I just can't memorize *kanji*. It is really a pain.)
私はどうしても新しい車が欲しいんです。
　　(I definitely want a new car.)

● 聞く　　3-6

So far, we have learned two ways of using this verb.

1．N を聞く　　(listen to ～)
　　私は毎朝天気予報を聞いてから，学校へ来ます。
　　(I come to school every morning after listening to the weather forecast.)
　　あの人はレコードを聞くのが好きです。(He likes to listen to records.)

Lesson 15

2．N1 を N2 に聞く　　(ask N2 about N1)

先生に時間を聞きましたが，先生は時計を持っていませんでした。
(I asked Sensei the time, but he did not have a watch.)

わからないところを加藤さんに聞きました。
(I asked Kato san about the part I could not understand.)

練習(れんしゅう)

練習(れんしゅう)　1　　　　Nのこと

例　来週の試験　⇨先生，来週の試験のことなんですが…。
(Sensei, about the exam next week ...)

1．この前の試験　　　2．昨日の宿題　　　3．この前，お願いしたリポート
4．奥さんの病気　　　5．来年の奨学金　　6．来月ある講演

練習(れんしゅう)　2　　　　～ておく

例　お酒を買う　⇨今晩，友達が来るから，お酒を買っておいてください。
(Please buy some *sake* (have some *sake* bought) since my friends will come tonight.)

1．部屋を掃除する　　　　2．覚える　　　　3．忘れない
4．加藤さんに電話をする　5．買い物をする　6．加藤さんに言う

練習(れんしゅう)　3　　　　～てしまう

例　宿題を忘れる　⇨宿題を忘れてしまいました。(Unfortunately, I forgot my homework.)

1．つまらない本を買う　2．ビールを十本飲む　3．その言葉を忘れる
4．十分でお風呂を出る　5．三年で大学を卒業する　6．リポートが簡単過ぎる
7．加藤さんには困る　　8．五時間もテレビを見る　9．家の犬が死ぬ

練習(れんしゅう)　4　　　　～ていい

例　食べる　⇨これ，食べてみていいですか。(May I try a bite of this?)

1．飲む　　2．着る　　3．読む　　4．書く　　5．使う　　6．乗る

練習(れんしゅう) 5	お＋stem＋する

例　それを持つ　⇨先生，それをお持ちしましょうか。
　　　　　　　　　(Sensei, shall I carry that for you?)

1．この本を返す　　　　2．ここで待つ　　　　　3．学生の名前を調べる
4．お手紙を出す　　　　5．ドアを開ける　　　　6．窓を閉める

練習(れんしゅう) 6	S＋じゃないですか

例　とてもいいです。⇨とてもいいじゃないですか。(It's certainly very good!)

1．遅いです。　　　　　2．全然わからないです。　3．とても読みやすいです。
4．ちっとも勉強していない。　5．宿題をして来ない。　6．大変よく勉強する。

練習(れんしゅう) 7	～過ぎる

例　これは簡単です。⇨これは簡単過ぎますよ。(This is too simple.)

1．あの人は静かです。　　　　2．この部屋は寒いです。
3．この教科書は難しいです。　4．あの人はたばこをすいます。
5．あの人はお酒を飲みます。　6．あの人は何でも食べます。
7．あの人は料理を作ります。

練習(れんしゅう) 8	～方がいい

例　今日は早く寝る　⇨今日は早く寝た方がいいですよ。(You should sleep early today.)

1．宿題は今する　　　2．明日の朝は早く来る　　3．図書館の本は早く返す
4．漢字は覚える　　　5．その映画は見ない　　　6．今，あの人に何も言わない

練習(れんしゅう) 9	stem＋方

例　この漢字を読む　⇨この漢字の読み方を教えてください。
　　　　　　　　　(Please teach me how to read this *kanji*.)

1．この料理を作る　　　2．辞書を引く　　　　　3．この仕事をやる
4．リポートを書く　　　5．この器械(きかい)を使う　6．ハンバーガーを食べる

Lesson 15

練習(れんしゅう)　10　　　〜てある

例　窓を開けておいてください。⇨はい，窓は開けてあります。
　　(Please leave the window open. ⇨ Yes, the window is left open.)

1．宿題をやっておいてください。　　　　2．辞書を買っておいてください。
3．先生の奥さんに電話をしておいてください。　4．この言葉は覚えておいてください。
5．料理を作っておいてください。　　　　6．買い物はしておいてください。
7．部屋を掃除しておいてください。　　　8．それは調べておいてください。

練習(れんしゅう)　11　　　S＋ところだ

例　晩御飯を食べている　⇨今，晩御飯を食べているところなんですよ。
　　　　　　　　　　　　(I am just now eating dinner.)
　　手紙を書いた　　　　⇨今，手紙を書いたところなんですよ。
　　　　　　　　　　　　(I have just written a letter.)
　　電話をする　　　　　⇨今，電話をするところなんですよ。
　　　　　　　　　　　　(I am just about to make a phone call.)

1．部屋を掃除している　　2．上野さんに聞いてみた　　3．試験の勉強をする
4．困っている　　　　　　5．図書館で調べてきた　　　6．リポートを書き直す

練習(れんしゅう)　12　　　NかN

例　ビールを飲みましょう。(ワイン)　⇨ビールかワインを飲みましょう。
　　　　　　　　　　　　　　　(Let's drink beer or wine.)

1．上野さんに聞きました。　（加藤さん）　2．今日，行きましょう。　（明日）
3．お金が要ります。　　　　（時間）　　　4．猫の子が欲しいです。　（犬の子）
5．今週，返した方がいいですよ。（来週）　6．映画を見るつもりです。（テレビ）
7．今週の週末，行きます。　（来週）　　　8．百ドル貸してください。（二百ドル）

練習(れんしゅう)　13　　　〜に聞く／〜を聞く

例　加藤さん　⇨悪いけど，加藤さんに聞いてくれませんか。
　　　　　　　(Sorry to trouble you, but won't you please ask Kato san?)
　　このテープ　⇨悪いけど，このテープを聞いてくれませんか。
　　　　　　　(Sorry to trouble you, but won't you please listen to this tape?)

1．今日の天気予報　　　　2．私の言うこと　　　　　3．先生
4．家内(かない)　　　　　5．加藤さんの言うこと　　6．主人(しゅじん)

練習(れんしゅう) 14　　　　　Counters

例　鉛筆(えんぴつ)を買いました。(5,6)　⇨鉛筆を五,六本買いました。
　　　　　　　　　　　　　(I bought 5 or 6 pencils.)

1. 紙(かみ)が欲しいんです。　(20,30)　　　2. 辞書が要ります。　　(1,2)
3. じゃがいもを下さい。(2,3)　　　　4. 休みが欲しいんです。(4,5日)
5. 学生がいます。　　　(7,8)　　　　6. 時間を下さい。　　　(1,2分)

十六課

内容表

文法	Honorific Expressions		おっしゃる，いらっしゃる
	Noun-Modifiers With Perfect Form		眼鏡をかけた方
	Plural Modifiers		眼鏡をかけたやせた方
	Indirect Quotation		see P. 190
	S (with Perfect form)＋ことがある		見たことがありません。
	では＋Negative Expressions		運動靴じゃ合いません。
	「に」in the potential sentence		私にわかること
	S1 ために S2 (S2 so that S1)		のんびりするために着る。
	S＋ことが多い／少ない／ない		着ることが多い (Occasion)
	S1 し(それに) S2		Besides, in addition to
	Verbs for "Put on / Take off / Wear"		着る，はく，する，かぶる／脱ぐ，とる
	Sんじゃないですか		多いんじゃないですか。
	N1 は，N2 が，Predicate		あの人は背が高い。
	こ，そ，あ，どういう		What sort of, what kind of
	こ，そ，あ，どんな		What sort of, what kind of
機能	Stating Factual Information (Describing appearance)	1-2	着る，はく，かける，する…
	Inquiring About Intentions	2-10	何を着て行くんですか。
	Stating Intentions	2-9	行こうと思っている／行くつもりです
	Expressing Certainty	2-19	ハイヒールをはいて行くんですね。
	Stating Factual Information (Experience)	1-2	はいたことはありません。
	Stating Factual Information (Frequency)	1-2	ことが多い／少ない／ある／ない
	Expressing a Belief / Opinion	2-33	Sんじゃないですか。
	Asking About Factual Information (Type, Kinds)	1-3	どういうN
	Reporting Information	1-6	いらっしゃるとおっしゃっていました。
	Telling Jokes	6-16	運動靴じゃ合いませんからね。

Lesson 16

会話 (かいわ)

1

A：ローレンスさん，さっき中村さんとおっしゃる方がいらっしゃいました。

B：中村さん？ どんな方でした？

A：背が高くて，眼鏡をかけたやせた方でした。

B：さあ，誰だろう。中村何ていうか聞きませんでした？

A：ええ。ひげをはやして，長い髪をした男の人でしたが…。

B：わかりませんね。誰だろう。

A：あとで，またいらっしゃるとおっしゃっていました。

B：それじゃ，その時にわかりますね。

2

A：ハーディさんの結婚式のことなんですけど，[ええ。]何を着て行くんですか。

B：私は背広を着て，ネクタイをして行こうと思っていますが…。東山さんは？

A：私はドレスを着て行くつもりです。

B：そうですか。東山さんがドレスを着ているのは見たことがありませんから，楽しみにしていますよ。[ありがとうございます。]それじゃ，もちろん，ハイヒールをはいて行くんですね。

A：ええ，あまりはいたことはありませんが，運動靴じゃ合いませんからね。

1

A：Lawrence san, someone by the name of Nakamura san came (to see you) a while ago.

B：Nakamura san? What was he like?

A：He was a tall, thin man with glasses.

A：Well, who could that be? Did you ask Nakamura who?

A：No. He was a man with a beard and long hair ...

B：I just don't know. Who could he be?

A：He said that he would come by again later.

B：Well, we'll find out then, won't we?

2

A：It's about Hardy san's wedding ... [Yes?] ... what will you wear to it?

B：I'm thinking about wearing a suit and a tie ... but what about you, Higashiyama san?

A：I plan to wear a dress.

B：Is that so? I've never seen you wearing a dress, Higashiyama san — I'm looking forward to it. [Thank you.] Then, of course, you're going to wear high heels?

A：Yes. I haven't worn them very often, but sneakers just won't match (my dress).

Lesson 16

3

A：北川さん、ちょっと質問してもいいですか。

B：何でしょう。私にわかることですか。

A：日本人の若い人は、ふだん着物を着ますか。

B：着ないでしょう。私は着物を着たこともないし、それに一枚も持っていませんよ。

A：そうですか。じゃ、男の人で着物を着る人はどういう人ですか。

B：中年以上の人が、家でのんびりするために着ることが多いんじゃないですか。

A：女の人はどうですか。

B：若い女の人たちは、改まった時に着ることが多いですね。

単語表（たんごひょう）

1

おっしゃる	言う
方(かた)	人
いらっしゃる	来る、行く、いる
どんな	what kind of
背(せ／せい)が高(たか)い	tall
眼鏡(めがね)をかける	wear glasses II
やせた	slim（やせる—lose weight）
(ひげを)はやす	have a beard, mustache, or whiskers
長(なが)い	long
髪(かみ)	hair
長い髪をする	have long hair
あとで	later

2

結婚式(けっこんしき)	wedding
背広(せびろ)	men's suit
ネクタイをする	wear a tie
東山(ひがしやま)	a surname
～を楽(たの)しみにする	look forward to
ハイヒールをはく	wear high-heels
運動靴(うんどうぐつ)	sneakers, athletic shoes
合(あ)う	fit, match

3

A: Kitagawa san, may I ask you a brief question?

B: What is it? Is it about something I know?

A: Do young Japanese people normally wear *kimono*s?

B: Not generally. I have never worn a *kimono,* and I don't even own one.

A: Is that so? Then what kind of men wear *kimono*s?

B: I would say mostly middle-aged and older men wear them to relax at home.

A: How about the women?

B: Young women mostly wear them on formal occasions.

3

質問(しつもん)	a question	中年(ちゅうねん)	middle age
ふだん	普通, normally	(中年)以上(いじょう)	above
着物(きもの)を着る	wear kimono Ⅱ	のんびりする	relax
それに	in addition, what's more	多(おお)い	many, majority
どういう人	what kind of person	改(あらた)まった	formal

関連語句 (かんれんごく)

頭(あたま)がいい／悪(わる)い	(頭—brain, head) smart / dumb		
背(せ)が低(ひく)い／高(たか)い	short / tall		
忙(いそが)しい	busy	体(からだ)	body (*cf.* 休み)
短(みじか)い	short	太(ふと)った	fat, chubby
目(め)	eye	太(ふと)る	gain weight
青(あお)い	blue	高(たか)い	expensive
黒(くろ)い	black, dark	説明(せつめい)	explanation
辞(や)める	quit, resign	万年筆(まんねんひつ)	fountain pen

Lesson 16

文法 (ぶんぽう)

● 敬語(けいご)

In Japanese, people shift their speech according to the relationship they have with the listener and the people or things in the topic of conversation. This system of speech is called *keigo*. The inability to use proper *keigo* would be considered similar to the lack of knowledge of *kanji*. A person without the ability to handle *keigo* would be considered uneducated or childish.

You may ask, then, if speaking in *keigo* all the time constitutes the perfect speaker of Japanese. Unfortunately this is not the case. Such a person sounds too polite and, consequently, unfriendly, because the essence of *keigo* is to keep psychological distance between the speaker and the person in the topic of conversation. The important thing, in this case, is to be able to differentiate the forms of speech according to the person, topic, and place of the conversation.

Keigo has three properties:

尊敬(そんけい)—To exalt the position of the person in the topic.

Honorific	Neutral
おっしゃる	言(い)う
いらっしゃる	来(く)る，行(い)く，いる
方(かた)	人(ひと)
お国	国(くに)
お名前	名前(なまえ)
御両親	両親(りょうしん)
御兄弟	兄弟(きょうだい)

(This person can be the listener or a third person, but never the speaker.) This use is "honorific," and, from here on, will be marked by the following symbol: ☝

The left column contains some of the honorific words we have already seen.

謙譲(けんじょう)—To lower the position of the speaker or those related to the speaker. We have not yet seen many of these. The only expression we have encountered in this form is お返(かえ)しします (L. 15). This is called the "humble form," and words in this category will hereafter be marked with a ⬇.

丁寧(ていねい)—お酒(さけ)，お金(かね) are examples of this form of *keigo*. The prefix is not used to show respect to the items or to their owner. These expressions are used to avoid giving a vulgar impression to people and possibly offending them.

In L. 30, we will go into the details of *keigo* usage.

● おっしゃる   1-1   ☞ L. 13, ことばの使い方「いらっしゃる」

This is an honorific equivalent of 言う.

Base	Pl. neg.	Stem	Dic. form	て-form
おっしゃ	ら	い	る	って

1．こちらは中村さんとおっしゃいます。(This is Nakamura san.)
2．北川さんは，今日は，忙(いそが)しくて行けないとおっしゃいました。
(Kitagawa san said that he was too busy to go today.)

● どんな　　　1-2

This word belongs to the series of こんな，そんな，あんな，どんな．
　　こんな——like this, this kind of　　そんな——like that, that kind of
　　あんな——like that, that kind of　　どんな——like what, what kind of

Note　To understand the difference between そんな and あんな, see L. 14 文法「それまで」．

1．A：加藤(かとう)さんてどんな人ですか。(What is Kato san like?)
　　B：おとなしい，いい人ですよ。(He is a quiet, good person.)
2．A：私，こんな眼鏡(めがね)が欲しいんです。(I want glasses like this.)
　　B：学生には，高過(たかす)ぎますよ。(They are too expensive for a student.)

● 背が高い　　　1-3

Use the following pattern to describe the characteristics of persons or things:

　　　N1 は N2 が Predicate（です）。

The は in this sentence indicates that the topic is N1. In this pattern, N2 must be, in a sense, a particular part of N1. "N2 が Pred.," as a whole, works as a compound adj. Note the following to see how negative and interrogative sentences are formed:

1．ローレンスさんは目(め)が青(あお)い。
　　(As for Lawrence san, his eyes are blue. — Lawrence san has blue eyes.)
2．あの人は頭(あたま)がいいですか。
　　(As for that person, is his brain good? — Is he smart?)
3．この辞書(じしょ)は説明(せつめい)がよくありません。
　　(As for this dictionary, its explanations are not good. — The explanations in this dictionary are not good.)

● 眼鏡をかけたやせた方　　　1-3

In L. 13, we studied the pattern "て＋いる." One of its two functions is to describe the continuation of a state. When this pattern is used in this capacity as a noun modifier, the form ～た can be used instead of ～ている. Even though ～ている as a noun-modifier is grammatically and stylistically correct, the ～た form is more frequently used.（☞文法, L. 13）

　　晴(は)れている空(そら)　　⇨晴れた空 (clear sky)
　　眼鏡をかけている人　　⇨眼鏡をかけた人 (a person wearing glasses)
　　やせている人　　　　　⇨やせた人 (a slim person)

● Plural Modifiers　　　1-3

As you can see in the headline above, the 方 in the phrase "眼鏡をかけたやせた方" has two modifiers; in "背が高くて，眼鏡をかけたやせた方" it has three modifiers. The last phrase can also be rendered: "背が高い，眼鏡をかけたやせた方." Here is another sentence "ひげをはやして，長い髪をした人."

In Japanese, it is not difficult to tell the end of a noun modifying phrase. (There is a noun preceded by a plain form.) Finding the beginning of the phrase, however, demands considerable attention. In order to interpret a sentence correctly, it is important to understand its

189

Lesson 16

whole structure, and the function of each contained phrase.

When we say "modifier," we tend immediately to think of a "noun-modifier," but we must not forget that there is also a "verb-modifier" which is usually called an adverbial phrase. In the following sentence from the second dialogue, "背広を着て，ネクタイをして行こう," 行こう is modified by 背広を着て and ネクタイをして.

● **Indirect Quotation**　　　1-7

To present a direct quotation of a person's speech, the words are put between Japanese quotation marks as shown below:

「今日は寒いですね。」と中村さんは田中さんに言いました。

(Nakamura san said to Tanaka san, "It is cold today, isn't it?")

私は北川さんに「友達が来ませんでしたか。」と聞きました。

(I asked Kitagawa san, "Didn't my friend come?")

In L. 14 we learned the form "S と思います," to express "I think that ..." The contents of your thoughts (i.e. "S") take the plain form, and precede と思います. Expressing indirect quotations is basically the same. Take a look at the 文法 in L. 12 so that you can refresh your memory on plain forms.

But how do we quote questions? Here are some examples:

Question asked	Quoted question	Particle	Verbs
あの人は学生ですか	あの人は学生	か	と (って)
寒くありませんでしたか	寒くなかった		言う
どこへ行きましたか	どこへ行った		聞く
来るでしょうか	＊来るだろう		質問する
行きましょうか	＊行こう		

＊These were not introduced in L. 12. They are the plain forms. For 行こう see the explanation which comes later in this section.

In quoting questions, remember the following major points:

1. The plain form だ has to be deleted. (In an affirmative quotation, it stays.)
2. The quotational particle と can be omitted when it is used before 聞く and 質問する. (Never in affirmative quotations.)
3. Do not forget か after the plain forms.

● 着て行く　　　2-1　☞L. 13, 文法　6．て＋Verb

● 行こうと思う　　　2-2　☞P.156「行こう」

| Pl. volitional＋思う | ⇨ "I think I will V," "I intend to V" |

Note that this is used to refer to the action of the speaker himself.

● (行こうと)思っています　　　2-2

In comparison to 思います, 思っています is slightly different: 思っています indicates that the speaker has been thinking of the content of the preceding clause for some time, while 思います does not have this kind of specification. This difference can be found in the following pair of sentences that denote habitual action.

私は毎朝七時に起きます。
(I get up at seven every morning. — There is no explanation when this began.)
私は一か月前から，毎朝七時に起きています。
(I have been getting up at seven every morning since a month ago.)

● 見たことがありません　　2-4

$\boxed{\text{S (ending with plain perfect)}＋ことがある／ない}$

This pattern literally means that S has happened or has not happened before, depending on whether ある or ない is used. It is often used to express one's experience or inexperience in a situation.

1．私は中村さんという方にまだ会ったことはありません。
　　(I have not yet met the gentleman named Nakamura san.)
2．加藤さんは東京に住んだことがありますか。
　　(Kato san, have you ever lived in Tokyo?)
3．私は子供の時から，朝御飯を食べなかったことはないんですよ。
　　(I have never missed breakfast since I was a child, you know.)

● 運動靴じゃ合いません　　2-7

This じゃ is the contracted form of では; は, as you know, often accompanies negative expressions. The sentence can be analyzed according to the following two patterns:

$\boxed{\text{N＋で＋favorable statement}}$ ⇨ N is O.K. / N is acceptable.

The sentence from the dialogue is its negative counterpart:

$\boxed{\text{N＋では＋unfavorable statement}}$ ⇨ N is not good / O.K.

What is meant by these ambiguous terms, "favorable" and "unfavorable?" Expressions such as "good," "not too bad" are some of the favorable, and "bad" "terrible" and "doesn't fit" (as in the dialogue) are unfavorable. Many other "unfavorable" expressions can be substituted in these phrases. See the example below.

A：すみませんが，お金を貸してくれませんか。
B：今，あまりないので，十ドルでいいですか。
A：十ドルじゃ困るんですよ。十二ドル，お願いしますよ。
　　(A：May I borrow some money?)
　　(B：I don't have so much now. Is ten dollars all right?)
　　(A：Ten is not enough. May I ask for twelve?)

● 私にわかる（ことですか）　　3-2　☞P.158「話しにくい」
この雑誌は，子供にはよくありません。
　(This magazine is not good for children.)
これは私にはわかりませんね。(This is incomprehensible to me.)

● S1 し(それに)S2　　3-4　☞P.81
今日は，雪は降るし寒い。嫌な天気だ。
　(It is snowing, and what's more, it is cold today. Terrible weather!)
明日の試験の勉強はよくしてあるし，お金もあるから遊びに行こう。

Lesson 16

(Since I am well-prepared for tomorrow's test, and moreover, since I have money, I will go out to have fun.)

● 一枚も持っていません　　3-4

|1＋(counter)＋も…ない|　⇨　not even one, none at all

も in 一枚も is functionally the same as the も in お邪魔してもいいですか, which means "even." (☞L. 13 "て(も)いいです.")

　　私は東京へ行ったことは一度もありません。
　　　(I have never once been to Tokyo.)
　　あの先生の講演はひとつもわかりませんでした。
　　　(I understood nothing of that professor's lecture.)

● 男の人で着物を着る人　　3-5

で is the particle to limit perspective or scope.
It can be illustrated in the diagram below.

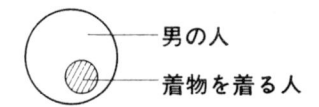

　　　　　　　　　　―男の人
　　　　　　　　　　―着物を着る人

　　このクラスの学生でAをもらった人は何人いますか。
　　　(How many students in this class received As?)

● のんびりするために　　3-6

|S1 (with dic. form)＋ために S2|　⇨　for the purpose of, in order to

Note that the subjects in S1 and S2 must be identical.
　　伊藤さんは、ハーディさんの結婚式に出るために着物を買いました。
　　　(Ito san bought a *kimono* in order to attend Hardy san's wedding.)
　　秋山さんは、結婚するために会社を辞めました。
　　　(Akiyama san quit her company to get married.)

● 着ることが多い　　3-6

This pattern can be used to express the frequency of an action, or to express whether or not something, in fact, takes place; substitute 多い with 少ない (a few / a little) or with ある／ない. Don't confuse this with "S (plain perfect)＋ことがある" on the previous page.

　　A：北川さんは着物を着ることが多いですか。
　　B：夏、ゆかたを着ることはありますが、他には着ることは少ないですね。
　　　(A：Kitagawa san, do you have many occasions to wear a *kimono*?)
　　　(B：I have occasion to wear *yukata* sometimes in the summer; aside from that, I have very little opportunity to wear it.)

Note that the next two sentences do not share this pattern. When the verb is related to mental activities such as わかる, 思う, 言う, and 聞く, two interpretations are possible: "there are occasions when …," and "there is something that …."

　　先生：何かわからないことがありますか。
　　　(Is there something you don't understand?)

学生：いいえ，わからないことは，何もありません。
(There isn't anything that I don't understand.)

● 多いんじゃないですか　　3-6

This pattern can be generalized as "S＋んじゃないですか," which indicates that the speaker's assertion of what he/she is thinking. It is, therefore, close in meaning, to "Sと思います" or "S＋でしょう." Don't confuse this with "いいじゃないですか" in L. 15.

ことばの使い方 (ことばのつかいかた)

● **Japanese verb for "putting on," "taking off," or "wear"**

Several different verbs are used in Japanese, depending on which part of the body you are dressing or undressing.

| 着る | ⇨to wear something on the upper half (above the waist) or the whole of your body.

1．あの黒いオーバーを着ている人は中村さんですか。
   (Is the person in the black overcoat Nakamura san?)
2．北川さんはきれいなセーターを着ていますね。
   (Kitagawa san, you are wearing a beautiful sweater.)

| はく | ⇨lower half of your body

1．そんな汚い靴下ははかないでください。
   (Don't put on such dirty socks!)
2．佐藤さんはいつもスカートをはかないで，ジーンズをはいています。
   (Sato san never wears a skirt; she always wears jeans.)

| する | ⇨other small items and accessories

   ネクタイ，バンド (band)，ベルト (belt)，イヤリング (earring)，コンタクトレンズ

| かぶる | ⇨only hats and caps (帽子)

| かける | ⇨only glasses

The antonyms to the above verbs are as follows:
   着る，はく　　←→脱ぐ
   かぶる，する←→とる (in the case of ぼうし, 脱ぐ is acceptable.)
   かける　　　　←→はずす

● さあ，誰だろう　　1-4

For an explanation of さあ, see L. 7. 誰だろう is uttered like a monologue. For this reason, the more polite expression, 誰でしょう is not used here.

● 長い髪をする　　1-5

する here is used to describe the physical characteristics of a person.

Lesson 16

　　１．日本人はみんな黒い目をしていますか。
　　　　(Are the eyes of all Japanese dark?)
　　２．ハーディさんはバスケットボールの選手で、とてもいい体をしています。
　　　　(Hardy san is a basketball player and has a great body.)

● 楽しみにしている　　　2-4

This phrase meaning "to look forward to ～," follows a noun in a sentence. When a whole sentence is used as an object in this pattern, the nominalizer の must precede the object marker を.

　　１．私は春休みを楽しみにしています。
　　　　(I am looking forward to spring break.)
　　２．私は春休みに友達が遊びに来るのを楽しみにしています。
　　　　(I am looking forward to my friend coming to visit me during spring break.)

● どういう　　　3-5

This is basically the same as どんな that we studied in the first part of this lesson. This series is also used as a noun modifier to mean "this kind of," "that kind of," etc. In most cases, both series are interchangeable, but occasionally, こんな, そんな, and あんな may imply an unfavorable attitude on the part of the speaker; こういう, そういう, and ああいう are objective expressions, and are free of negative nuances.

　　１．こんな車には乗りませんよ。
　　　　(I won't drive this kind of car. — This car might be unsuitably fancy or too out of shape, and so on.)
　　２．こういう車には乗りませんよ。
　　　　(I won't drive this kind of car. — The speaker simply states a fact about what kind of car he would not drive.)

● 中年以上の人　　　3-6

～以上 means "more than ～," (including ～). The opposite is 以下.
　　中年というのは何才以上ですか。(Above what age is "middle age?")
　　この映画は十八才以下の人にはよくありません。
　　　　(This movie is not good for those younger than eighteen.)

● 改まった　　　3-8

This is used as a noun modifier, and means "formal." The opposite is くだけた.
　　あの人はいつも改まった話し方をしますね。
　　　　(That person always speaks formally.)
　　昨日のパーティーはとてもくだけたおもしろいパーティーでした。
　　　　(Yesterday's party was a very casual and enjoyable one.)

練習 (れんしゅう)

練習 (れんしゅう) 1　　　　いらっしゃる／おっしゃる

例　中村先生が来ました。⇨中村先生がいらっしゃいました。(Nakamura sensei has come.)
　　中村先生は行かないと言いました。
　　　　⇨中村先生はいらっしゃらないとおっしゃいました。
　　　　　(Nakamura sensei said that he won't go.)

1．中村先生はいませんでした。　　　　2．中村先生はそう言いました。
3．中村先生は明日行きません。　　　　4．中村先生はそう言うでしょう。
5．中村先生は行かないと言いました。　6．中村先生は明日来ないと言いました。
7．中村先生は部屋にいません。　　　　8．中村先生はどこにもいませんでした。

練習 (れんしゅう) 2　　　　着る，はく，する，かける

例　背広　　⇨東山さんは背広を着ています。
　　　　　　(Higashiyama san is wearing a suit.)
　　イヤリング　⇨東山さんはイヤリングをしています。
　　　　　　(Higashiyama san is wearing earrings.)

1．セーター　2．靴下　3．眼鏡　4．ドレス　5．ジーンズ　6．オーバー

練習 (れんしゅう) 3　　　　着る，する，はく，かける

例　中村さん，ひげ　⇨中村さんはひげをはやした人です。
　　　　　　(Nakamura san is the person with the beard.)
　　東山さん，ドレス　⇨東山さんはドレスを着た人です。
　　　　　　(Higashiyama san is the person wearing the dress.)

1．北川さん，ジーンズ　　2．佐藤さん，眼鏡　　3．秋山さん，短い髪
4．ハーディさん，運動靴　5．東山さん，ネクタイ　6．中村さん，背広

練習 (れんしゅう) 4　　　　Indirect quotation

例　大学院生です。⇨中村さんは，あの人は大学院生だと言いました。
　　　　　　(Nakamura san said that that person is a graduate student.)

1．大学院生でしょう。　2．大学院生でした。　3．頭がいいです。
4．目が青くありません。　5．何でも食べます。　6．何も食べません。

Lesson 16

| 練習(れんしゅう)　5 | Indirect quotation |

例　大学院生ですか。⇨中村さんは，あの人に大学院生かと聞きました。
(Nakamura san asked that person if he is a graduate student.)

1．遊びに来ませんか。　　2．大学院生でしたか。　　3．この大学はいいですか。
4．いい図書館がありませんか。　5．何でも食べますか。　6．何も食べませんか。

| 練習(れんしゅう)　6 | N1 は N2 が Pred. |

例　この大学の図書館はいいです。⇨この大学は図書館がいいですね。
(The library at this university is good. ⇨ Speaking of this university, the library is good.)

1．中村先生の説明はわかりやすいです。　　2．佐藤さんの目は黒いです。
3．北川さんの背は高いです。　　　　　　4．東山さんの体は大きいです。
5．リンさんの目は青いです。　　　　　　6．この机の引き出しは大きいです。
7．この辞書の説明はわかりにくいです。　　8．この大学の図書館はいいです。

| 練習(れんしゅう)　7 | Plain volitional |

例　手紙を書く　⇨私は手紙を書こうと思います。(I think I will write a letter.)
　　映画を見る　⇨私は映画を見ようと思います。(I think I will see the movie.)

1．加藤さんに会う　　2．日本語で話す　　3．この本を全部読む
4．ビールを飲む　　　5．ここで泳ぐ　　　6．新しい背広を買う
7．先生に質問する　　8．食べてみる　　　9．明日は歩いて来る
10．前に買った本を読み直す　11．今日は遅く寝る

| 練習(れんしゅう)　8 | Volitional＋と思う |

例　ネクタイをして行く　⇨私はネクタイをして行こうと思っています。
(I plan to wear a tie [to the occasion].)

1．ひげをはやす　　2．眼鏡をかける　　3．ドレスを着て行く
4．先生に質問する　5．部屋の掃除をする　6．自転車に乗って来る

十六課

| 練習(れんしゅう)　9 | Pl. Past＋ことはない |

例　着物を着る　⇨私は着物を着たことはありません。
　　　　　　　　　(I have never worn a *kimono*.)

1．日本語を教える　2．英語を習う　3．ハイヒールをはく　4．中村さんに会う
5．先生に質問する　6．結婚式に行く　7．テニスをする　　8．車の運転をする

| 練習(れんしゅう)　10 | Pl. Past＋ことがある |

例　着物を着る　⇨私は子供の時，着物を着たことがあります。
　　　　　　　　　(I had occasion to wear a *kimono* as a child.)

1．日本語で話す　2．英語を習う　3．ハイヒールをはく　4．中村さんに会う
5．先生に質問する　6．結婚式に行く　7．テニスをする　　8．車の運転をする

| 練習(れんしゅう)　11 | NP を楽しみにしている |

例　夏休み　　⇨私は夏休みを楽しみにしています。
　　　　　　　　(I am looking forward to the summer holidays.)
　　東京へ行く　⇨私は東京へ行くのを楽しみにしています。
　　　　　　　　(I am looking forward to going to Tokyo.)

1．春休み　　　　　2．感謝祭　　　　　3．学期末試験
4．友達の結婚式　　5．明日のパーティー　6．友達が遊びに来る
7．春休みに家へ帰る　8．新しいことを習う

| 練習(れんしゅう)　12 | 一＋counter もない |

例　着物は持っていません。(I don't have *kimono*s.)
　　⇨着物は一枚も持っていません。(I don't have a single *kimono*.)

1．日本語の辞書はありません。
2．人類学の学生はいません。
3．ビールは買いませんでした。
4．授業は休みません。　　　　　　(一日)
5．日本へは行ったことはありません。(一回)
6．じゃがいもは使いません。　　　　(ひとつ)

Lesson 16

練習(れんしゅう)　13 　　　　　S1 し（それに）S2

例　今日は天気が悪い，寒い　⇨今日は天気が悪いし，それに寒いんです。
(Today the weather is bad, and on top of that, it's cold.)

1．あの人は病気だ，仕事がない
2．加藤さんの奥さんは静かだ，頭がいい
3．この漢字は難しい，調べ方もわからない
4．この説明はつまらない，簡単すぎる
5．この教科書は漢字が多すぎる，説明が長すぎる
6．今日は雨が降っている，とても寒い
7．この町は寂しい，嫌いだ

練習(れんしゅう)　14 　　　　　S ために

例　のんびりする，着物を着る　⇨のんびりするために着物を着ます。
(I wear a *kimono* to relax.)

1．御飯を食べる，お箸を使う　　　2．結婚する，料理を習う
3．料理を習う，学校へ行く　　　　4．運転を覚える，車の本を買う
5．大学へ行く，近道を通る　　　　6．手紙を書く，万年筆を使う

十七課

内容表

文法	Causes, Reasons		から，ので，て，んです
	Selective Questions		S1 か S2 か
	Expressing Duty		〜なければならない
	Omission of Particles		は，が，を
	て-form＋もらう		Having s.b. do a favor
	S1 のに，S2		作り方はやさしいのにおいしい
	お＋stem＋する (Humble)		お待たせする
	Conjunctional Words		それが，それで，それと
機能	Apologizing	4-1	すみません，お待たせして。
	Inquiring About Preference	3-11	コーヒー／紅茶がいいですか。
	Stating Preference	3-10	紅茶，いただきます。
			コーヒー，お願いします。
			要りません。
	Reason for Action / Non-Action	2-41	ダイエットをしているので
	Extending an Invitation / Offer	2-5	
	(1)		どうぞ
	(2)		是非，〜てください
	(3)		〜がいいですか
	Telling Secrets	6-25	実は
	Expressing Concern	6-21	あなたのこと，心配していたんですよ。
	Justifying / Presenting Excuses	2-52	止まっていたし，遠くて見えなかった。
			論文の準備で忙しくて
	Inviting Others to Perform	5-12	是非，読んでみてください。
	Expressing Compliments	6-19	おいしそう，おいしい
	Expressing Surprise	3-8	作り方はやさしいのに味がいい。
	Remembering	2-37	あ，そうだ

Lesson 17

会話 (かいわ)

1

A：すみません。お待たせして。

B：どうしたんですか。何かあったんですか。あなたのこと，心配していたんですよ。

A：ええ，途中で，交通事故があって，それで…。

B：どんな事故だったんですか。

A：それが自動車がずっと止まっていたし，遠くて見えなかったんですよ。

2

A：西川さん，この本読みました？

B：この頃，小説はほとんど読んでいないんですよ，論文の準備で忙しくて。

A：ああ，大変でしょう。私も久しぶりに読んだんですけど，とてもいい小説ですから，是非読んでみてください。

B：じゃ，借りてもいいですか。［ええ，どうぞ。］週末にでも，読んでみましょう。

A：ええ。きっと気に入ると思いますよ。

3

A：コーヒーがいいですか，紅茶がいいですか。それとも，緑茶がいいですか。

B：そうですね。紅茶，いただきます。［はい。］あ，そうだ，今晩遅くまで勉強しなければならないので，コーヒー，お願いします。

A：お砂糖やミルクは入れますか。

B：ダイエットをしているので，要りません。

1

A: I'm sorry to have kept you waiting.

B: What's wrong? Did something happen? We were worried about you.

A: Yes. On the way there was a traffic accident and ...

B: What kind of accident was it?

A: Well, I couldn't see it because the cars were stopped all the way, and it was too far in the distance.

2

A: Nishikawa san, have you read this book?

B: Lately I have hardly read any novels — I've been busy with preparations for my thesis.

A: Oh, what a chore that is! I haven't read anything in a while either, but since this is a very good novel, you should, by all means, try reading it.

B: Then, may I borrow it? [Why, certainly.] I'll try reading it, perhaps, during the weekend.

A: Yes. I think you'd probably like it.

3

A: Would you like coffee or black tea? Or would you like green tea?

B: Let me see. I'll have some black tea, please. [Certainly.] Oh yes, I would like some coffee, please, since I must study until late tonight.

A: Would you like sugar and milk?

B: Since I'm on a diet, I don't need any.

Lesson 17

4

A：これ，新(あたら)しい作り方で作ったケーキなんですよ。召(め)し上(あ)がってみてください。

B：おいしそうなケーキですねえ。

A：ええ，とてもおいしいですから，食べてみてください。

B：いただきます。[どうですか。]おいしいですねえ。

A：そうでしょう。実(じつ)は北村(きたむら)さんの奥(おく)さんに教(おし)えてもらったんですよ。

B：そうですか。じゃ，私にも教えてくれません？

A：ええ，いいですよ。作り方はとてもやさしいのに，とても味(あじ)がいいんですよ。

単語表 (たんごひょう)

1

待(ま)たせる	make s.b. wait II
あなた	☞ことばの使い方
心配(しんぱい)する	worry, be concerned
途中(とちゅう)	middle, in the midst of
交通事故(こうつうじこ)	traffic accident
それで／それが	☞ことばの使い方
自動車(じどうしゃ)	automobile, car
ずっと	all the way, all through the time
止(と)まる	stop
遠(とお)い	far, distant
見(み)える	can see

2

西川(にしかわ)	a surname
この頃(ごろ)	lately, recently
論文(ろんぶん)	thesis, dissertation
準備(じゅんび)	preparation
久(ひさ)しぶり	after a long time, a long time since …
是非(ぜひ)	by all means
借(か)りる	borrow, rent II

3

紅茶(こうちゃ)	black tea
それとも	☞ことばの使い方
緑茶(りょくちゃ)	green tea
いただく	receive, take ⬇
お砂糖(さとう)	sugar
ミルク	milk
入(い)れる	pour, put in

4

A：This is a cake I made with a new recipe. Please have some.

B：It looks delicious.

A：Yes, it's very good, so please have a bite.

B：I will. [How is it?] It's good!

A：Isn't it? To tell you the truth, I had Mrs. Kitamura teach me.

B：I see. Won't you please teach me, too?

A：Yes, certainly. It's very easy to make, but it tastes very good.

4

召し上がる(めしあがる)	☞ことばの使い方	北村(きたむら)	a surname
おいしそうだ	look delicious, seem tasty	もらう	receive て＋もらう ☞文法
実(じつ)は	☞ことばの使い方	味(あじ)	taste

関連語句 (かんれんごく)

病院(びょういん)	hospital	元気(げんき)だ	be healthy / be fine
火事(かじ)	fire	オーブン	oven
白(しろ)い	white	黒(くろ)い	black
青(あお)い	blue	緑色(みどりいろ)	green
茶色(ちゃいろ)	brown	灰色(はいいろ)	gray (lit. ash color)

Lesson 17

文法 (ぶんぽう)

● **Giving Reasons**

In response to a statement like "昨日来なかったですね," you can give any of the following answers to explain "why you could not come."

　　1．友達が来たから，来られませんでした。
　　2．友達が来たので，来られませんでした。
　　3．友達が来たんです。
　　4．友達が来て，（それで）来られませんでした。
　　5．友達が来ました。だから，来られませんでした。

Of these, the first sentence hardly has an apologetic tone. The fourth sentence combines the two expressions loosely to make a cause-effect impression.

Note that the agents in the causal clause are marked by "が" when the agents in S1 and S2 are different.

● **Selective Questions**　　3-1

A selective question is one in which you ask the listener to make a choice from two or more possibilities: "Do you like A or B?" In Japanese this is expressed as "S1? S2?" If you find it necessary to insert a word, use それとも ("or") before the second sentence. In answering, you would probably choose one of the given options.

　　1．映画を見に行きましょうか，それとも家でのんびりしましょうか。
　　　　(Shall we go to see a movie or stay at home and relax?)
　　2．コーヒーがいいですか，お茶がいいですか。
　　　　(Would you care for coffee or tea?)

To make these questions indirect quotations, simply use plain endings.

　　コーヒーがいいか，紅茶がいいか聞きました。
　　　　(I asked if he/she'd like coffee or tea.)

● **勉強しなければならない**　　3-2

| Pre-ない-form ＋ なければならない |　⇨　must, ought to, should

The meaning implied by this pattern is that you are doing something out of your own sense of commitment and obligation, and not out of pressure from some outside source.

　　今日，子供が生まれるので，病院へ行かなければならないんですよ。
　　　　(I have to go to the hospital since my baby is going to be born today.)

● **コーヒー，お願いします (Omission of particles)**　　3-3

There are some particles that are often dropped when the sentence can be clearly understood without them. Those which can be omitted are は, が, を and occasionally に and へ (the latter two can be deleted only if motion verbs are used in the sentences). These particles, however, are not dropped in writing unless they appear in a casual letter between friends. (☞L. 11 文法「文房具です」)

　　1．私（は），明日東京（へ or に）行きます。

2．さっき加藤さん(が)来ましたよ。
3．コーヒー(を)お願いします。

● 読んだんですけど　　2-3

けど is a conjunction derived from けれども, which means "but" or "though." The derivation can be traced back to けれども⇨けれど⇨けど. This is also the order of formality it conveys, from the most to the least formal. This is usually used as a sentence connector (S1 け〔れ〕ど〔も〕S2), but sometimes it is used at the beginning of a sentence to introduce a statement opposing a view given in a preceding sentence.

1．今日は寒いですけど，いい天気ですね。
　　(It's cold today, but the weather is nice.)
2．A：奥さん，お元気ですか。
　　B：ええ。おかげさまで。けど，子供が病気で…。
　　(A：Is your wife well?)
　　(B：Yes. She is fine, thank you. But my child is ill ....)

● おいしそう(なケーキ)ですね　　4-2

おいしい is an adjective that means "delicious" and おいしそう is a な-adj. meaning "look delicious." (We will study this more in detail in L. 27.)

おいしい　　　　　　⇨おいし—そう
　　　　　　　　Exception：いい→よさそう，ない→なさそう
簡単だ　　　　　　　⇨簡単—そう
雨が降ります　　　　⇨雨が降りそうです。

This pattern is often used to convey a manifest description of a condition that, in all appearance, seems to show how a person is feeling, his/her physical condition or his/her needs. In Japanese, as seen in L. 11「欲しい」you cannot describe the feelings, physical conditions and desires of a third person as you can your own. In order to talk about these elements in a third person, you must resort to giving a description of his/her appearance, or showing what you surmise based on how he/she looks, behaves, and acts.

○　私はちょっと寒いです。　　(I feel a little chilly.)
○　あなたは寒いですか。　　(Do you feel chilly?)
×　あなたは寒いです。　　(You feel chilly.)
×　あの人はちょっと寒いです。　　(That person feels chilly.)
○　あの人はちょっと寒そうです。(He looks to be feeling chilly.)
　　　　　　　　　　　　　　　　(He seems cold.)
○　私は友達が欲しいです。　　(I want to have friends.)
×　彼は友達が欲しいです。　　(He wants friends.)
○　彼は友達が欲しそうです。　(It appears that he wants friends.)

Note that the sentence with あの人 or 彼 in both groups will become acceptable if you change the ending to んです, which makes the whole sentence your explanation.

● 教えてもらった　　4-5

1．私は北村さんの奥さんにケーキの作り方を教えてもらいました。
　　R.　　　　　　　G.
2．北村さんの奥さんは(私に)ケーキの作り方を教えてくれました。
　　G.　　　　　　　R.

Lesson 17

Both sentences indicate that the "I" (私) has received a favor from "Mrs. Kitamura's instruction." 私 is the recipient; the giver of the favor is Mrs. Kitamura. The difference between the two is that the first one shows what "I" did, the second one defines what Mrs. Kitamura did. In other words, attention is placed on the recipient in the first case, while it is focused on the giver in the second sentence. The restrictions on the giver and the recipient mark another difference between these sentences. In the first sentence pattern, the <u>giver</u> cannot be "I" or "someone closer to me" than the recipient. In the second sentence pattern, the <u>recipient</u> has to be "I" or "someone closer to me" than the giver.

● 作り方はやさしいのに、とても味がいい   4-7

S1 のに S2   ⇨   Although S1, (to the speaker's surprise), S2.

S1 ends with a plain form. The exception is (like の／んです、ので、) that だ has to be changed to な. This pattern expresses the speaker's surprise, and therefore, contains an emotional tone; it is usually not used in ordinary writing, though it appears frequently in conversation.

1. 彼はスポーツは何もしないのに、いろいろなことをよく知っています。
   (Although he does not play any sports, he knows very well about them.)
2. これは昨日習ったのに、もう忘れてしまいました。
   (Though I learned this yesterday, I have already forgotten it!)
3. 母がたばこをやめたのに、父はまだすっています。
   (or 父は、母がたばこをやめたのに、まだすっています。)
   (My father is still smoking, though my mother has quit!)

ことばの使い方 (ことばのつかいかた)

● お待たせして   1-1

お＋V stem＋する   ☞L. 15 文法「お返しします」

The verb 待たせる is derived from 待つ; it means "to have someone wait" or "to make someone wait," which we will study in the last lesson.

● あなた   1-2

The usage of あなた, meaning "you," is much more restricted and limited than the English "you." It is more often used by women than by men. Wives often use this word to call their husbands, while husbands call their wives by their names.

For future reference, here are a few other words which are used for second person reference:

君　—Used by men to address people of the same or lower social level than themselves. Not suitable for use in reference to superiors. Rather formal.

お宅—Used mostly business people to mean "you" or "your company." The original meaning of this word is "your house," and it is still used in this sense occasionally, not necessarily restricted to people in business.

お前—Used only between very close male friends in informal situations. Some people may consider it vulgar. The use of this word is not recommended.

As you can see from the explanations, not one of the usages of these words is free of restrictions. The best way to address a person, after all, is his/her name followed by 〜さん or his/her title.

● 交通事故があって　　1-3

We have already learned a couple of usages of this verb:

1．机の上に黄色い封筒がありますか。

(Is there a yellow envelope on the desk?)

2．私には兄が三人と姉が一人と妹が一人あります。

(I have three elder brothers, an elder sister, and a younger sister.)

In this lesson, ある means "happen," "take place," or "break out." The particle in this case is not に but で.

昨日の夜，家の近くで火事がありました。

(There was a fire near my house last night.)

来週の月曜日に，この教室で試験があります。

(An examination will be held next Monday in this classroom.)

● それで　　1-3

This is a conjunctive expression which describes temporal consequence, and means "and" or "and then." There is another それで which is made up of a demonstrative それ＋で ("by means of"), and together its meaning is "because of that," or "with that." In this dialogue, both interpretations work.

● それが　　1-5

This is also a conjunctive expression which indicates that the sentence which follows is quite different from what would be expected.

A：明日，結婚式ですね。　(Your wedding is tomorrow, isn't it?)
B：それが，やめたんですよ。(Well, I gave it up.)

● この頃　　2-2

This is read as「このごろ」, and means: "these days" or "recently."

1．この頃，西川さん，大学にいますか。全然見ませんね。

(Has Nishikawa san been at school lately? I haven't seen him at all.)

2．この頃の若い学生はよく勉強しますね。

(Young students these days study hard, don't they?)

● 是非　　2-4

This means "definitely" and is usually followed by a request or an expression of desire.

北村さんておもしろい人ですから，是非一度会ってくださいよ。

(Since Kitamura san is a very interesting person, by all means, please meet him.)

● 週末にでも　　2-5

This でも indicates that the preceding word or expression is one item or one example that can be chosen from a number of possibilities.

Lesson 17

1．ジュースでも，あげましょうか。
　　(Shall I give you, say, some juice?)
2．退屈(たいくつ)だから，テレビでも見ませんか。
　　(It's so boring. Shall we, perhaps, watch some TV?)

The particles が，は，を must be replaced by でも. Other particles, such as に, must be retained.

● 気に入る　　2-6

The complete pattern using this expression is "N が気に入る," and the phrase means that the noun (N) is appealing to the speaker and he/she comes to like it.

1．私はこの小説がとても気に入りました。
　　(This novel is very appealing to me. — I like this novel very much.)
2．あの人の話し方は，私は気に入りません。
　　(His manner of speech is not appealing to me. — I don't like the way he talks.)

● それとも　　3-1

This is a conjunction used to cite alternatives, and is very often dropped.

お昼(ひる)は何(なに)がいいですか。御飯(ごはん)がいいですか。(それとも)おそばがいいですか。
　　(What is good for lunch? Rice, or buck-wheat noodles?)
行くんですか，(それとも)行かないんですか。(Are you going or not?)

● お願いします　　3-3

This expression is used when you want something, or more generally, when you want someone to do something for you. The phrase can be used, for instance to draw the attention of a teller at a bank or a clerk at a post office.

ビールとこれ，お願いします。
　　(Beer and this, please. —[at a restaurant.])

● 召し上がる　　4-1

This is the honorific form of 食べる，飲む.

● いただきます　　4-4 / 3-2

This is a common greeting used when you eat or drink something that is offered to you. Even in the relaxed atmosphere of a family meal, each person usually says this before beginning to eat. If somebody says いただきます to you, greet that person back with どうぞ.

● 実は　　4-5

実は, roughly translatable as "the fact is ...," is a conjunctive expression which implies that what follows is something that you, as speaker, find difficult to put into words for psychological, emotional, or other reasons. In this dialogue, the speaker thinks that the praise should go not to herself but to Mrs. Kitamura. She is correcting her friend's assessment. This is why she hesitates to be assertive, and resorts to using the conjunctive phrase to preface the "truth" which she is about to reveal. When you make a request that might cause trouble or inconvenience someone, this is a helpful expression.

西川さん，実はちょっとお願いがあるんですが…。
　　(Nishikawa san, I have a little favor to ask of you.)

● **Names of Colors**

Some representative colors are as follows:

1. 黒い　　　(black)　　　白い　　　(white)
   赤い　　　(red)　　　　青い　　　(blue)
   黄色い　　(yellow)

2. 茶色　　　(brown)　　　緑色　　　(green)
   灰色　　　(gray)　　　　紫色　　　(purple)
   水色　　　(light blue)　桃色　　　(pink)

The words in the first group are い-adjs., whereas those in the second group are nouns. It is, therefore, necessary to add の in order to use the words in the second group as modifiers.

　　赤いセーター　　(red sweater)　　　茶色のセーター　　(brown sweater)
　　青いセーター　　(blue sweater)　　　紫色のセーター　　(purple sweater)

練習 (れんしゅう)

練習(れんしゅう) 1	～て／～ないで、すみません

例　お待たせする　⇨すみません、お待たせして。(Sorry to keep you waiting.)

1．遅れる　　　　　　2．何も持って来ない　　　3．この本を二週間もお借りする
4．名前を忘れてしまう　5．電気をつけておかない　6．よく話を聞いていない
7．わからない　　　　　8．ネクタイをして来ない　9．汚い靴をはいて来る

練習(れんしゅう) 2	S1 て、それで S2

例　日本語を勉強する、日本へ行く
　　⇨あの人は日本語を勉強して、それで日本へ行ったんですよ。
　　(That person studied Japanese, and then, went to Japan.)

1．授業に遅れる、家へ帰ってしまう
2．交通事故がある、電話をする
3．家へ帰らない、友達の家へ行く
4．御飯を食べに行く、今の奥さんに会う
5．友達にケーキの作り方を教えてもらう、今日作る
6．朝の三時まで小説を読んでいる、授業に来られない

Lesson 17

練習(れんしゅう)　3	それが

例　あの映画はどうでしたか。(How was that movie?)
　　　（行かない）　⇨それが，行かなかったんですよ。(The thing is, I didn't go.)

1．ダイエットはどうですか。　　　　　（やめてしまう）
2．昨日のパーティは大変でしたか。　　（誰も来ない）
3．ケーキの味はどうでしたか。　　　　（オーブンがこわれてしまう）
4．北村さんに教えてもらいましたか。　（いらっしゃらない）
5．休みにはのんびりしましたか。　　　（とても忙しい）
6．ダイエットをしてやせましたか。　　（太る）

練習(れんしゅう)　4	S1，それともS2

例　右へ行く，左へ行く　⇨右へ行きましょうか，それとも，左へ行きましょうか。
　　　　　　　　　　　　(Shall we go to the right, or shall we go to the left?)

1．テレビを見る，遊びに行く　　　　　2．背広を着て行く，セーターを着て行く
3．辞書を引く，西川さんに聞く　　　　4．図書館で借りる，本屋で買う
5．御飯の前に食べる，御飯の後で食べる　6．これを聞いてみる，それを聞いてみる

練習(れんしゅう)　5	～なければならない

例　今晩，遅くまで勉強する　⇨今晩，遅くまで勉強しなければならないんですよ。
　　　　　　　　　　　　　　　(I must study until late tonight.)

1．明日の朝早く起きる　　　　　　2．週に二十マイル走る
3．八時二十分に教室に行く　　　　4．毎日，自分で料理する
5．毎日，朝御飯を作る　　　　　　6．八時間くらい寝る
7．授業の後，すぐ家へ帰る　　　　8．家へ帰って，掃除をする

練習(れんしゅう)　6	～なければならないので

例　今晩，遅くまで勉強する
　　⇨今晩，遅くまで勉強しなければならないので，大変なんですよ。
　　　　(It's really a hassle because I have to study until late tonight.)

1．明日の朝早く起きる　　　　　　2．週に二十マイル走る
3．八時二十分に教室に行く　　　　4．毎日，自分で料理する
5．毎日，朝御飯を作る　　　　　　6．八時間くらい寝る
7．授業のあと，すぐ家へ帰る　　　8．家へ帰って，掃除をする

十七課

練習（れんしゅう） 7	～ぶりに

例　田中さんに会った。（五年）　⇨五年ぶりに田中さんに会いました。
（I met Tanaka san for the first time in five years.）

映画を見に行った。（久しい）
　　⇨久しぶりに映画を見に行きました。
（I went to see a movie for the first time in a long while.）

1．お風呂に入った　（一週間）　　2．日本料理を食べた　　（半年）
3．日本へ行ってきた（三年）　　　4．ダイエットをやめた　（二か月）
5．小説を読んだ　（久しい）　　　6．西川さんに手紙を出した（一か月）

練習（れんしゅう） 8	S1 けど，S2

例　西川さんの御主人は来ました。奥さんは来ませんでした。
　　⇨西川さんの御主人は来ましたけど，奥さんは来ませんでした。
（Mr. Nishikawa came, but his wife did not.）

1．父は忙しいです。母はのんびりしています。
2．私はコーヒーが好きです。家内は紅茶が好きです。
3．兄はおもしろいと言いました。姉はつまらないと言いました。
4．弟は行くと思います。妹は行かないと思います。
5．加藤さんのお父さんはいらっしゃいます。お母さんはいらっしゃいません。
6．加藤さんのお父さんは背が高くありません。お母さんは高いです。

練習（れんしゅう） 9	S1 から是非～てください

例　いい小説，読む　⇨とてもいい小説ですから，是非読んでみてください。
（Since it's a very good novel, by all means please read it.）

1．おいしい料理，食べる　　2．おもしろい歌，聞く　　3．楽しい人，会う
4．いい所，行く　　　　　　5．いい自転車，乗る　　　6．いい人，電話する

練習（れんしゅう） 10	～でも

例　ジュースを飲む　⇨ジュースでも，飲みませんか。
（Shall we have some juice or something?）
　　映画に行く　　　⇨映画にでも行きませんか。
（Shall we go to the movies or something?）

1．レコードを聞く　　　2．西川さんに聞く　　　3．図書館で新聞を読む
4．小説を書く　　　　　5．北村さんに電話する　6．木村さんに教えてもらう

Lesson 17

練習(れんしゅう) 11　　　　い-adj.＋そうです

例　これ，おいしい　⇨これは，おいしそうですね。(This looks delicious.)

1．あの人，楽しい　　　　2．あの人，寂しい　　　　3．この本，おもしろい
4．その本，つまらない　　5．あの人，頭がいい　　　6．あの人，背が低い
7．このドレス，高い　　　8．あの人，忙しい　　　　9．これ，おいしい

練習(れんしゅう) 12　　　　～てもらう

例　加藤さんが英語を教えてくれました。
　　　⇨加藤さんに英語を教えてもらいました。(I had Kato san teach me English.)

1．加藤さんが漢字を調べてくれました。　　2．加藤さんが小説を貸してくれました。
3．加藤さんが本を借りてくれました。　　　4．加藤さんが手紙を読んでくれました。
5．加藤さんが結婚式に来てくれました。　　6．加藤さんが電話してくれました。

練習(れんしゅう) 13　　　　S1のに，S2

例　習った，覚えていない　⇨習ったのに，覚えていないんですか。
　　　　　　　　　　　　　　(You don't remember it although you learned it?)
　　勉強した，忘れた　　　⇨勉強したのに，忘れたんですか。
　　　　　　　　　　　　　　(Did you forget it even though you studied it?)

1．高かった，よくなかった　　　　　　　2．安かった，よかった
3．さっきここにいた，今いない　　　　　4．学生だ，キャデラックに乗っている
5．意味がわかる，読み方がわからない　　6．今日は試験だ，勉強して来なかった

練習(れんしゅう) 14　　　　色の名前

例　この赤いセーターは，誰のですか。(緑色)
　　　⇨この緑色のセーターは，誰のですか。(Whose is this green sweater?)

1．白い　　　　　2．灰色　　　　　3．黒い　　　　　4．茶色
5．青い　　　　　6．紫色　　　　　7．黄色い　　　　8．緑色

練習(れんしゅう) 15　　　　色の名前／着る，はく，する

例　緑色，セーター　⇨あの緑色のセーターを着た人は誰ですか。
　　　　　　　　　　　(Who is that person in the green sweater?)

1．白い，ズボン　　　　2．灰色，スカート　　　　3．赤い，帽子
4．紫色，シャツ　　　　5．黄色い，ネクタイ　　　6．茶色，オーバー

十八課

内容表

文法	S1 と S2		運動するとのどがかわく
	Spontaneous Change		な／い-adj., N＋なる
	V (perfect)＋ばかりだ		買い物をしたばかりです
	CL たら, CL		頭が疲れたら
	S ことにしている		寝ることにしている
	CL ば, CL		調べれば, わかりますよ。
	CL ば, いい		調べればいいんですよ。
	S って		東京へ行くんだって。
	もし, S なら		もし, 行くなら
	できる		何かできること
	もっと＋Adj. / Adv.		もっとはっきり
	Tense of "Verbs of Change"		疲れる／疲れた
	こ／そ／あ／どうやって		どうやって調べたら
	そして		
機能	Stating Factual Information (Physical Conditions)	1-2	のどがかわく, 痛い, 疲れた おなかがすく。
	Stating Generalization	1-5	S1 と S2
	Inquiring About One's Health/Welfare	6-20	元気がないですね。
	Making Advice	5-4	S のがいい
	Declining an Invitation	2-6	いいえ, 結構です。
	Taking Leave	6-2	お大事に
	Disrespect, Insult, Ridicule	3-25	調べれば, わかるでしょう。 今すぐ行ってみたら, どうですか。
	Stating Hypothesis	1-4	もし, S なら はっきりしたら, 知らせます。
	Reporting Information	1-6	〜さんから, 聞いたんですけど
	Making Suggestions	5-1	私の家に行きましょうか。
	Expressing Sympathy	3-15	それは大変でしたね。疲れたでしょう。
	Criticism, Blame, Accusation	3-26	こんないい天気なのに寝てしまう

Lesson 18

会話 (かいわ)

1

A：ああ，のどがかわいた。

B：私も。運動するとのどがかわくわね。そして，次の日，体が痛くなるの。

C：僕は運動すると，非常におなかがすく。ああ，おなかがすいた。

B：じゃ，昨日買い物をしたばかりで，食べ物も飲み物もあるから，家に行きましょうか。

2

A：どうしたんですか。元気がないですね。

B：今，試験を二つ終えたところなんですよ。

A：それは大変でしたね。疲れたでしょう。頭が疲れたら運動するのがいいですよ。テニスでもしませんか。

B：いいえ，結構ですよ。私は疲れたら寝ることにしています。これから帰って，少し寝ます。

A：こんないい天気なのに寝てしまうんですか。もったいないですね。

B：でも，実は頭も痛いんですよ。

A：そうですか。それは，いけませんね。じゃ，お大事に。明日，授業で。

3

A：西川さん，これ，わかりますか。

B：どれですか。さあ，私にはわかりませんが，調べればわかるでしょう。

A：どうやって調べたらいいでしょうね。

B：図書館に行って，そして，いい参考書を探せばいいんですよ。

A：しかし，何ていう本を見たらいいんでしょうね。

B：図書館の人に聞けば，ちゃんとわかりますよ。今すぐ行ってみたらどうですか。

1

A：Oh, I'm thirsty!

B：Me, too. I always get thirsty when I exercise. And the next day, my body aches.

C：I get very hungry when I exercise. Oh, I'm hungry.

B：Then, let's go to my house, since I just shopped yesterday, and I have food and drinks.

2

A：What happened? You're not in high spirits.

B：I just now finished two examinations.

A：That must have been hard. You're tired, I guess. When your mind is exhausted, it's good to exercise. Why don't we play tennis or something?

B：No, thank you. I make it a rule to sleep whenever I'm tired. I'll go home now and take a little nap.

A：You're going to sleep when the weather is so nice?! What a waste!

B：But, to tell you the truth, I also have a headache.

A：I see. That's too bad. Please take care. See you tomorrow in class.

3

A：Nishikawa san, do you understand this?

B：Let me see it. Well ... I don't, but (I'm sure) you'll understand it if you look it up.

A：How (do you think) I should look it up?

B：Go to the library and look for good reference books; that should do it.

A：I wonder which book I should use.

B：You can find out precisely what to use if you ask a librarian. Why don't you go right away?

Lesson 18

4

A：南さん，西川さんから聞いたんだけど，東京へ行くんだって。

B：いいえ，まだはっきりわからないんですよ。

A：そうですか。もし行くなら，お願いしたいことがあるんだけど。

B：いいですよ。何かできることでしたら。もっとはっきりしたら，知らせますよ。

単語表 (たんごひょう)

1

のどがかわく	get thirsty (Lit. のど-throat, かわく-get dry)
S と S	☞文法
そして	and
次(つぎ)	next
痛(いた)い	hurting, painful
なる	become, get
非常(ひじょう)に	very, とても
おなかがすく	become hungry (Lit. おなか-stomach, すく-become empty)
食べ物(たべもの)	food

2

元気(げんき)がない	have no energy
終(お)える	finish (v.t.) II
頭(あたま)	brain, head
疲(つか)れる	get tired II
いいえ，結構(けっこう)です	No, thank you.
寝(ね)ることにしている	☞文法
もったいない	wasteful
いけません	no good
お大事(だいじ)に	take care

3

どうやって	how
探(さが)す	look for, search
しかし	but
ちゃんと	in the way it should be, proper way
今(いま)すぐ	right now

4

もし	if
できること	s.t. that one can do
もっと(はっきり)	more (clearly)
知(し)らせる	tell, inform II

4

A：Minami san, I heard from Nishikawa san that you're going to Tokyo. Is it true?

B：It's not definite yet.

A：I see. If you're going, I have something I would like you to do.

B：Surely, if it is something I can do. I'll let you know when my plans are more definite.

関連語句 (かんれんごく)

風邪(かぜ)をひく	catch cold	眠(ねむ)れる	can sleep Ⅲ
眠(ねむ)くなる	become sleepy	祖父(そふ)	grandfather
嬉(うれ)しい	be happy	渡(わた)す	pass, hand out
芝居(しばい)	drama, play	もう少(すこ)し	a little more

Lesson 18

文法 (ぶんぽう)

● 運動するとのどがかわく　　1-2

　|S1 と S2|

　This と connects two sentences and means: "Whenever S1, S2." or "If S1, then S2." S1 normally ends with a plain imperfect form except in polite conversation, in which case です, ます are used.

　This pattern indicates that S1 and S2 have a "cause and effect" or "antecedent and consequent relationship"; whenever S1 occurs, S2 follows immediately without so much as a pause. S2, therefore, cannot convey a request, a command, a volition, a desire, or a permission.

　　この頃, 仕事をすると, とても疲れるんです。
　　　(These days I get very tired whenever I work.)
　　私は日本へ行くと, いつも帝国ホテルに泊まります。
　　　(When I go to Japan, I always stay at the Imperial Hotel.)
　　風邪をひくと, いつものどが痛くなります。
　　　(Whenever I catch cold, I get a sore throat.)

　You can see from these examples that these sentences give general statements, like habitual actions, rather than describe particular events.

● 痛くなる　　1-2

　痛く is the adverbial form of the adjective 痛い, and なる means "to become" or "to enter a new phase." Note how adjectives and nouns are changed into adverbial forms, as shown below.

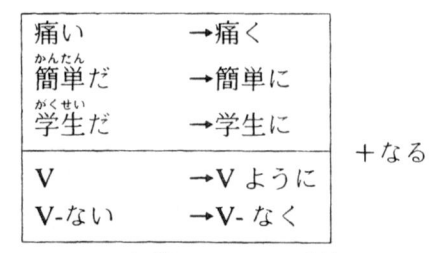

痛い	→痛く
簡単だ	→簡単に
学生だ	→学生に
V	→V ように
V-ない	→V- なく

＋なる

1. 四月になると, 暖かくなります。
　　(When April comes, it gets warm.)
2. 電子レンジを買ってから, 料理が簡単になりました。
　　(Since we bought a microwave oven, cooking has become easy.)
3. この頃, 子供が歩くようになりました。
　　(My child has started to walk recently.)
4. 日本語がわからなくなりました。
　　(I have become unable to understand Japanese——I am getting confused.)

● 買い物をしたばかりです　　1-4

　|V (perfect)＋ばかりだ|　⇨　have just done ~, did ~ quite recently

This pattern implies that the speaker feels almost no time has passed since the action expressed by the verb was completed. There is an overlap in meaning with this form and V（た）＋ところだ．(See L. 15, S＋ところだ). In the present pattern, the short time elapsing between the action and the utterance of the sentence is subjectively determined by the speaker. た＋ところだ, however, maintains a considerable degree of objectivity in expressing the time span between action and utterance.

1．A：長くお待たせしてしまいましたか。
　　B：いいえ。私も今来たばかりなんですよ。（○ところ）
　　　（A：Have I kept you waiting long?）
　　　（B：No. I just got here, too.）
2．A：何年くらいアメリカにいらっしゃるんですか。
　　B：三年前に来たばかりですよ。（×ところ）
　　　（A：How many years have you been in the States?）
　　　（B：I came here just three years ago.）

● 頭（あたま）が疲れたら　　2-3

For all practical purposes, we can say that this form is made by adding ら to a perfect form in both affirmative and negative.

学生です	→学生でした	→学生でしたら
学生だ	→学生だった	→学生だったら
行きます	→行きました	→行きましたら
行く	→行った	→行ったら
行かない	→行かなかった	→行かなかったら
寒い	→寒かった	→寒かったら

CL (Clause)1 たら, CL 2

This form expresses the speaker's idea or opinion, CL 2, which is dependent on the completion of the preceding clause, CL 1. In this pattern, CL 1 has to be well established before CL 2 takes place. (*cf.* In "S1 と S2," S1 and S2 are almost concurrent.)

The meaning portrayed by this pattern can generally be divided into two types: those in which the event, action, or state expressed in CL 1 has already taken place, and those in which they are yet to happen. In this lesson, we shall focus on the latter, the usage in which the agenda described in CL 1 has not yet taken place in reality, but is expressed in hypothetical form as if it has already been realized.

1．Uncertain future event, hypothesis:
　　寒かったら，窓を閉めてください。
　　　（If you feel cold, please close the window.）
　　今年日本へ行けたら，とても嬉しいんですが。
　　　（If I can go to Japan this year, I will be very happy.）
2．Future event that most certainly will be realized.
　　田中さんに会ったら，この本を渡してくれませんか。
　　　（If you see Tanaka san, won't you give this book to him?）
3．Giving or soliciting a suggestion or advice. CL 1 is a verbal clause and CL 2 is いい

Lesson 18

／どうですか. In conversation among friends, CL 2 can be dropped completely.

1．すぐ図書館へ行ったらどうですか。

(Why don't you go to the library right away? / How about going ~?)

2．A：どんな辞書を買ったらいいでしょうね。
　　B：この辞書を買ったらいいですよ。とても使いやすい辞書ですから。

(A：What kind of dictionary do you think I should buy?)
(B：You should buy this. It's very handy.)

● 寝ることにしています　　2-5

| V (plain form)＋ことにしている | ⇨ make ~ a rule, practice |

The pattern "V＋ことにする" that will be dealt with in L. 23, expresses the speaker's decision to do what the verb signifies. The て-form in ことにしています indicates that the state caused by a past event or action (in this case "the decision") still remains effective.

私は疲れたら寝ることにしています。

(I make it a rule to sleep whenever I feel tired.)

私はビールを飲んだらワインは飲まないことにしています。

(I have decided not to drink wine once I have beer.)

● こんないい天気なのに寝てしまうんですか　　2-7

こんな　　☞文法，L. 16「どんな」
のに　　　☞文法，L. 17「S1 のに S2」
て＋しまう　☞文法，L. 15「て＋しまう」

● 調べれば（ば-form）　　3-2

This form is created in the following way:

Group I verbs	Group II verbs	Group III verbs
会う ⇨会えば	起きる⇨起きれば	する ⇨すれば
書く ⇨書けば	見る ⇨見れば	来る ⇨来れば
話す ⇨話せば	寝る ⇨寝れば	
立つ ⇨立てば	食べる⇨食べれば	
死ぬ ⇨死ねば		
飲む ⇨飲めば		
終わる⇨終われば		
泳ぐ ⇨泳げば		
飛ぶ ⇨飛べば		

(Noun / な-adj.) だ／です		い-adj., Negative verb	
学生だ／です	⇨学生なら（ば）	寒い	⇨寒ければ
簡単だ／です	⇨簡単なら（ば）	行かない	⇨行かなければ

| CL 1　ば　CL 2 |

This pattern indicates that CL 1 makes CL 2 possible. Its usage can be separated into the following two types:

1．To explain the logic that CL 2 always happens whenever CL 1 takes place. This form describes natural phenomena, truth, and general "antecedent-consequent relationships," but not individual or unique events. CL 2, therefore, is never in the perfect tense. The matter described in CL 2 is not under the speaker's control. In this usage, ば may be replaced by と.

四月になれば，雪はなくなります。(When April comes, snow will disappear.)

調べれば，わかりますよ。(If you look it up, you'll understand.)

2. The second clause, CL 2, signifies the will, determination, evaluation, desire, etc. of the speaker. (Note that と cannot be used in these instances.)

忙しければ，明日でもいいですよ。

(If you are busy, tomorrow will be fine.)

時間があれば，今夜のパーティーに行くつもりです。

(I intend to go to the party tonight if I have time.)

● (いい参考書を)探せばいいんですよ　　　3-4

ば-form＋いいんです　⇨　all you have to do is ～, you had better only ～.

病気の時は，寝ていればいいんですよ。

(All you should do when you're sick, is lie in bed.)

● (東京へ行くんだ)って　　　4-1

This is a colloquial variant of the quotational と. It is used in the pattern "S＋って" which indicates that the speaker is quoting the speech of a third party. When it is directed as a question, with a rising intonation, it means："I hear that ～, but is it true?"

お父さん，お母さんが御飯ですって。

(Daddy, Mom says that dinner's ready.)

さっき，西川さんて人からお電話がありまして，今日少し遅くなりますって。

(A person named Nishikawa san called a while ago and said that he will be a little late today.)

● もし(行く)なら　　　4-3

もし gives emphasis to the fact that what follows is a hypothetical statement. It is used with たら, ば, と and 時. It is acceptable to drop もし in a hypothetical sentence. V＋なら constitutes a hypothesis.

(もし)日本へ行くなら，日本語を勉強した方がいいですよ。

(If you [plan to] go to Japan, you should study Japanese — before going.)

(もし)日本へ行ったら，日本語を勉強した方がいいですよ。

(If you are in Japan, you should study Japanese — in Japan.)

● (何か)できる(こと)　　　4-4

This verb is usually used with a noun or a nominalized phrase, and means "can." Note that the particle which marks the object is が, and not を.

1. A：英語を話すのは，難しいでしょう。

B：十年勉強したら，誰でもできますよ。

(A：Speaking English is difficult, isn't it?)

(B：Anybody can do it if they study it for ten years.)

2. 南さんはゴルフができますか。

(Can you [play] golf, Minami san?)

Lesson 18

- もっとはっきり　　　4-4

  | もっと＋Adj. / Adv. / V. | ⇒ to emphasize the degree or quantity of a thing / state indicated in the phrase.

  この背広(せびろ)がもっと安(やす)ければ，買(か)うんですが。
  (I would buy this suit, if it were more inexpensive.)
  もっと大(おお)きい声(こえ)で，もっとはっきり話してください。
  (Please speak louder and more clearly.)
  すみませんが，この紙(かみ)，もっとありませんか。
  (Excuse me, but do you have more of this paper?)

  The expression 'もう少し' which means "a little more" can be used in the same way as もっと.

  もう少しきれいに書いてくれませんか。これじゃ，目(め)が悪(わる)くなりますよ。
  (Would you please write a little more neatly? This will ruin my eyes.)

ことばの使い方 (ことばのつかいかた)

- のどがかわく／おなかがすく／疲れる　　　1-1

  The verbs in these expressions that describe various physical conditions are classified as verbs of change. In their dictionary forms, or ます-forms, they mean, "to **get** thirsty, hungry and tired," and not "**be** thirsty, hungry, and tired." To describe the latter — "I am thirsty, hungry, tired" — you must use the perfect form ました. ☞P. 59「困った」

  のどがかわきました。水(みず)を一杯(いっぱい)下さい。
  (I am thirsty. Give me a glass of water.)
  のどがとてもかわいた時はレモン・ジュースを飲むといいんですって。
  (I hear it is very good to drink lemon juice when you are very thirsty.)

- 結構です　　　2-5

  Use this expression to formally turn down an offer. Some people simply say 結構です without いいえ. Informally, you can say いいです.

  A：カリフォルニアのワインですが，飲みませんか。
  (This is California wine. Won't you have some?)
  B：車を運転しなければならないので，結構です。
  (No, thank you. I have to drive.)

- もったいない　　　2-7

  This is used often when someone has been wasteful. In this dialogue, the speaker feels that the hearer is wasting the sunny day.

- 頭も痛い　　　2-8

  This does not mean that the speaker physically has a headache as well as other kind of pain. Here in this dialogue, however, the speaker is tired and, moreover, he has a headache.

  あの人は，勉強もよくしますけど，頭もいいですよ。

(He studies hard but he is also smart.)

● それは、いけませんね　　2-9

On hearing (moderately) bad news, this phrase is used. If, on the contrary, you hear good news, (それは)よかったですね can be used as a response.

You may hear a mother prohibiting a child from doing something by saying いけません. Its original meaning is "no good."

● お大事に　　2-9

Use this expression when you are leaving someone who is ill or injured. It means "take care." Keep in mind that this usage in Japanese is much more limited than the English "take care."

● どうやって　　3-3

This is an interrogative phrase which questions the means by which to do a thing; that is, it asks about the order or procedure for accomplishing something: you can respond with こうやって、そうやって、ああやって. Don't confuse this with どう (L. 15「どう思いますか」) or どうして (L. 4).

　　学校までいつもどうやって来るんですか。
　　(How do you usually come to school?)
　　このケーキ、どうやって作ったか教えてくれませんか。
　　(Would you tell me how you made this cake?)

● そして　　3-4

This is originally そうして which literally means "(by) doing so"; in modern Japanese, it means "and" or "and then." It is similar in meaning to それから.

　　昨日は、デパートへ行って買い物をして、そして、芝居を見に行った。
　　(Yesterday I went to the department store, shopped, and went to see a play.)

● ちゃんと　　3-6

This is an adverb which means "in the way it should be," or "in the proper way." It is one of the most useful expressions for Japanese mothers when disciplining their children. When した is added to it, as in はっきりした, it is used as a noun modifier.

　1．太郎(boy's name)、遊ばないで、御飯をちゃんと食べて。
　　　(Taro, don't fool around. Eat your food properly.)
　2．A：あの人、どういう人ですか。変な人ですねえ。
　　　B：あの人の着ている物を見ると、そう思うんですけど、ちゃんとした人ですよ。
　　　(A：What kind of a person is he? Isn't he weird?)
　　　(B：If you look at his clothes, you may think so, but he is, in fact, a respectable man.)

Lesson 18

練習 (れんしゅう)

練習(れんしゅう) 1　　　　SとS

例　運動する，のどがかわく　⇨運動すると，のどがかわきますね。
　　　　　　　　　　　　(When I exercise, I get thirsty.)

1．運動する，体が痛くなる　　　　　　2．コーヒーを飲む，眠れなくなる
3．風邪をひく，のどが痛くなる　　　　4．車で行く，五分しかかからない
5．今，宿題をする，今晩遊びに行ける (can go)　6．アルバイトをする，疲れる
7．森さんに電話する，長く話してしまう　8．英語の芝居を見る，眠くなる

練習(れんしゅう) 2　　　　のどがかわく／おなかがすく

例　ケーキ　⇨おなかがすいたから，ケーキでも食べましょうか。
　　　　　　(Since I'm hungry, let's have cake or something.)
　　ジュース　⇨のどがかわいたから，ジュースでも飲みましょうか。
　　　　　　(Since I'm thirsty, let's have some juice or something.)

1．コーラ　2．チーズ　3．バナナ　4．水　5．サンドイッチ　6．紅茶

練習(れんしゅう) 3　　　　なる

例　今日は，寒い　⇨今日は寒くなりますよ。(It will get cold today.)

1．明日は暖かい　　　　2．この料理はおいしい　　　3．あの人は大学院生だ
4．家はきれいだ　　　　5．この辞書が欲しい　　　　6．日本語が嫌いだ

練習(れんしゅう) 4　　　　SとS～になる

例　運動する，体が痛い　⇨運動すると，体が痛くなりますか。
　　　　　　　　　　　(When you exercise, does your body ache?)

1．四月になる，暖かい　　　　　　　　2．今年，四年生だ，来年，大学院生だ
3．掃除をする，この家はきれいだ　　　4．二年生になる，この辞書が欲しい
5．日本語の授業を休む，日本語が嫌いだ　6．風邪をひく，頭が痛い
7．もう少し，塩(salt)を入れる，この料理はおいしい

練習（れんしゅう） 5　　　～たら

例　寒い，窓を閉めた方がいいですよ　⇨寒かったら，窓を閉めた方がいいですよ。
(If you're cold, you should close the window.)

1．暑い，窓を開けてください
2．お金がない，仕事をした方がいいですよ
3．長くお待たせする，失礼ですよ
4．図書館へ行く，これを調べてください
5．田中さんに会う，この本を渡してください
6．学生だ，少し安いですよ
7．風邪をひく，早く寝た方がいい

練習（れんしゅう） 6　　　～たら～

例　運動する，元気になる　⇨運動したら，元気になりますか。
(If you exercise, will you feel better?)

1．四月になる，暖かい
2．今年，四年生だ，来年，大学院生だ
3．掃除をする，この家はきれいだ
4．二年生になる，この辞書が欲しい
5．日本語の授業を休む，日本語が嫌いだ
6．風邪をひく，体が痛くなる
7．もう少し，塩を入れる，この料理はおいしい

練習（れんしゅう） 7　　　S ことにしている

例　疲れたら寝る　⇨私は，疲れたら寝ることにしています。
(I make it a point to sleep when I'm tired.)

1．一か月に一回部屋を掃除する
2．日曜日には車に乗らない
3．コーヒーには何も入れない
4．あの奥さんには何も教えてもらわない
5．ケーキは作らないし，食べない
6．英語の勉強のために毎日テレビを見る

Lesson 18

練習（れんしゅう） 8　　　　～ば～

例　運動する，元気になる　⇨運動すれば，元気になりますか。
(If you exercise, will you feel better?)

1. 四月になる，暖かい
2. 今年，四年生だ，来年，大学院生だ
3. 掃除をする，この家はきれいだ
4. 二年勉強する，日本語がもっとできる
5. 日本語の授業を休む，日本語が嫌いだ
6. もう少し，塩を入れる，この料理はおいしい

練習（れんしゅう） 9　　　　～ば～

例　忙しい，明日でもいいです　⇨忙しければ，明日でもいいです。
(If you're busy (today), tomorrow is fine.)

1. 忙しくない，行きましょう
2. つまらない，途中で帰りましょう
3. 時間がある，一緒に行くつもりです
4. あの人に聞く，わかるでしょう
5. よく寝る，元気になる
6. ちゃんと食べない，病気になる

練習（れんしゅう） 10　　　　～たらいいんでしょうか

例　どうやって調べる　⇨どうやって調べたらいいんでしょうか。
(How should I look it up?)

1. 誰に聞く　2. どこを探す　3. いつお邪魔する　4. 何時頃行く
5. どうやって帰る　6. 何を食べる　7. 誰と一緒に行く　8. どの新聞を見る

練習（れんしゅう） 11　　　　～たら，どうですか

例　図書館へ行って調べる　⇨図書館へ行って調べたらどうですか。
(Why don't you go to the library and look it up?)

1. 佐藤さんに聞く　2. そこの本屋で探す　3. 今日お邪魔する　4. 三時頃行く
5. 電車で帰る　6. これを食べる　7. 加藤さんと行く　8. この新聞を見る

| 練習(れんしゅう) 12 | Sって |

例　病気だ　⇨西川さんは病気なんですって。(Is it true that Nishikawa san is ill?)

1．昨日，買い物をしたばかりだ　　2．いい参考書を探している
3．試験を二つ終えたところだ　　　4．図書館でアルバイトをしている
5．学校をやめる　　　　　　　　　6．テニスを六時間もした

| 練習(れんしゅう) 13 | もし，Sなら |

例　大学院に入る，どこの大学院
　　⇨中村さんは，もし大学院に入るなら，どこの大学院に入るつもりですか。
　　(Nakamura san, if you go to graduate school, which school do you plan to attend?)

1．外国語を習う，何語　　　　　　2．今夜映画を見に行く，どんな映画
3．コンピューターを買う，どこの　　4．東京へ行く，いつ
5．着物を着る，どんな着物　　　　6．日本語で話をする，どんな話をする

| 練習(れんしゅう) 14 | Nができる |

例　英語　⇨私は英語が少しできます。(I can speak a little English.)

1．タイプ　2．スキー　3．スケート　4．料理　5．日本語　6．フランス語

| 練習(れんしゅう) 15 | もっと |

例　きれいに書く　⇨もっときれいに書いてください。(Please write more neatly.)

1．大きい声で言う　　2．はっきり質問する　　3．のんびりする
4．よく聞く　　　　　5．何度も練習する　　　6．早く来る
7．早く渡す　　　　　8．いい本を読む　　　　9．きれいに書く

| 練習(れんしゅう) 16 | もう少し |

例　きれいに書く　⇨もう少し，きれいに書いてください。
　　(Please write a little more neatly.)

1．大きい声で言う　　2．はっきり質問する　　3．のんびりする
4．よく聞く　　　　　5．くわしく話す　　　　6．早く来る
7．早く渡す　　　　　8．いい本を読む　　　　9．きれいに書く

十九課

内容表

文法	Formal Requests		お＋stem＋ください
	Humble Self-Introduction（名前）		～と申します。
	Potential		
	N ができる		英語ができる
	Potential forms of Verbs		英語が書ける
	Presenting a Topic /「なら」		少しなら
	Specifying conditions /「なら」		少しなら，二百字ぐらいなら
	Change, development, deterioration		V＋ようになる
	"Without ～ing"		～ないで
	Asking for Favors		て＋もらえませんか
	Inability Due to Certain Situations		S＋わけにはいかない
	Causing Change		Adj.＋する
	Indicating Limits		早くても
	"As ～ as possible"		なるべく（早く）
機能	Greeting	6-1	失礼します
	Making Requests	5-3	おかけください
			～てくれませんか。
			奥さんに頼んでもらえない？
	Introducing Oneself	6-7	～と申します。
	Starting Conversation	6-3	早速ですが
	Expressing Capability	2-15	少しならできます。
	Inquiring About Capability	2-16	日本語ができますか。
	Hesitating	2-45	少しならできます。
			まあ，読めます。
	Stating Hypothesis	1-4	勉強したら，話せます。
	Encouraging One to Perform	5-11	そんなこと言わないで，がんばって
	Expressing Impossibility	2-13	私が決めるわけにはいかない。
			無理でしょうね。
	Expressing Incapability	2-15	全く駄目だよ。
			全然できないんだ。

会話 (かいわ)

1

A: 失礼します。

B: どうぞおかけください。[ありがとうございます。]はじめまして。私は阿部と申します。どうぞよろしく。

A: ペリーと申します。こちらこそ、どうぞよろしく。

B: 早速ですが、ペリーさんは日本語ができますね。

A: はい、まだ下手ですが、少しならできます。

B: そうですか。漢字が読めますか。

A: 二百字ぐらいなら、まあ、読めます。

B: じゃあ、新聞や雑誌は？

A: あと二年くらい勉強しないと、十分には読めないだろうと思います。

2

A: 勝先生、日本語は一年勉強したら、自由に話せますか。

B: 一年？無理でしょうね、一年じゃ。少なくても、二、三年勉強して、それから日本へ行って、一、二年ぐらい生活しないと、自由に話せるようにはならないでしょうね。

A: そうですか。日本語というのは、ずいぶん時間がかかるんですね。[ええ。]ところで、先生、日本へ行くのは難しいでしょうか。

B: 奨学金がかなりあるから、がんばって勉強すれば、割合、簡単に行けますよ。

A: でも、私はあまりがんばれないんです。

B: そんなこと言わないで、がんばってください。ハリスさんはがんばれる人ですよ。

1

A：Excuse me.

B：Please sit down. [Thank you.] How do you do? I am Abe. It's nice to meet you.

A：I am Perry. It's nice to meet you.

B：Well, to come to the point, I see that you can speak Japanese.

A：Yes, I'm not very proficient yet, but I can speak a little.

B：I see. Can you read Chinese characters?

A：I can read, ... well, about 200 characters.

B：Then, how about newspapers and magazines?

A：I don't think I can read them satisfactorily until I study for about two more years.

2

A：Katsu sensei, if I study Japanese for a year, will I be able to speak it freely?

B：One year? I doubt if you can in a year. You probably won't be able to speak it freely until you study it for at least two or three years, and then go to Japan and live there for about one or two years.

A：I see. It takes a lot of time to master Japanese, doesn't it? [Yes.] By the way, sensei, is it difficult to go to Japan?

B：There are quite a few scholarships, so if you study hard, you can go rather easily.

A：But I can't study very hard.

B：Don't say that; please study hard. Harris san, you're a person who can study hard.

3

A：横井さん。[何ですか。]横井さんは，何か楽器が弾ける？

B：ええっ，楽器？ 全く駄目だよ。

A：ピアノは弾けない？

B：家内がピアノの教師なのに，僕は楽器は全然できないんだ。

A：じゃ，奥さんに頼んでもらえない？ 今度の集まりに，音楽がいるのよ。

B：僕が決めるわけにはいかないから，帰って聞いてみるよ。

A：そう。じゃ，返事は，なるべく早くしていただけない？ お願いね。[はい。]

単語表 (たんごひょう)

1

かける	sit (on a chair) Ⅱ
阿部(あべ)	a surname
申(もう)します	言う⬇
早速(さっそく)ですが	☞ことばの使い方
下手(へた)だ	poor in ~
読める	potential of 読む Ⅱ
まあ	☞ことばの使い方
あと二年	☞ことばの使い方
十分(じゅうぶん)に	fully, thoroughly

2

勝(かつ)	a surname
自由(じゆう)に	freely, easily
無理(むり)だ	impossible
少(すく)なくても	at least
生活(せいかつ)する	live
話(はな)せる	potential of 話す Ⅱ
割合(わりあい)	かなり, relatively
がんばれる	potential of がんばる Ⅱ

3

横井(よこい)	a surname
楽器(がっき)	musical instrument
弾く(ひく)	play
全く(まったく)	completely
駄目(だめ)だ	no good
教師(きょうし)	teacher
頼(たの)む	ask s.b. to do s.t.
今度(こんど)	☞ことばの使い方
集(あつ)まり	meeting
音楽(おんがく)	music
決(き)める	decide Ⅱ
~わけにはいかない	☞ことばの使い方
返事(へんじ)	answer, reply
なるべく	as ~ as possible
(て-form＋)もらう	ask ~ to do
いただく	polite equivalent of もらう⬇

3

A：Yokoi san. [Yes?] Can you play an instrument?

B：An instrument? Not a thing.

A：Can't you play the piano?

B：My wife is a piano teacher, but I can't play any instrument.

A：Well, then, won't you ask your wife to play (for us)? We need music at our next gathering.

B：Since I can't decide for her, I'll ask her when I get home.

A：I understand. Then, please let me know as soon as possible. [All right.]

関連語句 (かんれんごく)

上手(じょうず)だ	be good at ～, adept	学者(がくしゃ)	scholar
野球(やきゅう)	baseball	研究(けんきゅう)する	research
論文(ろんぶん)	thesis, paper	人生(じんせい)	life
運転(うんてん)する	drive		

Lesson 19

文法 (ぶんぽう)

● おかけください　1-2

お＋stem＋ください

This pattern is a formal request, more formal than て＋ください(ませんか).

It cannot be used with verbs whose stems are mono-syllabic, like 寝, 来, し, 見. Entirely different verbs are used with these latter forms.

寝る⇨お休みください　　　　　　する⇨なさってください
来る⇨おいで／いらっしゃってください　見る⇨御覧ください
食べる, 飲む⇨お召し上がりください

● **Potential forms**　1-5, 7

These forms basically indicate that a person has the internal ability to do something. "Can" or "be able to" is a good translation, but you should keep in mind that the English "can" has a wider range of meaning than the potential form in Japanese. For example, "can" that expresses permission does not have an equivalent in the Japanese potential form.

In Japanese potentiality can be expressed in two ways:

1. Noun＋できる：
   a) 英語ができますか。(Can you speak / read / etc. English?)
      英語はできません。(I cannot.)
2. Using the potential form of a verb:
   b) 英語が書けますか。(Can you write English?)
      英語は書けません。(I cannot write English.)

In the examples above, note that the particle signifying the object of a potential verb is が. The particle が becomes は in negative or contrastive sentences.

Potential Forms of Verbs

Group I verb		Group II verbs	
会う	⇨会える	起きる	⇨起きられる
書く	⇨書ける	見る	⇨見られる
話す	⇨話せる	寝る	⇨寝られる
立つ	⇨立てる	食べる	⇨食べられる
死ぬ	⇨死ねる		
飲む	⇨飲める	Group III verbs	
終わる	⇨終われる	来る	⇨来られる
泳ぐ	⇨泳げる	する	⇨できる
飛ぶ	⇨飛べる		

Exception　行く⇨行ける／行かれる

Note 1　In conversations among young people, the potential forms of Group II and 来る may become 起きれる, 来れる by dropping ら. This form has not yet met

十九課

Note 2　All the potential verbs belong to group II, regardless of their origin.

Note 3　There are some verbs that do not have potential forms. They are: わかる, 困る, 知る, ある, (のどが)かわく, (おなかが)すく, 疲れる, (雪が)降る and other verbs that express actions and states, over which the speaker does not have any control.

Note 4　In the case of compound verbs such as 書いている, 書いておく, 書いてしまう, 書いてもらう, 書き始める etc., the second verb is changed into the potential form.

● 少しならできます　　1-6

In L. 18 we learned "V＋なら" as a hypothetical expression. The なら in "N＋なら," which appears in this lesson is similar in meaning to the topical marker は. The only difference lies in the fact that なら still maintains a hypothetical tone.

1．A：今日，行けますか。(Can you go today?)
　　B：午後なら，行けますよ。(Yes, I can go, if it's in the afternoon.)
2．千字は書けませんが，三百字くらいなら書けます。
　　(I cannot write a thousand Chinese characters, but I can manage about three hundred.)

● あと二年くらい勉強しないと，読めないだろうと思います　　1-10

There are two と in this sentence: the one after しない is conjunctive and the other is quotational. The "quoted" part of this sentence includes everything which precedes と思います. The comma in the middle may be misleading since it may give the impression that the quotation begins with 読めない. If you pay close attention, however, you will recognize that 読めないだろう is the result of the preceding condition. The preceding part, therefore, has to be included as the content of the speaker's thought. You must be especially attentive to understand modification and quotation; don't let the little comma throw you off into a mistaken tangent.

1．佐藤さんは東京へ行ったら，いい参考書を買うつもりだと言っています。
　　(Sato san says that he plans to buy a good reference book when he goes to Tokyo.)
2．これは，父が若い時にお金がなくて友達から借りて買った辞書なんですよ。
　　(This is a dictionary which my father bought, when he was young, after borrowing money from his friend as he had had no money.)

● 話せるようにならない　　2-3

In L. 18, we learned how to use なる. (☞文法「痛くなる」) When a verb is used with なる, it has to be connected by ように. This pattern implies that the topical person undergoes a gradual change and attains a new level of competence in which his/her skill or situation begins to develop or deteriorate.

| V＋ように＋なる | ⇨ "come to V," "start to V" |

1．この頃，日本語がかなりわかるようになりました。
　　(I have come to understand Japanese quite well recently.)
2．私は小学校の一年生の時に，自転車に乗れるようになった。
　　(I learned to ride a bicycle when I was a first-grader.)

Lesson 19

  3．練習すればもっと話せるようになりますよ。
    (If you practice, you will be able to speak more proficiently.)

● そんなこと言わないで   2-8

  |V (pre-ない)＋ないで| ⇨ "without ～ing"

This adverbial phrase modifies the verbal phrase that follows it.
  1．名前を書かないで試験を出してしまいました。
    (I have submitted my test without writing my name.)
  2．ゆうべはとても疲れたので，何もしないで八時頃寝てしまいました。
    (Last night I went to bed at around eight without doing anything because I was very tired.)
  3．阿部さんは，さようならとも言わないで帰ってしまいました。
    (Abe san went home without even saying good-bye.)

● 奥さんに頼んでもらえない   3-5

頼んでもらえる is a potential form of 頼んでもらう. This is similar in meaning to 頼んでくれませんか, but the former sounds slightly more polite than the latter because of its indirectness. (See the example below.) In both cases, the person who asks the wife to play the piano is the hearer, Yokoi san. If you want a more polite expression than these, use the potential form of いただく, which is いただける. (☞L. 17 文法「教えてもらった」)

  横井さん，すみませんけど，明日八時に私の部屋に来て
   A）もらえませんか。
   B）くれませんか。
  (Sorry Yokoi san, A) may I ask you to come by my office at eight tomorrow?
        B) will you come by my office at eight tomorrow?)

● 僕が決めるわけにはいかない   3-6

  |S＋わけにはいかない| ⇨ "cannot ～" (for social, moral, or psychological reasons)

  1．今日は試験があるので，授業を休むわけにはいかない。
    (Because there is a test today, I cannot skip class.)
  2．学者になるなら，大学院へ行かないわけにはいかないでしょう。
    (In order to become a scholar, I suppose you cannot do without going to graduate school.)

● 早くする   3-7

In order to understand this phrase, compare it to「痛くなる」in L. 18 文法. Since both する and なる are verbs, they take adverbial forms as shown in the explanation of「痛くなる」.

なる is an intransitive verb that signifies a change spontaneously caused without a direct relation to people, whereas する is a transitive verb that signifies the intention or will of a topical person.
  1．部屋を暖かくしました。(I made the room warm.)
   部屋が暖かくなりました。(The room became warm.)
  2．私たちは加藤さんを議長にしました。(We made Kato san chairman.)
   加藤さんが議長になりました。(Kato san became chairman.)

十九課

ことばの使い方 (ことばのつかいかた)

● 早速ですが　　1-5

This expression signals that your conversation is about to take a turn from the superficial to something important and substantive. Before this, you may make small talk, give greetings talk about the weather, chat about mutual friends, etc. This phrase literally means "It is too abrupt or too soon." It implies that you are not supposed to delve into the central issue right in the beginning, and that for a little while you should engage in general conversation to develop a cordial atmosphere. The expression is formal and is used often in business talk.

● まだ下手です　　1-6　☞「もう」L. 13　ことばの使い方

● 下手です　　1-6

This is a な-adj. used to describe a person's incapabilities or lack of skills. The opposite expression is 上手だ. The particle denoting the object is が, not を. Like other が, it is often replaced by は.

　　私はいい車が欲しいんですが、まだ運転がとても下手なので買えないと思います。
　　　(Although I want a good car, I don't think I can buy one because I am still very poor at driving.)
　　阿部さんは、テニスは上手だけど、野球は下手だね。
　　　(Abe san, you are excellent at tennis, but terrible at baseball.)
　　勝さん、誰かピアノの上手な人を知りませんか。
　　　(Katsu san, don't you know someone who is good at playing the piano?)

● まあ、読めます　　1-8

This まあ is used to imply that the speaker is hesitant to say too conclusively that he can read. The speaker tries to avoid giving an impression that he is over-confident and tries to show his reserved attitude.

　　１．A：この仕事、今日終わりますか。(Can you finish this job today?)
　　　　B：まあ、無理ですね。　　　　　(Impossible, I should say.)
　　２．A：これ、全部わかりましたか。　(Did you understand all of this?)
　　　　B：ええ、まあ、わかりました。　(Well, I guess so.)

● あと二年　　1-10　☞P. 128「あと六日」
　　あと五分で、終わりですよ。(In another five minutes, time will be up.)
　　あと二年くらい、研究して、それから論文を書こうと思っています。
　　　(I have been thinking of writing my thesis after doing research for another two years.)
　　あと三人は、かけられますよ。
　　　(There are seats for three more.)

Lesson 19

● 無理です　　2-2

This is a な-adj. which means "hardly possible."

この論文は，まだ無理ですよ。あと二年くらい日本語を勉強したら，読めると思いますが。

(This paper is still over your head. I think you'll be able to read it if you study Japanese for about two more years.)

一年で，漢字を二千覚えるのは，普通(ふつう)の人には無理なことですよ。

(It is an impossible task for ordinary people to memorize two thousand *kanji* in a year.)

● 少なくても　　2-2

The expression **Adj.**＋ても is used to show limits.

少ない⇨少なくても(at least)　　遅(おそ)い⇨遅くても(at the latest)
多い　⇨多くても　(at most)　　早(はや)い⇨早くても(at the earliest)
高(たか)い　⇨高くても　(at the highest / most expensive)
安(やす)い　⇨安くても　(at the cheapest)

1．この本は日本で買うと，安くても五万円ぐらいですよ。

(This book would cost at least ¥50,000 if you buy it in Japan.)

2．A：明日の朝，何時頃，学校に来ますか。
　　B：そうですねえ。遅くても九時半には来るつもりです。

(A：What time will you come to school tomorrow morning?)
(B：Well, I intend to come, at the latest, by nine-thirty.)

● 生活する　　2-3

While 住(す)む "to live," expresses living or residing in a static, abstract sense, 生活する, also "to live," describes an active life that includes getting up, having breakfast, going to school, meeting people, and so on.

● 日本語というのは　　2-4

This phrase from the dialogue can be replaced by 日本語は without substantially changing its meaning. The difference is that the speaker referring to 日本語 keeps a distance when he says 日本語というのは. This form of speech can be seen in topic-introducing sentences, defining sentences, or in the concluding sentence of a paragraph. というのは may be replaced by "って" in informal conversation.

先生，日本語というのはどんな言葉(ことば)なんですか。

(Sensei, what kind of language is Japanese?)

人生(じんせい)って，いろいろおもしろいことがありますね。

(There are many exciting things in life, aren't there?)

● ところで　　2-4　☞P. 41

● 楽器を弾く　　3-1

弾(ひ)く is a word that means "to play" stringed instruments. (A piano is thought to be a stringed instrument and, an organ, though it does not have strings, takes this verb.) With wind instruments, use 吹(ふ)く.

● 駄目です　　　3-2

駄目 is a widely used expression whose basic meaning is "no good." It is often used to describe the bad quality of something and as an expression of prohibition as seen in the examples.

1．A：この辞書はいいですか。(Is this dictionary good?)
　　B：全く駄目ですよ。　　　(It is completely useless!)
2．子供：お母さん、もう食べてもいい？
　　母親：まだ駄目ですよ。あと五分くらいでお父さんが帰ってきますから、それまで、待ちましょうね。
　　(Child ： Is it all right if I start eating now, Mom?)
　　(Mother: Not yet. Daddy will be back in about five minutes. Let's wait until then.)

● 教師　　　3-4

While 先生 has a respectful tone and is used to refer to other people, 教師 does not have that sort of tone, and, consequently, it can be used to refer to the speaker himself/herself or his/her family members.

1．A：阿部さんの奥さんは先生ですって？
　　B：ええ。家内は小学校の教師ですよ。
　　(A：I hear your wife is a teacher. Is that true?)
　　(B：Yes. She is a teacher at an elementary school.)
2．A：失礼ですが、どんなお仕事をしていらっしゃいますか。
　　B：私ですか。中学校の教師です。
　　(A：Excuse me, what kind of job do you do?)
　　(B：Me? I am a teacher at a junior high school.)

● 奥さんに頼む　　　3-5

頼む is "to ask s.b. to do ～." Don't confuse this with 聞く which means "to ask somebody about ～."

　　勝さん、この仕事を横井さんに頼んでください。
　　(Please ask Yokoi san to do this, Katsu san.)

● 今度の集まり　　　3-5

When this word is used to refer to the future, it means "next time," and when it signifies a state or event in the past, it can be translated "this time." In other words, the interpretation of this word is determined by the tense of the sentence.

1．今度、いつ横浜に行くんですか。(When will you go to Yokohama next?)
2．先生、今度の試験はずいぶん難しかったですね。
　　(Sensei, this last test was extremely hard, wasn't it?)

Lesson 19

練習 (れんしゅう)

| 練習(れんしゅう) 1 | Nができる |

例　料理　⇨横井さんは料理ができますか。(Yokoi san, can you cook?)

1．日本語　　　2．テニス　　　3．運動　　　4．この車の運転
5．野球　　　　6．ソフトボール　7．この仕事

| 練習(れんしゅう) 2 | Potential Form |

例　フランス語の新聞を読む
　　⇨横井さんはフランス語の新聞が読めますか。
　　　(Yokoi san, can you read French newspapers?)

1．この国で生活する　2．三時まで学校にいる　3．ケーキを作る　　　4．着物を着る
5．今晩図書館に行く　6．これを調べる　　　　7．明日の夜,家に来る　8．楽器を弾く

| 練習(れんしゅう) 3 | ～なら, Potential Form |

例　この新聞が読めますか。(Can you read this newspaper?)
　　⇨この新聞なら読めると思います。
　　　(If it's this paper, I think I can read it.)

1．明日早く来られますか。　　　　2．七時まで仕事ができますか。
3．このケーキが作れますか。　　　4．この問題が調べられますか。
5．日本語で手紙が書けますか。　　6．ピアノが弾けますか。
7．来週アルバイトができますか。　8．明日の夜八時頃,先生の家に行けますか。

| 練習(れんしゅう) 4 | Potential Form |

例　これ,読みますか。(Will you read this?)
　　⇨それは,読めませんよ。(I can't read that.)

1．これ,食べますか。　　2．これ,飲みますか。　　3．これ,使いますか。
4．これ,買いますか。　　5．これ,借りますか。　　6．これ,調べますか。
7．これ,しますか。　　　8．これ,入れますか。　　9．これ,着ますか。

練習(れんしゅう) 5　　　Object-marker が

例　中村さん，テニス，上手　⇨中村さんはテニスが上手です。
(Nakamura san is good at tennis.)

1．私，テニス，下手
2．私，いい友達，欲しい
3．私，勉強，好き
4．中村さん，野球，嫌い
5．石井さん，テニス，下手じゃない
6．私，テニス，上手じゃない
7．私，勉強，好きじゃない
8．中村さん，野球，嫌いじゃない

練習(れんしゅう) 6　　　なら

例　漢字が読めますか。(二百字)　⇨二百字くらいなら，読めます。
(Can you read *kanji*?　⇨ If it's about two hundred characters, I can.)

1．今，時間がありますか。（一時間）
2．もう少し，食べられますか。（あと一つ）
3．明日，行けますか。（三時頃）
4．今日の授業，休めますか。（一時間）
5．まだ入れますか。（あと三人）
6．少し待てますか。（二，三日）
7．安いですか。（学生）
8．説明できますか。（明日）

練習(れんしゅう) 7　　　Vようになる

例　着物が着られる　⇨着物が着られるようになりました。
(I've come to be able to wear a *kimono*.)

1．日本語が聞いてわかる
2．漢字が二百字くらい読める
3．教科書が割合簡単に読める
4．ピアノがかなり弾ける
5．運動すると体が痛くなる
6．研究がおもしろいと思える
7．森さんにギターが教えてもらえる
8．論文が書き始められる

練習(れんしゅう) 8　　　ないで

例　話をしない，食べる　⇨話をしないで，食べた方がいいですよ。
(You should eat without talking.)

　　鉛筆で書かない，ボールペンで書く
　　　⇨鉛筆で書かないで，ボールペンで書いた方がいいですよ。
(You should write with a ball point pen, not with a pencil.)

1．車で行かない，歩いて行く
2．英語を使わない，日本語で言う
3．家で勉強しない，図書館でする
4．学者にならない，小説を書く
5．授業を休まない，毎日出る
6．あまりがんばらない，のんびりする

Lesson 19

練習(れんしゅう) 9	～てもらえる

例 これ，教えてくれませんか。⇨これ，教えてもらえませんか。
　　　　　　　　　　　　　　　(Won't you teach me this?)

1．この漢字，説明してくれませんか。　　2．ここに，名前を書いてくれませんか。
3．その本，貸してくれませんか。　　　　4．ピアノを弾いてくれませんか。
5．ワインを一本買ってきてくれませんか。　6．勝さんにこれを頼んでくれませんか。
7．これを図書館で調べてきてくれませんか。8．この本を探してきてくれませんか。

練習(れんしゅう) 10	S わけにはいかない

例　明日，試験がある，授業を休む
　　⇨明日試験があるから，授業を休むわけにはいかないんですよ。
　　(Since there's an exam tomorrow, I can't quite skip class.)

1．今夜，友達が来る，映画に行く　　　　2．家内がたばこが嫌いだ，たばこを吸う
3．ピアノを買った，練習しない　　　　　4．みんな行く，行かない
5．来週決める，今日返事をする　　　　　6．今夜パーティーをする，掃除しない

練習(れんしゅう) 11	～する

例　お風呂，熱い　⇨お風呂を熱くしました。(I made the bath hot.)

1．部屋，暖かい　　　2．試験の時間，早い　　　3．覚える漢字，多い
4．宿題，簡単だ　　　5．パーティー，にぎやかだ　6．授業の時間，長い

練習(れんしゅう) 12	～ないと～ない

例　たくさん食べると大きくなります。(You'll grow big if you eat a lot.)
　　⇨たくさん食べないと大きくなりませんよ。
　　(If you don't eat a lot, you won't grow big.)

1．調べるとわかります。　　　　　　　　2．勉強するとよく読めるようになります。
3．毎日，運動すると病気になりません。　4．奨学金をもらうと日本へ行けます。
5．論文を書くと卒業できます。　　　　　6．加藤さんに聞くとわかります。

十九課

| 練習(れんしゅう) 13 | ～て |

例　辞書を引く，調べた　⇨辞書を引いて調べました。(I looked it up in the dictionary.)

1．テレビを見る，遅くまで起きていた　　2．新聞を読む，そのニュースを知った
3．秋山さんに聞く，全部わかった　　　　4．がんばる，試験の勉強をした
5．電話をする，そのことを言った　　　　6．車を運転する，親戚の家へ行った

| 練習(れんしゅう) 14 | VP の |

例　今年，日本へ行く
　　⇨私，今年日本へ行くのは，無理でしょうか。

(Do you think it would be impossible for me to go to Japan this year?)

1．奨学金をもらう　　　　　　　　2．ピアノを習う
3．それを加藤さんにお願いする　　4．明日までに返事をもらう
5．漢字を毎日二十覚える　　　　　6．この論文を本にする

| 練習(れんしゅう) 15 | なるべく |

例　返事は，早くしていただけませんか。
　　⇨返事はなるべく早くしていただけませんか。

(Can you answer as soon as possible?)

1．多くの学生に聞いてください。
2．漢字はきれいに書いてください。
3．漢字はたくさん覚えた方がいいですよ。
4．電話は短くお願いします。
5．家を早く出た方がいいんじゃないですか。
6．明日は，ちゃんとした洋服を着てきてください。

二十課

内容表

文法	Receiving s.t. from s.b.		友達にもらった
	Desiderative form		が／を＋V stem＋たい
	NP＋が 嫌いだ		音楽が嫌いなんですか。
	S わけじゃない		そういうわけじゃありませんよ。
	S ことができる		学校に来ることができる。
	て Indicating a weak "cause-effect" relationship		早く治って，よかった。
	NP に感心，驚く，びっくりする		予習復習をするのに感心した。
	Indirect quotation (Questions)		S (with an interrogative) か知らない。
	CL たら CL (Past Event)		会ったら，テープを聞いていた。
機能	Inquiring About an Opinion	2-34	一緒にどう。
	Commenting on a Topic	7-11	悪いけど
	Rejecting (a Fact, Situation)	2-38	そういうわけじゃないわ。
	Expressing Likes / Dislikes	3-1	ロックが大嫌いなの。
	Pleasure / Displeasure		友達が来てくれたのは，嬉しかった。
	Inquiring About Likes / Dislikes	3-2	音楽が嫌いなの？
			寂しかったでしょう。
	Expressing Congratulations	6-19	よかったですね。
	Acknowledging Polite Comments	6-24	おかげさまで。
	Expressing Possibility	2-13	学校に来ることができる。
	Expressing Agreement	2-1	その通りですよ。
	Expressing Capability	2-15	英語が上手／下手です。
	Expressing Surprise	3-8	あの人の英語には，驚きました。
	Evaluating	2-39	英語がお上手ですね。
			発音がとてもいい。
			文法は正確ですし
			言葉の使い方も自然です。
			真面目に予習復習をする。

会話 (かいわ)

1

A：長井さん，ロックのコンサートの切符を二枚，友達にもらったんだけど，一緒にどう。僕，このコンサートのことを聞いてから，ずっと行きたかったんだ。

B：悪いけど，ロックには興味がないの。聞きたいと思わないの。

A：音楽が嫌いなの？

B：そういうわけじゃないわ。好きな音楽も，嫌いな音楽もあるわ。

A：でも，このグループは歌が上手だし，とても人気があるんだよ。行こうよ。

B：実は，私はロックが大嫌いなのよ。他の人を誘って行ってください。すみません。

2

A：やあ，青木さん。病気は，もう治ったんですか。よかったですね。

B：ええ，おかげさまで。今日初めて学校に来ました。[本当によかったですね。] ええ，やっと学校に来ることができるようになりました。

A：御両親のいらっしゃらない病院で，一人で寝ているのは，寂しかったでしょう。

B：ええ，まあ，少しは。でも，毎日，寮の友達が来てくれたのは，嬉しかったですね。

A：寮に住んでいるのも，悪くありませんか。

B：ええ，全くその通りですよ。

A：でも，早く治って，安心したでしょう。

B：ええ。元気でいるのが，一番ですね。病気はしたくないと思いました。

1

A：Nagai san, a friend gave me two tickets to a rock concert; would you like to go? After hearing about this concert, I have been dying to go.

B：I am sorry but I have no interest in rock music. I just don't feel like listening to it.

A：You don't like music?

B：No, that's not the case. Some music I like, and some, I don't.

A：But the members of this group sing well, and they are very popular. So let's go!

B：The fact is, I hate rock music. Please invite someone else along. I'm sorry.

2

A：Hi there, Aoki san! Are you completely well now? That's great.

B：Yes, thank goodness. This is my first day back in school. [That's really great.] I am finally well enough to come back to school.

A：It must have been lonely to be sick in bed in a hospital away from your parents.

B：Yes, well, just a little. But it really made me happy that my friends from my dormitory came to visit me every day.

A：So, living in the dormitory isn't too bad?

B：Yes, that's absolutely true.

A：But, you must feel relieved that you've recovered so quickly.

B：Yes. There's nothing better than being healthy. I don't ever want to get sick again.

Lesson 20

3

A：マッケンジーさん，今，話していた方はどなたですか。

B：私の英語の学生なんですよ。

A：あの方は英語がお上手ですね。

B：ええ，あの人は発音がとてもいいし，文法は正確ですし，言葉の使い方も自然ですし，それに，何しろ真面目に予習復習をするのに感心しました。

A：どうやって発音の練習なんかしているんでしょう。

B：さあ。どうやって練習しているのかよく知りませんが，でも，昨日バーで会ったら，テープを聞きながらビールを飲んでいました。

A：素晴らしいですね，本当に。私，あの人の英語には全く驚きました。

単語表（たんごひょう）

1

長井(ながい)	a surname
切符(きっぷ)	ticket
もらう	receive
一緒(いっしょ)に	together, with
ずっと	all through the time, throughout
行きたい	☞文法
(に)興味(きょうみ)がある	be interested in ~
音楽(おんがく，おんがく)	music
わけ	☞文法
歌(うた)	song
人気(にんき)がある	popular
大嫌(だいきら)いだ	hate
他(ほか)の人	other people
誘(さそ)う	ask to do ~ together, invite along

2

青木(あおき)	a surname
治(なお)る	recover, be cured
寂(さび)しい	lonely
嬉(うれ)しい	happy, glad
寮(りょう)	dormitory
全(まった)く	completely
その通(とお)りだ	That's exactly right!
安心(あんしん)する	feel relieved

3

どなた	who, whom
発音(はつおん)	pronunciation
お上手(じょうず)な	上手だ🔝
正確(せいかく)な	accurate
自然(しぜん)な	natural
何(なに)しろ	above all

3

A：McKenzie san, who is the person you were talking with just now?

B：He's my English student.

A：He speaks English very well.

B：Yes, his pronunciation is very good, his use of grammar is accurate, and he speaks very naturally; and, more than anything, I'm impressed by the way he seriously prepares for class and reviews material which has been covered.

A：I wonder how he practices — pronunciation, for example.

B：Well, I don't exactly know how he practices, but when I met him at a bar yesterday, he was listening to a tape while he was drinking his beer.

A：That's really wonderful. I am utterly impressed by his English ability.

真面目(まじめ)な	serious	やっと	☞ことばの使い方
予習(よしゅう)する	prepare for class	Sことができる	Ⅱ ☞文法
復習(ふくしゅう)する	study again, review	一緒(いっしょ)に	together, with
感心(かんしん)する	be impressed	素晴(すば)らしい	wonderful, great
なんか	☞ことばの使い方	驚(おどろ)く	be surprised
おかげさまで	☞ことばの使い方	いつでも	anytime, always
初(はじ)めて	for the first time		

関連語句(かんれんごく)

寝坊(ねぼう)する	oversleep	びっくりする	be surprised, be startled
腹(はら)が立(た)つ	get angry	がっかりする	be disappointed
けがをする	get injured	(〜を)見つける	find (and get) 〜 Ⅱ

Lesson 20

文法 (ぶんぽう)

● 友達にもらった　1-1

In L. 17, we studied 「て＋もらう」. (☞P.205 教えてもらった). Without the て-forms, the verbs もらう, くれる, and あげる (which we have not yet covered) present different forms which mean either "giving" or "receiving." We will study these verbs in the next lesson. Review the grammar for 「て＋もらう」.

● 行きたかった　1-2

V (pre-ます)＋たい

行きたかった is the perfect form of 行きたい, which is a combination of the stem of the verb 行く and the desiderative (showing desire) suffix たい.

Like other expressions portraying feelings, desires, and emotions (*e.g.* 疲れた, 頭が痛い, 欲しい, 嬉しい, 楽しい, 好きだ, 嫌いだ), this pattern cannot be used to refer to the third person, except by adding のです, みたい etc., at the end, which indicates that you are explaining or making a conjecture based on seemingly solid evidence.

A question using this pattern can be used to address a second person only if that person and you are very close. In Japanese, asking about feelings or desires is considered rude; adults in Japan traditionally and customarily do not express their feelings and desires in a straight-forward manner unless they are dealing with those with whom they are reasonably intimate.

English speakers in the beginning stages of learning Japanese tend to say "コーヒーを飲みたいですか," thinking that it is equivalent to "Would you like some coffee?" This is, however, not the case. You should say "コーヒー、どう／いかがですか" or "コーヒー、飲みませんか."

Note 1　The pattern as a whole functions as a compound adjective and conjugates like an い-adj.
　　　　病気をしてから、全然お酒は飲みたくありません。
　　　　　(Even since I became ill, I don't want to drink at all.)
　　　　私は子供の時、パイロットになりたかったんですよ。
　　　　　(When I was a child, I wanted to be a pilot, you know.)

Note 2　To designate an object, this form takes が as long as the object being desired is positioned close enough in the sentence to the predicate たい. Otherwise, it takes を.
　　　　ワインが飲みたいですよ。(I want some wine.)
　　　　私はワインを紙コップで飲みたいとは思いません。
　　　　　(I don't think I want to drink wine with a paper cup.)

Note 3　In comparing "V＋たい" with 欲しい, note that 欲しい takes a noun.
　　　　私はいい車が欲しい。(I want a good car.)
　　　　私はいい車が買いたいんですよ。(I want to buy a good car.)

Note 4　と思います is often attached at the end to buffer the directness of this phrase.

● 音楽が嫌いなの　　1-4

This な-adj. 嫌いだ is used in exactly the same way as 好きだ, 大好きだ, and 大嫌いだ. The object is designated by が, which turns into は in negative or contrastive sentences.

 Note: Don't confuse this with い-adj. Even though it ends in い, this is a な-adj. きれいだ is another な-adj. which is often mistaken for an い-adj.

 1．私はお酒は嫌いじゃありませんが，あまり好きでもありません。
  (I don't hate *sake* but don't really like it either.)
 2．これは私の大好きなレコードです。(This is a record I really like.)

● そういうわけじゃないわ　　1-5

In L. 19, we learned S＋わけにはいかない. The わけ used in this pattern is the same as that used in this lesson, which means "reason, cause, or logical relationship." The speaker of this sentence is rejecting the hasty interpretation made by his acquaintance in the dialogue, who seems to have the mistaken idea that disliking rock is the same as disliking music altogether. The speaker disagrees with his logic. If you agree with his logic, 〜わけです can be used. Other phrases can also precede わけ, as shown below:

 1．A：遅かったですね。寝坊したんでしょう。
   B：いや，そういうわけじゃありませんよ。交通事故があったんですよ。
   (A：You are late! You must have overslept.)
   (B：No. That's not the case. There was a traffic accident.)
 2．A：どうしたの。もっと食べて。この料理，おいしくない？
   B：いいえ，おいしくないわけじゃないの。昼御飯をちょっと食べ過ぎて。
   (A：What's the matter? Eat more! Is this dish not good?)
   (B：It is not that, you know. I ate too much for lunch …)

● 学校に来ることができる　　2-3

The pattern "S＋ことができる" also signifies "potentiality." The difference between this and potential forms 〜れる, られる in L. 19 is that, while れる and られる emphasize internal abilities, the pattern means that something is allowed or sanctioned by rules, regulations or customs. In the sentence from the dialogue, the speaker may be allowed by the doctor to attend classes. If he wanted to say that he has recovered so well that he could come to school, he would say 来られる.

● 早く治って，安心したでしょう　　2-9

As we saw in L. 13 (文法 6. て＋VP) the て-form before a verbal phrase in a sentence can be either a verbal modifier (i.e. an adverbial phrase) or a connector, "and." The sentence under discussion contains an example of the latter use of て as connector. In this example, however, the two phrases 早く治る and 安心した are not simply put side by side; the first phrase signifies "cause," and the second signifies "effect." This "cause-effect" interpretation is made when the second phrase expresses a psychological state.

 1．時間がなくて，困っているんですよ。
  (I don't have time, and it drives me crazy.)
 2．長井さんが来てくれて，とても嬉しかったですよ。
  (I was very happy that you kindly came by.)
 3．この論文ははっきりしていて，とてもわかりやすいですね。
  (This article is clearly written and is very easy to understand.)

Lesson 20

● 真面目に予習復習をする<u>のに</u>感心しました　　3-5

Pay special attention to the phrase 感心する. It is preceded by NP (including an ordinary noun)＋に, but never を. The following words belong to the same group:

驚く，びっくりする (colloquial equivalent of 驚く)
腹が立つ (get angry)
がっかりする (get disappointed)

1．あの人の発音には感心しました。(I was impressed by his pronunciation.)
2．あの人の発音のいいのには感心しました。
　　(I was impressed by the fact that his pronunciation was so good.)

Note: Don't confuse this with the conjunctive のに which means "although."

● どうやって練習しているの<u>か</u>知りません　　3-7

This is basically the same as the indirect quotation of a question. (☞L. 16 文法) The content of the verb 知る is shown in the plain form.

北川さんはどうして来ないんですか。(Why isn't Kitagawa san coming?)
⇨北川さんがどうして来ないのか知っていますか。
　　(Do you know why Kitagawa san isn't coming?)

● バーで会ったら…ビールを飲んでいました　　3-7

CL 1 たら，CL 2

This is a new usage of "たら"; it is followed by a sentence describing a past event. (☞L. 18「頭が疲れたら」)

In this pattern, the speaker recollects past events. CL 1 took place prior to CL 2, and, therefore, CL 2 cannot be under the speaker's control.

CL 2 is usually not anticipated by the speaker, and so, it contains elements of unexpectedness, discovery, or surprise.

CL 1 and CL 2 do not particularly have a "cause and effect" relationship.

あの問題は青木さんに聞いたら，はっきりしました。
　　(That question became clear when I asked Aoki san.)
昨日映画を見に行ったら，先生が奥さんと一緒に来ていました。
　　(I went to see a movie yesterday and Sensei was there with his wife.)
ゆうべ，佐藤さんに電話をしたら，元気がなかったですよ。
　　(Last night I called Sato san and he did not seem to be in high spirits.)

ことばの使い方 (ことばのつかいかた)

● 一緒に　　1-1

When this word means "together with 〜," it is always preceded by と.

A：週末，友達と一緒に中華料理を食べに行ってきましたよ。
B：誰と一緒に行きました？

A：田中さんとですよ。
　　　　（A：Last weekend, I went to eat Chinese food with my friend.）
　　　　（B：Who did you go with?）
　　　　（A：With Tanaka san.）

● コンサートのこと　　1-2　☞L. 15　ことばの使い方「Nのことなんですが」

● ずっと　　1-2

This adverb means "throughout the time" or "without a break."
　　１．私は，大学の四年間一日も休まずにずっと授業に出ました。
　　　　（I attended classes through four years of college without missing a single day.）
　　２．今日の試験のために，今朝までずっと勉強をしていました。
　　　　（I studied through this morning for today's exam.）
　　３．交通事故で，自動車がずっと止まっていました。
　　　　（Cars were stopped all the way because of the accident.）

● ロックには興味がない　　1-3

To designate the object of your interest, use に.
　　私は漢字の意味に興味があるので，中国語の研究をしたいと思っています。
　　　　（Since I am interested in the meaning of *kanji*, I want to research the Chinese language.）

● 誘う　　1-7

This word means "to ask s.b. to do something with the speaker."
　　１．昨日青木さんを誘って，デパートへ買い物に行きました。
　　　　（Yesterday I invited Aoki san along to go shopping at the department store.）
　　２．クラシック音楽のコンサートに長井さんを誘ったのですが，長井さんは忙しくて，来られませんでした。
　　　　（I invited Nagai san to a classical music concert, but she could not come because she was very busy.）

● やあ　　2-1

This is a casual greeting used by men to acknowledge old acquaintances and friends. Women would say あら or こんにちは in the same situation.

● おかげさまで　　2-2

This is a common response that is used to tell people that you are fine or that something turned out well. It literally means "thanks to you" and indicates that things are fine due to the kind concern of people including the hearer.
　　１．A：しばらくですね。お元気ですか。
　　　　B：ええ，おかげさまで。佐藤さんは？
　　　　　（A：I haven't seen you in a long time! How are you?）
　　　　　（B：Fine, thanks to you. How about you, Sato san?）
　　２．A：奨学金，もらえたんだって。
　　　　B：ええ，おかげさまで。
　　　　　（A：I heard you got the scholarship. Did you?）
　　　　　（B：Yes. Thank you.）
　　Note:　In Japanese, お元気ですか is not used as often as the English greeting "How are

Lesson 20

you?" It is used only when you see or talk to somebody after a long absence.

● やっと　　2-3

This adverb indicates that a thing or an event for which you have waited a long time finally arrives or happens. It cannot be used in reference to something negative because it portrays a sense of long-awaited yearning for something.

1．やっと試験が終わりました。(The exams are finally over.)
2．やっとこの問題がわかりました。
　　(I have finally come to understand this question.)

● 病気はしたくない　　2-10

In order to say "to become ill" or "to get injured," the words 病気 and けが (injury) are followed by をする. In the case of 病気, you can also say 病気になる. The difference between 病気をする and 病気になる is that 病気をする has to do with carelessness, while 病気になる is a natural, unavoidable phenomenon. This is probably why けが cannot be followed by なる.

● どなた　　3-1

This is the polite form of 誰.

　A：あちらにいらっしゃる方は，どなたですか。(Who is that person over there?)
　B：さあ，どなたでしょう。わかりません。(I wonder who he is. I don't know.)

● どうやって発音の練習なんかしているんでしょう　　3-6

なんか signifies that what precedes it is a typical example from a score of many similar or related items. It takes the place of は, が, and を. Pay special attention to the position of なんか in relation to other particles.

You may get the impression that this usage of なんか is the same as でも. They may share the same meaning but their usages are different: でも is usually used when you are offering or suggesting something; it cannot be used in the examples below:

1．どうやって漢字なんか覚えるんですか。
　　(How do you memorize, say, *kanji*?)
2．私は東京になんか住みたくありません。
　　(I don't want to live in a place like Tokyo.)
3．図書館でなんか勉強できませんよ。
　　(I can't study in a place like the library.)

● 真面目に　　3-5

This is a な-adj. often used to describe a person's diligence and seriousness.

1．あの人は，真面目な人ですね。授業に遅れたことも，休んだこともないでしょう。
　　(He is a diligent person, isn't he? I suppose he has never been late for or absent from classes.)
2．中村さんが真面目なことは，よくわかります。でも，勉強の仕方がよくないんじゃないですか。
　　(I know you are serious and diligent, Nakamura san, but maybe your study habits need some improvement.)

練習(れんしゅう)

練習(れんしゅう) 1　　　　くれる／もらう

例　友達が私に辞書を一冊くれました。　　　　(A friend gave me a dictionary.)
　　⇨私は友達に辞書を一冊もらいました。　　(I received a dictionary from a friend.)
　　友達が私に漢字を教えてくれました。　　　(A friend taught me *kanji*.)
　　⇨私は友達に漢字を教えてもらいました。(I had a friend teach me *kanji*.)

1．友達が私に切符を二枚くれました。　　2．長井さんが私に新しい歌を教えてくれました。
3．友達が私に切符を買ってくれました。　4．長井さんが私にレコードを貸してくれました。
5．友達が病院に来てくれました。　　　　6．長井さんが映画に誘ってくれました。

練習(れんしゅう) 2　　　　もらう／くれる

例　私は友達に辞書を一冊もらいました。　　　(I received a dictionary from a friend.)
　　⇨友達が私に辞書を一冊くれました。　　　(A friend gave me a dictionary.)
　　私は友達に漢字を教えてもらいました。　　(I had a friend teach me *kanji*.)
　　⇨友達が私に漢字を教えてくれました。(A friend taught me *kanji*.)

1．私は友達においしいケーキをもらいました。
2．私は長井さんに買い物に行ってもらいました。
3．私は友達に芝居の切符を買ってもらいました。
4．私は長井さんに参考書を貸してもらいました。
5．私は友達にリポートを読んでもらいました。
6．私は長井さんに部屋を掃除してもらいました。

練習(れんしゅう) 3　　　　Nのこと

例　青木さん　⇨青木さんのことを何か聞きましたか。
　　　　　　　　(Have you heard something about Aoki san?)
　　知っている　⇨青木さんのことを何か知っていますか。
　　　　　　　　(Do you know something about Aoki san?)

1．来週の試験　　2．聞いた　　　3．覚えている　　4．子供の時
5．リンさん　　　6．知っている　7．覚えている　　8．聞いた

Lesson 20

練習(れんしゅう)　4　　　　　　　～に興味がある

例　言語学(げんごがく)，ある　⇨私は言語学に興味があります。
　　　　　　　　　　(I am interested in linguistics.)
　　人類学(じんるいがく)，ない　⇨私は人類学には興味がありません。
　　　　　　　　　　(I have no interest in anthropology.)

1．この問題，ある　　　　2．新聞や雑誌，ない　　　3．音楽，ある
4．ピアノ音楽，ない　　　5．あの人の返事(へんじ)，ある　6．漢字の意味，ない

練習(れんしゅう)　5　　　　　　　～てから

例　それを聞いた，ずっと行きたいと思っていた
　　　⇨それを聞いてから，ずっと行きたいと思っていました。
　　　　(After hearing about it, I've been wanting to go.)

1．御飯(ごはん)を食(た)べ終(お)わった，新聞を読んだ　2．漢字を研究し始めた，漢字が好きになった
3．大学院生になった，部屋を借(か)りている　　4．暖(あたた)かくなった，オーバーを買ってしまった
5．この大学に入った，ここに住んでいる　　　　6．目(め)が悪(わる)くなった，テレビを見なくなった

練習(れんしゅう)　6　　　　　　　～たい

例　ジャズのコンサートに行く　⇨ジャズのコンサートに行きたいですね。
　　　　　　　　　　　　　　　(I want to go to a jazz concert.)
　　ジャズを聞く　　　　　　　⇨ジャズが聞きたいですね。
　　　　　　　　　　　　　　　(I want to listen to jazz.)

1．暖かい所に住む　　　　2．ベリーさんに会う　　　　3．日本語を自由に話す
4．日本で二，三年生活する　5．英語の新聞を読む　　　　6．おいしいワインを飲む
7．奨学金をもらう　　　　8．なるべく早く返事をする　9．ピアノを弾く

練習(れんしゅう)　7　　　　　　　～たくない

例　病気をする　⇨病気はしたくないですね。(I don't want to become ill.)
　　下手なジャズを聞く　⇨下手なジャズは聞きたくないですね。
　　　　　　　　　　　　(I don't want to listen to bad jazz.)

1．寒い所に住む　　　　　2．青木さんに会う　　　　　3．加藤さんと話す
4．怪我(けが)をする　　　5．授業を休む　　　　　　　6．つまらない映画を見る

練習(れんしゅう) 8　　　～たいと思わない

例　ジャズを聞く　⇨ジャズは聞きたいと思わないんですよ。
(I don't feel like listening to jazz.)

1．寒い所に住む　　　　2．青木さんに会う　　　　3．加藤さんと話す
4．テニスをする　　　　5．授業を休む　　　　　　6．映画を見る
7．学者になる　　　　　8．ロー・スクールに入る　9．日本で勉強する

練習(れんしゅう) 9　　　VPのは

例　病気で寝ている，寂しい　⇨病気で寝ているのは，寂しいです。
(It is lonely to be sick in bed.)

1．友達が来てくれた，嬉しい　　　　　2．漢字が読めるようになる，楽しい
3．寮に住んでいる，悪くない　　　　　4．病気が早く治った，よかった
5．友達が遠くへ行ってしまう，寂しい　6．奨学金がもらえた，嬉しい
7．仕事が楽しい，よかった　　　　　　8．勉強で忙しい，悪くない

練習(れんしゅう) 10　　　～が一番だ

例　病気をしない　⇨病気をしないのが，一番ですね。
(There's nothing better than not being ill.)

1．元気でいる　　　　　　　　　2．雪を見ながら，お酒を飲む
3．嫌いだとはっきり言う　　　　4．家でおもしろい小説を読んでいる
5．毎日，元気で勉強ができる　　6．怪我をしないで元気でいる

練習(れんしゅう) 11　　　～のに感心する

例　あの人はよく勉強する，感心する
　　⇨あの人のよく勉強するのに感心しました。
(I was impressed by how hard that person studies.)

1．あの人は頭がいい，驚く
2．あの人はよく練習する，びっくりする
3．あの人はいつも遅れる，腹が立つ
4．奨学金がもらえなかった，がっかりする
5．あの人は言葉の使い方が自然だ，感心する
6．あの人が怪我をした，びっくりする

Lesson 20

練習(れんしゅう)　12	なんか

例　どうやって練習をしているんですか。
　　　　⇨どうやって練習なんかしているんですか。
　　　　　(How do you practice, for example?)
　　横浜へ行きたくありません。⇨横浜へなんか行きたくありません。
　　　　　　　　　(I don't want to go to a place like Yokohama.)

1．ジュースを飲みますか。　　　　2．加藤さんは行きますか。
3．中華料理がいいですね。　　　　4．東京に住みたくありません。
5．図書館で勉強したくないです。　6．学者になりません。

練習(れんしゅう)　13	Indirect Quotation

例　どうやって練習しているんでしょう。(I wonder how he/she practices.)
　　　⇨さあ、どうやって練習しているのかわかりません。
　　　(Well, I don't know how he/she practices.)

1．あの人，いつ来たんでしょう。　　2．この仕事，何時頃終わりますか。
3．加藤さん，どうして来ないんでしょう。4．彼，どこに住んでいるんですか。
5．あの人，何年生ですか。　　　　6．彼，どんな仕事をしているんですか。

練習(れんしゅう)　14	CL たら CL

例　バーに行った，あの人がいた　⇨バーに行ったら，あの人がいました。
　　　　　(When I went to the bar, that person was there.)

1．参考書を見た，わかった　　　　2．教科書を見た，書いてあった
3．病気で寝ていた，寂しかった　　4．予習をしていた，田中さんが遊びに来た
5．ゴルフをしてみた，おもしろくなかった　6．御飯を食べていた，彼から電話があった

練習(れんしゅう)　15	S ことができる

例　学校に来る　⇨学校に来ることができました。
　　　　(I was able to come to school.)

1．大学院に入る　　2．奨学金をもらう　　3．日本で勉強する
4．大学を卒業する　5．いい仕事を見つける　6．安くてよいアパートを見つける

二十一課

内容表

文法	Giving and Receiving Things		あげる，くれる，もらう
	Giving and Receiving Favors		て＋あげる，くれる，もらう
	S＋はずだ		手帳に書いてあるはずです。
	「で」—unit		全部で
	"Only, Merely"		それだけ
	"Another ～"		もう＋numerals
	目—Order		三ページ目
	なかなか…ない		なかなか見つからない。
	～の方 (One of the Two)		お宅の方に電話してみます。
	Contractions		て＋いる／いく
	Kinship terms		娘／息子
機能	Stating Factual Information	1-2	あげる，くれる，もらう
	Seeking Factual Information (Giving and Receiving Things/Favors)	1-3	て＋あげる，くれる，もらう
	Indicating Knowledge / Ignorance	2-50	電話番号を知っていたら 何番かわかりますか。
	Stating Factual Information (Giving Telephone Number)	1-2	3753の2640です。
	Expressing Certainty	2-19	手帳に書いてあるはずです。
	Taking Leave / Departing	6-2	あとのことはお願いします。 どうぞ御心配なく。 じゃ，行ってきます。 行っていらっしゃい。
	Stating Hypothesis	1-4	もし，問題があったら わかったら，お願いします。
	Listing / Classifying	2-48	これとこれでしょう。 それと，もう一ページ，これ
	Remembering (Recalling, Reminding)	2-37	忘れずに，…連れてって 水をやるのを忘れないでください。

会話 (かいわ)

1

A：松川さん，これをくれませんか。

B：ああ，すみませんが，それはあげられません。友達からもらった物なので。

2

A：先生，この本を貸してくださいませんか。

B：ああ，その本は貸してあげられないんですよ。森先生に貸していただいた物なので。

3

A：竹井さん，試験の問題，全部もらった？

B：これとこれでしょう。

A：それだけじゃないよ。それともう一ページ。これ。

B：あら，私，これしかもらってないわ。全部で三ページ？

A：うん。じゃ，これをあげるよ。[ありがとう。]先生，三ページ目の問題，もう一枚下さいませんか。

4

A：梅田さん，先生の電話番号を知っていたら，教えてくれませんか。

B：ええ。手帳に書いてあるはずですから。先生のお宅の電話番号は，ちょっと待ってくださいね。なかなか見つからないですね…，ああ，ありました，3753の2640です。[3753の2640ですか。]はい。

A：研究室の電話番号は何番かわかりますか。わかったらそれもお願いします。

B：ええと…，研究室の方は書いてないですね。

A：そうですか。それじゃ，お宅の方にお電話してみます。

1

A：Matsukawa san, won't you give me this?

B：Oh, I'm sorry, but I can't give you that. It's something I got from a friend.

2

A：Sensei, won't you lend me this book?

B：Oh, I can't lend it to you. I borrowed it from Mori sensei.

3

A：Takei san, did you get all the exam questions?

B：This and this, right?

A：That's not all. There's one more page. This one.

B：Well, I only got these. Are there three pages in all?

A：Yes. Then I'll give you this. [Thank you.] Sensei, may I have another third page of problems?

4

A：Umeda san, would you tell me Sensei's phone number if you know it?

B：Yes. It should be written in my memo book. Sensei's home number is … wait a second … I'm having trouble finding it … oh, here it is! It's 3753-2640. [3753-2640?] Yes.

A：Do you know his office phone number? If you do, please tell me that as well.

B：Let's see … I don't have his office number written down.

A：I see. Then I'll try calling him at home.

Lesson 21

5

A：それじゃ，これからでかけますが，あとのことは，よろしくお願いしますね。

B：ええ，どうぞ御心配なく。あとのことは引き受けましたから。

A：忘れずに，犬を散歩に連れてってやってくださいね。[はい。]それから，花や植木に水をやるのを忘れないでくださいね。[はい，わかりました。]もし，何か問題があったら，娘の所に電話をして，相談してください。[はい。]じゃ，行ってきます。

B：お気をつけて。行っていらっしゃい。

単語表 (たんごひょう)

1
松川(まつかわ)	a surname
あげられる	can give Ⅱ

3
全部(ぜんぶ)	all (of things)
だけ	☞ことばの使い方
それと	besides, and
三ページ目	third page
もう	☞ことばの使い方

4
梅田(うめだ)	a surname
電話番号(でんわばんごう)	telephone number
手帳(てちょう)	memo book
はずだ	☞文法
お宅(たく)	someone's house ⬆
なかなか…ない	☞ことばの使い方
見つかる	be found
研究室(けんきゅうしつ)	professor's office
方(ほう)	☞ことばの使い方

5
でかける	go out, set out Ⅱ
あとのこと	☞ことばの使い方
御心配(ごしんぱい)なく	☞ことばの使い方
引き受ける(ひきうける)	take on, take responsibility for Ⅱ
散歩(さんぽ)	a walk
花(はな)	flower
植木(うえき)	plant, potted plant
水(みず)	water
やる	give ⬇
娘(むすめ)	daughter
相談(そうだん)する	consult

5

A：Well then, I'll be off now. You'll take good care of things in my absence, won't you?

B：Yes, please don't worry. I'll take over the responsibilities.

A：Please don't forget to walk the dog. [Yes.] And also, please don't forget to water the flowers and plants. [I understand.] If there's a problem, please call my daughter and ask her what to do. [Yes.] Well, I'm going now.

B：Take care. Good-bye.

関連語句 (かんれんごく)

時計(とけい)	watch, clock	手伝(てつだ)う	help
行(ぎょう)	line, sentence	怒(おこ)る	get mad, angry
動物園(どうぶつえん)	zoo	息子(むすこ)	son
水をかける	sprinkle water II	食べさせる	feed, have ~ eat II
魚(さかな)	fish		

Lesson 21

文法 (ぶんぽう)

● **Verbs of Giving and Receiving**
We have already studied くれる／くださる and もらう／いただく：
- て＋くれる，くださる ☞L. 13
- もらう ☞L. 20
- て＋もらう ☞L. 17

くれる, くださる	もらう, いただく
↓くださる くれる→ R ↑くれる	↓いただく もらう→ R ↑もらう

Note 1　R stands for a recipient who must be "I," "we," or somebody closer to the speaker (*e.g.* family-members or co-workers) than the giver. (See examples 5 and 6 below.)

Note 2　The giver cannot be "I" or "we."

Note 3　In the case of もらう and いただく, the giver is designated by に or から. See the examples below. に and から are interchangeable only when the verb signifies movement or direction in the interaction between the giver and recipient.

　　私は先生に漢字を教えてもらいました。(○から)
　　　(I had my teacher teach me *kanji*.)
　　私は大工さんに家を建ててもらいました。(✕から)
　　　(I had carpenters build a house.)

Note 4　The distinctions apparent in these verbs are regulated by such things as the superior-inferior relationship between the involved parties, the degree of familiarity between the speaker and topical person, the difference in age, station, and gender of the person to whom you are talking, and the situation in which the exchange takes place.

　　For example, you may say 「先生にいただきました」 in a very formal setting or when you are talking to the teacher directly. If you talk about him/her with a friend, however, you will probably say 「先生にもらいました」.

1．父はこの時計を私にくれました。(Father gave me this watch.)
　Giver　　　　Rec.

2．私はこの時計を父に(から)もらいました。(I received this watch from my father.)
　Rec.　　　　　　Giver

3．先生がこの字の読み方を私たちに教えてくださいました。
　　(Sensei taught us how to read this character.)

4．私たちは先生に(から)この字の読み方を教えていただきました。
　　(We had Sensei teach us how to read this character.)

5．友達は母に映画の切符をくれました。
　　(My friend gave my mother a movie ticket.)

264

6. 母は私の友達に切符を買ってもらいました。
   (My mother had my friend buy a movie ticket.)

```
やる, あげる, さしあげる
         ↑ さしあげる
あげる ← [ G ]
         ↓ やる
```

Note 1　G stands for the giver who can be anyone.

Note 2　The recipient cannot be "I" or "we."

1. 何をさしあげましょうか。
   (Lit. What shall I give you? / May I help you? [at a store])
2. 父に誕生日のプレゼントをあげました。
   (I gave my father a birthday present.)
3. 花に水をやりましたか。
   (Did you give water to the flowers? i.e. Did you water the flowers?)
4. 知らない人に道を教えてあげました。
   (I gave directions to a stranger.)
5. 弟に宿題を手伝ってやりました。
   (I helped my younger brother do his homework.)

Note 3　さしあげる is often used by people working in shops and restaurants, and by polite women.

Note 4　Avoid using て＋あげる (さしあげる) with your superiors since it may sound patronizing or condescending. In situations with superiors, use the question form お＋stem＋する.

　　×先生, そのかばん持ってあげましょうか。
　　⇨先生, そのかばん, お持ちしましょうか。／お持ちします。

Note 5　Men prefer やる rather than あげる in conversations with close friends, while women tend to avoid using やる.

● 手帳に書いてある<u>はず</u>です　　4-2

はず is a dependent noun that means the preceding part is expected as a due course of events or a logical result.

Since this is a dependent noun (that always needs a modifier), modifiers take the regular noun modifier forms.

	Verb	い-Adj.	な-Adj.	Noun
Imperf.	行く	寒い	簡単な	学生の
Perfect	行った	寒かった	～だった	

あの人は, 今日, 東京へ行くから, 来ないはずですよ。
(Since he is going to Tokyo today, I don't expect him to come.)

これは, わかるはずですよ。前に勉強したでしょう。
(You should know this. You have studied it before, haven't you?)

あの人，ニューヨーク出身のはずですよ。大学はニューヨーク大学だったはずです。

(I am quite certain that he is from N.Y. He went to, I believe, N.Y. College.)

The negative form of this sentence is S はずがない, and not じゃない. Compare the two sentences below.

1．あの人は来ないはずです。

(We don't expect him today, though there is some possibility that he will come.)

2．あの人が来るはずはないですよ。(There is no possibility of his coming.)

ことばの使い方 (ことばのつかいかた)

● 全部　　3-1

全部 is a quantity noun. It is important to note that quantity nouns are not followed by a regular object-marker (i.e. を，が); they can be followed, however, by the contrastive は and も which means "even."

A：全部わかりましたか。　(Did you understand everything?)
B：全部はわかりませんね。(Not everything.)

● 全部で　　3-4

This で indicates a unit of numbers.

1．この鉛筆，一本いくらですか。一ダースでいくらですか。

(How much is it for one pencil? How much is it for a dozen?)

2．アメリカ合衆国は，はじめ十三州で始まりました。

(The United States of America began with thirteen states.)

3．これは，みんな五ドルです。(Every item is five dollars.)

4．これは，みんなで五ドルです。(These are five dollars all together.)

● それだけじゃ ない(ありません) よ　　3-3

This だけ limits the preceding word or clause to itself; its function is similar to the English "only."

1．私がもっているお金はこれだけです。(This is all the money I have.)

2．来たのは松川さんだけです。(The only person who came was Matsukawa san.)

● もう一ページ　　3-3

もう used with numerals means "another ～." It shares some similarities with あと (☞L. 19 ことばの使い方「あと二年」), but もう simply means "another ～"; unlike あと, it does not have the nuance of making something complete or perfect.

1．コーヒー，もう一杯どうですか。

(How about another cup of coffee?)

2．すみませんけど，もう三日だけ待ってくれませんか。

(Would you please wait just three more days?)

● 三ページ目　　　3-5

This 目, placed after a numeral and counter, stands for ordinal numbers. (i.e. first, second, third ...) When you mean "third page," you can simply say 三ページ. This, however, can cause a misunderstanding ("three pages" as opposed to "page three," for example). To avoid confusion, it is useful to add 目 to cardinal numbers to create ordinal numbers.

  三ページ読んでください。(Read three pages.)
  三ページを読んでください。／三ページ目を読んでください。(Read the third page.)
  五行読んでください。(Please read five lines.)
  五行目を読んでください。(Please read the fifth line.)

 Note: In 三ページを読んでください, を may be dropped in ordinary conversation and the sentence can become the same as that which means, "Read three pages." The addition of 目, therefore, functions to clarify the meaning of such sentences.

● 電話番号の言い方　　　4-3

The Chinese reading for numerals is used in giving a telephone number. Please note that the last vowel of the mono-syllabic numbers, in other words, of those written in one *hiragana*, is lengthened in speech.

  1　いち　　　　　6　ろく
 ☆2　にい(に)　　　7　なな
  3　さん　　　　　8　はち
  4　よん　　　　　9　きゅう
 ☆5　ごお(ご)　　　0　ゼロ, れい(零), まる(〇)

For example. The number 123-4567 reads いち, にい, さん の よん, ごお, ろく, なな. The hyphen is read as "の" in spoken Japanese.

There are two special telephone numbers that are read differently:

  110　(ひゃくとお番)　　　Police station
  119　(ひゃくじゅうきゅう番)　Fire station, Ambulance

Note that the telephone numbers in the metropolitan Tokyo area are now two sets of four digit numbers. The first number in the first four digits is 3 or 5, as shown in the dialogue.

● なかなか見つからないですね　　　4-3

This is an adverb indicating that it takes time to complete the action or reach the state described by the verb. (なかなか used in this sense is always followed by a negative.)

  竹井さん, どうしたんでしょうね。なかなか来ませんね。
  (What's happened to Takei san? He hasn't arrived yet.)
  大きくて, 安い家はなかなか見つからないですね。
  (A large and inexpensive house is hard to find.)

● 見つかる　　　4-3

As this verb is an intransitive verb, the object to be found is designated by が. The corresponding transitive verb is 見つける. The difference between them is that the intransitive verb indicates a natural, spontaneous occurrence, whereas the transitive verb signifies intentional action.

  A：あの本, 見つかりましたよ。(That book has been found.)

Lesson 21

　　　　B：どこで見つけたんですか。(Where did you find it?)
　　　　A：神田の古本屋で，偶然見つけました。
　　　　　　(I found it by accident at a second-hand bookstore in Kanda.)

● お宅　　　4-7

This is the formal equivalent of 家 and is used to refer to someone's house. It is also used as a second person pronoun (to mean "you") among business people and some college students.

● （お宅の）方　　　4-7

This 方 is used in referring or pointing to one of two items and is very important in making comparisons. We will learn about comparisons in L. 22.
　　　　A：昨日帰らなかったので，お父さん，怒ったでしょう。
　　　　B：いいえ，母の方が怒りました。
　　　　　　(A：Your father must have gotten mad at you because you didn't go home yesterday.)
　　　　　　(B：No, it was mother who got angry at me.)

● でかける　　　5-1

This word means "to go out." The destination of the speaker is usually not specified.

● あとのこと　　　5-1

This phrase means "things to be done after something is done (here, one is gone)."

● よろしくお願いします　　　5-1

This expression is used to conclude your request(s). It literally means: "Now that I leave everything to you, please handle it in a favorable way."

● どうぞ御心配なく　　　5-2

This phrase is used to reassure the hearer that you are worthy of his/her trust. Use this expression when you feel that the hearer seems dubious or unconvinced that you are capable of handling something.
　　　　A：明日，必ず四時に来てくださいよ。遅れないでくださいね。
　　　　　　(Please be sure to come at four tomorrow. Don't be late.)
　　　　B：どうぞ御心配なく。(Don't worry.)

● 忘れずに　　　5-3

This adverbial phrase, meaning "without ～ing," modifies the verbal phrase that follows it. The form is a carry-over from classical Japanese and is used as frequently as its modern version ～ないで. (☞L. 19「そんなこと言わないで」) The only irregularity with this form is that when used with the verb する the す turns to せ; せずに is a correct phrase.
　　　　風邪を引いたので，今日は，勉強せずに早く寝ます。
　　　　　　(Since I caught cold, I will go to bed early without studying.)

● 連れて行く　　　5-3

In contrast to 持って行く whose object must be inanimate, 連れて行く takes an animate object which can move around with you. The object is usually dependent on and inferior to the subject who takes the leadership or initiative.

　　　The object of this phrase, therefore, can be deemed weaker than the subject who is taking the lead. If you want to avoid this sense of power relationships, use 〜と一緒(いっしょ)に行く, "to go with."

1．昨日(きのう)は，子供(こども)を連れて動物園(どうぶつえん)に行きました。
   (I took my children to the zoo yesterday.)
2．明日のパーティーに友達を連れて来てもいいですか。
   (May I bring a friend to the party tomorrow?)

● 連れてってやってくださいね　　5-3

This is a slightly complicated pattern though it is basically the same as what we have been studying in this lesson. First of all, 連れてって is the contracted form of 連れて行って, which is explained at the end of this section.

Secondly, the expression 連れて行って＋やる means "Doing (the dog) a favor by taking it out for a walk." Thirdly, て＋ください means "Do me (the speaker) a favor by doing something." In sum, this sentence literally means: "Do me a favor by doing the dog a favor by taking it out for a walk."

● 娘　　5-5

Since this is a kinship term, its form varies, depending on whose daughter is in question. To refer to your own daughter, use 娘. To refer to another person's daughter, use 娘さん or お嬢(じょう)さん.

With a son, use 息子(むすこ)／息子さん.

● 行ってきます　　5-5

This is a greeting used when leaving a place where you will return to later. It is used every morning by those going off to school or work to bid farewell to those who are still at home. The polite equivalent is 行ってまいります in which まいります is the humble form of 行きます and 来ます.

● 行っていらっしゃい　　5-6

This is an expression used in response to 行ってきます.

● お気をつけて　　5-6

This is the polite form of 気をつけて which means "Be careful in doing 〜." Some older people may insist that this should be お気をおつけになって, but お気をつけて has been established as an acceptable expression.

[On Contractions]

Take a look at the following dialogue sentences from this lesson:

　　　私，これしかもらってません。　　　　3-4　⇨もらっていません
　　　犬を散歩に連れてってやってくださいね。　5-3　⇨連れて行ってやって

In these sentences, い is missing from the underlined parts. The first and second sentences should orthographically be read as the forms indicated by the arrows. The expressions following the arrows are the correct written forms, but the dialogue sentences represent the most common patterns in normal spoken Japanese. These phenomena are called "contractions," and we will encounter more of them in later chapters. Contractions are formularized as shown in the following page.

Lesson 21

Remember that these forms are for speaking and not for writing.

て＋いる，いらっしゃる	⇨	て＋る，らっしゃる(読んでる)
て＋いたら	⇨	て＋たら(知ってたら)
て＋いく	⇨	て＋く(持ってく)

練習(れんしゅう)

練習(れんしゅう) 1 　　　　やる／あげる／さしあげる

例　松川さん，これ　⇨松川さんにこれをあげましょうか。
　　　　　　　　　　　(Shall I give this to Matsukawa san?)
　　先生，この本　　⇨先生にこの本をさしあげましょうか。
　　　　　　　　　　　(Shall I give this book to Sensei?)
　　猫，御飯　　　　⇨猫に御飯をやりましょうか。(Shall I feed the cat?)

1．竹井さん，日本語の教科書　　　2．先生，このテープ
3．花，水　　　　　　　　　　　　4．秋山さんのお母さん，この雑誌
5．犬，食べる物　　　　　　　　　6．石井さん，この背広
7．秋山さんのお父さん，いいウィスキー　8．梅田さん，自転車

練習(れんしゅう) 2 　　　　～て＋やる／あげる，お＋stem＋する

例　松川さん，これを貸す　⇨松川さんにこれを貸してあげましょうか。
　　　　　　　　　　　　　　(Shall I lend this to Matsukawa san?)
　　先生，この本を貸す　　⇨先生にこの本をお貸ししましょうか。
　　　　　　　　　　　　　　(Shall I lend this book to Sensei?)
　　猫，御飯を食べさせる　⇨猫に御飯を食べさせてやりましょうか。
　　　　　　　　　　　　　　(Shall I feed the cat?)

1．竹井さん，日本語の教科書を買ってくる
2．先生，音楽のテープを作る
3．花，水をかける
4．秋山さんのお母さん，この雑誌を貸す
5．犬，食べる物を作る
6．秋山さんのお父さん，ウィスキーを持つ
7．梅田さん，自転車を貸す
8．石井さん，このニュースを教える

練習(れんしゅう) 3　　　あげる／もらう

例　この本を貸してあげる
　　　⇨この本は，貸してあげたいんだけど，貸してあげられないんですよ。
　　　　(I want to lend you this book, but it's not possible.)
　　この本を貸してもらう
　　　⇨この本は，貸してもらいたいんだけど，貸してもらえないんですよ。
　　　　(I want to borrow this book, but I can't.)

1．おいしいケーキを作ってあげる　　　2．友達に宿題を手伝ってもらう
3．もう一回試験をしてあげる　　　　　4．手紙を書いてもらう
5．電話番号を調べてあげる　　　　　　6．散歩に連れて行ってもらう

練習(れんしゅう) 4　　　もう＋number

例　本，一冊　⇨この本を一冊下さい。ああ，そうだ，もう一冊，お願いします。
　　(Please give me a copy of this book. Oh, yes, give me one more copy.)

1．カード，百枚　　　2．じゃがいも，一つ　　　3．ジュース，二本
4．クリップ，一箱　　5．魚，一匹　　　　　　　6．紙，一枚

練習(れんしゅう) 5　　　だけ

例　これを作りました。　⇨これだけ作りました。(I made only this.)
　　加藤さんが来ました。⇨加藤さんだけ来ました。(Only Kato san came.)

1．これがわかりました。　2．これが欲しいんですが。　3．この本が嫌いです。
4．切符をもらいました。　5．日本語の授業を休みました。　6．発音がいいです。

練習(れんしゅう) 6　　　quantity＋で

例　このクラス，全部，五十人　⇨このクラスは全部で五十人です。
　　(In total, this class has fifty people.)

1．この教科書，二冊，六十ドル　　　2．この紙，五百枚，八ドル
3．この料理，全部，二千円　　　　　4．このたばこ，一箱，三ドル
5．この大学の学生，全部，一万人　　6．この消しゴム，二つ，百円

Lesson 21

練習(れんしゅう)　7　　　　　number＋目

例　三ページ目の問題　⇨三ページ目の問題を下さい。
(Please give me the problems on the third page.)

欲しいんですが　⇨三ページ目の問題が欲しいんですが。
(I would like the problems on the third page.)

1．ないんですが　　　　2．三つ目の質問　　　　3．よくわからないんですが
4．三行目の漢字　　　　5．はっきりしないんですが　6．二枚目の問題
7．二人目の人が言ったこと　8．四行目の字　　　　9．よく見えないんですが

練習(れんしゅう)　8　　　　　はず

例　梅田さんは来る，そう言った
　　⇨梅田さんは来るはずですよ。そう言いましたから。
(Umeda san should be coming. He said that he would.)

1．全部あげた，全部ない　　　　2．書いてある，前に聞いた
3．これに書いてある，前に調べた　4．梅田さんは行く，そう言った
5．この部屋にある，昨日見た　　6．あそこで売っている，先週買った
7．梅田さんはわかる，前に教えた　8．梅田さんは日本語が話せる，日本で生まれた

練習(れんしゅう)　9　　　　　なかなか

例　先生のお宅の電話番号，見つからない
　　⇨ちょっと待ってくださいね。先生のお宅の電話番号がなかなか見つからないんですよ。
(Please wait a second, I'm having trouble finding Sensei's home number.)

1．この問題，わからない　2．眼鏡，見つからない　3．梅田さん，「行く」と言わない
4．竹井さん，来ない　　　5．予習，終わらない　　6．病気，治らない

練習(れんしゅう)　10　　　　　Sかわかる

例　先生のお宅の電話番号，何番
　　⇨先生のお宅の電話番号が何番かわかりますか。わかったらお願いします。
(Do you know Sensei's phone number at home? If you do, please tell me.)

1．宿題，何ページ　　　　　2．あの人，何という人
3．試験，いつ　　　　　　　4．松川さんのお宅，どこ
5．竹井さん，どうして休んでいる　6．梅田さん，どこに住んでいる

練習(れんしゅう) 11　　　ないで⇨ずに

例　御飯を食べないで来てくださいね。
　　⇨御飯を食べずに来てくださいね。(Please come without having dinner.)

1．忘れないで切符をもらってくださいね。
2．竹井さんを誘わないで映画に行きましょうね。
3．勉強しないで遊びましょう。
4．遊ばないで勉強しましょう。
5．驚かないで聞いてくださいね。
6．電話をしないで帰りましょう。

練習(れんしゅう) 12　　　Contraction／ている⇨てる

例　何を食べているんですか。⇨何を食べてるんですか。(What are you eating?)

1．勉強していますか。
2．何を書いているんですか。
3．誰と会っていましたか。
4．何をしていらっしゃるんですか。
5．雑誌を読んでいらっしゃるんですか。

二十二課

内容表

文法	Comparing Two Things： 　"Between A and B, which is ～er?" 　"A is ～er than B." 　"A is not as ～ as B." Comparing More Than Two Things： 　"Which / What is the ～est?" 　"A is the ～est." S＋かもしれない (Possibility) S＋といけない (Duty, obligation) 「と」Showing mutuality		AとBとでは，どちらが～。 Aの方が(Bより)～。 AはBほど～ない。 ～の中で，どれ／何が一番～。 Nが一番～。 そうかもしれませんね。 シカゴへ行かないといけない 私と同じですね。
機能	Comparing	2-36	どちらがお金がかかりますか。 どっちが経済的ですか。 家賃はアメリカの方が日本より高い。 アメリカの家の方が大きい。 シカゴは東京ほど物価は高くない。 私と同じですね。
	Expressing Obligation	2-20	行かないといけない 運動した方がいいんでしょうけど
	Expressing Possibility	2-13	そうかもしれません。
	Giving/Citing Examples	2-47	例えば，家賃はどうですか。 物価はどうですか。
	Indicating Knowledge/Ignorance	2-50	はっきりとはわかりませんが
	Expressing Agreement	2-1	それはそうでしょうね。 私もそう思います。
	Stating Hypothesis	1-4	できれば
	Requesting Permission	2-22	～てよろしいでしょうか。
	Granting Permission	2-21	結構です。

Lesson 22

会話 (かいわ)

1

A：私，今度，仕事でシカゴへ行かないといけないんですが。[ああ，いいですね。]シカゴと東京とでは，どちらがお金がかかりますか。どっちが経済的ですか。

B：シカゴと東京ですか。その比較は難しいですね。

A：そうかもしれませんね。でも，例えば，家賃はどうですか。

B：家賃はアメリカの方が日本より高いですが，でも，アメリカの家の方が，ずっと大きいし広いですからね。

A：それは，そうでしょうね。物価はどうですか。

B：はっきりとはわかりませんが，シカゴは東京ほど物価は高くないでしょう。

2

A：大宮さんは，スポーツの中で何が一番好きですか。

B：スポーツの中でですか。そうですねえ。野球が一番好きですね。

A：自分でするのとテレビで見るのとでは，どちらが好きですか。

B：テレビで見る方が好きですね。

A：じゃ，私と同じですね。本当はもっと運動した方がいいんでしょうけどねえ。

B：ええ，私もそう思います。

1

A：I have to go to Chicago soon on business ... [Well, how nice.] ... but between (living in) Chicago and Tokyo, which would be more expensive? Which would be more economical?

B：Between Chicago and Tokyo? That's a difficult comparison.

A：That may be so. But what about rent, for example?

B：Rent in America is more expensive than rent in Japan, but American houses are larger and more spacious.

A：I can understand that. How about the cost of living?

B：I'm not sure, but the cost of living in Chicago is probably not as high as that in Tokyo.

2

A：Omiya san, of all sports, which do you like best?

B：Of all sports? Well, I like baseball best.

A：Between playing it yourself and watching it on television, which would you prefer to do?

B：I prefer watching it on television.

A：Then you're like me. I suppose it would be better for us if we got more exercise, but ...

B：Yes, I think so, too.

Lesson 22

3

A：寺山先生，夏休みに日本語を勉強するつもりなんですが，[はい。]ここで，勉強するのと日本へ行くのと，どっちがいいでしょうか。

B：それは，できれば日本へ行く方がいいですが，何か奨学金はありますか。

A：まだ，調べてありませんが，きっと何かあると思います。

B：ええ，何かあるはずですよ。もしあったら日本へ行くのが一番いいですね。日本人の家に住んで，日本語の学校へ通うのが一番いいですよ。

A：そうですか。それじゃ，奨学金のことをもう少し調べてから，また来ます。推薦状が必要な時はお願いしてよろしいでしょうか。

B：ええ，結構ですよ。

単語表 (たんごひょう)

1

どちら	which (one of two)
お金がかかる	cost money
どっち	colloquial equivalent of どちら
経済的(けいざいてき)だ	economical
比較(ひかく)	comparison
そうかもしれない	it may be so
例(たと)えば	for example
家賃(やちん)	rent
高(たか)い	expensive
広(ひろ)い	spacious, wide
物価(ぶっか)	prices
ほど	☞文法

2

大宮(おおみや)	a surname
(と)同(おな)じだ	same as

3

寺山(てらやま)	a surname
できれば	if possible
きっと	certainly, most probably
一番(いちばん)いい	best
通(かよ)う	commute
推薦状(すいせんじょう)	a letter of recommendation
必要(ひつよう)だ	necessary
よろしい，結構(けっこう)だ	☞ことばの使い方

3

A：Terayama sensei, I plan to study Japanese during the summer holidays, but ... [Yes?] ... which would be better, studying here or going to Japan?

B：It would certainly be better to go to Japan if it's possible, but do you have access to a scholarship?

A：I haven't looked into that yet, but I'm sure there's something available.

B：Yes, there should be something. If you can find something, it's best to go to Japan. It's best to live with a Japanese family and commute to a Japanese language school.

A：I see. Then, I'll come back after I've done a little more research on scholarships. If I need a letter of recommendation, may I ask you (to write one for me)?

B：Yes, certainly.

関連語句 (かんれんごく)

バス	bus	払(はら)う	pay
乗り物(のりもの)	transportation	電車(でんしゃ)	(electric) train
すし	sushi	安全(あんぜん)だ	safe
交通(こうつう)が便利(べんり)だ	transportation (system) is convenient	考(かんが)え	idea, thought
隣(となり)の家	house next-door		

Lesson 22

文法 (ぶんぽう)

● **Comparison**

In this lesson, we are going to learn how to compare two items and how to say that something is the best. In other words, we will learn how to express ideas that, in English, are related to comparative and superlative cases (i.e. 〜er and 〜est.)

1) Comparing Two Items

When you want to know which is the larger between A and B, the question is:

$$\begin{Bmatrix} AとBとでは \\ AとBでは \\ AとBと \end{Bmatrix} \begin{Bmatrix} どちら \\ どっち \end{Bmatrix} が大きいですか。$$ (Between A and B, which is larger?)

As the basic pattern, let's adopt the first expression, even though you may hear sentences with other alternatives. In this basic sentence, と is the same as the と in "N1 と N2," but in old Japanese, a second と appears after the second noun; it is a remnant of classical Japanese. で functions to limit the scope or frame to A and B. This restriction can be expanded, as you will see in the following section, by simply adding C, D, and so on.

The difference between どちら and どっち: the former is formal and the latter is colloquial. どちら is recommended for use in writing. It means: "which of the two?" Both words belong to the following series of words:

こちら	こっち	(this one)
そちら	そっち	(that one)
あちら	あっち	(that one over there)
どちら	どっち	(which one of the two)

Note 1   There are no particular comparative cases in this pattern as there are in English. Use ordinary words without adding suffixes.

Note 2   The words that can be used in this pattern are not limited to adjectives; adverbs and some adjectival expressions such as お金がかかる appearing in the first dialogue can also be used.

Note 3   The particle following どちら, どっち, and the noun in answering questions, as shown below, is always が.

Here are a few possible answers to the above question:

1) Aが大きいです。　　　(A is large(r).)
2) Aの方が大きいです。　(A is larger.)
3) Aの方がBより大きいです。 (A is larger than B.)

1. A：ダウンタウンへ行くのに、バスと電車ではどちらが便利ですか。
   B：バスの方が便利ですね。
   A：値段はどうでしょう。
   B：値段は電車の方がバスより安いと思いますよ。

   (A：Which is more convenient to go downtown, taking the bus or the train?)
   (B：The bus is more convenient.)
   (A：How about the fare?)

(B：In terms of the fare, I think the train is cheaper than the bus.)
2．A：このコンピューターとそれと，どっちがいいでしょう。これですか。
　　B：それよりこっちの方がいいですよ。
　　　（A：Which computer is better, this or that one? This one?）
　　　（B：This is better than that one.）

2) Comparing More Than Two Items

When comparing more than two things, どちら can no longer be used. Depending on the type of question, どれ, どの＋N or 何 is used.

1．AとBとC（の中）で，どれ／どの＋N／何が一番～ですか。
2．N (showing category)（の中）で，何／誰／どこ／いつ etc. が一番～ですか。

If the items to be compared are arranged in such a way that you can physically point them out, use どれ or どの＋N. Otherwise, use 何, 誰, どこ, いつ, etc.

1．ここにあるケーキの中でどれが一番おいしそうですか。
　　（Of all the cakes here, which one looks the tastiest?）
2．アメリカの町の中でどこが一番住みやすいですか。
　　（Of all the towns in the United States, which is the most comfortable to live in?）
3．乗り物の中で，何が一番安全ですか。
　　（Of all forms of transportation, which is the safest?）

The possible answers to such questions are:

1．Aです。
2．Aが一番です。
3．Aが一番～です。

Be aware of the presence and position of the particle が in the questions and answers.

● そうかもしれませんね　　1-4

　S＋かもしれません

This pattern indicates that there is a slight possibility of S. The sentence endings should be as follows: (Compare this with the diagram in L. 21「はず」. P. 265)

	Verb	い-Adj.	な-Adj.	Noun
Imperf.	行く	寒い	(だ) 0	
Perfect	行った	寒かった	だった	

Note 1　There is a "0" between the な-adjs. and nouns. It indicates that だ has to be deleted here when it is connected with かもしれない.

Note 2　Negative sentences in plain form can precede かもしれない as shown in the first example.

1．大宮さんは，ゆうべ帰って来なかったかもしれませんよ。
　　（It is possible that Omiya san did not come home last night.）
2．今夜は，大雨かもしれないと天気予報で言っていましたよ。
　　（The weather forecast said that there may be heavy rain tonight.）

Lesson 22

● シカゴは東京ほど物価は高くない　　　1-8

　　N1 は N2 ほど~ない

This pattern is also used to compare two items, but in a slightly different way from what we have so far seen. It signifies that "N1 is not as ~ as N2," and the adjectivals are always used in the negative forms.

　　大宮さんは，寺田さんほど真面目じゃありません。
　　　(Omiya san is not as diligent as Terada san.)
　　大宮さんは，寺田さんほど真面目に勉強しません。
　　　(Omiya san does not study as hard as Terada san.)

ことばの使い方 (ことばのつかいかた)

● 今度　　　1-1　　☞ L. 19 ことばの使い方「今度の集まり」

● 行かないといけない　　　1-1

In L. 17, we studied the "Pre-ない form＋なければならない" which expresses a voluntary sense of obligation or duty. The pattern we are learning here, on the contrary, signifies obligation and duty, but forced upon by others in the form of an order, rules, or expectations. The same idea can be expressed by the "Pre-ない form＋なければいけない."

　　さっき家内から電話があったので，すぐ帰らないといけないんですよ。
　　　(I had a telephone call from my wife a short while ago, so I have to go home right away.)

● 例えば　　　1-4

This expression is used to solicit or give examples of something.

1．A：今夜はいろいろしなければならないことがあって，遊びには行けませんよ。
　　B：例えば，どんなことですか。
　　　(A：There are so many things I have to do tonight I can't go out with you.)
　　　(B：For example, what things? / Like what?)

2．私は日本料理が大好きです。例えば，すしなら，毎日食べたいですね。
　　　(I love Japanese food. For example, I don't mind having *sushi*, every day!)

● ずっと　　　1-5

This is an adverb used to emphasize the degree of an adjectival in a comparative sentence like the English words "much" and "far." The following adverbs showing the degree of adjectivals can be used in this pattern: ちょっと, 少し (a little), もう少し (a little more), ずっと (far).

　　A：東京はニューヨークよりずっと大きいですか。
　　B：いいえ，少し大きいだけですよ。
　　　(A：Is Tokyo far bigger than New York?)
　　　(B：No, it is just a little bigger.)

● それはそうだ　　　1-7

それ is a vague reference to the topic of a preceding sentence or thought; it functions to set it up again as a topic, and what follows expresses the opinion of the speaker concerning the topic. それはそうだ is more emphatic than simply saying そうだ.

1．A：昨日、隣の家が火事になりましてね。
　　B：それは、驚いたでしょう。
　　　（A：Fire broke out at my neighbor's house yesterday …）
　　　（B：That must have surprised you!）
2．A：明日の授業、出ますか。(Will you attend class tomorrow?)
　　B：それは出ますよ。　　　(Of course, I will!)

● はっきりとはわからない　　　1-8

This expression means the same thing as はっきりはわからない. Adverbs such as はっきり, which end in り, are followed by と, as in: はっきりとする、はっきりと言う. The presence or absence of と does not affect the meaning of the sentence.

● 私と同じですね　　　2-5

Note that the particle this word takes is と. The opposite expression is 〜と違う which means "different from 〜." This と represents a "mutuality," a reciprocity in the actions or states of an exchange or situation. In other words, it does not describe a one-directional interplay, as can be evidenced in the following sentences:

1．大宮さんは、寺山さんと結婚しました。
　　(Omiya san got married to Terayama san.)
2．昨日、森さんと会って、買い物に行きました。
　　(I met with Mori san yesterday and went shopping.)
3．A：「僕」は「私」と意味が同じですか。
　　B：ええ、意味は同じですが、使う人が「私」と違いますね。
　　　（A：Is "boku" the same in meaning as "watashi?"）
　　　（B：Yes, the meaning is the same but a person who uses it would be different from one who uses "watashi."）

● もっと運動する　　　2-5　☞ L. 18「もっとはっきり」. P. 222

● 運動した方がいいんでしょうけど　　　2-5

All that the speaker of this sentence is doing is guessing that doing more exercise would benefit himself. ん＋です／でしょう signifies conjecture based on solid evidence.

(Looking down from a room in a tall building at people running helter-skelter, holding bags and other things over their heads, you can say:)
1．雨が降り始めたんですね。(I guess it has started to rain.)

(Seeing that your friend, as usual, has not come to class on time, you say:)
2．また、寝坊しているんでしょう。(I suppose he has overslept again.)

● できれば　　　3-3

This expression and できたら share almost the same meaning. できれば, however, may sound slightly more formal than できたら.

Lesson 22

A：明日，私の研究室にちょっと来てくれませんか。
B：はい。何時頃，行ったらいいでしょうか。
A：できれば，九時半頃がいいですね。
　　(A：Will you drop in at my office tomorrow?)
　　(B：Yes. Around what time shall I come?)
　　(A：If you can, around nine-thirty would be the best.)

● お願いしてよろしいでしょうか　　3-8

よろしい is the formal equivalent of いい. Its usage, which is "to receive permission or approval" from someone, is limited to the pattern "て＋よろしい."

● 結構です　　3-9

This phrase generally means: "It's perfect." or "There is nothing more to be desired." 結構 is interchangeable with いい, but cannot be used in question forms. Use this expression when you are asked to give your opinion, permission, or approval.

練習 (れんしゅう)

| 練習(れんしゅう)　1 | 〜ないといけない |

例　仕事でシカゴに行く　⇨仕事でシカゴに行かないといけないんですよ。
　　　　(I have to go to Chicago on business.)

1．今夜は早く家に帰る　　　　　2．友達に，今，電話する
3．もっと運動する　　　　　　　4．夏休みに日本語の勉強をする
5．奨学金をもらう　　　　　　　6．奨学金のことを調べる
7．日本語の学校に通う　　　　　8．推薦状をお願いする

| 練習(れんしゅう)　2 | N1 と N2 とでは，どちらが〜 |

例　シカゴ，東京，お金がかかる
　　　⇨シカゴと東京とでは，どちらがお金がかかりますか。
　　　(Which would be more costly, being in Chicago or Tokyo?)

1．シカゴ，東京，経済的だ　　　2．シカゴ，東京，大きい
3．シカゴ，東京，安全だ　　　　4．シカゴ，東京，物価が高い
5．シカゴ，東京，交通が便利だ　6．シカゴ，東京，好きだ

練習(れんしゅう) 3　　　　N1 の方が (N2 より)〜

例　東京，お金がかかる　⇨東京の方がお金がかかりますよ。
　　　　　　　　　　　　　([Being in] Tokyo is more costly.)

1．シカゴ，経済的だ　　　　2．東京，大きい　　　　　3．東京，安全だ
4．東京，物価が高い　　　　5．東京，交通が便利だ　　6．シカゴ，好きだ

練習(れんしゅう) 4　　　　N1 の方が N2 より〜

例　東京，シカゴ，お金がかかる
　　⇨東京の方がシカゴよりお金がかかりますか。
　　　　(Is [being in] Tokyo more costly than [being in] Chicago?)

1．東京，シカゴ，経済的だ　　　　2．東京，シカゴ，大きい
3．東京，シカゴ，安全だ　　　　　4．東京，シカゴ，物価が高い
5．東京，シカゴ，交通が便利だ　　6．東京，シカゴ，好きだ

練習(れんしゅう) 5　　　　〜かもしれません

例　そうだ。(That is so.)　⇨そうかもしれませんね。(That may be so.)

1．その比較は難しい。　　　2．あの人は野球が好きだ。
3．今夜，大雪が降る。　　　4．その問題は前に調べたことがある。
5．新しい方が経済的だ。　　6．大宮さんは家賃(やちん)を払(はら)っていない。
7．寺山さんは病気(びょうき)だった。

練習(れんしゅう) 6　　　　〜の方が〜かもしれない

例　家賃，アメリカ，日本，高い
　　⇨家賃はアメリカの方が日本より高いかもしれませんね。
　　　　(Rent in America may be more expensive than that in Japan.)

1．勉強，大宮さん，寺山さん，する　　　　2．漢字(かんじ)，この教科書(きょうかしょ)，それ，多い
3．背(せ)，大宮さん，寺山さん，高い　　　4．頭(あたま)，大宮さん，寺山さん，いい
5．着物(きもの)，中年(ちゅうねん)の人，若(わか)い人，よく着る　　6．漢字(かんじ)，あの人，私，書ける

Lesson 22

練習(れんしゅう)　7　　　　　　　Intensifying Adverbs

例　少し　⇨シカゴの方が少し大きいですね。
　　　　　　　(Chicago is slightly larger.)

1．ちょっと　　　2．もう少し　　　3．ずっと　　　4．もっと
5．少し　　　　　6．もうちょっと

練習(れんしゅう)　8　　　　　　　N1 は N2 ほど〜ない

例　シカゴ，東京，お金がかかる
　　　⇨シカゴは東京ほどお金がかからないでしょう。
　　　([Being in] Chicago is probably not as costly as [being in] Tokyo.)

1．東京，シカゴ，経済的だ　　　　　　2．シカゴ，東京，大きい
3．シカゴ，東京，安全だ　　　　　　　4．シカゴ，東京，物価が高い
5．東京，シカゴ，交通が便利だ　　　　6．シカゴ，東京，好きだ

練習(れんしゅう)　9　　　　　　　〜の中で一番〜

例　授業，おもしろい　⇨授業の中で，何が一番おもしろいですか。
　　　　　　　(Which of all your classes is most interesting?)
　　この辞書，使いやすい　⇨この辞書の中で，どれが一番使いやすいですか。
　　　　　　　(Which of all these dictionaries is easiest to use?)

1．授業，退屈だ　　　　　　　　　　2．アメリカの町，住みやすい
3．このクラス，背が高い　　　　　　4．この家，あの家，その家，広い
5．ここにある小説，人気がある　　　6．ここにいる人，早く来た
7．若い学生の遊び，人気がある

練習(れんしゅう)　10　　　　　　VP と VP とでは，どっちが

例　自分でする，テレビで見る
　　　⇨自分でするのと，テレビで見るのとではどっちが好きですか。
　　　(Which do you prefer, doing it yourself or watching it on television?)

1．自分で料理を作る，レストランで食べる　　2．旅行する，家でのんびりする
3．自分で運転する，ほかの人に運転してもらう　4．お風呂に入る，シャワーを浴びる
5．友達と電話で話す，手紙を書く　　　　　　　6．宿題が多い，全然ない

二十二課

練習(れんしゅう) 11　　　　～と同じ／違う

例　この本，同じ　⇨この本は私のと同じですね。(This book is the same as mine.)

1．このコンピューター，違う　　　2．あの人の漢字の書き方，同じ
3．父の考え，同じ　　　　　　　　4．あの人の考え，違う
5．妹(いもうと)の話し方，同じ　　6．加藤さんの考え，違う

練習(れんしゅう) 12　　　　て＋あります

例　奨学金のこと，調べる
　　⇨奨学金のことは，まだ調べてありません。
　　(I have not yet looked into scholarships.／Scholarships have not yet been researched.)

1．推薦状，書いてもらう　　　　　2．部屋(へや)，掃除(そうじ)する
3．今日の宿題，やる　　　　　　　4．文法(ぶんぽう)の説明(せつめい)，読(よ)む
5．今日のパーティーの料理，作る　6．日本語学校のこと，調べる

練習(れんしゅう) 13　　　　もっと～した方がいいんでしょう

例　運動する　⇨もっと運動した方がいいんでしょうけど，したくないんですよ。
　　(I suppose I should exercise more, but I don't want to.)
　　いろいろな所に行く
　　⇨もっといろいろな所に行った方がいいんでしょうけど，行きたくないんですよ。
　　(I suppose I should go to many more places, but I don't want to.)

1．旅行する　　　2．友達と一緒(いっしょ)に遊びに行く　　3．テープを聞いて練習する
4．たくさん本を読む　5．両親(りょうしん)に手紙を書く　　6．いろいろな本で調べる

練習(れんしゅう) 14　　　　もし，～たら

例　奨学金がある，教える　⇨もし，奨学金があったら，教えてください。
　　(If you find a scholarship, please let me know.)

1．興味(きょうみ)がある，来る　2．時間がある，調べる　　3．わかる，すぐ教える
4．必要(ひつよう)だ，知らせる　5．日本へ行く，私の友達に会う　6．田中さんが来る，電話する

二十三課

内容表

文法	なる，する 　　い／な -adj.＋なる，する 　　S＋ことになる，する 　　S＋ことにしている，なっている て＋くる S みたいだ 　　Figurative 　　Feeling, Impression 「〜たい」と object N1 を N2 にする NP＋について NP が気になる 〜なくては＋Negative Statement		Change (Natural, Deliberate) 暖かくなる 行くことにする 走ることにしている。 暖かくなってきました。 今日はハワイみたいです。 今日は寒いみたいです。 父は私をサラリーマンにしたくない。 テーブルを机にする。 ベッドがなくちゃ困る。
機能	Stating Factual Information 　　(Change)	1-2	暖かくなる etc. 暖かくする etc.
	Comparing	2-36	まるでハワイみたいですね
	Commenting on a Topic/Subject	7-11	何だか／気のせいかもしれませんが
	Stating Factual Information 　　(Telling of Occupation)	1-2	Name of Occupation＋をしている
	Expressing Surprise	3-8	本当に増えましたね。
	Stating Generalization	1-5	S ことにしている。
	Expressing Certainty	2-19	間違いなく〜でしょうね。
	Stating Factual Information 　　(Decision)	1-2	〜ことにする／なる
	Focusing on a Topic	7-3	NP について
	Expressing Fear/Worry	3-6	NP が気になる
	Complaint	3-28	知らせてくれたら，よかったのに。
	Stating Intentions	2-9	行こうかなと思っている。
	Asking for/Offering Help	6-15	よかったら
	Inquiring About an Opinion	2-34	ベッドはどうするんですか。
	Expressing Compliments	6-19	それは，いい考えですね。

会話 (かいわ)

1

A：このところ、随分暖かくなってきましたね。今日なんか、まるでハワイみたいですね。

B：ええ、四月になると、大分いい気候になりますね。何だか、この辺も賑やかになったみたいですね。そう思いませんか。

A：そうですね。運動している人が、冬よりずっと多くなったからでしょう。

B：ああ、それででしょうね。本当に増えましたね。高橋さんは、何か運動は？

A：ええ、一月ほど前から、毎日二マイル走ることにしているんですよ。気のせいかもしれませんが、体の調子がよくなったみたいですよ。体重も二キロ減りました。

2

A：フォードさん、あと二か月で、卒業ね。[ええ。] 間違いなく、卒業できるんでしょう。

B：ええ、おかげさまで、六月に卒業できることになったよ。

A：卒業したら、どうするの。大学院、それとも、就職するの。

B：一年ほど会社に勤めて、それからビジネス・スクールに行くことにしたんだけど。

A：御両親は、何とおっしゃっているの。ビジネス・スクールに行くことについて。

B：父は、医者をしているんだけど、僕をサラリーマンにはしたくないみたい。はっきり反対はしないけど、ちょっと気になってね。母は、賛成してくれたんだけどね。

3

A：この部屋、きれいになったわねえ。驚いたわ。全部、一人でやったの？

B：ええ。昨日、朝から晩まで一日かけてきれいにしたんですよ。いやあ、参りました。

1

A: It's become quite warm these days, hasn't it? It's just like being in Hawaii today.

B: Yes, the weather becomes quite nice in April. This area seems to have become lively. Don't you think so?

A: I think so. It's probably because there are many more people exercising now than during the winter.

B: Yeah, that's probably why. The number certainly has increased. Do you do some kind of exercise, Takahashi san?

A: Since about a month ago, I've made it a regular practice to jog two miles a day. It may be just my imagination, but I seem to be in better physical condition. I've even lost two kilograms.

2

A: Ford san, you graduate in two months, don't you? [Yes.] You are graduating for certain, right?

B: Yes, things have worked out so that I can graduate in June.

A: What will you do after graduation? Will it be graduate school, or will you work?

B: I've decided to work for about a year, and then go to business school.

A: What do your parents say about your decision to go to business school?

B: My father, who is a doctor, doesn't seem to want to make me a businessman ... although he doesn't come right out and say that he's opposed. That worries me a little. My mother has agreed with me.

3

A: This room has become clean! I'm surprised. Did you do it alone?

B: Yes. I spent the whole day yesterday cleaning from morning till night. It was exhausting!

Lesson 23

A：そりゃあ、疲れたでしょう。［ええ。今日は、体中痛くて。］でも、私に知らせてくれたら、よかったのに。何かお手伝いできたのに。［でも、悪いから。］そんなことないわ。ところで、家具はまだ？

B：時間がなかなかなくて…。今日の午後、買いに行こうかなと思っているんです。

A：机はどうするの。もし、よかったら、家に一つ使ってないのがあるけど。

B：しばらく、このテーブルを机にします。あまり広くないでしょう、ここ。

A：それは、そうね。でも、ベッドはどうするの。ベッドがなくちゃ。

B：布団にしました。その方が部屋が広く使えるし、お金もかからないでしょう。

A：布団？ それはいい考えね。

単語表 (たんごひょう)

1

このところ	these days
なって ⇨ なる	☞文法
まるで〜みたいだ	just like 〜
大分(だいぶ)	かなり
気候(きこう)	climate, weather
何(なん)だか	somehow, for some reason
この辺(へん)	this area, around here
賑(にぎ)やかだ	lively
それで	because of that
増(ふ)える	increase (v.i.) Ⅲ
高橋(たかはし)	a surname
一月(ひとつき)ほど	一か月くらい
〜ことにしている	☞L.18, p.220
気(き)のせい	imagination
調子(ちょうし)	condition
体重(たいじゅう)	weight (of body)
減(へ)る	decrease (v.i.)

2

間違(まちが)いなく	without a mistake
就職(しゅうしょく)する	have a full-time job
(に)勤(つと)める	work for Ⅲ
〜ことにする	☞文法
医者(いしゃ)	(medical) doctor
サラリーマン	businessman (salaried-man)
(〜に)反対(はんたい)する	oppose 〜
(〜が)気(き)になる	be worried about
(に)賛成(さんせい)する	agree

3

きれいだ	☞ことばの使い方
一人(ひとり)で	without any help, by oneself
(〜に)一日かける	spend a day on 〜 Ⅲ
(〜に)参(まい)る	be exhausted, have a hard time with
そりゃあ	☞ことばの使い方

A：You must certainly be tired. [Yes, my whole body hurts.] You should have told me. I could have helped you. [It would've been troublesome for you.] Not at all. By the way, what about furniture?

B：I can hardly find any time ... I am thinking of going out to buy some pieces this afternoon.

A：What will you do about a desk? If you like, I have one at home that I'm not using.

B：For a while, I'll use this table as a desk since it's not very spacious here.

A：That's true. But what will you do about a bed? You can't do without a bed.

B：I've decided on a *futon*. That way, I will have more space in my room, and it won't be costly.

A：A *futon*? What a great idea!

体中(からだじゅう)	all over (one's body)	しばらく	for the time being, for a while
お手伝(てつだ)いする	help s.b. do work	広(ひろ)い	spacious, wide
家具(かぐ)	furniture	なくちゃ	☞文法
よかったら	☞ことばの使い方	布団(ふとん)	*futon*
家(うち)	my house		

関連語句 (かんれんごく)

冷(つめ)たい	cold (tangible)	枕(まくら)	pillow
会社員(かいしゃいん)	office worker	工員(こういん)	factory worker
弁護士(べんごし)	lawyer	会計士(かいけいし)	accountant

文法 (ぶんぽう)

● 暖かくなる　　1-1

The intransitive verb なる, together with the transitive verb する, is one of the topics we will cover in this lesson. The examples below should help you understand the difference between the two.

  1．祖父は，父を医者にしました。　(Grandfather made my father a medical doctor.)
   父は医者になりました。　　　　(My father became a doctor.)
  2．母はテレビの音を小さくしました。(Mother turned down the TV.)
   テレビの音が小さくなりました。　(The sound of the TV went down.)
  3．私は部屋をきれいにしました。　(I made my room clean. / I cleaned my room.)
   部屋がきれいになりました。　　　(My room has become clean.)

From these examples, you may conclude that sentences with する signify the will of the agents, while those with なる do not specify such a thing, and the results are stated in such a way as if they came about naturally. In other words, なる is preferred over する when the speaker is more concerned about the result itself than about who takes responsibility for it.

Note that なります can mean "become ～ on one's own accord." In this case, only the will of the speaker is involved to make the decision.

  私は貧しい(poor)人のために，医者になります。
   (I will become a doctor for the sake of poor people.)

From the above examples, you can also get information on what forms are taken by the nouns, な-adjs., and い-adjs. so that each of them can make a grammatical form with する and なる.

● 行くことにする　　2-5

  V ＋ ことに ＋ する／なる

This pattern with する expresses the speaker's decision to do what the verb signifies.

This sentence suggests that it is no one other than the speaker who makes the decision. On the contrary, the pattern with なる indicates that the speaker has little to do with the decision; the decision is made by others.

  来月の終わりで，会社を辞めることにしました。
   (I made up my mind to quit the company at the end of next month.)
  来月の終わりで，会社を辞めることになりました。
   (It has been decided that I will quit the company at the end of next month.)

Note that sometimes people use the expression with なる as a humble form of speech. If you feel that the will of others was involved in the decision or that the things came out in such a way naturally, you may want to use sentence 1 below rather than sentence 2. In saying sentence 1, you acknowledge that other people helped you reach the conclusion.

  1．佐藤さんと結婚することになりました。(It happens that ...)
  2．佐藤さんと結婚することにしました。　(I have decided to marry ...)

● 走ることにしている　　1-7

<pre>V ＋ ことに ＋ して／なって いる</pre>

This て-form stands for a state that is the result of a past action, or, in this case, a past decision. These patterns show that the result of a decision made previously still remains in effect.

1．私は朝起きたら，まずコーヒーを二杯飲むことにしています。

(When I wake up in the morning, I make it a practice to have two cups of coffee before anything else.)

2．日曜日の朝御飯は，主人が作ることになっています。

(It is arranged that my husband prepares breakfast on Sundays.)

● 暖かくなってきました　　1-1

<pre>て-form ＋ くる</pre>

This pattern signifies that something began in the past and is still continuing in the present.

1．雨が降ってきましたよ，北村さんの奥さん。

(Mrs. Kitamura, it has started raining!)

2．私は，今まで，三十年もパン屋をしてきました。

(I have been a baker for thirty years.)

Note that this pattern has other meanings as well. Do not get them confused.

1．宿題をやって来ましたか。

(Have you finished the homework [and come?] i.e. Did you come after having completed your homework?)

2．ワインを一本持って来ましたよ。

(I have brought a bottle of wine.)

● ハワイみたいです　　1-1

みたい appears several times in the three dialogues. It is used often in daily conversation. It is a dependent word that always needs modifiers and acts like a な-adj.

学者みたいな人　　(a person who is like a scholar)
学者みたいに勉強する人　　(a person who studies like a scholar)
青木さんは学者みたいです。　　(Aoki san is like a scholar.)

To construct a modifier, it is necessary to change the ending of the preceding part just as you would with かもしれない. (☞L.22 「そうかもしれませんね」P. 281)

This expression signifies either subjective judgment not particularly based on evidence, or opinions based on intuition. The judgment may or may not be true. When the pattern is "A は B みたいだ," the meaning may be slightly confusing. In this case, two interpretations are possible:

ここはハワイみたいです。　　1) This place is like Hawaii.
　　　　　　　　　　　　　　2) It seems that this place is Hawaii.

The first interpretation is possible if we read the sentence figuratively: "This place resembles Hawaii." Then, the place cannot be Hawaii.

The second interpretation is not related to figurative speech. It indicates the speaker's un-

Lesson 23

confirmed judgment. He is not yet certain whether or not he is in Hawaii; however he is inclined to believe that he is in Hawaii.

"A は B みたいだ" is the only pattern for which the two interpretations described above are possible. Only the second interpretation applies to all other uses of みたい.

1. 加藤さんは ┌ 病気みたいですね。　　　(It seems Kato san is ill.)
　　　　　　　│ 病気だったみたいですね。(It seems Kato san was ill.)
　　　　　　　│ 病気みたいでした。　　　(It seemed Kato san was ill.)
　　　　　　　└ 病気だったみたいでした。(It seemed Kato san had been ill.)

2. 田中さんは、歌を歌うのが、好きみたいですね。
(Tanaka san seems to be fond of singing.)

3. この町は、いつも風が吹いているみたいですね。
(It seems that it's always windy in this town.)

● 父は、僕をサラリーマンにはしたくないみたい　　2-7　☞P. 250

In Japanese, it is generally inappropriate to talk about a third person's desires, feelings, will, and frame of mind; however, it is acceptable if the speaker indicates that what is said about the third person is his/her opinion, impression or conjecture. This is accomplished by adding such expressions as; みたい, 〜のです and 〜と思います.

● 知らせてくれたら、よかったのに　　3-3

のに here is the same as のに we studied in L. 17 (P. 206). This pattern literally means "If you had notified me, it would have been good," or "I wish you had let me know." The speaker is unhappy because the hearer did not inform him that he was cleaning the apartment alone.

今日、試験があると教えてくれたら、よかったのに。
(I wish you had told me that there was going to be an exam today.)

● 買いに行こう　　3-6　☞L. 13 文法「遊びに行く」(P. 144)

● 行こう　　3-6　☞L. 16 文法「行こうと思う」(P. 190)

● 行こうかなと思っている　　3-6

Compared to 行こうと思う, this expression indicates that the speaker is less positive about going. In terms of inclination, 行こうと思う corresponds to "probably," and 行こうかなと思っている to "maybe."

On some occasions かな can be replaced by the feminine かしら. As for the meaning of 思っている in comparison to 思う, see「気になる」in this lesson.

● このテーブルを机にします　　3-8

The literal meaning of this sentence is "to make this table a desk" which, in fact, means "to use this table as a desk."

1. 加藤さんは厚い英語の辞書を枕にして寝ていました。
(Kato san was sleeping with a thick English dictionary as a pillow.)

2. 子供たちはオレンジ・ジュースのかん(can)を電話にして遊んでいます。
(Children are playing, using cans of orange juice as telephones.)

● ベッドがなくちゃ　　3-9

Here, ちゃ means the same thing as the では in 「運動靴じゃ合いません」. (☞L. 16 文法 「運動靴じゃ合いません」 P. 191) The example in L. 16 uses the て-form of です with は; however, in this lesson the て-form of the adjective is used.

Generally speaking, the pattern て-form ＋ は signifies the condition of the following negative statement. Since this rule (i.e. that a negative statement follows て＋は) is very consistent, the negative statement can often be omitted. In this example, the deleted statement is something like 困るでしょう.

You may be wondering how て＋は is contained in the above example. ちゃ is the contracted form of ては, and じゃ is the contracted form of では.

1. それは薬ですから，飲んじゃいけませんよ。
   (Don't drink it; it's medicine!／[lit.] It is not good to drink it, as it is medicine.)
2. 今日返してくれなくちゃ，困りますよ。
   (I'll be in trouble if you don't return it today.)
3. 明日の試験に遅れちゃ駄目ですよ。
   (Don't be late for tomorrow's exam.)

ことばの使い方 (ことばのつかいかた)

● このところ　　1-1

This phrase is rarely used to mean "this place"; ここ is more commonly used for that purpose. このところ means "these days."

　このところ，松本さん，学校に来ていないみたいですね。
　　(It seems Matsumoto san has not been coming to school these days.)

● まるで　　1-1

This adverb is often used together with みたいです to portray a figurative meaning.

　昨日はとても寒くて，まるで冬みたいでした。
　　(It was so cold yesterday that it seemed like [felt like] winter.)

● 何だか　　1-3

This phrase indicates that the speaker is unclear about or puzzled by the reason for the statement which follows.

　松本さん，どうしたんでしょうね。何だか泣いているみたいでしたよ。
　　(I wonder what's wrong with Matsumoto san. I don't know why but he seemed to be in tears.)
　テニス，もうやめましょう。何だかとても疲れました。
　　(Let's quit playing tennis. For some reason, I am tired out.)

● 一月ほど前　　1-7

Like くらい, the dependent noun ほど shows the approximate quantity of various items. The only difference between くらい and ほど is stylistic: ほど is more formal than くらい.

Lesson 23

● 気のせい   1-7

You may have noticed that the word 気 also appears in the second dialogue in another phrase. 気, in fact, is a word used in numerous idiomatic expressions. In reference to human beings, 気 may be interpreted to mean "state of mind." The expression 気のせい, as a whole, means "because of (one's) imagination or sense."

  A：あっ, 何の音ですか。変な音ですね。
  B：音なんか何もしませんよ。気のせいでしょう。
    (A：Oh, what is that noise? Isn't it a strange noise?)
    (B：There's no noise. It must be your imagination.)

● 体の調子がいい   1-8

This is a colloquial expression that literally means "one's physical condition is good." The opposite expression is 調子が悪い. By substituting 体 with various words, you can create discussions on a wide range of topics.

 1．A：今日は, のどの調子がよくないんですよ。
  B：風邪ですか。
    (A：My throat doesn't feel right today.)
    (B：Is it a cold?)
 2．私の車は, このところ調子が悪くて困るんですよ。
   (My car has been in poor condition lately and gives me a headache.)

● 間違いなく   2-1

間違い is a "mistake," and なく is the adverbial form of the い-adj., ない. The phrase, as a whole, means "without a mistake," "unmistakably," or "definitely."

 1．A：あの人, 松本さんみたいですね。
  B：ああ, あの歩き方は間違いなく松本さんですよ。
    (A：That guy looks like Matsumoto san, doesn't he?)
    (B：That's his walk. He is definitely Matsumoto san.)
 2．A：明日, 八時までに間違いなく来てくださいね。
  B：はい, 間違いなく。
    (A：Please come without fail tomorrow by eight o'clock.)
    (B：Yes, I'll definitely 〔come〕.)

● (ビジネス・スクールに行くこと)について   2-6

"～について" following a noun or a noun phrase means "concerning" or "about." To make a noun phrase with this pattern, use こと instead of の.

 先生はこのことについて, どうお考えになりますか。
  (What do you think of this, Sensei?)
 奨学金のことについて, ちょっとお聞きしたいことがあります。
  (I have something to ask of you concerning scholarships.)

● 医者をしている   2-7 ☞P. 142 "Other uses of て＋いる"

This pattern is used to describe what one does for a living: Name of occupation ＋をしている.

 父は大学の教師をしていて, 母は医者をしています。
  (My father is a college professor, and my mother is a doctor.)

● 気になる　　2-8

This expression means "to be worried about," and the cause is marked by が. In this dialogue, the speaker could have said 気になります in place of 気になっています without changing the basic meaning.

て＋いる used with verbs that signify mental activities such as 思う, 考える, 驚く, 困る, etc. indicates that the condition or the speaker's state began in the past and is continuing in the present. Without て＋いる, this temporal nuance disappears, and there is no specification as to the beginning of the state.

　　西川さんが昨日言ったことが、とても気になっているんだよ。
　　　　(What Nishikawa san said yesterday has been bugging me.)
　　明日、ソフト・ボールの試合があるので、天気が気になります。
　　　　(I am worried about the weather since we have a softball game tomorrow.)

● きれいになる　　3-1

We have learned that one of the meanings of きれいだ is "beautiful," as in きれいな女の人. きれいだ in this dialogue means "clean"; another meaning is "neat," as is exemplified in the first example:

　　１．御飯を食べる時はきれいに食べなさい。
　　　　(When you eat meals, be neat.)
　　２．このブラウスは、洗濯してもきれいにならないんですよ。
　　　　(This blouse doesn't get clean even though I wash it.)

● いやあ　　3-2

This is an exclamatory expression used mostly by men. まあ is a feminine equivalent.

　　Ａ：いやあ、久しぶりですね、佐藤さん。お元気そうですね。
　　Ｂ：ええ、おかげさまで。北村さんも、本当にお元気そうで。
　　　　(Ａ：Oh, it's been a long time, Sato san. You look great!)
　　　　(Ｂ：Thank you. Kitamura san, you look great, too.)

● 参りました　　3-2

This is a colloquial expression for 疲れました. Women usually prefer 疲れる which is much less colloquial than 参りました.

● そりゃあ　　3-3

This is a contracted form of それは. (☞L. 22 ことばの使い方「それはそうだ」P. 283)

　　これは　⇨　こりゃあ　　　あれは　⇨　ありゃあ

● もし、よかったら　　3-7

This phrase means "if you like" or "if you don't mind," and is used when offering something to someone in such a way as not to offend the receiver's feelings.

よろしかったら is a polite alternative that can be used with superiors.

　　１．もし、よかったら、今夜一緒に芝居を見に行きませんか。
　　　　(If you like, won't you go with me to see a play tonight?)
　　２．先生、もし、よろしかったら、家でパーティーをしますので、来てくださいませんか。
　　　　(Sensei, would you please come to the party at my house if you have time?)

Lesson 23

● お金がかかる　　3-10

The verb かかる is an intransitive verb and should be learned in conjunction with its transitive counterpart かける. There have been quite a few such pairs of verbs in the lessons we have covered. A list summarizing them appears below.

A. (-aru) と (-eru)

| | | 例文 ||
v.i.	v.t.	v.i.	v.t.
終わる	終える	仕事が〜	サラリーマンが仕事を〜
始まる	始める	授業が〜	私たちが授業を〜
止まる	止める	タクシーが〜	私がタクシーを〜
集まる	集める	家族が〜	父が家族を〜
閉まる	閉める	ドアが〜	私がドアを〜
決まる	決める	考えが〜	私たちが考えを〜
かかる	かける	時間が〜	宿題に時間を〜

B. (-ru) と (-su)

| | | 例文 ||
v.i.	v.t.	v.i.	v.t.
起きる	起こす	家内が〜	私が家内を〜
こわれる	こわす	窓が〜	私が窓を〜
はえる	はやす	ひげが〜	田中さんがひげを〜
増える	増やす	宿題が〜	先生が宿題を〜
減る	減らす	宿題が〜	先生が宿題を〜
出る	出す	風呂から〜	子供を風呂から〜
通る	通す	車が道を〜	警官が車を〜

Note: 警官（policeman）

C. (-eru) と (-u)

| | | 例文 ||
v.i.	v.t.	v.i.	v.t.
生まれる	生む	子供が〜	家内が子供を〜

D. (-u) と (-eru)

		例文	
v.i.	v.t.	v.i.	v.t.
入る	入れる	お風呂に〜	子供をお風呂に〜
育つ	育てる	子供が〜	母親が子供を〜
開く	開ける	ドアが〜	猫がドアを〜
つく	つける	電気が〜	私が電気を〜
建つ	建てる	家が〜	私が家を〜

練習 (れんしゅう)

練習 (れんしゅう) 1　　　なる

例　暖かい　　　⇨暖かくなりましたね。　(It's become warm.)
　　退屈だ　　　⇨退屈になりましたね。　(It's become boring.)
　　いい天気だ　⇨いい天気になりましたね。(The weather has become nice.)

1. 運動している人が多い　　2. 部屋がきれいだ　　　3. 十九才だ
4. 髪が長い　　　　　　　　5. この辺はにぎやかだ　6. 明日の授業は休みだ
7. 加藤さんは大学院生だ　　8. この辺はハワイみたいだ　9. 毎朝，暖かい

練習 (れんしゅう) 2　　　なって＋くる

例　暖かい　　　⇨暖かくなってきましたね。(It's been getting warm.)
　　退屈だ　　　⇨退屈になってきましたね。(It's been getting boring.)
　　いい天気だ　⇨いい天気になってきましたね。(The weather has been getting nice.)

1. 運動している人が多い　　2. 部屋がきれいだ　　　3. いい気候だ
4. 髪が長い　　　　　　　　5. この辺はにぎやかだ　6. 授業が大変だ
7. 加藤さんは真面目だ　　　8. この辺はハワイみたいだ　9. 毎朝，暖かい

Lesson 23

練習(れんしゅう)　3	Figurative, みたい

例　あの人，学者　⇨あの人はまるで学者みたいですね。(He is just like a scholar.)

1．あの先生，学生　　　　2．このビール，水　　　　3．この電話，二十年前の電話
4．私の書いた字，子供の字　5．あの人のギター，プロ(professional)
6．この部屋，駅(えき)　　7．この本，辞書　　　　8．このパン，一週間前のパン

練習(れんしゅう)　4	S＋みたい

例　このところ，暖かくなってきましたね。
　　⇨このところ暖かくなってきたみたいですね。
　　(It seems to have become warm these days.)
　　明日は天気が悪いですね。
　　⇨明日は天気が悪いみたいですね。
　　(It seems the weather tomorrow will be bad.)

1．大宮(おおみや)さんはアメリカへ行きますよ。　　2．もっと運動した方がいいですね。
3．シカゴは東京(とうきょう)ほど物価(ぶっか)は高(たか)くありません。　4．寺山(てらやま)さんはテレビがとても好きです。
5．松川(まつかわ)さんは，今年卒業します。　　6．秋山(あきやま)さんは日本へ帰りました。
7．昨日(きのう)，竹井(たけい)さんは授業を休みました。　8．私，塩を入れるのを忘れました。

練習(れんしゅう)　5	S＋ことにする

例　毎日二マイル走ります。⇨私は毎日二マイル走ることにしました。
　　(I've made a decision to run two miles a day.)

1．たばこをやめます。　　　　　　2．お酒(さけ)を飲みません。
3．寮(りょう)(dorm.)に住みます。　4．大学院(だいがくいん)に行きません。
5．その問題(もんだい)は友達に相談(そうだん)します。　6．何でも手帳(てちょう)に書いておきます。

練習(れんしゅう)　6	S＋ことにしている

例　毎日二マイル走ります。⇨私は毎日二マイル走ることにしています。
　　(I make it a rule to run two miles a day.)

1．自分でたばこは買いません。　　2．お酒はあまり飲みません。
3．経済的だから，寮(dorm.)に住みます。　4．授業は，休みません。
5．そういう問題は友達に相談します。　6．何でも手帳に書いておきます。

練習(れんしゅう) 7　　　　　　〜の調子

例　この頃，体の調子がよくなったみたいですよ。
　　悪い　⇨この頃，体の調子が悪くなったみたいですよ。
　　　　　　(My physical condition seems to have deteriorated lately.)
　　頭　⇨この頃，頭の調子が悪くなったみたいですよ。
　　　　　　(My brain seems to have deteriorated lately.)

1．とてもいい　　2．体　　3．車　　4．エンジン　　5．かなり悪い　　6．いい

練習(れんしゅう) 8　　　　　　S＋ことになる

例　六月に卒業できる　⇨六月に卒業できることになりました。
　　　　　　(It was decided that I can graduate in June.)

1．大きい会社に就職できる　　　2．少し運動してもいい
3．自分のアパートが借りられる　4．車の運転ができる
5．一緒に遊びに行けない　　　　6．今月の終わりに国へ帰らなければならない

練習(れんしゅう) 9　　　　　　する

例　部屋がきれいだ　⇨部屋をきれいにしました。(I made the room clean.)

1．部屋が暖かい　　　2．ジュースが冷たい　　3．テレビの音が小さい
4．靴がきれいだ　　　5．論文が短い　　　　　6．説明が簡単だ
7．辞書が枕だ　　　　8．テーブルが机だ　　　9．ピザが昼御飯だ

練習(れんしゅう) 10　　　　　　〜について

例　ビジネス・スクール
　　⇨ビジネス・スクールについて，お聞きしたいことがあるんですが。
　　　　　　(I have something to ask of you about the business school.)
　　ビジネス・スクールで勉強する
　　⇨ビジネス・スクールで勉強することについてお聞きしたいことがあるんですが。
　　　　　　(I have something to ask of you about studying in the business school.)

1．ビジネス・スクールの奨学金　　2．奨学金をもらう
3．日本で日本語を習う　　　　　　4．京都の日本語学校
5．アジアを旅行する　　　　　　　6．よい辞書
7．安くて良いアパート

Lesson 23

練習(れんしゅう)　11　　　～が気になる

例　それ　⇨それが気になるんですよ。(I am worried about that.)
　　彼から電話がなかった　⇨彼から電話がなかったことが気になるんですよ。
　　　　　　　　　　　　　　(I am worried about the fact that he didn't call me.)

1．父が反対している　　　　　2．病気の後，体重が増えない　　3．この背広の色
4．母がはっきり反対している　5．このケーキの味　　　　　　6．車の調子

練習(れんしゅう)　12　　　Volitional, かなと思う

例　勝さんと買い物に行く　⇨勝さんと買い物に行こうかなと思っています。
　　　　　　　　　　　　(I think that, maybe, I'll go shopping with Katsu san.)

1．明日の晩，また映画を見に行く　　2．日本語の勉強は，もうやめる
3．来年，就職する　　　　　　　　4．明日は，部屋をきれいにする
5．ベッドじゃなくて，布団にする　　6．ビジネス・スクールへ行く前に，会社に勤める

練習(れんしゅう)　13　　　よかったら／よろしかったら

例　明日，家に来ない？
　　　⇨もしよかったら，明日家に来ない？
　　　　(If it's convenient, won't you come over tomorrow?)
　　明日，家にいらっしゃいませんか。
　　　⇨もしよろしかったら，明日家にいらっしゃいませんか。
　　　　(If it's convenient, wouldn't you please come over tomorrow?)

1．このセーター貸してくれない？　　2．今晩，電話下さいませんか。
3．もう一枚いただけませんか。　　　4．これをコピーしてもらえない？
5．この本，読まない？　　　　　　　6．召し上がりませんか。

練習(れんしゅう)　14　　　～ては＋Neg.

例　食べる　⇨食べてはいけませんよ。
　　　　　　(It's not good if you eat it. — You mustn't eat it.)
　　食べない　⇨食べなくてはいけませんよ。
　　　　　　　(It's not good if you don't eat. — You must eat.)

1．体重を減らさない　　2．六月に卒業しない　　3．会社に勤めない
4．運動する　　　　　　5．たばこをすう　　　　6．体重を増やす

練習(れんしゅう)　15	ては ⇨ ちゃ

例　食べる　　⇨食べちゃ駄目ですよ。
　　　　　　　(It's not good if you eat it. — You mustn't eat it.)
　　食べない　⇨食べなくちゃ駄目ですよ。
　　　　　　　(It's not good if you don't eat. — You must eat.)

1．体重を減らさない　　2．六月に卒業しない　　3．会社に勤めない
4．運動する　　　　　　5．たばこをすう　　　　6．体重を増やす

練習(れんしゅう)　16	～くれたら，よかったのに

例　教える
　　⇨どうして，教えてくれなかったんですか。教えてくれたら，よかったのに。
　　　(Why didn't you tell me? I wish you had told me.)

1．話す　2．手紙で知らせる　3．電話する　4．家にいる　5．見せる　6．貸す

二十四課

内容表

文法	Quotation (Direct, Indirect)		
	Embedded Questions		Sかどうか
			Interrogative＋か(教えてください)
	Interrogative＋(Particle)＋でも		誰とでも
	て＋くる		
	Action / State starting in the past continues.		聞けるようになってきた
	Action toward s. b.		電話がかかってくる
	Nができる (come into being)		友達ができる
	Nについて (a topic)		日本語について
	～て欲しい (I want s. b. to ～)		(あなたに)言って欲しいんです。
	Imperative		帰りなさい。
	S間に，Nの間に (While S, N)		お留守の間に
	N中に (Within N)		明日中に終わらせる
	N, Sまでに (By N, S)		明日の朝までに終わらせる
	Sのに		約束したのに。
	Kinds of shops (～屋)		本屋
	Appositional の		本屋の大田さん
機能	Reporting Information	1-6	友達ができたかどうかは書いてない。
	Passing on Information	7-13	十一時頃帰ると伝えておいてください。
			終わらせるとのことでした。
			お電話が欲しいとの伝言でした。
	Expressing Relief	3-35	安心しました／それはよかった
	Focusing on a Topic	7-3	日本語について
	Making Requests	5-3	いないと言って欲しいんです。
	Taking Leave	6-2	行ってらっしゃい(ませ)。
	Giving Instructions	5-8	お帰りなさい。
	Sequencing Communication	7-2	まず初めに…次に…最後に
	Criticism, Blame, Accusation	3-26	しようがないなあ／約束したのに
	Deadline	2-40	明日中に終わらせる
	Stating Want/Desire	3-16	いないと言って欲しい

Lesson 24

会話 (かいわ)

1

A：大江さん，メイラーさんからやっと手紙が来ましたよ。

B：着いたら，すぐ手紙を下さいと言っておいたのに，ずいぶん時間がかかりましたね。メイラーさん，お元気ですか。

A：ええ。「とても元気で，毎日楽しく勉強しています。」と書いてありますよ。

B：そうですか。安心しました。日本語について何と言っていますか。

A：ええ，「日本語もだいぶ楽に聞けるようになってきました。」と言っていますよ。

B：それはよかった。日本人の友達はできたんでしょうか。

A：友達ができたかどうかは書いてありませんね。今度手紙を出す時，友達ができたか聞いてみますよ。あの人なら誰とでもすぐ友達になれますよ。

2

A：佐藤さん，私，ちょっと急用で出掛けるんですが。[はい。]もし，家内から電話がかかってきたら，今夜十一時頃帰ると伝えておいてくれませんか。

B：はい，十一時頃ですね。

A：それから，西さんから電話があると思いますが，今いないと言って欲しいんですが。

B：西さんですね。わかりました。行ってらっしゃいませ。

A：ああ，それから，佐藤さんももうお帰りなさい。じゃ，また明日。

3

A：石原さん，お留守の間にいろいろお電話がありました。

B：ああ，そうですか。じゃ，誰からあったか教えてください。

A：まず初めに，遠藤さんとおっしゃる方が，今夜行こうとおっしゃってました。次に，出版社の中川さんから，仕事は明日中に必ず終わらせるとのことでした。

1

A：Oe san, a letter has finally arrived from Mailer san.

B：I asked him to write us as soon as he arrived, but he's taken a long time. Is Mailer san well?

A：Yes. He writes, "I am doing well, and am enjoying my studies every day."

B：Is that so? I'm relieved. What does he say about Japanese?

A：Yes. He says, "I can now listen to and understand Japanese quite comfortably."

B：That's great. I wonder if he's made any Japanese friends.

A：He hasn't written whether or not he's made friends. Next time I write, I'll ask him if he's made friends. He is one person who can make friends easily with anyone.

2

A：Sato san, I'm going out briefly on urgent business ... [Yes.] If my wife calls, would you tell her that I'll return home tonight around eleven?

B：Yes, around eleven, is it?

A：Also, I'm expecting a call from Nishi san, but I want you to tell him that I'm not in now.

B：From Nishi san. I understand. I'll see you soon.

A：Oh yes, and Sato san, why don't you call it a day for today? Then, I'll see you tomorrow.

3

A：Ishihara san, there were a few calls while you were out.

B：Is that so? Tell me who I received them from.

A：First of all, someone by the name of Endo san said he wanted to go out with you tonight. Then, Nakagawa san from the publishing company said that he will definitely complete the work by the end of the day tomorrow.

Lesson 24

B：そう言っていましたか。しようがないなあ、明日の朝までにって約束したのに。

A：最後に、もうお一人、本屋の大田さんが、明日の朝八時頃までに、お電話が欲しいとの伝言でした。八時過ぎると、出掛けてしまうからとおっしゃってました。

B：わかりました。じゃ、今電話かけてみましょう。じゃ、まず遠藤から。

単語表 (たんごひょう)

1

大江(おおえ)	a surname
(〜に)着(つ)く	arrive (at)
楽(らく)に	with ease
友達(ともだち)ができる	make friends II
(〜に)手紙(てがみ)を出す	send a letter (to)
(と)友達になる	become friends with

2

急用(きゅうよう)	urgent business
出掛(でか)ける	go out, set out II
伝(つた)える	pass words to, relay a message II
お帰りなさい	☞文法

3

石原(いしはら)	a surname
留守(るす)	being away from home
間(あいだ)に	during, while
初(はじ)めに	at first
遠藤(えんどう)	a surname
次(つぎ)に	next
出版社(しゅっぱんしゃ)	publishing co.
中川(なかがわ)	a surname
明日中(あしたじゅう)に	within tomorrow, during tomorrow
必(かなら)ず	surely
終(お)わらせる	have s.t. finished II
しようがない	hopeless, cannot be helped
朝(あさ)までに	by morning
(〜と)約束(やくそく)する	promise s.b.
最後(さいご)に	at the end
本屋(ほんや)	bookstore
大田(おおた)	a surname
伝言(でんごん)	message

B：He said that? What does he think he's doing? He promised to have it ready by tomorrow morning.

A：And finally, one more person, Ota san, the owner of the bookstore, left a message that he wanted you to return his call by eight tomorrow morning. He said that he will be going out after eight.

B：I see. Then I'll try calling now. First of all, (I'll begin with) Endo.

関連語句 (かんれんごく)

石井さん		電話		
	に		をかける／する	call Ishii san
	に／から		をもらう	receive a call from Ishii san
	から		がある	there is a call from Ishii san
	が		を切る	Ishii san hangs up the phone
	が		をくれる	Ishii san calls me/us
	が		をしてくる	Ishii san calls me/us
	と		で話す	talk to Ishii san over the telephone

文法 (ぶんぽう)

● 友達ができたかどうか   1-8

We learned about quotations in L. 16 (☞P.190 文法「Indirect Quotation」) but there is one pattern we did not cover in that section.

When you want to change a directly-quoted selective question like the following:

1. 大江さんは, メイラーさんに「友達ができましたか, できませんか。」と聞きました。

    (Oe san said to Mailer san, "Have you made friends with somebody or haven't you?")

There are two possible ways of formulating the sentences:

2. 大江さんは, メイラーさんに友達ができたか, できないか(と)聞きました。

    (Oe san asked Mailer san whether he had made friends with somebody or whether he had not.)

3. 大江さんは, メイラーさんに友達ができたかどうか(と)聞きました。

    (Oe san asked Mailer san whether or not he had made friends with somebody.)

As in the English indirect quotation in which "whether" or "if" does not concur with interrogative words, the Japanese 〜かどうか cannot be used with question forms. This is because selective questions demand an answer from two possible choices, while questions with interrogative words require replies with a specific frame of reference.

Note that this is a noun phrase so it should be handled like all other nouns.

彼が来るかどうかはわかりません。(It is unknown whether or not he will come.)

その日あなたがどこにいたかを話してくれませんか。

(Could you tell us where you were on that day?)

● 〜と書いてあります   1-4 ☞P. 174「て-form＋ある」

● 何と言っていますか   1-5

Obviously, this does not indicate that the action is continuing, but that the result of the action done in the past still remains. This form is often used to quote a person.

1. トーマス・ジェファソンは, 人間は平等だと言っています。

    (Thomas Jefferson said that men are equal.)

2. ナポレオンは, 私の辞書には「不可能」という言葉はないと言っている。

    (Napoleon said, "The word 'impossible' does not exist in my dictionary.")

● 聞けるようになってきました   1-6

This is the verbal equivalent of く＋なる(い-adj.) and に＋なる(な-adj., nouns) which we studied in L. 23 and L. 18. (☞P. 218 文法「痛くなる」)

This pattern signifies gradual change unless otherwise specified.

1. この頃, 子供が歩けるようになりました。

    (Recently my child has come to be able to walk.)

2. 前より, 日本語がわかるようになってきたみたいです。

    (I think I have come to understand Japanese better than before.)

● 友達ができた　　　1-7

This できる means that something marked by が has come into being.

1．急用ができたので，帰ります。
　　(Since something urgent has come up, I'll go home.)
2．晩御飯ができましたから，食べましょう。(Since dinner is ready, let's eat.)
3．この家は，八十年以上前にできた家ですよ。
　　(This house was built more than eighty years ago.)

● 誰とでも，友達になれる　　　1-9

Interrogative ＋でも

This form can be better understood through examples using two question words in the pattern phrase.

	＋か	＋も…ない	＋でも
誰	somebody	nobody	anybody, whoever
何	something	nothing	anything, whatever

(☞P. 79 「interrogative ＋か／も」)
(☞P. 95 「何か用事でも」)

1．図書室は学生なら誰でも入れます。
　　(Anybody can enter the library, if he/she is a student.)
2．私は嫌いな物がありません。ほとんど何でも食べます。
　　(I have no dislikes. I eat almost anything.)

Notice the position of the particles in the following sentences, and you will understand why と is used in the sentence from the dialogue.

1．長井さんは，誰とでも，楽しく話ができます。
　　(Nagai san can talk pleasantly to anybody.)
2．あの人は，何にでも興味を持ちます。気持ちが若いんですねえ。
　　(He gets interested in anything. He is young at heart.)

● 電話がかかってきたら　　　2-1

This form of て＋くる is different from other usages such as：暖かくなってきましたね。(It's warming up, isn't it?). Here, くる simply signifies the imaginary movement of the telephone call from someone to the speaker. To indicate from whom or from whence the call comes, the particle から is used. Without くる in the sentence, the receiver of the call would remain unclear.

1．日本の友達が，ビデオ・テープを送ってきたよ。
　　(My friend in Japan sent me a videotape.)
2．石原さんが来月の二日に結婚すると書いてきたよ。
　　(Ishihara san wrote us that he is getting married on the second of next month.)

● 言って欲しい　　　2-4

We learned the pattern N が欲しい in the previous lesson. (☞P. 111「欲しい」) In this lesson, we shall learn the following new pattern:

N1 が N2 に＋て＋欲しい　　⇨　N1 would like N2 to ～.

Lesson 24

Both N1 and N2 must be animate, and it seems safe to say that they usually represent people. The person who has the desire is N1, and the person who is responsible for the action is N2. The restrictions on the specifications of N1 are the same as those described in the previous usage in P. 111.

The same idea can be expressed more politely, if it is appropriate, by replacing 〜て欲しい with 〜ていただきたい. This replacement does not work in the second example below because「〜ていただく」is an honorific expression that cannot be applied to the speaker himself/herself.

1. 加藤さん，明日三時に食堂へ来て欲しいんですが，どうですか。
 (Kato san, I want you to come to the dining room at three tomorrow, but would it be O.K.?)
2. 父は私に医者になって欲しかったみたいですね。
 (It seems that my father wanted me to become a doctor.)

Compare:
3. 父は私を医者にしたいみたいですね。
 (It seems that my father wants me to become a doctor.)

● お帰りなさい　　2-6

Pre- ます form ＋ なさい

This pattern is an imperative form which is often used by mothers with their children, or in such impersonal writings as instructions on a test. It is, however, not suitable to use with your friends, and, needless to say, with your superiors.

By adding お, as in the dialogue, the sentence may sound slightly less harsh than without it, but it still indicates a high-low relationship. It is not recommended that you use this pattern at this point.

The same expression is used as a daily greeting when a member of your family or in-group arrives home; it means "welcome back." This greeting is exactly the same in form as the imperative form, but the two usages are rarely confused.

● お留守の間に　　3-1

The word 間 is a noun that can take various noun modifiers to create temporal expressions:

S1 (or N の) 間に，S2. ⇨ While S1 (or N), S2.

In this pattern, S1 or N has to signify some length of time, and S2 has to take place during that period. Without に after 間, S2 takes place all through the time of S1(or N) as seen in the fourth example. (☞P. 68「月曜日に」)

1. 西さんが出掛けている間に，大江さんから二回電話がありましたよ。
 (While you were out, Nishi san, Oe san called you twice.)
2. この子は，私たちがアメリカにいる間に生まれたので，英語は上手ですよ。
 (Since this child was born while we were in the United States, she speaks English well.)
3. 私は，夏休みの間に日本語の復習をするつもりです。
 (I intend to review Japanese during summer vacation.)

4．私は、夏休みの間祖母の家にいるつもりです。

(I intend to stay at my grandmother's house all through summer vacation.)

● 明日中に　　　3-4

中に, used with temporal expressions, excluding those that refer to the past, means that something happens or is completed within a specified time.

The reading of 中に is usually じゅうに, but with such words as 今週, 夏休み, and 授業, it is ちゅうに. As for the function of に, see P. 68「月曜日に」.

1．来週中に試験をします。まだ何曜日か決めていませんが、必ずしますから。

(I will give you a test sometime next week. I haven't decided on the day, but I will definitely give you the exam.)

2．仕事中にたばこをすってはいけませんよ。

(Don't smoke while you are at work.)

● 終わらせるとのことでした　　　3-4

S＋とのことです

This pattern is often used to convey a message in a rather formal fashion and is too formal for conversation among friends; って is preferred in informal situations. (☞P. 221 文法「東京へ行くんだって」)

A distinction between です and でした is made depending on whether the speaker regards the issue as a past event or one which still belongs to the present.

● 明日の朝までに　　　3-5

We learned まで, as it was used in a sentence such as "朝から晩まで、勉強しました." まで shows a temporal or spatial limit. までに, however, means "by (the time)," and signifies the completion of an action by a specified time.

1．八時まで、テレビを見ました。(I watched TV until eight o'clock.)

2．明日の八時までに、東京駅に来てください。

(Come to Tokyo Station by eight tomorrow.)

● 約束したのに　　　3-5

We have already covered のに in L. 17 (P. 206) and L. 23 (P. 296); it was used in the sentence pattern "S1 のに S2" which expressed surprise on the part of the speaker. Surprise is its core element, but anger, disappointment, and resentment are secondary emotions contained in the nuance of sentences using this word. In this sentence, the speaker is disappointed, if not resentful about the broken promise. When S2 is clearly understood, it can be omitted.

1．昨日、どうして来なかったの。必ず来るって言っていたのに。

(Why didn't you come yesterday? You said you would definitely come.)

2．今朝まで寝ないで勉強したのに。

(I studied without sleeping 'til this morning! [but it didn't work.])

3．こんなこと、先学期習ったのに。

(We learned this sort of thing last quarter!)

Lesson 24

ことばの使い方 (ことばのつかいかた)

● あの人　　1-9　☞P. 157「それまで」

● 行ってらっしゃいませ　　2-5

This is a common greeting used when seeing off someone who is temporarily leaving the place to which he/she belongs: home, country, company, etc. The literal meaning of this expression is "go and come back." This phrase, therefore, cannot be used with a person whose return is not anticipated.

The suffix ませ makes this expression very polite, and 行ってらっしゃい without ませ is a non-polite form used among family members and co-workers.

When leaving for work or school, a Japanese person would usually hear "行ってらっしゃい(ませ)," and upon his/her return, the person would be greeted by "お帰りなさい。" (Note that お帰りなさい, as used in the dialogue, is different from the way it is used here, as explained in the 文法 section.)

● まず初めに　　3-3

This expression, combined with 次に and 最後に, is a word used to indicate the order in which something should be done; these words are often used in such things as describing recipes and giving instructions. まず means "first of all," and 初めに means "in the beginning."

● 終わらせる　　3-4

We have already learned 終わる(v.i.) and 終える(v.t.). 終わらせる is the causative form of the verb, and simply means "to make something end." This form expresses more determination than that indicated in the form 終える. We will study "causatives" in L. 31.

● しょうがないなあ　　3-5

This word has the same literal meaning as しかたがない(L. 8): "there is no way of doing 〜." The speaker in the dialogue was very disappointed in the person who could not keep his promise to complete an assignment by the following morning. He felt that there was no way of curing his irresponsible behavior.

● しょうがないなあ　　3-5　☞P. 59「困ったなあ」

● 本屋　　3-6

The following is a list of some specialty stores.

米屋 (rice shop)	風呂屋 (public bath)
花屋 (florist)	おもちゃ屋 (toy shop)
魚屋 (fish shop)	クリーニング屋 (laundry, cleaners)
薬屋 (pharmacy)	菓子屋 (cake shop, confectionery)
文房具屋 (stationery shop)	八百屋 (green grocer)
本屋 (bookstore)	布団屋 (*futon*-shop)
パン屋 (bakery)	カメラ屋 (camera shop)
靴屋 (shoe store, cobbler)	電気屋 (home appliance shop)
果物屋 (fruit shop)	そば屋 (noodle shop)

私の家は、東京で薬屋をしています。(My family operates a pharmacy in Tokyo.)

● 本屋の大田さん   3-6

The nouns 本屋 and 大田さん are appositives. This phrase means "the owner of the bookstore, Ota san" or "Ota san who is the owner of the bookstore." (Note that Ota san need not necessarily be the owner; he might be just a person working at the store.)

　　こちらは，私の友達の遠藤さんです。(This is my friend, Endo san.)
　　主人(しゅじん)の佐藤(さとう)です。(This is my husband, Sato.)

練習(れんしゅう)

練習(れんしゅう) 1　　　　S1 のに S2

例　すぐ手紙をくれると言った，なかなかくれない
　　⇨遠藤さんは，すぐ手紙をくれると言ったのに，なかなかくれません。
　　(Although Endo san said he would write soon, he has not written promptly.)

1. 病気(びょうき)が治(なお)った，学校(がっこう)に来(こ)ない
2. 病気だ，学校に来ている
3. 発音(はつおん)がいい，文法(ぶんぽう)がよくない
4. 英語が上手だ，英語で話さない
5. 全然，友達と話さない，人気(にんき)がある
6. テープを聞(き)かない，発音が素晴(すば)らしい

練習(れんしゅう) 2　　　　～てある

例　手紙に元気だと書く　⇨手紙に元気だと書いてあります。
　　　　　　　　　　　　(It's written in the letter that he is fine.)
　　宿題をする　　　　　⇨宿題はしてあります。(The homework is done.)

1. コンサートの切符(きっぷ)を二枚(にまい)買う
2. 先生(せんせい)に推薦状(すいせんじょう)をもらう
3. もう十分予習(よしゅう)をする
4. この課(か)のテープを何度(なんど)も聞く
5. 佐藤さんに，明日八時に会(あ)おうと言う
6. 大江さんの電話番号(でんわばんごう)を調(しら)べる

練習(れんしゅう) 3　　　　～について言っている

例　大江さん，日本語　⇨大江さんは，日本語について何と言っていますか。
　　　　　　　　　　　(What does Oe san say about Japanese?)

1. 長井さん，昨日のコンサート
2. 医者(いしゃ)，青木(あおき)さんの病気
3. 学生，新(あたら)しくできた教科書(きょうかしょ)
4. 友達，あなたの今度(こんど)の仕事
5. 最近(さいきん)の学者(がくしゃ)，この問題(もんだい)
6. 佐藤先生，あなたの考(かんが)え

練習(れんしゅう) 4　　　V ようになる, adj. くなる

例　日本語がよくわかる　⇨このところ，日本語がよくわかるようになってきました。
(Recently, I have come to understand Japanese well.)

日本語がよくわからない
⇨このところ，日本語がよくわからなくなってきました。
(Recently, I have become unable to understand Japanese well.)

1．二マイル泳げる
2．二マイル泳げない
3．朝早く起きられる
4．朝早く起きられない
5．ロックがおもしろいと思える
6．ロックがおもしろいと思えない

練習(れんしゅう) 5　　　〜かどうか

例　奨学金がもらえた，聞く
⇨奨学金がもらえたかどうか聞いてください。
(Please ask him whether or not he has received a scholarship.)

1．元気で勉強している，聞く
2．明日の朝までにできる，教える
3．この説明でいい，聞く
4．西さんから，電話があった，知らせる
5．明日来られる，教える
6．明日着く，知らせる

練習(れんしゅう) 6　　　誰(と)でも

例　誰と話をしますか。⇨誰とでも話をしますよ。(I talk to anybody.)

1．誰から教えてもらえますか。
2．いつから始めますか。
3．何時にできますか。
4．どこで買えますか。
5．どこから手紙を出しますか。
6．誰と相談しますか。

練習(れんしゅう) 7　　　〜て欲しい

例　佐藤さんが言う　⇨私は佐藤さんに言って欲しいんですよ。
(I want you, Sato san, to say it.)

1．今すぐ西さんが行く
2．長井さんが切符を買う
3．友達が私の家に来る
4．西さんがもっと練習をする
5．ジョンソンさんが英語を教える
6．誰かがこの手紙を出す
7．子供が医者になる

練習(れんしゅう) 8		～なさい		

例　帰る　⇨帰りなさい。(Go home.)

1．読む　　　2．書く　　　3．入れる　　　4．聞く　　　5．言う
6．調べる　　7．食べる　　8．する　　　　9．来る

練習(れんしゅう) 9	間に

例　お留守，電話があった　⇨お留守の間に，電話がありました。
　　　　　　　　　　　　(There were some phone calls while you were out.)
　　いらっしゃらない，お電話があった
　　　⇨いらっしゃらない間に，お電話がありました。
　　　　　　(There were phone calls while you were not here.)

1．子供が寝ている，買い物に行く　　　2．新聞を読んでいる，家内が起きた
3．友達がテレビを見ている，料理を作った　　4．友達に電話をしている，料理ができた
5．日本に住んでいる，日本語を覚えた　　6．アメリカにいる，キャデラックに乗りたい
7．両親が出掛けている，父の酒を飲んだ　　8．弟が学校に行っている，手紙を書いた

練習(れんしゅう) 10	～中に

例　明日，終わらせる　⇨明日中に，終わらせます。(I'll finish it by tomorrow.)

1．今月，国へ帰る　　　2．今週，一度お邪魔する　　　3．今年，卒業する
4．夏休み，東京へ行く　5．授業，寝てはいけない　　　6．今晩，お知らせする

練習(れんしゅう) 11	S とのことです

例　大江さんは，病気だ　⇨大江さんは病気だとのことです。
　　　　　　(Oe san said he is ill./The story is that Oe san is ill.)

1．遠藤さんは，今日来られない　　　2．石原さんは，明日いらっしゃれない
3．先生は，いらっしゃれる　　　　　4．西さんはお出掛けだ
5．中川さんが電話が欲しい　　　　　6．来週の授業はない

練習(れんしゅう) 12	S のに。

例　すぐ手紙をくれると言った(なかなかくれない)
　　　⇨遠藤さんは，すぐ手紙をくれると言ったのに。
　　　　　(Endo san said he would write soon〔but he has not〕.)

Lesson 24

1．病気が治った（学校に来ない）　　　2．病気だ　　　　　（学校に来ている）
3．発音がいい　（文法がよくない）　　4．英語が上手だ　　（英語で話さない）
5．前に勉強した（覚えていない）　　　6．テープを聞かない（発音が素晴らしい）

練習（れんしゅう）　13	Appositional の

例　私の友達，大江さん　⇨こちらは，私の友達の大江さんです。
　　　　　　　　　　　　　(This is my friend, Oe san.)

1．本屋，中川さん　　2．英語の先生，ダン先生　　3．家内，直子
4．主人，ジョン　　　5．弟，二郎　　　　　　　　6．友達，西さん

練習（れんしゅう）　14	初めに，次に，最後に

例　大江さん，遠藤さん，石原さん，来た
　　⇨初めに大江さんが来ました。次に，遠藤さんが来ました。最後に，石原さんが来ました。
　　　(First, Oe san came. Next, Endo san came. At the end, Ishihara san came.)
　　友達に聞く，新聞で調べる，切符を買う
　　⇨初めに，友達に聞きます。次に，新聞で調べます。最後に，切符を買います。
　　　(First, I ask my friends. Next, I check it in the newspaper. Finally, I buy tickets.)

1．手，顔，頭，洗う
2．ワイン，コーヒー，ブランデー，飲む
3．友達，先生，図書館の人，聞く
4．ジョギングをする，シャワーを浴びる，ビールを飲む
5．朝御飯を食べる，テニスをする，テレビを見る
6．アルバイトをする，旅行に行く，勉強をする

練習（れんしゅう）　15	Omission of V

例　何時に来るって言っていましたか。（九時半）
　　⇨九時半に（来る）って言っていました。(At nine-thirty, he said.)

1．何月に始まると書いてありますか。　　　　　　（四月）
2．誰と行くっておっしゃっていましたか。　　　　（佐藤先生）
3．どこでやるって聞きましたか。　　　　　　　　（図書館）
4．いつ帰って来ると書いてありますか。　　　　　（今週）
5．何を買って欲しいっておっしゃっていましたか。（ワイン）
6．何で来るって聞きましたか。　　　　　　　　　（車）

二十五課

内容表

文法	Perfect form for Recollection		確か交番がありましたよ
	N 中 (in the process of 〜)		工事中
	Interjection		ですね，ね
	Connecting Clauses with て-form		行って…曲がって…
	Embedded Questions		駅はどこか御存じですか。
	Honorific, Humble "to know"		御存じですか／存じません。
	「を」 (along, through)		信号を左に曲がる，その通りを行く
	「と」 of Discovery If S1, (then one finds) S2.		真っ直ぐ行くと，信号があります。
	"This side" vs. "the other side"		「こちら」と「向こう」
	N でいい (avoiding causing trouble)		この辺で結構／いい です。
機能	Commenting on a Topic/Subject	7-11	あのう，すみませんが ちょっとお聞きしたいんですが
	Giving Directions/Instructions	5-8	☞会話
	Narrating	2-46	その通りを行って…東急ですよ。
	Remembering	2-37	確か交番がありましたよ。
	Terminating Conversation	6-5	ありがとうございました。
	Stating Factual Information (Distance)	1-2	二キロぐらいあります。
	Seeking Factual Information (Price)	1-3	おいくら／いくら ですか。
	Expressing Confirmation	2-25	その道ですか。 ああ，そこの広い道ですね。 橋のこちら側…ですね。
	Indicating Knowledge/Ignorance	2-50	駅はどこでしょうか。 東急…はどこか御存じでしょうか。
	Justifying/Presenting Excuses	2-52	細かいのがないので

Lesson 25

会話 (かいわ)

1

A：あのう，すみませんが，[はい。]駅へ行きたいんですが，駅はどこでしょうか。

B：実は，私もこの辺は今日が初めてで，道は全然わからないんですよ。[そうですか。]すみませんが，他の人に聞いてください。そこに，工事中の所がありますね。[はい，そこですね。]ええ，その横の所に確か交番がありましたよ。

A：わかりました。じゃ，そこの交番で聞いてみます。ありがとうございました。

2

A：あのう，ちょっとお聞きしたいんですが，[はい，何でしょう。]東急デパートは，どこか御存じでしょうか。[東急ですか。]ええ，道がわからなくなってしまったものですから…。

B：そうですか。ちょっと遠いですけどね，その通りを真っ直ぐ行って，[その道ですか。]いいえ，次の大通りですよ。[ああ，そこの広い道ですね。]ええ，そうです。その通りを真っ直ぐ行って，[はい。]三つ目の信号を左に曲がってですね，[はい。]また，そうですねえ，十分ぐらい真っ直ぐ行くとですね，[はい。]橋の手前に西武があって，それから，橋を渡った所が東急ですよ。

A：はあ，そうですか。わかりました。橋のこちら側が西武で，向こう側が東急ですね。

B：ええ，そうです。二キロぐらいありますが，簡単にわかると思いますよ。[どうも。]

3
〔タクシーに乗る〕

A：横浜まで，お願いします。

B：横浜のどの辺に行きますか。

A：プリンス・ホテルの近くです。

B：はい，わかりました。

1

A : Um, excuse me ... [Yes?] I want to go to the station, but can you tell me where it is?

B : I'm afraid I'm also in this area today for the first time, and I don't know my way around at all. [I see.] I'm sorry; please ask someone else. Do you see that spot under construction? [Yes, over there?] Yes. I thought I saw a police box next to that.

A : I see. Then I'll ask at that police box. Thank you.

2

A : Excuse me, may I ask you ... [Yes?] Do you know where Tokyu Department store is? [Tokyu?] Yes. I have lost my way.

B : I see. It's a little far from here, but go straight down that street. [That street?] No, the next main street. [Oh, it's that wide street there.] Yes, that's right. Go straight down that street, [OK.] turn left at the third light, [Yes.] and go straight again for ... well ... about ten minutes, [OK.] and then, you'll find Seibu Department store on this side of the bridge. And right across the bridge is Tokyu Department store.

A : I see. This side is Seibu, and the other side is Tokyu?

B : Yes, that's right. It is about two kilometers but you can find it easily, I guess. [Thank you.]

3 [Taking a Taxi]

A : To Yokohama, please.

B : Where in Yokohama shall I go?

A : Near the Prince Hotel.

B : Yes, very well.

Lesson 25

〔目的地に近づく〕

A：あの銀行の所で，左に曲がってください。[はい。]それから，二百メートルくらい行ってください。[はい。]そこの道を，入ってください。[ここですねえ。]はい。その角で，また，右に曲がってください。[はい。]その辺で止めてください。[この辺でよろしいですか。]もう少し行ってください。ああ，この辺で結構です。おいくらですか。[千五百五十円です。]はい。細かいのがないので，一万円でお願いします。[じゃ，八千四百五十円のおつりですね。ありがとうございました。]

〔タクシーを降りる〕

単語表（たんごひょう）

1

道(みち)	road, street, way
工事中(こうじちゅう)	under construction
横(よこ)	by, beside, side
確(たし)か	I may be wrong but ~
交番(こうばん)	police box

2

東急(とうきゅう)デパート	name of a department store
御存(ごぞん)じですか	☞文法
〜ものですから	☞文法
通(とお)り	street
真(ま)っ直(す)ぐ	straight
大通(おおどお)り	main street
広(ひろ)い	broad, wide
信号(しんごう)	traffic signal
(を)曲(ま)がる	turn, curve (v.i.)
橋(はし)	bridge
手前(てまえ)	this side
西武(せいぶ)	name of a department store
(を)渡(わた)る	cross
こちら側(がわ)	this side
向(む)こう側(がわ)	the other side
二キロある	☞文法

3

タクシー	taxi
どの辺(へん)	where, around where
目的地(もくてきち)	destination
(に)近(ちか)づく	come close to, approach
銀行(ぎんこう)	bank
角(かど)	corner
(を)止(と)める	stop, halt Ⅲ
おいくら	how much
細(こま)かいの	small note, change
おつり	change (to return)
(を)降(お)りる	get off, disembark Ⅱ

〔Approaching the destination〕

A： Please turn left at that bank. [Yes.] And then, please go about 200 meters. [Yes.] Please turn into that street. [Yes.] Please turn again to the right at that corner. [Yes.] Stop around there, please. [Is this a good place to stop?] Please move up a bit. Yes, this will do. How much is the fare? [It's ¥1550.] Here. Since I don't have anything smaller, here's ¥10,000. [Then, the change is ¥8450. Thank you.]

〔Get out of the taxi〕

関連語句 (かんれんごく)

曲(ま)がり角(かど)	corner	バスの停留所(ていりゅうじょ)	bus stop
映画館(えいがかん)	movie theater	⇨バス停(バスてい)	
駅前(えきまえ)	open space in front of a station	電気屋(でんきや)	home appliance store
		冷蔵庫(れいぞうこ)	refrigerator
地下鉄(ちかてつ)	subway	反対側(はんたいがわ)	opposite side
斜(なな)め前(まえ)	diagonal	突(つ)き当(あ)たり	dead end
富士山(ふじさん)	Mt. Fuji	身長(しんちょう)	person's height
体重(たいじゅう)	person's weight	JR(ジェイ・アール)	Japan Railways

Lesson 25

文法 (ぶんぽう)

● 交番がありました　　1-4

This use of the perfect form does not mean that there was a police box in the past. This form is used when you recollect something you heard or learned in the past. The speaker in the dialogue thinks he saw a police box and traces back his memory.

  1. 失礼ですが、前田さんでしたね。
   (Excuse me but you are Maeda san, aren't you?)
  2. 今、あそこに立っているのは森さんでしたね。
   (The person standing there now is Mori san, isn't he?)

● 御存じでしょうか　　2-2

This is the polite form of 知っていますか. The word 御存じ(御存知) is a honorific noun, and its negative form is 御存じじゃありません. Its affirmative form is 御存じです used to refer to the knowledge or information possessed by a third party who is deserving of the honorifics. If this question is addressed to you, however, you should not respond with honorific forms; simply say 存じています, to indicate that you know, and 存じません, to mean that you do not know.

	Affirm.	Neg.
Humble	存じています	存じません
Honorific	御存じです	御存じじゃありません
Neutral	知っています	知りません

● 三つ目の信号　　2-6　☞L. 21 ことばの使い方「三ページ目」P. 267

● 信号を左に曲がる　　2-6　☞L. 14 文法「家を出る」P. 157

● 道がわからなくなってしまったものですから　　2-2

The meaning of this pattern "S1 ものですから S2" is similar to "S1 から S2," but it sounds more like ので, much softer than から. This pattern is used to explain, make an excuse, or justify in a reserved manner. If S1 ends with "N だ," だ has to be changed to な just like before 〜のです. See the second example below.

もの is often pronounced もん in conversation.

  1. 私は料理が嫌いなものですから、毎日外で食べているんですよ。
   (Since I don't like cooking; I eat out every day.)
  2. このところ家内が病気なもんですから、早く帰らないといけないんですよ。
   (Since my wife has been ill these days, I have to go home early.)

● 左に曲がってですね　　2-6

ですね is an interjection that is often scattered in the middle and at the end of phrases, clauses, and sentences in a conversation. The function of this interjection is for the speaker to confirm that the listener is following what he/she is saying. If he/she is following, the listener should respond by saying はい or ええ.

In conversation among friends, the use of ね, without です, is more common than its formal counterpart ですね. Like the interjection "you know" in English, the presence of ですね or ね adds no meaning to the sentences or passages; excessive usage, however, would be annoying to the listener.

● 真っ直ぐ行くと，西武があって　　2-7

In L. 18 we learned the pattern "S1 と S2," which signifies a cause and effect or an antecedent and consequent relationship. It can be translated as "Whenever S1, S2." or "If S1, S2." In this lesson, this pattern is used to mean "S1, (and you will notice) S2." The S2 in this pattern usually describes a certain state of which you can become aware when S1 is established. There is no nuance of "whenever," and S2 can be used in the perfect form.

1．この問題は見ると簡単そうですが，やってみると難しいですよ。
　　(At first sight this question seems easy, but once you try to solve it, you will find it difficult.)
2．ドアを開けると，男が一人死んでいた。
　　(When I opened the door, I found a man lying dead.)

● 二キロぐらいあります　　2-10

This pattern is used to cite a measurement of distance, height, weight and so on. This expression gives a sense that the indicated number is large. It is necessary to use です／だ to avoid this sense. In order to give the smaller numbers and amount, use an expression such as しか…ない.

1．富士山は三千七百七十六メートルある。(Mt. Fuji is 3776 meters high.)
2．A：あの選手は，大きいですねえ。
　　B：ええ。身長は百八十センチしかありませんが，体重は百四十キロもあるそうですからね。
　　　(A：That player is really big.)
　　　(B：Right. I heard that he is only 180 cm. tall but weighs as much as 140 kilograms.)
3．A：暑いですね。今日は。　　(It's hot today!)
　　B：ええ。三十五度ありますよ。(Yes. It's 35°C.)

ことばの使い方 (ことばのつかいかた)

● 工事中　　1-3

This 中 means that the action described by the preceding word is still going on.

1．田中さんに電話をしてみたんだけど，お話し中でした。
　　(I gave Tanaka san a call, but he was in the middle of talking. … the line was busy.)
2．今は授業中ですから，静かにしてください。
　　(Please be quiet now, since class is in session.)

Lesson 25

3．先生は，今会議中です。あと五分くらいで終わると思います。
　　(Sensei is now in the middle of a meeting. I think he will be done in about five minutes.)

● 次の大通り　2-5

This word means "next" in terms of sequence.
　　Aの次は，Bで，Bの次はCです。
　　(B is next to A, and C is next to B.)

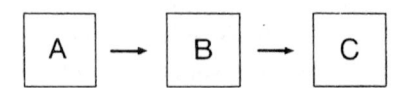

| A | → | B | → | C |

● こちら　2-9

This belongs to the following series of words: こちら, あちら, and どちら. The common meaning among these words is "direction" or "side." We have already learned that this series of words, particularly こちら, is used to refer politely to people when making introductions. The less polite expressions of this series are こっち, そっち, あっち, and どっち; this series is used among friends.

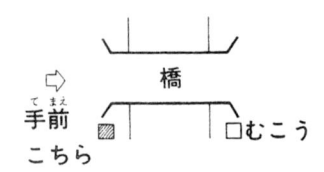

手前
こちら　　　　　橋　　　□むこう

● おいくら　3-10

おいくら means the same thing as いくら; the addition of お makes the word more polite than simply saying いくら. Women would use this form most of the time, while men would do so when an older person serves him; he would otherwise use the plain form, いくら.

練習 (れんしゅう)

| 練習（れんしゅう）　1 | Asking for directions |

例　駅に行きたい，駅
　　⇨あのう，すみませんが，駅に行きたいんですが，駅はどこでしょうか。
　　(Um, excuse me, I want to go to the station, but can you tell me where it is?)

1．映画が見たい，映画館　　　　　2．買い物がしたい，デパート
3．東京へ行きたい，駅　　　　　　4．バスに乗りたい，バスの停留所
5．テレビが欲しい，電気屋　　　　6．本が欲しい，本屋

練習(れんしゅう) 2　　　"The way to"

例　東京　⇨あのう，すみませんが，東京へ行く道を教えてくださいませんか。
(Excuse me, will you tell me the way to Tokyo?)

1．横浜　2．京都　3．ニューヨーク　4．シカゴ　5．ダウンタウン　6．デパート

練習(れんしゅう) 3　　　初めて

例　今日，初めてこの辺へ来ました。(I came to this area for the first time today.)
⇨この辺へ来たのは，今日が初めてです。
(Today is the first time that I have come to this area.)

1．今日，加藤さんに初めて会いました。　2．今週，初めて図書館へ行きました。
3．去年，森さんのお父さんと，初めて話しました。
4．明日，初めて病院へ行きます。　　5．来週，先生のお宅に初めてお邪魔します。
6．来月，初めて日本を旅行します。　7．今年，初めて奨学金をもらいます。

練習(れんしゅう) 4　　　て-form of です

例　今日，初めてこの辺へ来ました。
⇨この辺へ来たのは今日が初めてで，よく知らないんですよ。
(This is the first time I've been in this area, and so, I don't know my way around too well.)

1．今日，加藤さんに初めて会いました。　2．今週，初めて図書館へ行きました。
3．去年，森さんのお父さんと，初めて話しました。
4．明日，初めて病院へ行きます。　　5．来週，先生のお宅に初めてお邪魔します。
6．来月，初めて日本を旅行します。　7．今年，初めて奨学金をもらいます。

練習(れんしゅう) 5　　　Asking for locations

例　駅　⇨あのう，ちょっとお聞きしたいんですが，駅はどこか御存じでしょうか。
(Excuse me, may I ask you if you happen to know where the station is located?)

1．映画館　　2．デパート　　3．バスの停留所
4．本屋　　　5．電気屋　　　6．スーパー

Lesson 25

練習(れんしゅう)　6	Giving directions

例　その通りを真っ直ぐ行く，三つ目の信号を左に曲がる
　　　⇨その通りを真っ直ぐ行って，それから，三つ目の信号を左に曲がってください。
　　　(Go straight down that street, and then, turn left at the third light.)

1．その信号を右に曲がる，真っ直ぐ行く
2．十分くらい歩く，最初の信号で左に曲がる
3．駅まで来る，駅前(えきまえ)から電話する
4．タクシーで駅まで来る，そこで待っている
5．大通りを二キロくらい来る，文房具屋(ぶんぼうぐや)の前にいる
6．駅を出る，バスの停留所で待つ

練習(れんしゅう)　7	と indicating discovery

例　十分ぐらい真っ直ぐ行く，駅がある
　　　⇨十分ぐらい真っ直ぐ行くと，駅があります。
　　　(If you go straight ahead for about ten minutes, you'll find the station.)

1．教科書(きょうかしょ)を見る，書(か)いてある　　2．そこに行く，わかる
3．教室(きょうしつ)に行く，加藤さんがいる　　4．そこのパン屋に行く，売っている
5．森さんに聞(き)く，教(おし)えてくれる　　6．冷蔵庫(れいぞうこ)(refrigerator)を開(あ)ける，ビールがある

練習(れんしゅう)　8	Interjection ですね

例　十分ぐらい真っ直ぐ行く，駅がある
　　　⇨十分ぐらい真っ直ぐ行くとですね，駅がありますよ。
　　　(If you go straight ahead for about ten minutes, you'll find the station.)

1．教科書を見る，書いてある　　2．そこに行く，わかる
3．教室に行く，加藤さんがいる　　4．そこのパン屋に行く，売っている
5．森さんに聞く，教えてくれる　　6．冷蔵庫を開ける，ビールがある

練習(れんしゅう)　9	Confirmation

例　橋の手前がJRの駅で，向こう側が地下鉄の駅です。
　　　⇨ああそうですか。橋の手前がJRの駅で，向こう側が地下鉄の駅ですね。
　　　(I see. So this side of the bridge is the JR line station, and the other side is the subway station?)

1．この本が一年生の本で，この本が二年生の本です。
2．そこの方が田中さんで，あちらの方が伊藤さんです。
3．今日が十五日で，明日が十六日です。
4．あちらが先生で，そちらが学生です。
5．ここが銀行で，あれが駅です。
6．石井さんが大学院の学生で，中村さんが四年生です。

練習(れんしゅう) 10   "By means of"

例　タクシー　　　⇨タクシーで行きましょうか。(Shall we take a taxi?)
　　歩く　　　　　⇨歩いて行きましょうか。(Shall we walk there?)
　　タクシーに乗る　⇨タクシーに乗って行きましょうか。
　　　　　　　　(Shall we ride on a taxi to go there?)

1．地下鉄　　　2．走る　　　3．バスに乗る　　　4．自転車　　　5．車に乗る
6．地下鉄に乗る　7．バス　　　8．歩く　　　9．車　　　10．電車に乗る

練習(れんしゅう) 11   を，で

例　その角，右に曲がる　⇨その角を右に曲がってください。
　　　　　　　　　　　(Please turn right at that corner.)
　　その辺，止める　　　⇨その辺で止めてください。
　　　　　　　　　　　(Please stop around there.)

1．この道，真っ直ぐ行く　2．一つ目の信号，左に曲がる　3．病院の前，止める
4．その道，入る　　　5．信号の所，止まる　　　6．工事中の所，待つ

練習(れんしゅう) 12   Numeral ＋ある

例　二キロだ　⇨二キロあります。(It is two kilometers.)

1．彼は身長が一メートル九十センチだ　　2．リーさんは，体重が三百三十ポンドだ
3．夏休みは九十日だ　　　　　　　4．今日は三十二度だ
5．ワシントンまで千マイルぐらいだ　　　6．来なかった人が三十人だ

二十六課

内容表

文法	Indicating "Hearsay"		S＋そうだ，って，という話だ，と聞いた
	Adverbial Use of Verbs		
	〜と言って＋V		かわいいと言って喜んでいました。
	〜と思って＋V		何がいいだろうと思って相談に来た。
	〜たら，どうでしょう (Suggestion)		聞いてみたら，どうでしょう。
	Noun-modifier＋はずはない		勉強できるはずはない。
	さえ…ば (If only)		時間さえあれば
	どこ (to refer to an institution)		どこか他の大学
	Sといい		見つかるといいですね。
	方 (refering to one of the two)		勉強の方は問題ない。
	できる＋N		できる学生
	Spontaneity		見える，聞こえる
機能	Reporting Information	1-6	S＋そうだ，って，という話だ，と聞いた
	Describing, Narrating	2-46	かわいいと言って喜んでいました。
	Reason for Action/Non-Action	2-41	〜と思って相談に来た
	Making Suggestions	5-1	聞いてみたら，どうでしょう。
	Expressing Certainty	2-19	きっと見つかると思うわ。
	Expressing Agreement	2-1	それが一番いいかもしれませんね。
	Expressing Regret	3-34	できる学生だったのにもったいない。
	Expressing Impossibility	2-13	S＋はずはない
	Expressing Concern	6-21	松原さん，どうしたんでしょう。
	Expressing Sympathy	3-15	大変だよね。 いい大学が見つかるといいね。 気持ちはわかりますけどね。
	Predicting	2-44	あの人はいいお父さんになりますよ。 あとで困ることになりますから。

Lesson 26

会話 (かいわ)

1

A：田中さんの家に赤ちゃんが生まれたそうですね。

B：ええ，さっき聞きました。女の子ですってね。

A：ええ。田中さん，とてもかわいい赤ん坊だと言って喜んでいました。

B：あの人はいいお父さんになりますよね，間違いなく。

A：そうですね。それで，お祝いに何がいいだろうと思って相談に来たんですよ。

B：田中さんに，直接聞いてみたらどうでしょうね。必要な物，きっとあるでしょう。

A：そうですね。それが一番いいかもしれませんね。

2

A：バウマンさん，この大学，やめたんですって。

B：うん，授業料が高過ぎて，払えないという話だったよ。

A：そう。真面目なよくできる学生だったのに，もったいないわねえ。

B：先学期は毎週二十時間も働いていたそうだね。

A：じゃ，勉強できるはずはないわ。[ええ。]奨学金はなかったんでしょうか。

B：もらえなかったと聞いたよ。奨学金をもらわないで勉強するのは大変だよね。

A：ええ。あの人なら，時間さえあれば，勉強の方は問題ないんでしょうけど…。

B：どこか他のいい大学が見つかるといいですね。

A：今から探せば，秋学期の始まるまでには，きっと見つかると思うわ。

3

A：この頃，松原さん，見えませんが，どうしたんでしょうね。

B：ええ，あの犬が死んでしまって，非常にがっかりしているという話ですよ。

A：あの犬が…。あの犬は，松原さんが子供の時から飼っていたんだそうですね。

1

A : I hear that a baby was born to the Tanaka's.

B : Yes, I heard it just a little while ago. It's a girl, I hear.

A : Tanaka san was very happy and was saying that she's a very cute baby.

B : He'll be a good father ... without a doubt.

A : Yes, he will. And I've been wondering what would be a good congratulatory gift, and came to get your opinion.

B : Why don't we ask Tanaka san directly? I'm sure there are things he needs.

A : That's true. That may be the best thing to do.

2

A : I heard that Bauman san quit this university.

B : Yes, the story was that the tuition was too high and she couldn't pay it.

A : I see. She was such a serious, bright student. It's really too bad.

B : I heard that she was working as many as twenty hours a week last quarter.

A : Then, she certainly couldn't study. [Yes.] Didn't she have a scholarship?

B : I heard that she couldn't get one. It's difficult to study without receiving scholarship aid.

A : Yes. For her, as long as she has the time, she probably doesn't have any difficulty with the study material ...

B : I hope she finds another good university somewhere.

A : If she looks for one now, I am sure she can find it by the time fall quarter starts.

3

A : I haven't seen Matsubara san recently. I wonder what happened.

B : Well, the story is that that dog died, and he's feeling very sad.

A : That dog ... I understand that Matsubara san had had that dog since he was a child.

Lesson 26

B：あの人は優しい人ですから。授業にも全然出ていないんですって。

A：気持ちはわかりますけどねえ。今日，ちょっと彼の所に寄ってみましょうか。

B：ええ，そうしましょう。行って，元気づけてあげましょう。

A：そうですね。授業に出なくちゃ，あとで困ることになりますからね。

単語表（たんごひょう）

1

赤(あか)ちゃん	baby
～そうです	☞文法
女(おんな)の子(こ)	girl
かわいい	cute, lovely
赤(あか)ん坊(ぼう)	baby ☞ことばの使い方
喜(よろこ)ぶ	(look) happy, pleased
お祝(いわ)い	gift
相談(そうだん)する	consult
直接(ちょくせつ)	directly
必要(ひつよう)な	necessary
きっと	certainly

2

授業料(じゅぎょうりょう)	tuition
払(はら)える	can pay Ⅲ
～という話だ	☞文法
できる	be good at, be smart, be bright Ⅲ
先学期(せんがっき)	last term, previous term
(で)働(はたら)く	work at
～はずはない	☞文法
～と聞きました	☞文法
もらえる	can receive Ⅲ
さえ	☞文法
(が)見つかる	can be found

3

松原(まつばら)	a surname
犬(いぬ)	a dog
非常(ひじょう)に	とても
(を)飼(か)う	keep animals/pets
優(やさ)しい	kind, considerate
授業に出(で)る	attend class Ⅲ
気持(きも)ち	feelings
(に)寄(よ)る	drop in, visit
元気(げんき)づける	cheer up Ⅲ

B：He's such a kind-hearted person. I hear that he hasn't been to class at all.

A：I do understand how he feels, but ... Shall we briefly stop by his place today?

B：Yes, let's. Let's go and cheer him up.

A：Yes. If he doesn't come to class, he'll get into trouble later.

関連語句 (かんれんごく)

(名前を)付ける	name Ⅱ	高校生(こうこうせい)	high school student
(が)はやる	prevail, be popular	大雪(おおゆき)	heavy snowfall
(が)聞こえる	reach one's ear, can be heard	(が)見える	come into sight, can be seen Ⅱ
隣(となり)の家	the house next door	泣(な)き声(ごえ)	cry, sobbing

文法 (ぶんぽう)

● S＋そうだ　　1-1

In this lesson we are going to learn hearsay patterns that are used in relaying information from one source to another. The patterns appearing in this lesson are:

S＋そうだ／という話だ／と聞いた／って

The following describes the differences among the above expressions:

そうだ — is always used with the plain form of verbs, い-adjs., and the copula, but not in the perfect form. (i.e. そうでした is hardly ever used.) This expression can be used in both the written and spoken languages. Do not confuse this hearsay そうだ with the そうだ as used in おいしそうだ (L.17 文法), which we will study more in detail in the next lesson.

1．明日, 試験があるそうですね。

(I hear that there will be a test tomorrow.)

2．昨日, 試験があったそうですね。

(I hear that there was a test yesterday.)

という話だ — The 話 in this pattern means "rumor" or "report," and the sentence preceding という indicates the content of the 話. This can be used in both the written and spoken languages, though this form is most frequently used in the spoken language.

1．明日, 大雪が降るという話ですね。

(It is said that there will be a heavy snowfall tomorrow.)

2．試験はやさしいという話でしたよ。

(I heard that the test will be easy.)

と聞いた — This is normally used in the perfect form to report what has been heard.

って — This is the most colloquial of these expressions and not suitable for use in formal situations. ☞P. 221 文法「東京へ行くんだって」

● S＋と言って喜んでいました　　1-3

喜ぶ is used to describe a person's display of gratitude; this word, however, cannot be used to describe one's own feelings. (To describe one's own happiness, the adj. 嬉しい is used.) In the example from the dialogue, the reason 田中さん looked so happy is because his new born baby was so lovely. The sentence before と言って marks the approximate quotation which explains why he looked happy.

松原さんは, 犬が死んだと言って泣いていました。

(Because [saying that] his dog had died, Matsubara san was sobbing.)

西川さんは, 御両親から手紙が来たと言って喜んでいましたよ。

(Having received a letter from her parents, Nishikawa san was happy.)

A similar sentence can be found in this dialogue: that is,「お祝いに何がいいだろうと思って相談に来たんですよ。」. In this example, the reason for the speaker's visit is explained in the first part of the sentence. The て-form here functions as a verb-modifier.

● お祝いに　　　1-5　☞P. 296　文法「このテーブルを机にします」
● 聞いてみたらどうでしょう　　1-6　☞P. 219　文法「頭が疲れたら」3．
● S＋かもしれません　　1-7　☞P. 281　文法「そうかもしれませんね」
● S＋はずはない　　2-5　☞P. 265　文法「手帳に書いてあるはずです」

This pattern indicates that there is no possibility of S. Noun modifiers such as こんな, そんな, あんな, can take the place of the sentence.

1．A：あなたは，授業料を払ってないですね。
　　B：そんなはずはないですよ。先月払いましたよ。
　　　　(A：You haven't paid the tuition, have you?)
　　　　(B：That can't be. I paid it last month.)
2．今月はかなりアルバイトをしたから，こんなに金が少ないはずはないんだが。
　　　　(Since I did more part-time jobs this month [than before], it can't be that I have so little money.)

● S＋んでしょうか　　2-5

This pattern is used when you offer your conjecture or opinion in a reserved, hesitant way, as in: "I wonder if S." Since this is a variation of ん(の)です, the copula must be changed to な.

　南さん，どうしたんでしょう。遅いですね。時間を間違えたんでしょうか。
　　　　(I wonder what has happened to Minami san. He's so late. I wonder if he misunderstood the time.)
　風邪がはやっているんでしょうか。授業を休んでいる学生が多いですね。
　　　　(I wonder if there's a cold going around. There are many students absent from class.)

● 時間さえあれば　　2-7

This さえ is a particle that indicates the minimum requirement necessary to realize what follows. It takes the place of "が" and "を."

　が→さえ
　　これさえわかれば，いいんです。
　　　　(All I wanted to know is this. … Only if I can understand this, it is all right.)
　を→さえ
　　漢字の練習さえしていれば，こんなのは簡単に読めますよ。
　　　　(As long as you keep practicing *kanji*, you will be able to read this sort of thing easily.)

● どこか他のいい大学　　2-8

To ask the name of an institution to which one belongs, a person can use どこ, as follows:

1．北村さんの大学はどこですか。
　　　　(Kitamura san, from which university did you graduate?／Kitamura san, which university are you attending?)
2．A：あの人の会社は，どこですか。(Where does he work?)
　　B：確か，IBMでしたよ。(I may be wrong, but I think at IBM.)

These examples can also be interpreted as questions about the location of these institutions, but most such questions will be asked with にありますか。

Lesson 26

- S＋と＋いいですね　　2-8

The と of "S と、いいですね" is a conjunction. The pattern means: "If S, then it is good." This expression is used to describe wishes and desires; it can also be used to give advice.

1. 早く病気が治るといいですね。(I hope you recover soon.)
2. 明日が休みだといいですねえ。(I wish tomorrow were a holiday.)
3. 風邪をひいたら薬を飲むといいですよ。
　　(If you catch cold, you should take medicine.)

- 秋学期の始まるまでに　　2-9　☞P. 315 「明日の朝までに」

ことばの使い方 (ことばのつかいかた)

- 赤ちゃん，赤ん坊　　1-1, 3

Although the English translations of these words are identical, there is a slight difference in their Japanese usage: 赤ちゃん is tinged with a feeling of respect like that contained in お父さん. 赤ん坊, like 父, does not have that same nuance of respect.

To talk about your own baby with someone who is not a member of your family, 赤ん坊 can be used; this, however, is not a hard and fast rule like that between 父 and お父さん. If the child is older than a baby, 子供, お子さん, can be used.

- できる学生　　2-3

We learned できる in L.19. This usage of できる is derived from what we studied in that lesson. If you say できる学生 it usually means a student who excels in studying, that is, a bright student.

The opposite expression is できない学生, an incapable student.

- 勉強の方は問題ない　　2-7

When we studied how to compare two things, we learned the usage of 方. The use of 方 here is related to what we have already learned. Comparing two aspects of a student's life — studying and supporting herself, the phrase 勉強の方は picks up "study" as a topic. The speaker says that there is no problem on this matter, and leaves the other aspect (namely, supporting herself) unmentioned; this indicates that she may have problems supporting herself.

- 松原さん(が)，見えません　　3-1

This 見える is derived from 見る. It signifies the spontaneous action or events over which the agent has no control. Although this spontaneity is different in concept from that of the English potentiality or passivity, it may be translated into the passive potential form as in "can be seen." The original meaning of this phrase is, however, somewhat closer to "come into sight."

It is also used as a respectful expression for 来る.

Another example of this spontaneity, important at this level, is 聞こえる, which means "reach one's ear."

1．あのビルの一番高い所に登ると，冬なら富士山が見えますよ。
   (If you go up to the top of that building in winter, Mt. Fuji is visible.)
2．前に背の高い人がすわったから，映画がよく見えませんでした。
   (I couldn't see the movie well because a tall person sat in front of me.)
3．日曜日の朝は，いつも隣の家の高校生の弾くピアノの音が聞こえる。
   (On Sunday mornings we can always hear the high school student next door playing the piano.)

In these examples, you may have noticed that the object is marked by が, like in the potential cases.

● 授業に出なくちゃ　　3-7　☞P. 297　文法「ベッドがなくちゃ」．

練習（れんしゅう）

練習（れんしゅう）1　　そうです, Hearsay

例　田中さんの家に赤ちゃんが生まれました。
　⇨田中さんの家に赤ちゃんが生まれたそうです。
　(I hear that a baby was born to the Tanaka's.)

1．赤ちゃんは女の子です。
2．赤ちゃんは男の子じゃありません。
3．田中さんは喜んでいます。
4．田中さんは早く会社から帰ってきます。
5．赤ちゃんはまだ小さいです。
6．名前はまだ付けていません。
7．赤ちゃんは二週間早く生まれました。
8．奥さんも赤ちゃんも問題ありません。

練習（れんしゅう）2　　～んですって

例　バウマンさんが大学をやめました。
　⇨バウマンさんが大学をやめたんですって。
　(I heard that Bauman san has quit the university.)

1．授業料が払えませんでした。
2．バウマンさんはよくできる学生でした。
3．先学期は二十時間も働いていました。
4．奨学金はもらえませんでした。
5．勉強の方は問題はありませんでした。
6．授業料が高過ぎました。

Lesson 26

練習(れんしゅう)　3　　　　　　　～という話だ

例　田中さんの家に赤ちゃんが生まれました。
　　　⇨田中さんの家に赤ちゃんが生まれたという話ですよ。
　　　　(The story is that a baby was born to the Tanaka's.)

1. 赤ちゃんは女の子です。
2. 赤ちゃんは男の子じゃありません。
3. 田中さんは喜んでいます。
4. 田中さんは朝早く仕事に行かなくなりました。
5. 赤ちゃんはまだ小さいです。
6. 名前はまだ付けていません。
7. 赤ちゃんは二週間早く生まれました。
8. 奥さんも赤ちゃんも問題ありません。

練習(れんしゅう)　4　　　　　　　～と言って

例　とてもかわいい赤ん坊です，喜ぶ
　　　⇨とてもかわいい赤ん坊だと言って喜んでいました。
　　　　(He was pleased and said that she was a very lovely baby.)

1. 試験が難し過ぎます，怒る　　　2. 仕事が簡単です，喜ぶ
3. 学生がよくできます，感心する　4. 授業料が安いです，驚く
5. 犬が死にました，がっかりする　6. あの人が早く来ました，びっくりする
7. 今日はまるで春のようです，喜ぶ　8. この頃日本語がおもしろくなりました，喜ぶ

練習(れんしゅう)　5　　　　　　　～と思って

例　何がいいだろう，相談に来ました
　　　⇨何がいいだろうと思って相談に来ました。
　　　　(I've been wondering what would be good, and came to get your opinion.)

1. 昼御飯を食べよう，レストランに入りました
2. 先生に相談しよう，お宅に電話しました
3. 田中さんに直接聞こう，手紙を書きました
4. どこかいい大学を見つけよう，参考書を調べました
5. 今年から真面目に勉強しよう，新しい机を買いました
6. 風邪を治そう，お酒を飲みました

練習(れんしゅう) 6　　　～たら，どうでしょう／Suggestion

例　田中さんに直接聞いてみる　⇨田中さんに直接聞いてみたら，どうでしょうね。
(Why don't we ask Tanaka san directly?)

1．お祝いを持って行く　　　　　　2．必要な物を買ってあげる
3．田中さんと相談してみる　　　　4．授業料を安くしてもらう
5．働く時間を少なくする　　　　　6．もっとアルバイトを探す

練習(れんしゅう) 7　　　～かもしれない

例　あの人は，この大学の大学院の学生です。
　　⇨あの人は，この大学の大学院の学生かもしれませんね。
(That person over there may be a graduate student at this university.)

1．この犬はもうすぐ死にます。　　　2．松原さんががっかりしています。
3．この猫は今週中に子供を生みます。4．この猫は誰かが飼っていたんです。
5．そうするのが一番いいです。　　　6．あの人は授業に出ていません。

練習(れんしゅう) 8　　　～はずはない

例　二十時間も働いていた，勉強できる
　　⇨二十時間も働いていたんですから，勉強できるはずはないですよ。
(Since she was working as many as 20 hours, she could not have been able to study.)

1．毎朝十時に起きる，授業に出られる　2．漢字の練習をしない，覚えられる
3．赤ちゃんが生まれた，今夜遊びに行く4．みんなで相談した，変なお祝いだ
5．辞書で調べた，間違っている　　　　6．新聞で見た，そんなだ

練習(れんしゅう) 9　　　～さえ，あれば

例　時間，勉強の方は問題ない
　　⇨時間さえあれば，勉強の方は問題ないんでしょう。
(As long as she has the time, she probably doesn't have any difficulty with the study material.)

1．お金，嬉しい　　　　　　　　　2．授業料，生活はできる
3．アルバイト，授業料は払える　　4．仕事，どんな仕事でもいい
5．奨学金，もう一年で卒業できる　6．電話，すぐ行ける

Lesson 26

| 練習(れんしゅう) 10 | S と、いい |

例 どこかいい大学が見つかる
　　⇨どこかいい大学が見つかると、いいですねえ。
　　　(I hope she finds a good university somewhere.)

1. 早く病気が治る　　　　2. 試験が簡単だ　　　　3. いいアルバイトがある
4. 今年、卒業できる　　　5. 仕事が見つかる　　　6. 犬が元気になる
7. 元気づけてあげられる　8. 彼が家にいる　　　　9. 奨学金がもらえる

| 練習(れんしゅう) 11 | 見える、聞こえる／Spontaneity |

例 何が見えますか。(What can you see?／[lit.] What is visible?)
　　（富士山）⇨富士山が見えます。(I can see Mt. Fuji.)
　　何が聞こえますか。(What can you hear?／[lit.] What is heard?)
　　（音楽(おんがく)）⇨音楽が聞こえます。(I can hear music.)

1. いつ、富士山が見えますか。　　　　　　（冬の朝）
2. いつ、ピアノの音が聞こえますか。　　　（日曜の朝）
3. どこから、富士山が見えますか。　　　　（このビルから）
4. どこから、ピアノの音が聞こえますか。　（隣の家から）
5. 何時頃(なんじごろ)、富士山が見えますか。　　　　　（八時から九時頃まで）
6. 何時頃、ピアノの音が聞こえますか。　　（八時から九時頃まで）

| 練習(れんしゅう) 12 | ～ちゃ、いけない |

例 授業に出ない　⇨授業に出なくちゃいけませんね。
　　(It's not good not to attend class. / You must attend class.)

1. お祝いをあげない　　　2. いいお父さんにならない
3. 学校をやめる　　　　　4. 授業料を払わない
5. 二十時間も働く　　　　6. そんなことで、がっかりする

| 練習(れんしゅう) 13 | ～と聞きました |

例 Q：バウマンさんが大学をやめたんですって。
　　A：ええ、やめたと聞きました。
　　　(Q：I heard that Bauman san has quit the university. Is it true?)
　　　(A：Yes, I heard that she quit.)

1. 授業料が払えなかった　　　　2. バウマンさんはよくできる学生だった
3. 先学期は二十時間も働いていた　4. 奨学金はもらえなかった

5．勉強の方は問題はなかった　　　6．授業料が高過ぎた

練習（れんしゅう）　14　　　　〜までに

例　五時，私の部屋に来る　⇨五時までに，私の部屋に来てくださいね。
(You will come to my room by five, won't you?)
　　寝る，新聞を全部読む　⇨寝るまでに，新聞を全部読んでくださいね。
(Please read all of the newspaper before going to bed.)

1．金曜日，レポートを書く　　　　2．今月の終わり，新しいアパートを見つける
3．卒業する，いい論文を一つ書く　4．今年の秋，仕事を見つける
5．結婚する，料理を習っておく　　6．夏休みが始まる，この仕事を全部やる

二十七課

内容表

文法	〜なら (Judging from〜)		この天気なら，大丈夫だ
	N によると (According to N)		テレビによると，明日は雨が降る。
	〜らしい		明日は雨が降るらしい。
	〜そうだ (It looks〜)		降りそうには見えない。
	〜ようだ／みたいだ		筋肉を痛めたようだ／みたいだ
	V (Stem)＋始める／終わる		降り始める
	V (Pre-ない) ずに (without 〜ing)		準備運動をせずに
	〜じゃなくて〜です		足りなかったんじゃなくておいしかった。
	たとえ〜ても／〜たって		たとえ家の子が手伝ってくれたって
	V＋(の)には (in order to V)		作る(の)には時間がかかります
	こ，そ，あ，どれだけ (As much as)		あれだけ作るには，時間がかかった
	Honorific "to do"		なさる
	とても…ない (Even if I try)		とても，できそうもありません。
機能	Expressing Confirmation	2-25	この天気なら大丈夫ですよ。
	Reporting Information Through the Media	7-15	今朝のテレビによると テレビでそう言っていました。
	Expressing Surprise	3-8	ふうん
	Expressing Certainty	2-19	降りそう(には見えない) できそうもありません
	Reporting Information	1-6	〜と言っています。
	Expressing a Belief/Opinion	2-33	〜らしいですよ。 〜ようです／〜みたいです 大丈夫ですよ。
	Expressing Thanks	6-17	昨日は色々ありがとうございました。
	Expressing Corrections	5-10	〜じゃなくて，…ですよ
	Stating Hypothesis	1-4	たとえ〜ても／たって

347

Lesson 27

会話 (かいわ)

1

A：この天気なら，明日のソフトボールの試合，大丈夫だろうね。
B：でも，今朝のテレビによると，明日は雨が降るらしいわよ。
A：ええっ。こんな晴れた空なのに。ほんとう。降りそうには，見えないけどね。
B：ええ，夕方から曇り始めて，明日の朝から雨が降り始めるそうよ。テレビの天気予報でそう言っていたわ。
A：ふうん，そうか。こんなにいい天気なのに。

2

A：どうしました，大分疲れているようですね。
B：いいえ，疲れたわけじゃありませんが，ちょっと腕の筋肉を痛めたみたいなんです。
A：どこですか。ああ，痛そうですね。だいぶ腫れていますね。
B：準備運動をせずに，すぐ始めたのがいけなかったんでしょうね。
A：そうかもしれませんね。冷やした方がよさそうですね。それより，病院で診てもらった方がいいですね。
B：ええ，これから，病院に行こうと思っているんですよ。

3

A：渡辺さん，昨日は色々ありがとうございました。準備にずいぶん時間がかかったでしょう，あれだけ作るには。[いえいえ。]全部で何人くらい来たんですか。
B：一番多い時は六十人ぐらいいたらしいですね。子供がそう言ってました。
A：みんな，とても楽しかったようでしたよ。帰る時に，まだ歩きながら歌を歌っている人がいましたよ。
B：そうですか。そうだといいんですが。食べ物はちょっと足りなかったみたいでしたね。十分ありましたか。

1

A：If the weather is like this, I think the softball game tomorrow will be all right.

B：But, according to the TV this morning, it's supposed to rain tomorrow.

A：Really? When the sky is so clear? Is that true? It doesn't look as if it might rain.

B：Yes. I heard that it is going to start getting overcast this evening, and that it's going to start raining tomorrow morning. That's what they said on the weather forecast on TV.

A：Well, is that so? The weather is so nice, though.

2

A：What happened? You look very tired.

B：No, it's not that I'm tired; I think that I may have slightly hurt a muscle in my arm.

A：Where? Oh, it looks painful. It's quite swollen.

B：I think I shouldn't have started off right away without doing preparatory exercises.

A：Perhaps. It might be best to ice it. Better than that, you should have them take a look at it at the hospital.

B：Yes, I'm thinking about going to the hospital now.

3

A：Watanabe san, thank you for everything yesterday. It must have taken you quite a while to make all that. [No, not really.] About how many people showed up in all?

B：When there were the most people, it seems that there were about 60. That's what my child was saying.

A：It seemed like everybody had a good time. There were people on their way home who were still singing as they walked.

B：Really? I hope they did (have a good time). It seemed we were a little short on food. Did you have enough?

A：もちろんですよ。足りなかったんじゃなくて，おいしかったんですよ。奥さん，お一人で準備なさったんですか。私にはとてもできそうもありませんわ。

B：子供も手伝っていたようですね。

A：たとえ家の子供が手伝ってくれたって，作れそうもないわ，あんなにたくさん。

単語表（たんごひょう）

1
試合(しあい)	match, game
大丈夫(だいじょうぶ)だ	all right
空(そら)	sky
降りそうだ	☞文法
見える	II ☞文法
夕方(ゆうがた)	time of sunset, dusk
天気予報(てんきよほう)	weather forecast
ふうん	☞ことばの使い方

2
大分(だいぶ)	かなり
～わけじゃない	☞文法
腕(うで)	arm
筋肉(きんにく)	muscle
(を)痛(いた)める	hurt, injure II
(が)腫(は)れる	get swollen II
準備運動(じゅんびうんどう)	preparatory exercises
(を)冷(ひ)やす	to cool, chill, refrigerate

3
渡辺(わたなべ)	a surname
色々(いろいろ)ありがとう	Thank you for everything.
準備(じゅんび)する	prepare
足(た)りない	be lacking II
十分(じゅうぶん)だ	enough, sufficient
なさる	☞ことばの使い方
とても…ない	☞ことばの使い方
手伝(てつだ)う	help, assist
たとえ…ても／たって	☞文法

A：Of course. It's not that there wasn't enough; it was simply delicious! Did your wife prepare that all by herself? I couldn't possibly do that!

B：It seems my child was helping.

A：Even with the help of my child, I don't think I could possibly make that much.

関連語句 (かんれんごく)

研究(けんきゅう)	research	世界(せかい)	world
貧乏(びんぼう)だ	poor	麻雀(マージャン)	mahjong
財布(さいふ)	wallet, purse		

頭(あたま)
目(め)
鼻(はな)
口(くち)
歯(は)
耳(みみ)
首(くび)
肩(かた)
腕(うで)
肘(ひじ)
手(て)
指(ゆび)
胸(むね)
腹(はら)
腰(こし)
脚(あし)
膝(ひざ)
足(あし)

Lesson 27

文法 (ぶんぽう)

● この天気なら　　1-1

なら has various functions, but here it indicates that the part that follows is the speaker's opinion, judgment or advice that is based on what he sees. In this example, the speaker makes a judgment that the weather tomorrow will be alright after looking up at the sky. (☞ P. 221「もし, 行くなら」and P. 235「少しなら, できます」)

　　寒いなら窓を閉めてもいいですよ。
　　　(If you're cold, you can close the window.)
　　おなかがすいているなら, 冷蔵庫に何か食べる物がありますよ。
　　　(If you are hungry, there is something to eat in the refrigerator.)
　　車に乗るのなら, 気をつけて運転してね。
　　　(If you're going to take the car, drive safely.)

The speakers in the above examples observed the listeners and offered advice to them.
です or だ must be deleted before なら, since なら is a derived form of です.

● N によると　　1-2

N によると indicates that the noun (N) is the source of some information. This pattern is often used with expressions of hearsay.

　　今日の新聞によると, 今年は春の来るのが早いそうですね。
　　　(According to today's paper, spring will arrive early this year.)
　　最近の研究によると, 背の高い子供は, 頭がいいんですって。
　　　(According to recent research, tall children are smart.)

● 雨が降るらしい　　1-2

An important focus of this lesson is to learn to differentiate the meaning and usage of the following patterns:

　　S＋らしい　／　S＋ようだ(みたいだ)　／　CL＋そうだ

　ようだ／みたいだ

It is safe to say that ようだ is the same in meaning as みたいだ which we studied in L.23. Both ようだ and みたいだ relate the subjective opinion, impression, or judgment of the speaker. The difference between the two is that みたいだ is basically for colloquial use, while ようだ is mainly limited to formal conversation and writing.

There were two possible interpretations of the sentence "ここは, ハワイみたいです." One was figurative, while the other represented the "unconfirmed opinion" of the speaker. If みたいだ is substituted with ようだ, the same two interpretations are possible.

　らしい

In contrast to みたいだ and ようだ which express the "subjective" and "unconfirmed," らしい describes the opinion, impression, or judgment of the speaker with somewhat more objectivity than the two former words.

そうだ

This そうだ here is entirely different from the hearsay そうだ which takes the plain forms of the copula, adjs., and verbs. The use of そうだ in this lesson is identical to that which appears in the phrase おいしそうだ.

```
Verb (stem)   雨が降り―
い-adj.        今日は寒―       ＋ そうだ
な-adj.        ここは静か―
Noun          ×
```

This pattern means: Judging from one's observation of things, events and people, and so forth, "it is likely that S."

今夜は，雨が { 降るみたいだ（ようだ）。…（1）
　　　　　　　　降るそうだ。 ……………（2）……hearsay
　　　　　　　　降るらしい。 ……………（3）
　　　　　　　　降りそうだ。 ……………（4）

The differences among these forms are as follows:

The first sentence (1) with ようだ or みたいだ can be used when the speaker conceives of the likelihood of rain in some way other than through objective means. If he/she is asked why he/she thinks so, it is quite possible that he/she will not be able to give a satisfactory reason. His/her answer might be something like, "For some reason, I feel that way." Sentences with みたいだ or ようだ allow the speaker to be completely subjective.

Since ようだ is a dependent noun, the forms that can precede it are exactly the same as those which come before regular nouns. See the chart below:

〔ようだ〕

	Verb	い-adj.	な-adj.	Noun
Imperf.	行く	寒い	静かな	学生の
Perfect	行った	寒かった	～だった	

The third sentence (3) with らしい has more or less objective substantiation. The speaker may have heard or read the weather forecast, or watched it on TV. In his case, his answer will probably be credible and satisfactory to the person who asks him about the weather.

The forms required in front of らしい are identical to those preceding かもしれない, なら, and みたいだ.

〔らしい〕

	Verb	い-adj.	な-adj.	Noun
Imperf.	行く	寒い	(だ) 0	
Perfect	行った	寒かった	～だった	

Finally the sentence (4) with そうだ indicates that based on the speaker's observation and judging from the appearance of things, he/she feels that the action or state described in the phrase preceding そうだ is possible or likely to happen. Before the speaker says "今夜は

Lesson 27

雨が降りそうだ," he/she may look up at the sky to see how things look, and, perhaps, observe the clouds, before making a judgment.

Note that in this case the words ない and よい take slightly different forms: なさ and よさ.

1. 私には，私の生まれた所が世界で一番よさそうだ。
   (My native town is likely to be best place in the world for me.)
2. 先生が病気で休んだので，今日の試験はなさそうだ。
   (Since Sensei is absent due to an illness, the test today is likely to be cancelled.)
3. 急用ができたので，明日の会議には行けそうもない。
   (It is unlikely that I can attend tomorrow's meeting, as something urgent has come up.)

For the negative form, see the next page:「できそうもない」.

〔そうだ〕

	Verb	い-adj.	な-adj.	Noun
Imperf.	行き	寒	静か	not used
Perfect	not used			

● 降りそうには，見えない   1-3

This そう is the same as the one we studied above. This is a dependent word always in need of a precedent. It conjugates like a な-adj, taking な to modify a noun and taking に to function as an adverbial phrase. This is true of ようだ as well.

While そうだ and ようだ are like な-adjs., らしい conjugates like an い-adj.

1. 今日は，雨が降りそうな天気ですね。
   (The weather today seems as if it might rain.)
2. 松原さんは死んだ犬のことを話すと，泣きそうになります。
   (Whenever Matsubara san talks about the dead dog, he sounds as if he is about to cry.)
3. 先生，さっき先生のお友達らしい方から，お電話がありました。
   (Sensei, there was a call a little while ago from somebody who sounded as if he might be your friend.)

● 降りそうには，見えない   1-3

This 見える means "to look," and is different in meaning from the 見える which we studied in L.26. The particle that marks the object, however, is still が.

1. 空が青く見えます。(The sky looks blue.)
2. 黒い背広を着ると，学者に見えますよ。
   (If you wear a dark suit, you look like a scholar.)

● 降り始める   1-4

V (stem)＋始める／終わる： This pattern indicates the beginning and ending of an action. This 始める can never be used interchangeably with 始まる.

この本は，昨日の六時半に読み始めて，今朝の三時に読み終わりました。
(I started reading this book at six-thirty yesterday and finished it at three this morning.)

- 疲れたわけじゃありません　　　2-2　☞P. 251「そういうわけじゃないわ」
- 準備運動をせずに　　　2-4　☞P. 236「そんなこと，言わないで」

ずに is a remnant from classical Japanese, and is used quite often even in conversation today. This expression is the same in meaning as V (Pre- ない) ＋ないで which we studied in L.26. If ないで is substituted with ずに, it will make a correct form; the only exception is する, which becomes せ before ず (a classical equivalent of the modern ない).

1．何も食べずに運動するのは，体によくありませんよ。
(It is not good for you to exercise without eating anything.)
2．あの人は全然勉強もせずに，毎日何をしているんでしょう。
(What is he doing every day, without studying at all?)

- いけなかったんでしょうね　　　2-4　☞P. 283「運動した方がいいんでしょうけど」
- 足りなかったんじゃなくて，おいしかったんですよ　　　3-8

Unlike the pattern V＋ないで／ずに, which modifies the final verb, this phrase, the て-form of ない, indicates the continuity of the sentence; it means "and" or "but."

1．リーさんは，中国人じゃなくて，韓国人ですよ。
(Lee san is not Chinese, but he's Korean.)
2．父は，東京に行くんじゃなくて，大阪に行くんですよ。
(My father is going, not to Tokyo, but to Osaka.)

- できそうもありません　　　3-9

As in the case of はずだ, there are two possible negative sentences when そうだ, which represents likelihood, is used with a verb. The forms are そうもない and なさそうだ. Although both are acceptable, the former, そうもない, is more widely used than the latter, as is illustrated in the dialogue.

- たとえ家の子供が手伝ってくれたって　　　3-11

This pattern is used to hypothesize an extreme case; it means: "even if." Sometimes たとえ can be omitted without affecting the meaning of the whole sentence. Its function is to signal that a hypothetical sentence will follow.

たって is the colloquial equivalent of ても, which we studied in L.13 when we learned the patterns used to get permission from someone. When used in a form to solicit permission, たって and ても are not interchangeable, but in the present pattern they can be used interchangeably.

1．辞書を引いても，こんなにたくさんの漢字は調べられませんよ。
(Even if I consult a dictionary, I cannot check this many *kanji*.)
2．私は，貧乏でも，好きなことができる生活がいいです。
(Even if I were poor, I would prefer a life in which I could do the things I like.)

Lesson 27

ことばの使い方 (ことばのつかいかた)

● でも　　1-2

This conjunction signals that the sentence or statement that follows is difficult to predict from the information contained in the preceding sentences. でも is the same in meaning as しかし and けれども, but it is more colloquial than the latter two words, and cannot be used in formal writings and speeches.

おなかはすいています。でも，何も食べたくありません。
(I am hungry, but I don't feel like eating anything.)

● ええっ　　1-3

This is an indicator of surprise. The final「っ」shows that there is a glottal stop, similar to the action you would do before clearing your throat.

● ふうん　　1-6

This exclamatory expression indicates that the speaker has finally come to understand something. Its function is similar to ああ，そうですか, but it is used in informal conversations, and very often in monologues.

● 昨日は色々ありがとうございました　　3-1

Use this pattern when you thank someone for something; you may substitute 色々 with other words.

Suppose your friend gave you a ticket for a concert:

切符，どうもありがとう(ございました。)

If it is difficult to single out a specific item (like wanting to thank a person for various things you enjoyed about a party), use the greeting which appears in the dialogue.

● あれだけ作るには　　3-2

作る here can be used either in the dictionary form or with の (作るの).

● あれだけ　　3-2

When だけ is combined with これ, それ, あれ, どれ, it means "as much as this" or "to this extent." This だけ combination can be used interchangeably with the あんなに series.

● 全部で　　3-2　☞P. 266「全部で」
　1．これは，一つ五十円ですから，二つで百円です。
　　　(This is fifty yen a piece and, so, it's one hundred yen for two.)
　2．麻雀(マージャン)は四人(よにん)でします。(Mahjong is played with four people.)

● なさる　　3-9

This is an honorific expression that means する. This verb belongs to the same group as いらっしゃる and おっしゃる and り becomes い before "masu": that is, なさいます, instead of なさります.

● とてもできそうもありません　　3-9

This pattern, とても…ない, means: "Even if one forces himself/herself to do something, he/she cannot."

356

このような仕事は，私にはとてもできないと思います。
(I think that this kind of job is impossible for me to do even if I try.)

練習(れんしゅう)

練習(れんしゅう) 1　　　なら

例　この天気だ，大丈夫でしょう。　⇨この天気なら，大丈夫でしょう。
(If the weather is like this, it'll be alright.)

1．寒い，ドアを閉めた方がいいですよ。　　2．貧乏が嫌だ，もっと働いてください。
3．全部できた，帰っていいですよ。　　　　4．何もわからない，もう一度調べましょう。
5．筋肉を痛めた，冷やした方がいいです。　6．明日試合だ，早く寝なくちゃいけません。
7．この空だ，心配はいりませんよ。　　　　8．日本へ行く，私の友達に会ってください。

練習(れんしゅう) 2　　　～によると

例　テレビによると，明日は雨だそうです。(らしい)
　　⇨テレビによると，明日は雨らしいです。
(According to the television, it's likely to rain tomorrow.)

1．新聞　　2．大雪が降る　　3．みたいだ　4．らしい　5．そうだ(likelihood)
6．ようだ　7．天気はよくない　8．そうだ(hearsay)　　　9．そうだ(likelihood)

練習(れんしゅう) 3　　　らしい

例　明日は雨が降る　⇨明日は雨が降るらしいですよ。
(It is likely that it will rain tomorrow.)

1．あの人は大学院の学生だ　　　　　2．渡辺さんは東京へ行った
3．加藤さんは宿題に困っている　　　4．明日の試合は大丈夫だ
5．昨日のパーティーは賑やかだった　6．先生は今日は休みだ

練習(れんしゅう) 4　　　そうだ

例　明日は雨が降る　⇨明日は雨が降りそうですね。
(It looks like it will rain tomorrow.)

Lesson 27

1．明日の試合は大変だ
2．この仕事は疲れる
3．この準備は時間がかかる
4．今夜は天気がいい
5．あの人は時間がない
6．渡辺さんのアパートは便利だ
7．明日の朝は暖かい
8．このケーキはおいしい

練習(れんしゅう)　5　　　　そうです　(Hearsay, Likelihood)

例　雨が降る　⇨雨が降りそうですが，降らないそうですよ。
　　　　(It looks like rain but I hear it won't.)

1．この仕事は大変だ
2．今度の試験は楽だ
3．あの先生は優しい
4．あの先生の試験は非常に難しい
5．あのレストランはいい
6．この料理はおいしくない

練習(れんしゅう)　6　　　　V ＋始める

例　明日の朝，雨が降る
　　⇨明日の朝くらいから雨が降り始めるそうですよ。
　　(I heard that it'll start raining sometime tomorrow morning.)

1．来週，新しい教科書を使う
2．来月，中国語を習う
3．今日，病院に行く
4．先週，歩いた
5．去年，日本語がわかった
6．一年前，漢字が読めるようになった

練習(れんしゅう)　7　　　　ようだ

例　明日の朝，雨が降る
　　⇨明日の朝くらいから雨が降り始めるようですよ。
　　(It looks as if it will start raining sometime tomorrow morning.)

1．来週，新しい教科書を使う
2．来月，中国語を習う
3．今日，病院に行く
4．先週，歩いた
5．去年，日本語がわかった
6．一年前，漢字が読めるようになった

練習(れんしゅう)　8　　　　わけじゃない

例　疲れましたか。(Are you tired?)
　　⇨いいえ，疲れたわけじゃありません。(No, it's not that I'm tired.)

1．もう帰りますか。
2．今日の会議に行きませんか。
3．あの人は貧乏なんですか。
4．明日の試験の準備はできましたか。

5．麻雀が嫌いですか。　　　　　　　　　6．お金が足りませんか。

練習(れんしゅう)　9　　　～ずに

例　準備運動をしない，運動をする
　　⇨準備運動をせずに運動をするのは，よくありませんよ。
(It's not good to exercise without doing preparatory exercises.)

1．何も食べない，運動をする　　　　　2．よく考えない，論文を書く
3．よく寝ない，勉強する　　　　　　　4．予習しない，授業に出る
5．料理を手伝わない，遊んでいる　　　6．電話をしない，友達の家に遊びに行く

練習(れんしゅう)　10　　　～方がいい

例　病院で診てもらう　⇨病院で診てもらった方がいいですよ。
(You should be checked at the hospital.)

1．天気予報を見ておく　　　　　　　　2．仕事を全部終えてしまう
3．料理を作り始める　　　　　　　　　4．子供に手伝ってもらう
5．テレビを見ながら勉強しない　　　　6．あの人に言わずに行く

練習(れんしゅう)　11　　　～，ありがとう

例　色々　⇨昨日は色々ありがとうございました。
(Thank you for everything yesterday.)

1．お金　　2．電話　　3．本　　4．宿題　　5．お手紙　　6．お料理

練習(れんしゅう)　12　　　S＋に

例　あれだけ作る，時間がかかった
　　⇨あれだけ作るには，時間がかかったでしょう。
(It must have taken you a long time to make that much.)

1．ソフトボールをする，ボールが必要だ
2．明日，パーティーをする，準備を始めた方がいい
3．病院で診てもらう，お金を持って行かなければならない
4．腫れた所を冷やす，水じゃだめだ
5．麻雀をする，もう一人いる
6．東京へ行く，地下鉄(subway)が一番早い

Lesson 27

練習(れんしゅう) 13　　　〜んじゃなくて

例　足りなかった，おいしかった
　　⇨足りなかったんじゃなくて，おいしかったんですよ。
　　(It isn't that we didn't have enough, but rather, that it was delicious.)

1．学生だ，先生だ
2．ボーイフレンドだ，普通の友達だ
3．研究が好きだ，研究しかできない
4．ドアを閉めた，ドアが閉まった
5．いいレストランだ，他に食べられる所がない
6．暖かい，暑い

練習(れんしゅう) 14　　　〜そうもない

例　この仕事できますか。(Can you do this work?)
　　⇨その仕事はできそうもないですね。(I doubt if I can do that work.)

1．これ，食べられますか。
2．この水，飲めますか。
3．この論文，今日読めますか。
4．これだけ食べ物が作れますか。
5．明日までに準備できますか。
6．明日の会議，行けますか。

練習(れんしゅう) 15　　　たとえ〜たって

例　家の子供が手伝ってくれる，作れない
　　⇨たとえ，家の子供が手伝ってくれたって，作れません。
　　(Even if my child helps me, I don't think I can make it.)

1．友達に手伝ってもらう，できない
2．今すぐ始める，終わらない
3．図書館(としょかん)で調べる，わからない
4．車で行く，三時間(さんじかん)はかかる
5．毎日，休まないで読む，一年かかる
6．筋肉を痛める，やめない
7．何も食べない，コンピューターを買う

二十八課

内容表

文法	Passive (Introduction)		言う⇨言われる
	ただの N (a mere～)		ただの疲れ
	S (affirmative) ＋ことはない 　No need to ～		心配することはない。
	～しなければ／しないと…いけない／ならない／駄目だ etc.		規則正しい生活をしなければいけない。
	N 中に (Sometime before N is over)		今日中に
	～までに (by～)		何時までに出すんですか。
	Embedded question		間違いがないかどうか目を通す
機能	Inquiring About One's Health/Welfare	6-20	お医者さんに何て言われましたか。
	Expressing Obligation	2-20	～しなければ／しないと／しなくては 　…いけない／ならない／だめだ etc.
	Expressing Surprise	3-8	もうこんな時間ですか。
	Rejecting	2-38	まだ，そんな時間じゃないでしょう。
	Taking Leave	6-2	そろそろ失礼しなければ…。
	Offering Invitations	5-6	また，近いうちにいらしてください。
	Accepting Invitations	5-7	また，お邪魔します。
	Greeting	6-1	奥様によろしく。
	Offering Help	6-15	何か手伝えることはありませんか。
	Stating Want/Desire	3-16	持って行ってほしい。
	Expressing Need	2-17	心配することはないよ。

会話 (かいわ)

1

A：お医者さんに何て言われましたか。

B：ただの疲れだから、心配することはないって言われました。

A：それだけですか。よかったですね。

B：いえいえ。それで夜更かしをしないで、規則正しい生活をしなければいけないって、厳しく言われました。[そうですか。]それから、栄養を考えて食事をしなければ本当に体をこわすよって言われてしまいました。

2

A：(腕時計を見ながら)ああ、もうこんな時間ですか。ずいぶん長い間、お邪魔してしまいました。そろそろ、失礼しなければ…。

B：まだ、そんな時間じゃないでしょう。十一時前じゃないですか。

A：ええ。でも、今帰らないと、バスがなくなってしまいますので。

B：そうですか。それじゃ、また近いうちにいらしてください。

A：ええ、ありがとうございます。またお邪魔します。それじゃ、失礼します。

B：お休みなさい。お気を付けて。奥様によろしく。[はい。お休みなさい。]

二十八課

1

A：What did the doctor tell you?

B：He told me that it's just fatigue and that I don't need to worry.

A：That was all? I'm so happy for you.

B：Well. I was told very strictly that I should not stay up until late at night, and that I should lead a healthy, well-regulated life. [I see.] And then, I was warned that I would really ruin my health if I'm not nutrition-conscious about my meals.

2

A：(Looking at his wrist watch) My, it's getting late! I've stayed for such a long time. I must be on my way ... .

B：It's not that late yet. It's still before eleven o'clock.

A：Yes, but if I don't leave now, the buses will stop running.

B：I see. Well then, please come by again soon.

A：Yes. Thank you very much. I'll visit again. Then, I'll be on my way.

B：Good night. Be careful. Say hello to your wife. [Yes, I will. Good night.]

Lesson 28

3

A：ずいぶん忙しそうね，リンさん。

B：今日中に出さなくてはならないリポートが二つあるんだけど，それが，間に合わないかもしれないんでね。

A：今日中に。何時までに出すの。

B：締め切り？　一つは四時までで，もう一つは七時までなんだけど。

A：もう三時半ですよ。

B：知ってる。知ってる。ああ，気が狂いそうだよ。ゆうべ徹夜して，今日も朝から全然寝てないので，眠いしくたびれたし目は痛いし。ああ，参った。参った。

A：それは大変ねえ。何か手伝えることは，ない？

B：じゃ，悪いけどね，その原稿，字の間違いがないかどうか，目を通してくれない？　それから，先生の所へ持って行ってほしいんだけど。［ええ，いいわよ。］

単語表（たんごひょう）

1

（何）て	colloquial variation of quotational と
言われる	passive form of 言う III
ただのN	mere, simple
Sことはない	☞文法
（それ）だけです	That's all.
夜更（よふ）かしをする	fool around until late at night
規則正（きそくただ）しい	orderly, well-regulated
生活（せいかつ）をする	lead a life, live
厳（きび）しく	strictly
栄養（えいよう）	nutrition
考（かんが）える	think, consider III
食事（しょくじ）をする	have meals, dine
体をこわす	harm one's health

2

腕時計（うでどけい）	wrist watch
そろそろ失礼する	I'd better be on my way
近（ちか）いうちに	in the near future
奥様（おくさま）	☞ことばの使い方
〜によろしく	Give my regards to 〜. Say hello to 〜.

3

A：Lin san, you seem to be very busy.

B：I have two reports that I must hand in today. And I might not finish in time.

A：Today? By what time do you have to hand them in?

B：The deadline? One is by four and the other is by seven o'clock.

A：It's already three-thirty.

B：I know, I know. I'm almost going crazy. I stayed up all night last night, and I haven't slept a wink this morning either. I am sleepy, exhausted and my eyes are sore. Oh, my!

A：That's terrible. Is there anything I can do to help?

B：Then, if you don't mind, would you take a quick look through that manuscript to check for spelling errors? And then I would like you to take it to Sensei's place. [Yes, certainly.]

3

〜に間(ま)に合(あ)う	be in time for
締め切り(しめきり)	deadline
気(き)が狂(くる)う	become insane
ゆうべ	last night
徹夜(てつや)する	stay up all night, pull an all-nighter
くたびれる	get exhausted II
眠(ねむ)い	sleepy
原稿(げんこう)	manuscript
間違(まちが)い	mistake
〜に目(め)を通(とお)す	take a quick look, skim through

関連語句(かんれんごく)

外(そと)	outside
目覚まし時計(めざましどけい)	alarm clock
不規則(ふきそく)だ	irregular, unregulated

Lesson 28

文法 (ぶんぽう)

● 言われる　　1-1

　This is the passive form of 言う and is made up of the Pre -ない form of the verb and the suffix れる. The person who did the talking is the doctor, and に indicates the agent of the action. The passive voice will be explained in further detail in the next lesson.

● S＋ことはない　　1-2

　The S in this pattern is a sentence ending in the affirmative imperfect. The meaning of the phrase is "There is no need to S." The same idea can be expressed by an alternative phrase 必要(ひつよう)はない. Note that the S＋ことはない pattern is always used in the negative ことはない.

　　ただの風邪(かぜ)ですから，病院(びょういん)に行く ことはないですよ。／必要はないですよ。
　　(Since it's just a cold, there's no need to go to the hospital.)

● しなければいけない　　1-4

　We have already covered this pattern in L.17. In this lesson, we shall study several variations of the pattern which have similar meanings.

　　規則正しい生活をしなければいけない。……………(1)
　　食事(しょくじ)をしなければ体をこわすよ。……………(2)
　　そろそろ，失礼しなければ(いけません)。…………(3)
　　先生の部屋(へや)に持って行かないといけないんです。……(4)

　When these sentences are divided and analyzed, it becomes clear that the first portion represents a hypothetical clause such as: "If one does not～," and the second part means: "～ is no good, bad." The first portion is often marked by "～なければ" or "～ないと." The second portion signifies something negative in meaning; the words most often used are いけない and ならない. As shown in example (2), the second part of this pattern need only convey a negative sense; the words いけない and ならない do not necessarily have to be used.

　The first portion of the sentences above can be replaced by ～ては, which appeared in L.23. (☞P. 297「ベッドがなくちゃ」) As a matter of fact, なくては(ちゃ), なければ, and ないと can be used interchangeably; they all mean: "If one does not～, it is not good," as is exemplified in (A) below.

　One instance in which they are not interchangeable: when the first part of the pattern contains no negative element. In such a case, only ～ては(ちゃ) can be used, as is shown in (B).

　　病気(びょうき)なんだから，家(いえ)に ｛いなくては, いないと, いなければ,｝ いけませんよ。……(A)
　　(You must stay home, since you are ill.)
　　病気なんだから，外(そと)で遊(あそ)んではいけませんよ。……………(B)
　　(You must not play outside, since you are ill.)

　In the same way that ては is contracted in the spoken language to ちゃ (and では becomes じゃ), なければ can become either なけりゃ or なきゃ when it is used in conversation among friends.

| なければ ⇨ なけりゃ, なきゃ |

- ～までに　　　3-4　☞P. 315　文法「明日の朝までに」
- 気が狂いそうだ　3-7　☞P. 352　文法「雨が降るらしい…そうだ」
- ～かどうか　　3-10　☞P. 312　文法「友達ができたかどうか」

ことばの使い方 (ことばのつかいかた)

- **お医者さん**　1-1

In addressing or referring to a person, words which denote that person's occupation or title can be used instead of his/her name. Addressing the owner of a fish shop as 魚屋さん is commonly done. In the case of a medical doctor, お医者さん is more often used by women when referring to him/her as a third person while men would use 医者. In addressing the doctor directly, the word 先生 must be used. School teachers and professors are always called 先生, but never 先生さん.

- **何て**　1-1

The quotational と is often pronounced て after ん; otherwise it becomes って. Note that these are used only in speech, and never in writing.

- **ただの**　1-2

ただ followed by の is a noun modifier which means: "a mere～." Coupled with だけ, this word can become an adverb meaning: "merely."
　　1．ああ、これはただの風邪ですよ。　(This is just a cold.)
　　2．ああ、ただ風邪を引いただけですよ。(You have merely caught cold.)

- **それだけですか**　1-3

This phrase means "Is that all (he said)?" or "Is that the only thing?" When だけ takes a modifier such as a noun, it means "only."
　　A：たくさん買い物をしたんですか。
　　B：いいえ。これを買っただけですよ。／これだけですよ。
　　　(A：Did you do a lot of shopping?)
　　　(B：No, I just bought this./It's only this.)

- **そろそろ、失礼しなければ**　2-2

When you are leaving of someone's company, you cannot suddenly say, "Good-bye," and take off. You must first give a signal that you plan to leave soon. This phrase is such a signal. The unwritten second portion of the expression is なりません or いけません, but it is usually omitted.

Lesson 28

● 十一時前じゃないですか　　2-3　☞ P. 172　文法「とてもいいじゃないですか」

● 奥様　　2-7

　This 様 is the same as 〜さん. They both show respect for the person in question, but 様 is more formal than さん. The name of an addressee in a letter must always be followed by 様, except for the names of teachers, in which case 先生 is preferred. In ordinary conversation, さん is most commonly used. When formality is required, however, 様 is preferred. In shops and department stores, this can be heard quite frequently in the word お客様 which means : a customer or visitor.

● 今日中に　　3-2　☞ P. 315　文法「明日中に」

練習 (れんしゅう)

練習(れんしゅう)　1	S ことはない

例　心配する　⇨心配することはありませんよ。
　　　　　　　(There is no need to worry.)

1．そんなに毎日運動する　2．徹夜して書き終える　3．締め切りまでに論文を出す
4．こんなに早く帰る　　　5．その原稿に目を通す　　6．体をこわすまで勉強する

練習(れんしゅう)　2	S って言っておいて〜

例　心配する　⇨渡辺さんに，心配することはないって言っておいてくれませんか。
　　　　　　　(Won't you tell Watanabe san that there's no need to worry?)

1．毎日運動する　2．体をこわすまで勉強する　3．締め切りまでに論文を出す
4．早く帰る　　　5．その原稿に目を通す　　　　6．徹夜して書く

練習(れんしゅう)　3	だけ

例　本を買った　　　⇨本だけ買いました。　　(I bought only books.)
　　加藤さんが来た　⇨加藤さんだけ来ました。(Only Kato san came.)
　　先生に話した　　⇨先生にだけ話しました。(I told it only to Sensei.)

1．今日は晴れている　2．佐藤さんが元気づけてくれた　3．家賃を払った
4．先生と相談した　　5．父に言っておいた　　6．佐藤さんが試験に間に合わなかった

練習（れんしゅう） 4　　　　近いうちに〜ませんか

例　先生のお宅にお邪魔する　⇨近いうちに，先生のお宅にお邪魔しませんか。
　　　　　　　　　　　　　　(Shall we visit Sensei's house sometime soon?)

1．食事を一緒にする　　　　2．論文について相談する　　　3．芝居を見に行く
4．デパートに買い物に行く　5．みんなでパーティーをする　6．東京に遊びに行く

練習（れんしゅう） 5　　　　〜しては(ちゃ)いけません

例　夜更かしをする　⇨夜更かしをしちゃいけませんね。
　　　　　　　　　　(It's not good to stay up until late at night.)

1．心配し過ぎる　　　　　　2．夜更かしをする　　　　　　3．好きな物だけ食べる
4．不規則な生活をする　　　5．遅くまでお邪魔する　　　　6．締め切りに遅れる

練習（れんしゅう） 6　　　　〜なくてはいけない

例　規則正しい生活をする　⇨規則正しい生活をしなくちゃいけませんね。
　　　　　　　　　　　　　(We must lead an orderly life.)

1．栄養を考える　　　　　　2．そろそろ失礼する　　　　　3．締め切りに間に合う
4．今夜は十分寝る　　　　　5．書いたあと目を通す　　　　6．栄養のある食事をする

練習（れんしゅう） 7　　　　S ば S

例　規則正しい生活をしない，体をこわす
　　　⇨規則正しい生活をしなければ，体をこわしますよ。
　　　　(If you don't lead an orderly life, you'll ruin your health.)

1．栄養を考えない，病気になる　　　　2．風邪の時は早く寝ない，ひどくなる
3．締め切りに間に合わない，駄目だ　　4．書いたあと目を通さない，間違いがある
5．体に気を付けない，風邪をひく　　　6．今帰らない，バスがなくなる

練習（れんしゅう） 8　　　　S と S

例　規則正しい生活をしない，体をこわす
　　　⇨規則正しい生活をしないと，体をこわしますよ。
　　　　(If you don't lead an orderly life, you'll ruin your health.)

1．栄養を考えない，病気になる　　　　2．風邪の時は早く寝ない，ひどくなる
3．締め切りに間に合わない，駄目だ　　4．書いたあと目を通さない，間違いがある

Lesson 28

5．体に気を付けない，風邪をひく　　　　6．今帰らない，バスがなくなる

練習（れんしゅう）　9	～なくてもいい

例　もう帰らなければ。　⇨まだ，帰らなくてもいいじゃありませんか。
　　　(I must be going.　⇨You don't have to go back yet, do you?)

1．もう論文を書き終えなければ。　　　　2．もう失礼しなければ。
3．もう食事を作らなければ。　　　　　　4．もうこの原稿を渡さなければ。
5．もう仕事を始めなければ。　　　　　　6．もう寝なければ。

練習（れんしゅう）　10	までに

例　何時，リポートを出す　⇨何時までにリポートを出すんですか。
　　　　　　　　　　　　　(By what time do you have to hand in your report?)

1．今週の終わり，その仕事を終える　　　2．来週の初め，全部に目を通す
3．いつ，書き終える　　　　　　　　　　4．今日の四時，先生の部屋に持って行く
5．何時，お医者さんに行く　　　　　　　6．締め切り，間に合う

練習（れんしゅう）　11	て-form　(cause)

例　仕事が大変だ，気が狂う
　　　⇨仕事が大変で，気が狂いそうですよ。
　　　　(I'm so overwhelmed by my work that I'm almost going crazy.)

1．寒い，病気になる　　　　2．おなかがすく，死ぬ
3．宿題が多い，終わらない　4．疲れる，授業中寝てしまう
5．忙しい，行かれない　　　6．寂しい，気が狂う

練習（れんしゅう）　12	～ことはありませんか

例　手伝う　⇨何か私に手伝えること，ありませんか。
　　　　　　(Is there something I can do for you?)

1．する　2．してあげる　3．お手伝いする　4．調べる　5．準備する　6．手伝う

練習(れんしゅう) 13	〜かどうか

例　間違いがない，目を通す
　　　⇨間違いがないかどうか目を通してくれませんか。
　　　　(Won't you take a quick look through [it] to check for mistakes?)

1．答えが正しい，見る　　2．値段が安い，比べる　　3．そのやり方でいい，考える
4．西さんがいる，見てくる　　5．西さんがいる，聞く　　6．味がいい，食べてみる

練習(れんしゅう) 14	〜かどうか，Interrogative ＋か

例　間違いがない，目を通す
　　　⇨間違いがないかどうか目を通してくれませんか。
　　　　(Won't you take a quick look through [it] to check for mistakes?)
　　どれが正しい，目を通す
　　　⇨どれが正しいか目を通してくれませんか。
　　　　(Won't you take a quick look through [it] to spot the correct one?)

1．どの答えが正しい，見る　　2．どれが安い，比べる　　3．そのやり方でいい，考える
4．西さんがいる，見てくる　　5．誰と誰がいる，聞く　　6．味がいい，食べてみる

練習(れんしゅう) 15	〜によろしく

例　your father　⇨お父さんによろしく。
　　　　(Please say hello to your father.)

1．your husband　　　　　2．your mother　　　　　　3．your elder sister
4．your father　　　　　　5．your younger brother　　6．your wife

二十九課

内容表

文法	Polite Imperative		授業にちゃんと出なさい 全部するように

	Passive
	  1) Neutral passive
	  2) Suffering passive
			この歌は日本人によく歌われる。
			田中さんは泥棒にステレオを盗まれた。

	CL たり(CL たり)する		家が壊されたり橋が流されたりする。
	S＋ように(と)言う／頼む		全部するように言われました。
	Conjugation of 〜てしまう(ちゃう)		盗まれちゃいました。
	Omission of the Predicate		(この歌は)この頃は，あまり…
機能	Expressing Certainty	2-19	多分…と思いますよ。
	Changing a Topic	7-12	ところで
	Expressing a Belief/Opinion	2-33	よく聞かれているようですね。 好きなようですね。
	Giving/Citing Examples	2-47	アメリカには…ありますが，日本ではどうですか。
	Stating Generalization	1-5	毎年，壊されたり流されたりしますよ。
	Inquiring About Certainty	2-19	怒られたんでしょう。
	Giving Orders	5-23	授業にちゃんと出なさい。 全部するように
	Requesting Explanation	7-9	どんなことですか，〜っていうのは。
	Expressing Dislikes	3-1	Suffering Passive 〜てしまいました(〜ちゃいました)。
	Expressing Sympathy	3-15	いけませんね。 ひどいことをするのがいるんですね。
	Rejecting	2-38	とんでもない

Lesson 29

会話 (かいわ)

1

A：日本人はスティーブン・フォスターの歌をよく知っていますね。

B：小学校の時から教えられますからね。アメリカではあまり歌われないんですか。

A：昔は歌われたかもしれませんが、この頃はあまり…。

B：フォスターは、たぶんアメリカ人の作曲家の中で一番よく知られていると思いますよ。

A：そうですか。ところで、西洋の音楽は日本でもよく聞かれますか。

B：ええ。若い人の間ではよく聞かれているようですね。

A：お年寄りはどうですか。西洋の音楽をよく聞きますか。

B：普通のお年寄りは、日本の歌の方が好きなようですね。家の母などやはり民謡ですね。

2

A：アメリカには、ハリケーンとか竜巻とかありますが、日本ではどうですか。

B：竜巻はあまり聞いたことがありませんが、台風がありますよ。

A：台風で家が壊されたりしますか。

B：ええ。毎年、家が壊されたり、橋が流されたりしますよ。

3

A：ニューマンさん、先生に呼ばれたそうですね。怒られたんでしょう。

B：ええ、呼ばれて怒られました。

A：何て怒られたんですか。あの先生は、あまり怒ったりしないやさしい先生なのに。

B：授業にちゃんと出なさいって叱られました。そして、見てくださいよ。こんなにたくさん宿題を渡されました。週末に全部するようにって言われてしまいました。

1

A: Japanese people seem to know Stephen Foster's songs very well.

B: We are taught (his songs) from the time we are in elementary school. Aren't they sung very often in America?

A: Perhaps they were sung in the past, but not recently ...

B: I think that of all the American composers, Foster is probably the best known (in Japan).

A: I see. By the way, is Western music listened to very much in Japan?

B: Yes. I think it's listened to a lot by young people.

A: How about the older people? Do they often listen to Western music?

B: Most older people seem to prefer Japanese songs. My mother, for example, prefers Japanese folk songs.

2

A: In America we have hurricanes and tornadoes, but do you have them in Japan?

B: We don't hear of tornadoes very often, but we have typhoons.

A: Do houses get destroyed by typhoons?

B: Yes. Every year houses get destroyed and bridges get washed away.

3

A: Newman san, I heard you got called in by Sensei. You got scolded, didn't you?

B: Yes, I was called in and scolded.

A: What did he say when he scolded you? He's a gentle teacher who doesn't scold very often.

B: He chided me and told me to come to class regularly. And, take a look at this! I was given this huge load of homework. I was told to do all of this during the weekend.

Lesson 29

4

A：旅行はどうでした。楽しい旅行でしたか。

B：ええ、まあ、おもしろい経験をいろいろしました。

A：どんなことですか、おもしろい経験っていうのは。

B：生まれて初めて、スピード違反で罰金を取られました。[そうですか。]そして、その次の日に、カー・ステレオを盗まれちゃいました。買ったばかりのですよ。

A：いけませんね。ひどいことをするのがいるんですね。でも、天気はよかったでしょう。

B：とんでもない。毎日雨に降られましたよ。でも、おもしろい人にたくさん会いましたよ。

単語表 (たんごひょう)

1

スティーブン・フォスター	Stephen Collins Foster (1826〜64)
小学校(しょうがっこう)	elementary school
教(おし)えられる	be taught Ⅱ
歌(うた)われる	be sung Ⅱ
昔(むかし)	long time ago, in the past
作曲家(さっきょくか)	composer
西洋(せいよう)	West
〜の間(あいだ)で	among〜
お年寄(としよ)り	the elderly
民謡(みんよう)	traditional folk songs

2

ハリケーン	hurricane
竜巻(たつまき)	tornado
〜とか〜とか	☞ことばの使い方
台風(たいふう)	typhoon
家(いえ)	house (hold)
壊(こわ)される	be broken, damaged Ⅱ
〜たりする	☞文法
橋(はし)	bridge
流(なが)される	be washed away Ⅱ

3

呼(よ)ばれる	be called, summoned Ⅱ
怒(おこ)られる	be scolded, chided Ⅱ
出(で)なさい	☞文法
叱(しか)られる	be scolded, chided Ⅱ
Sように	☞文法

376

4

A: How was your trip? Did you have a good time?

B: Yes, well, I had many interesting experiences.

A: These interesting experiences ... what sort of things were they?

B: For the first time in my life I got a speeding ticket and was fined. [I see.] And the next day my car stereo was stolen. And I had just bought it too!

A: That's too bad. There are terrible people, aren't there? But the weather must have been nice.

B: Not at all! I was rained on every day. But I met many interesting people.

4

旅行(りょこう)	trip, travel
経験(けいけん)	experience
生(う)まれて初(はじ)めて	for the first time in one's life
スピード違反(いはん)	speeding violation
罰金(ばっきん)	fine
取(と)られる	be collected, taken, stolen Ⅱ
盗(ぬす)まれる	be stolen Ⅱ
買ったばかりの	one that I just bought
ひどい	terrible, cruel
とんでもない	not at all

関連語句(かんれんごく)

(泥棒(どろぼう)が)入(はい)る	(thief) enter, rob, steal
なくす	lose
警官(けいかん)	policeman
建(た)てる	construct, build Ⅱ
汚(よご)す	soil, make dirty

Lesson 29

文法 (ぶんぽう)

● **The Passive Voice** （受動態—じゅどうたい，受身—うけみ）

In Japanese, there are two types of passive sentences: one is called the neutral passive; it takes transitive verbs and is similar to the English passive voice. The other is the "suffering passive," used with both transitive and intransitive verbs.

$\boxed{\text{Passive forms of Verbs}}$

Group I Verbs: **pre-ない form ＋れる**
買う ⇨ 買われる
書く ⇨ 書かれる
話す ⇨ 話される

Group II Verbs: **same as potential form** (☞P. 234)
食べる ⇨ 食べられる
起きる ⇨ 起きられる

Group III Verbs: 来る ⇨ 来られる
する ⇨ される

Note that in this list, there are some intransitive verbs such as 起きる and 来る which may make you question the necessity or use of the passive form of such verbs. Once you read the explanation of the "suffering passive," however, you will understand why these forms are necessary.

$\boxed{\text{Neutral passive}}$

This passive is similar to the English passive voice. Each neutral passive sentence has a corresponding active sentence, and the verb used in the passive here is a transitive verb.

The relationship between the active and passive sentences in this case is as follows: the object on which the speaker puts his/her focus in an active sentence can be made the topic of a passive construction. See the examples below. The difference between sentences (1) and (2) is what is considered the main concern of the speaker. In (1) he/she wants to talk about the "Japanese," while in (2) he/she sets up "song" as the topic.

　　　日本人は　　　この歌を　　　よく　　　歌う。　……(1)

　　　この歌は　　　日本人に　　　よく　　　歌われる。……(2)

In other words, by setting a word or phrase as the topic of a sentence, the speaker makes it clear that his major concern is that word or phrase. There are, therefore, some sentences such as the following which violate this rule;

　　　×この歌は私に歌われた。　⇨私はこの歌を歌った。
　　　×このレコードは私に買われた。⇨私はこのレコードを買った。

The passive sentences on the left are unacceptable. Although these sentences are grammatically possible, they are awkward and unacceptable in terms of normal usage. When the speaker places 歌 and レコード as the topics of the sentences, he/she is yielding his/her own presence in the topic; it is highly unnatural for the self and another object or person to share a position in the topic.

In the dialogue, the main focus is placed on the songs of Foster, and "who sings them" is self-apparent. In compliance with the rule in Japanese grammar that "things which can be understood from the context are omitted," either the topic or the object can often be omitted, and full sentences are very uncommon.

The agent or the person who does the action described by the verb is usually indicated by the particle に, but there are some sentences which take から and 〜によって.

　　　私は，先生 から／に 怒られた。
　　　友達 に／から 仕事を頼まれた。

In the case of から, the verbs have interpersonal factors in them, and there is a psychological movement from the person in the topic to the object of the passive sentence. (☞ P. 264, Note 3.)

Suffering Passive

This is different from other passive forms in the following ways:
1. it always means that the topic, usually a person or a personified noun, suffers as a result of what is described in the part of the sentence which follows it.
2. this passive form can take intransitive verbs.
3. it does not have corresponding active sentences which include the topics of the passive sentences.
4. the agent and the object remain in place. Pay attention to the arrows in the diagram, and compare them to those in the neutral passive examples on the previous page.

```
            雨が      降った。(It rained.)
  ↓          ↓        ↓
私は        雨に      降られた。(It rained and I didn't like it.)
```

```
            泥棒が    カーステレオを   盗んだ。     (A thief stole a car stereo.)
  ↓          ↓        ↓              ↓
田中さんは  泥棒に    カーステレオを   盗まれた。
```
(Tanaka san had his car stereo stolen, and he was unhappy.)

● 台風で家が壊される　　　2-3

This is a passive sentence, but the agent 台風 is indicated by で, not に. It is because 台風 is thought to be a cause, rather than an agent. In passive sentences, various natural phenomena take the particle で more often than に.

● 壊されたり，流されたりします　　　2-4

We must first learn how to construct this form before we use the pattern. For all practical purposes, simply add り to the plain perfect form.

The basic meaning of this pattern is that the first event happens sometimes, and at other times, the second event takes place. (See the first example.) The number of agents in this form can be either one or two. The pattern implies that many events of a similar nature take place, and that the two described (can be more than two) are just representatives of all the possibilities. In the third sentence, the topical person must have done other things, but he exemplified what "yesterday" was like for him by describing these activities. Because of the im-

Lesson 29

plication that what is given indicates a few examples of a large number of possibilities, 〜たり is sometimes used only once and is not repeated, as is shown in the fourth sentence below.

1. この辺は，四月には暖かかったり，寒かったりします。
   (This area, in April, is sometimes warm and sometimes cold.)
2. 台風で，家が壊されたり，橋が流されたりします。
   (Because of typhoons, houses are destroyed, bridges are washed away, and so on.)
3. 私は，昨日は本を読んだり，テレビを見たりしていました。
   (Yesterday I did such things as read books and watch TV.)
4. 台風で家が壊されたりしますか。
   (Do houses get destroyed [among other things] by typhoons?)

● 何て怒られたんですか　　3-3　☞P. 338　文法「S＋と言って喜んでいました」

In the above sentence て is the same as 〜と言って. The speaker here is soliciting the listener for the words by which he/she (the listener) was scolded by the teacher.

● 全部するようにって言われました　　3-5

S＋ように＋と言う／頼む, etc.

This pattern indirectly signifies the imperative form. The speaker conveys the gist of what was said. The と can be omitted or replaced in conversation by its colloquial equivalent て.

1. 友達のお母さんが，「今日は台風が来るから，早くお帰りなさい。」と言いました。
   (My friend's mother said, "Because a tyhpoon is coming, you should go home early today.")
2. 友達のお母さんが，今日は台風が来るから，早く帰るように(と)言いました。

● 盗まれちゃいました　　4-5

We studied in L.23 that ては in "ベッドがなくては" often becomes ちゃ and では becomes じゃ in informal spoken language. In the same way, 〜てしまう and 〜でしまう become 〜ちゃう and 〜じゃう respectively. This is a colloquial style, unsuitable for use in formal writing or speech.

書いてしまわない	⇨	書いちゃわない	飲んでしまわない	⇨	飲んじゃわない
書いてしまいます	⇨	書いちゃいます	飲んでしまいます	⇨	飲んじゃいます
書いてしまう	⇨	書いちゃう	飲んでしまう	⇨	飲んじゃう
書いてしまえば	⇨	書いちゃえば	飲んでしまえば	⇨	飲んじゃえば
書いてしまおう	⇨	書いちゃおう	飲んでしまおう	⇨	飲んじゃおう

● 買ったばかりのですよ　　4-5

This の replaces the noun カー・ステレオ. For information on 〜ばかり, see P. 218.

A：あそこにある，青い車は，新しく買った車ですよ。
B：あの，青いのですか。立派な車ですね。キャデラックですね。
   (A：The blue car over there is the one I newly bought.)
   (B：That blue one? What a gorgeous car! It's a Cadillac, isn't it?)

● ひどいことをするのがいるんですね　　4-6

This の is a substitute for the noun 人, but it portrays a slightly impersonal, distancing sense. It is, therefore, a little awkward to use this の to replace a noun in a situation in which a description of fond, personal feelings is required.

ことばの使い方（ことばのつかいかた）

● 家の母　　1-9

私の母 is acceptable, but is not used as often as 家の母. 家の〜 is used to refer to family members; it is also used with things belonging to a family in general, and not with the possessions of a particular person.

● この頃はあまり…　　1-3

Since it is common knowledge that あまり takes a negative predicate, the phrase following あまり is often omitted in the spoken language. The following are some words like あまり, whose negative predicates can be omitted in speech: 全然，少しも，ちっとも，ほとんど.

1．A：これ，何だかわかる？ (Do you know what this is?)
　　B：全然。　　　　　　　(Not at all.)
2．A：疲れた？　　　　　　(Tired?)
　　B：ちっとも。　　　　　(No way!)

● やはり　　1-9

This word is often used in conversation in its colloquial form やっぱり, or sometimes in its more degenerated form: やっぱし (using this last form is not recommended.) The basic meaning of やはり is: "as expected."

日本語はやはり難しいですね。(As expected, Japanese is difficult.)

● ハリケーンとか竜巻とか　　2-1

とか is a particle that is used to enumerate several things as examples. It is used to form a pattern "N とか N とか" or "S とか S とか." It has some similarities in meaning with "N や N" but や cannot be used with sentences.

1．日本には，台風とか地震(earthquake)とか(が)あります。
　　(In Japan, there are typhoons, earthquakes, and so on.)
2．図書館で調べるとか，先生に聞くとかしたらどうですか。
　　(How about doing something like looking it up at the library or asking Sensei?)

● とんでもない　　4-8

This phrase indicates that the speaker strongly negates what was said. It is often used when someone is given a compliment, or when a person is told something unexpected.

1．A：あなたはピアノが上手ですねえ。　(You play the piano well.)
　　B：とんでもない。　　　　　　　　　(Oh, no. Not at all.)
2．A：この日本語の教科書はずいぶんやさしいですね。
　　B：とんでもありませんよ。学生はみんな大変だと言っていますよ。
　　(A：This Japanese textbook is very easy, isn't it?)
　　(B：No, way! All the students are saying that it's very tough!)

Lesson 29

練習 (れんしゅう)

練習(れんしゅう) 1　　　　Passive forms

例　知る　⇨知られる　(to be known)
　　読む　⇨読まれる　(to be read)

1. 書く　2. 入る　3. 買う　4. 話す　5. 死ぬ　6. 降る　7. 教える　8. 寝る
9. 来る　10. する　11. 売る　12. 聞く　13. 言う　14. 怒る　15. 叱る　16. 行く

練習(れんしゅう) 2　　　　Neutral pass.

例　日本人は，よくこの歌を歌う
　　　⇨この歌は，日本人によく歌われます。
　　　(This song is sung often by the Japanese.)

1. 父は，私にこの歌を教えた
2. 日本人は，フォスターの歌を知っている
3. 若い人は西洋の音楽を聞く
4. お年寄りは，民謡を歌う
5. 友達が私に仕事を頼んだ
6. 警官が(私から)罰金を取った
7. 先生が学生を叱った
8. 先生が私を呼んだ

練習(れんしゅう) 3　　　　Suffering pass.

例　毎日，雨が降る　⇨私は，毎日，雨に降られました。(I was rained on every day.)

1. 泥棒がカー・ステレオを盗む
2. 友達が嫌なことを言う
3. 弟が買ったばかりの背広を着る
4. 誰かが車を壊した
5. 友達が夜遅く遊びに来る
6. 泥棒が家に入る
7. 誰かがノートに変なことを書く
8. 知らない人がいろいろなことを聞く

練習(れんしゅう) 4　　　　〜たりする

例　家が壊される　⇨家が壊されたりしました。
　　　(Among other things, houses get destroyed.)

1. 大きい声で友達と一緒に歌を歌う
2. 長い間，見たかった映画を見る
3. 自分の部屋の掃除をする
4. のんびり新聞や雑誌に目を通す
5. 植木や花に水をやる
6. 母の料理の手伝いをする
7. とてもおもしろい人に会う
8. 買い物をする

練習(れんしゅう)　5	～たり～たりする

例　バスケットをする，ソフト・ボールをする
　　　⇨私は，昨日，バスケットをしたりソフト・ボールをしたりしました。
　　　　(Yesterday, among other things, I played basketball and softball.)

1．歌を歌う，夜遅くまで友達と話をする
2．映画を見る，おいしい料理を食べる
3．自分の部屋の掃除をする，植木や花に水をやる
4．新聞や雑誌に目を通す，母の料理の手伝いをする
5．書かなければいけない手紙を出す，読まなければいけない本を読む
6．友達に会う，先生のお宅にお邪魔(じゃま)する

練習(れんしゅう)　6	S ように

例　この宿題を全部しなさい　⇨この宿題を全部するように言われました。
　　　　(I was told to do all this homework.)

1．授業にもっとちゃんと出なさい　　2．スピードに気を付けなさい
3．栄養を考えて食事をしなさい　　　4．十二時までには必(かなら)ず帰って来なさい
5．教室(きょうしつ)で寝(ね)ないで，家で寝なさい　　6．若い人の聞いている音楽を聞いてみなさい

練習(れんしゅう)　7	S て

例　怒る　⇨何て怒られたんですか。
　　　　(What did he/she say when he/she scolded you?)

1．言う　　2．叱る　　3．書く　　4．説明する　　5．教える　　6．怒る

練習(れんしゅう)　8	～の間で

例　若い人は西洋の音楽を聞く
　　　⇨若い人の間では，西洋の音楽がよく聞かれますか。
　　　　(Is Western music listened to very much among young people?)
　　お年寄りは民謡を歌わない
　　　⇨お年寄りの間では，民謡はよく歌われませんか。
　　　　(Aren't folk songs often sung among older people?)

1．若い人は西洋の小説を読む　　　　2．中年(ちゅうねん)の人は新聞しか読まない
3．中年の女の人は着物を着る　　　　4．お年寄りはいろいろな運動をする
5．若い人は西洋の食べ物を食べる　　6．お年寄りは日本の歌しか歌わない

Lesson 29

練習(れんしゅう) 9	S て＋passive

例　もっと栄養のある物を食べた方がいい，言う
　　⇨もっと栄養のある物を食べた方がいいって言われました。
　　　(I was told that I should eat more nutritious food.)

1．運動しないと病気になる，叱る
2．これとこれは同じじゃない，説明する
3．もっと早く持って来ないとだめだ，怒る
4．使わないと覚えないよ，言う
5．なるべく早く授業料を払ってほしい，手紙に書く
6．ひどい病気じゃないから心配はいらない，言う

練習(れんしゅう) 10	S のに。

例　来ない　⇨どうして来なかったんですか。来ると言ったのに。
　　　(Why didn't you come? You said you'd come ...)

1．しない　　　　　　　2．行かない　　　　　　3．できない
4．旅行に行かない　　　5．手紙を書いてくれない　6．教えてあげない
7．推薦状を書いてもらわない　8．掃除をしてしまわない

練習(れんしゅう) 11	～のことですか，～って

例　どんな，おもしろい経験
　　⇨どんなことですか，おもしろい経験って。
　　　(What sort of thing is it, ... this interesting experience [of yours]?)
　　誰，フォスター
　　⇨誰のことですか，フォスターって。
　　　(Who is it, ... this [person called] Foster?)

1．どこ，楽しい所　　2．いつ，この前　3．何，あれ　　4．何時，この時間
5．どの田中さん，田中さん　6．どんな，罰金　7．どこ，あそこ

練習(れんしゅう) 12	～たばかりだ

例　このステレオは，昨日買いました。
　　⇨このステレオは，昨日買ったばかりです。(I just bought this stereo yesterday.)

1．この漢字は今日習いました。　　　　2．昨日，旅行から帰って来ました。
3．さっき先生に怒られました。　　　　4．今，佐藤さんと電話で話しました。
5．昨日，新しい車を盗まれました。　　6．一時間前に，雨が止みました。

練習（れんしゅう） 13　　　　～ばかりの N

例　買った，ステレオ，盗む　⇨買ったばかりのステレオを盗まれてしまいました。
　　　　　　　　　　　　　　　([Unfortunately,] the stereo I just bought was stolen.)

1．作った，料理，食べる　　　　　　2．買った，レコード，持って行く
3．建てた，家，壊す　　　　　　　　4．もらった，辞書，なくす
5．書いた，手紙，読む　　　　　　　6．作ってあげた，服，汚す

練習（れんしゅう） 14　　　　～とか

例　誰が来たんですか。（中村さん，加藤さん）
　　⇨中村さんとか加藤さんとかが来たんですよ。
　　　　(Nakamura san, Kato san, and others came.)
　　何をしたんですか。（買い物に行く，映画を見る）
　　⇨買い物に行くとか，映画を見るとかしたんですよ。
　　　　(We went shopping, watched a movie, and so on.)

1．何を買ったんですか。　　　　　　（バナナ，リンゴ）
2．誰に教えてもらったんですか。　　（友達，両親に）
3．どこから来たんですか。　　　　　（中国，韓国から）
4．どうするんですか。　　　　　　　（先生に聞く，友達に教えてもらう）
5．どうやって探すんですか。　　　　（友達に電話する，手紙を書く）
6．どこで調べるんですか。　　　　　（図書館で調べる，旅行会社へ行く）

練習（れんしゅう） 15　　　　Passive forms in composite expressions

例　ステレオを盗まれた（しまった）
　　⇨ステレオを盗まれてしまいました。(I had my stereo stolen.)

1．この音楽はよく聞かれる（いる）
2．今日は雨に降られる（かもしれない）
3．台風で家が流される（たりする）
4．父に怒られる（ことがあった）
5．妹に私の好きな服を着ていかれる（しまった）
6．あの人は，ガールフレンドに「もう会いたくない。」と言われた（そうです）

三十課

内容表

文法	敬語(けいご) 　　Formality of Words 　　Directness vs. Indirectness 　　Fluency and Politeness 　　Various Personal Pronouns 　　Humble Expressions 　　　ジョンソンと申します　失礼いたします 　　　お電話いたします　　　Sとありがたい 　　　出掛けております　　　拝見する，承知する 　　Honorific expressions 　　　おいでです 　　　　　　　　　　　Use of passive forms 　　　お帰りになる　　　　御指摘くださる 　　Use of です，ます-forms in the middle of a sentence 　　　　　　　　　　　ありまして／おいででしたら 　　Mixing Honorific Expressions with　あら，お待ちになってね。 　　　Plain Form Endings 　　〜ことは〜んですが　　　長いことは長いんですが	家(うち，いえ)vs. お宅 〜ですか vs. 〜でしょうか あのう 私(わたくし，わたし)，僕…
機能	Making a Telephone Call　　　　8-2 Answering a Telephone Call　　8-1 Requesting to Speak to Someone　8-3 Responding to Request to Speak 　with Someone　　　　　　　8-4 Stating Reason for Call　　　　8-10 Ending a Telephone Conversation　8-9 Putting a Caller on Hold　　　　8-6 Talking to a Caller after Hold　　8-7 Inquiring About a Message　　　8-12 Introducing Oneself　　　　　　6-7 Stating Hypothesis　　　　　　　1-4	もしもし，高橋先生のお宅でしょうか。 はい，高橋です。 先生がおいででしたら，恐れ入りますが。 実は，主人，三日程前から…。 お願いしたいことがありまして。 失礼いたします／ごめんください よろしくね／お休みなさい ちょっとお待ちになってね。 カーターさん，お待たせして，どうも 何かお伝えすることがございましたら 私，学生のジョンソンと申しますが もし，先生がおいででしたら

Lesson 30

会話 (かいわ)

1

A：もしもし、高橋先生のお宅でしょうか。[はい、高橋です。]
　あのう、私、学生のジョンソンと申しますが、先生にお願いしたいことがありまして。もし、先生がおいででしたら、恐れ入りますが…。

B：さようですか。実は、主人、三日程前から、学会で関西の方に出掛けておりまして明晩、帰って来る予定なんですが。何かお伝えすることが、ございましたら。

A：ありがとうございます。少々、複雑な問題ですので、先生がお帰りになってから、またお電話いたします。

B：はい。では、恐れ入りますが、そうなさってください。では、主人に、ジョンソンさんからお電話があったことだけ、お伝えしておきますので。

A：それでは、失礼いたします。[ごめんください。]

2

A：もしもし、池田さんのお宅ですか。

B：はい。池田でございます。あら、カーターさん。ちょっと、お待ちになってね。今、正子を呼びますので。[恐れ入ります。]

C：ああ、カーターさん。お待たせして、どうも。

A：ううん、大したことないよ。

C：今日は、何か特別な御用事でも。

A：特別というわけじゃないんだけど、明日か明後日、できたら僕の書いた手紙の日本語を直してもらえない？

C：ええ、いいわよ。明日の歴史の授業の後は、どう。

A：時間が空いているから、ちょうどいいな。[じゃ、その時に。]
　じゃ、よろしくね。[はい。]じゃ、また、明日。お休み。[お休みなさい。]

388

1

A：Hello, is this Prof. Takahashi's residence? [Yes, this is the Takahashi residence.] My name is Johnson, and I am his student. There is something I would like to ask of the professor. I'm sorry to trouble you, but if the professor is at home, may I ...

B：I see. My husband has been away for about three days now at a conference in Kansai, and he is expected back tomorrow evening. May I take a message?

A：Thank you. I have a rather complicated problem, so I'll call again when the professor has returned.

B：Fine. I'd appreciate it if you'd do so. Then, I'll tell my husband only that Johnson san called.

A：Well then, thank you very much. [Good-bye.]

2

A：Hello, is this the Ikeda residence?

B：Yes, this is Ikeda. Oh, you're Carter san. Wait just a minute, OK? I'll call Masako right away. [Please.]

C：Carter san, sorry to keep you waiting.

A：No, it's no big deal.

C：Has something special come up today?

A：It's not exactly special, but would it be possible for you to correct my Japanese in a letter I wrote, either tomorrow or the day after tomorrow?

C：Why certainly. How about tomorrow after history class?

A：I have time then, so that would be perfect. [Then, I'll meet you then.] Well, I appreciate it. [Sure!] I'll see you tomorrow. Good night. [Good night.]

Lesson 30

3

A：先生，恐れ入りますが，これ，御覧になってくださいませんか。

B：拝見します。ずいぶん長いのを書かれたんですね。

A：ええ，長いことは長いんですが，いろいろ問題があると思いますので，御指摘くださると，ありがたいのですが。

B：はい，承知しました。明日お返しすればよろしいですか。

A：はい。明日の今頃はいかがでしょうか。[結構です。]では，明日，参りますので。

単語表（たんごひょう）

There are three symbols used in the following lists. To review what they mean, reread P. 188.

- ⬆ Honorific　（尊敬—そんけい）
- ⬇ Humble　（謙譲—けんじょう）
- P Polite/formal（丁寧—ていねい）

1

おいでだ	いらっしゃる
恐(おそ)れ入(い)りますが	Pすみませんが
さようですか	Pそうですか
～程(ほど)	Pくらい
学会(がっかい)	(academic) conference
関西(かんさい)	Kansai area ☞ことばの使い方
おります	⬇います
明晩(みょうばん)	P明日の晩
予定(よてい)	schedule, plan
ございます	Pある
少々(しょうしょう)	P少し，ちょっと
複雑(ふくざつ)だ	complicated
いたす	⬇する

2

～でございます	Pです
お待(ま)ちになる	⬆待つ ☞文法
正子(まさこ)	女の人の名前
大(たい)したことはない	It's nothing to speak of.
特別(とくべつ)だ	special
明後日(あさって)	the day after tomorrow
直(なお)す	correct
歴史(れきし)	history

3

A：Sensei, I'm sorry to trouble you, but will you please take a look at this?

B：Let's see. You've written something quite long, haven't you?

A：Yes, it is long, but since I think there might be many problems, I'd really appreciate it if you'd point them out to me.

B：Yes, I understand. Would it be alright to return it to you tomorrow?

A：Yes. How about around this time tomorrow? [That's fine.] Then, I'll come again tomorrow.

空(あ)く	be unoccupied, vacant	指摘(してき)する	point out
ちょうどいい	just right	承知(しょうち)する よろしい	Pわかる Pいい
御覧(ごらん)になる	H見る	いかが	Pどう
拝見(はいけん)する	L見る	参(まい)ります	L来る, 行く

関連語句 (かんれんごく)

なさる	Hする	関東(かんとう)	Kanto area
一昨日(おととい)	the day before yesterday	写真(しゃしん)	photograph

Lesson 30

文法 (ぶんぽう)

```
敬　語
```

In this lesson, we are going to study how to use 敬語(けいご). You are advised to reread P. 188.

Keigo is one of the ways in which a speaker expresses respect toward a person (either the hearer or the third person) in the topic. Verbal expressions alone cannot convey this feeling of respect. The following factors must be incorporated into *keigo* speech activities: such things as your manner of speech, or body language (whether you stand or sit, whether you mumble or articulate when you talk with a person); the way in which you address someone (first name, surname, or title). Speaking very politely while chewing gum will certainly reduce the effects of *keigo*. Arriving late for an appointment with someone would probably cast doubt on your sincerity, no matter what polite expressions you may use later. These non-linguistic factors cannot be covered in this section.

In spite of understandable differences between American and Japanese societies, most values can be seen as similar in both cultures and are based on common sense.

An important difference, however, is that in Japanese society, it is unlikely that a vertical relationship between people will ever change. Once a person is your *Sensei*, he/she is always your *sensei*. The president of a company is treated no differently after his retirement. Even a relationship between peers would probably take a relatively longer time to develop into a close friendship in Japan than in English-speaking cultures.

There are many people in Japan who find it very difficult to manipulate *keigo* properly, but *keigo* will undoubtedly stay. However it might be more or less simplified in the future, if the society underwent drastic change as it did after the second World War.

● 高橋先生のお宅　　1-1

Compared to 家(うち，いえ), お宅 is an honorific word.

● 先生のお宅でしょうか　　1-1

While ですか represents a straight question, でしょうか in this case, injects a sense of indirectness. For this reason, its use is more appropriate here. Many people also use「高橋先生のお宅でいらっしゃいますか」in spite of criticism from various grammar-conscious people.

● はい，高橋です　　1-1

In the following way, the words for "yes" can be arranged according to the degree of politeness from high to low.

　　はい＞ええ＞うん

Similarly the words for "no" would be:

　　いいえ＞いや＞ううん

● あのう　　1-2

This expression indicates that the speaker is still thinking about how to express his thoughts. あのう can also be regarded as a device to show respect to a hearer. In Japanese, depending on the situation, speaking without fluency (interrupted speech) can be considered respectful.

● 私(わたくし)　　1-2

So far, the words we have seen for "I" are 私 and 僕. There are many other words which mean "I" in Japanese. The representative words for "I" used today are listed here.

Note that the sentences we have studied do not use the informal words and, therefore, they are not recommended for use at this level.

	Most formal	Formal	Less formal	Informal
男	私(わたくし)	私(わたし)	僕	俺
女			(あたし)	

● 学生のジョンソン　　1-2　☞P. 317　文法「本屋の大田さん」

● 私，学生のジョンソンと申します　　1-2

It is absolutely necessary in Japanese to say who is calling at the start of a telephone conversation. This is true even among family members.

The following three items —— in the shown order —— are criteria which must be established at the beginning of a telephone conversation unless the call is between two close friends or family members whose identities are absolutely unmistakable.

　　1. Make sure you got the correct household.
　　2. Tell who you are.
　　3. Tell the other party the person to whom you wish to talk when it is necessary.

● お願いしたい　　1-2　☞P. 172「お返しします」

This pattern, お＋stem＋する, signifies action done by the speaker or his in-group for the hearer or the person in the topic. Since the pattern means "to do something for someone" such intransitive verbs as 死ぬ, 歩く, 走る, 困る, 遅れる which do not involve another party cannot be used. It cannot be used with such transitive verbs as 忘れる, 覚える, 知る, 着る, 脱ぐ probably because these actions usually cannot be done for the sake of someone else.

お is replaced by 御 when the verb is a Chinese word like 指摘(point out).

いたす is used to increase the sense of humility in this pattern.

　　1．そのお荷物，お持ちしましょうか。(Shall I hold the luggage?)
　　2．明日，私の方からまたお電話いたします。(I will call you again tomorrow.)

● ありまして　　1-2

In addition to ありまして, there are similar forms in which 〜です, 〜ます are used instead of the plain forms. In formal speech and in formal letters, it is quite common to adopt the 〜です, 〜ます forms in non-final clauses.

　　　おいででしたら(おいでだったら)　　1-3
　　　お伝えしておきますので(しておくので)　　1-9

Lesson 30

● おいででしたら　　　1-3

This expression, おいでだ, is the same as いらっしゃる, the honorific form of 行く, 来る and いる. This pattern can be written as:

| お＋stem＋だ |

The stem here, いで, and its dictionary form, いづ, are classical forms and are not used in contemporary Japanese outside of this pattern.

For a discussion of the general use of this expression, see P.395.

● 出掛けております　　　1-4

Substituting いる with おる in the pattern て＋いる increases the humble nuance in the phrase. Note that this is a humble expression that refers to the action of the speaker or his in-group.

1．A：失礼ですが，何を研究していらっしゃるんですか。
　　B：私はアメリカの歴史を勉強しております。
　　　　（A：May I ask in what you are majoring?）
　　　　（B：I am studying American history.）
2．A：お父さん，今お宅においでですか。
　　B：もうすぐ出掛けると言っておりましたが，今はまだおります。
　　　　（A：Is your father at home now?）
　　　　（B：He said he would be going out soon, but he is still at home.）

The dictionary form おる rarely appears in conversation. In the second example above, you can theoretically say おると思います. In this case, however, いると思います sounds natural.

Note that おります takes the place of います in a pattern like 出掛けています as seen in the second dialogue above.

● お伝えすることが，ございましたら　　　1-5

ございます is the polite form of あります. This is different from〜でございます in the second dialogue「池田でございます」, which is the polite form of です. The dictionary form ござる, as well as でござる, are not used in modern Japanese.

● 先生がお帰りになる　　　1-6

| お＋stem＋になる |

This pattern is used to show the speaker's respect toward the person in the topic, who can be (but is not necessarily) a hearer. All verbs except those that have their own honorific forms such as 食べる（召し上がる），もらう（いただく），行く／来る／いる（いらっしゃる）can be used with this pattern.

To use this pattern effectively, let us summarize the verbs that have special honorific and humble equivalents.

Neutral Verb	Honorific	Humble
行く，来る	いらっしゃる	参る
いる	おいでだ	おる
見る	御覧になる	拝見する
言う	おっしゃる	申す
食べる，飲む	召し上がる	☆いただく
もらう		☆いただく
する	なさる	☆いたす
会う		☆お目にかかる，お会いする
訪ねる(visit)		☆お邪魔する
知っている	御存じだ	存じている
寝る	お休みになる	

In this lesson, the humble verbs without the symbol ☆ are for recognition only. At this point, even those verbs marked with ☆ should be used only in contexts similar to the ones in which they have already appeared. For all practical purposes, use the neutral verbs that are shown in the left column.

お＋stem＋だ

If になる is replaced by だ, we get the pattern お＋stem＋だ, as in おいででしたら. There is a slight difference in the degree of respect expressed by the two: になる is more polite than だ.

This pattern is used to relate habitual action, action in progress, and the perfect tense without changing its form.

1．毎日，何をお読みですか。（お読みになっていますか。）
2．今，この本，お読みですか。（お読みになっていますか。）
3．この本，もうお読みですか。（お読みになりましたか。）

● それでは　　1-10

The contracted form is usually avoided in formal speeches. In other words, to make what you say sound more formal, it is advisable to avoid using contracted forms.

● 失礼いたします　　1-10

This is more humble than 失礼します because of the addition of いたす. This sort of extremely humble and, therefore, highly formal form can often be heard in telephone conversations. In ordinary conversation, 失礼します is sufficiently polite.

● ごめんください　　1-10

Literally ごめん(御免) means "permission." This is a common greeting at the entrance to a person's house, alerting him/her that one has come. Another situation in which this greeting can be used is as a parting phrase, meaning "Allow me to leave." The greeting in the dialogue is its variation, and is heard often in telephone conversation.

Lesson 30

● あら、カーターさん。ちょっと、お待ちになってね　　2-2

The speaker shifted her manner of speech from the formal to the informal mode as soon as she recognized the voice on the phone. The use of あら, ちょっと and ね together with the omission of ください indicate immediately that the speaker adopted the mode of speech appropriate for someone who is close to her. Although the speaker, by speaking informally, indicates that she has close feelings for the hearer, she retains the use of the honorific expression お待ちになって. By mixing formal and informal speech, the speaker shows that she has feelings of both intimacy and respect for the hearer.

Expressions like お待ちになって can be used by women as well as by men. Adding ね at the end, however, makes the phrase sound feminine.

Note that Carter san does not change his mode of speech. He probably feels that it is most appropriate at this stage to use formal rather than informal expressions.

● 特別というわけじゃない　　2-7　☞ P.251 文法「そういうわけじゃないわ」

● 直してもらえない　　2-8

The polite form of this sentence is「直してもらえませんか」. The final particle か indicating a question can be substituted with either a rising intonation, かい (men), or かしら (mostly women) in conversations among friends. Leaving the particle か in speech among intimates, however, would sound arrogant or rough. When か, as in 行きましょうか, does not have as strong a sense of a question, it can remain intact in informal speech.

● 長いのを書かれた　　3-2

This is another way of showing respect for people. The form is exactly the same as that of passive. Pay special attention to the particles to tell it from the passive.

　　先生が来られた。　（先生がおいでになった。）
　　先生に来られた。　（Passive）

Women do not use this form as often as men because it indicates a lighter degree of respect than other patterns; feminine speech tends to be highly respectful and polite.

● 長いことは長いんです　　3-3

The pattern 〜ことは〜です indicates that the speaker has focused on whether or not something is 〜 and has concluded that it is 〜. It is usually followed by a statement that is opposite to 〜 in meaning.

1. A：この自動車、新しいですね。
   B：ええ、新しいことは新しいんですが、あまり調子がよくないんですよ。
   (It is new but it doesn't run smoothly.)
2. A：この問題、調べてくれましたか。
   B：調べたことは調べたんですが、どうもよくわからないんですよ。
   (I did check on it but I still don't quite understand.)

● 御指摘くださると　　3-3

御＋漢語＋ください is more formal than 〜てください. With Japanese verbs, the pattern is お＋stem＋ください.

1. その本は図書館にありますので、御安心ください。
   (Since we have that book in the library, please relax.)
2. サインをする前に全部お読みください。(Before you sign, please read everything.)

● S とありがたい　　3-4

This is a polite way of asking or telling a person to do something. The pattern 〜てほしい is not polite enough to use with your superiors. You can use this pattern with your superiors.

The sentence usually implies that you ask for and receive a favor from the hearer or a third person.

先生，恐れ入りますが，推薦状を書いていただけるとありがたいんですが。
(Sensei, I would appreciate it very much if you would kindly write a letter of recommendation for me.)

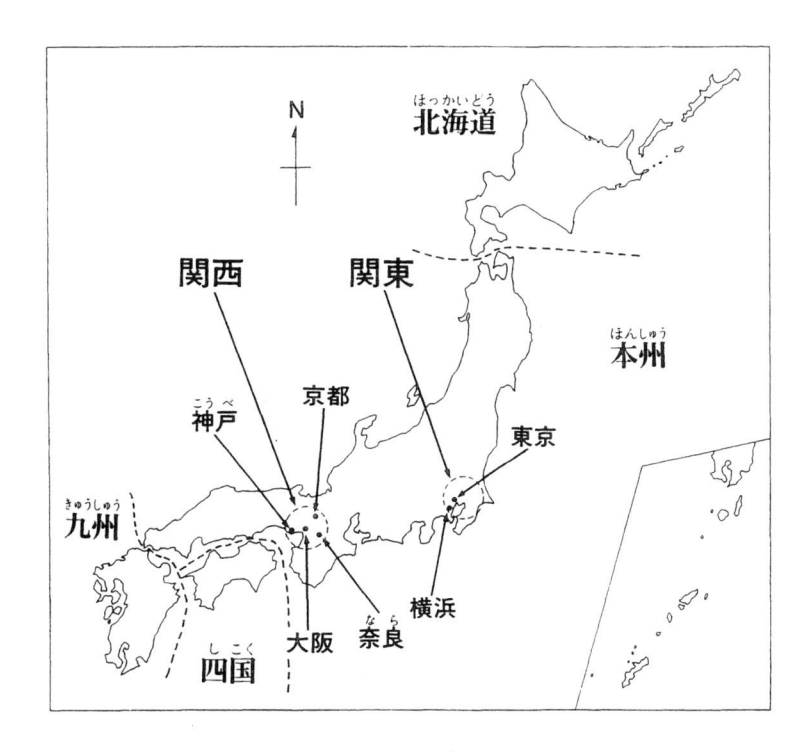

ことばの使い方 (ことばのつかいかた)

In this lesson, there are many expressions with different degrees of politeness or formality. Since the levels of politeness in *keigo* are difficult to distinguish, let us take a close look at the phrases in the present lesson with this point in mind. The symbol ＞ marks the relative degrees of politeness among the words printed horizontally across the page. Please note that a vertical comparison is not necessarily very accurate.

Lesson 30

Very polite / formal	Slightly polite / formal	Non-polite / formal
(～お宅)でしょうか >	(お宅)ですか >	お宅
～と申します >	～といいます > ～です >	～
おいでになる / いらっしゃる > おいでだ >	います >	いる
恐れ入りますが >	すみませんが > 悪いんですが >	悪いけど
さようでございますか > さようですか >	そうですか >	そう
	(三日)ほど >	(三日)ぐらい
	でかけております >	でかけています > でかけている
	明晩 >	明日の晩
	少々 >	ちょっと
	お電話致します >	(お)電話します > 電話する
	なさってください >	してください > して
お伝え致します > お伝えします >		伝えます
	致す / なさる >	する
ごめんください > 失礼します >		じゃ
恐れ入ります > どうもすみません >		どうも
～てくださいませんか > いただけませんか >		
Neg. question >	Affirm. question	
お休みなさいませ >	お休みなさい >	お休み
お＋stem＋になる >	お＋stem＋だ > ～られる	
承知しました >	わかりました >	わかった
よろしい / 結構だ >	いい	
いかが >	どう	

397

1-3
...valent of すみませんが, which is used in conjunction with expressions ...o something.

1-4
...xpression is the classical way of saying そう, which is used in さような... ...arded as a word which is more polite or fomal than そう.

- 三日程　1-4

程 is the same, in meaning, as くらい/ぐらい. There is, however, a stylistic difference between the two: 程 is the more formal and polite of the two.

- 関西（かんさい）　1-4

関西 refers to the area which includes 大阪（おおさか）, 京都（きょうと）, 奈良（なら）, 神戸（こうべ） while the area around 東京 is called 関東（かんとう）. There are considerable differences between the two regions in various aspects of culture, including dialects. The language we are learning, however, is perfectly understandable in both regions.

- 明晩　1-5

In Japanese, when there are two expressions that mean the same thing, the one with the Chinese reading (音読み) is considered more formal than the original Japanese word. 明日の晩, for example, is not as formal as 明晩（みょうばん）. This can also be applied to the pair ちょっと and 少々.

- 大したことはない　2-5

This is a noun-modifier that is usually used in the negative sense to mean "It is nothing to speak of," or "It's no big deal."

　　A：けがをしたんですって。
　　B：ええ。でも，大したことはありませんから，御心配なく。
　　　（A：Is it true that you got injured?）
　　　（B：Yes, but don't worry since it wasn't serious.）

- 明後日（あさって）　2-7

The day after tomorrow and the day before yesterday are:
　一昨日（おととい）　→昨日　→今日→明日　→明後日（あさって）

In order to indicate formality, they can be read in the Chinese readings (音読み). They are:
　いっさくじつ→さくじつ→本日（ほんじつ）→みょうにち→みょうごにち

Note that 本日 is used for "today."

- 拝見する　3-2

This is a humble way of saying "I will take a look at your concerns" (or those of your in-group). If what is under discussion is not related to the hearer (or his/her in-group), this word cannot be used.

　　お手紙，拝見しました。(I saw your letter.)

- 承知する　3-5

This is a humble expression meaning "to know, to accept, to be aware of." This phrase is often heard at stores, restaurants, hotels, and so forth.

- いかが　3-6

This is a formal version of どう; the meaning is the same.

Lesson 30

練習(れんしゅう)

練習(れんしゅう)　1	Polite forms in non-final clause

例　お願いしたいことがあって，お電話しました。
　　⇨お願いしたいことが<u>ありまして</u>，お電話しました。
　　　　(I am calling you because I have a favor to ask of you.)
　　私にできることがあったら，おっしゃってください。
　　⇨私にできることが<u>ありましたら</u>，おっしゃってください。
　　　　(Please let me know if there is something I can do for you.)

1．わかったら，すぐお知らせします。
2．雨が降っても，必ずお邪魔します。
3．旅行に行っていて，おりません。
4．今呼ぶので，お待ちください。
5．東京へ行ってから，すぐお電話します。
6．明日休みなので，遊びにいらっしゃいませんか。

練習(れんしゅう)　2	お＋stem＋になる

例　何を書くのか
　　⇨先生，何をお書きになるんですか。(What are you going to write, Sensei?)

（1〜3は「おいでになる」を使いなさい。）
　1．どこへ行くのか　　　　2．何時に大学へ来るのか　　　3．どこにいるのか
　4．何時に帰ったのか　　　5．いつ学会で話すか　　　　　6．その映画，いつ見たか
　7．たばこをやめたのか　　8．何を飲むか　　　　　　　　9．出掛けるか
　10．この人の電話番号，わかるか　　　11．どんなことを指摘したのか

練習(れんしゅう)　3	お＋stem＋になる

例　書いた本はいつ買えるか
　　⇨先生がお書きになった本は，いつ買えますか。
　　　　(When can we buy the book you wrote, Sensei?)

（1〜3は「おいでになる」を使いなさい。）
　1．行く学会は東京か　　　　　2．大学へ来たのは何時か　　　3．いる部屋はどこか
　4．帰った時間は何時頃だったか　　　　　5．今日見る映画は何か
　6．昼御飯を食べた所はよかったか　　　　7．たばこをやめたのは何才の時か
　8．飲んだのは何か　　　　　　　　　　　9．指摘したのはどんなことか

400

練習（れんしゅう） 4	Special honorific verbs

例　学会に行ったか
　　　⇨先生，学会にいらっしゃいましたか。
　　　　(Did you go to the conference, Sensei?)

1．何と言ったか　　　　　　　　　　2．たくさん本を持ってきた
3．関西にずっと住んでいるか　　　　4．今日の新聞を見たか
5．昼御飯はどこで食べるか　　　　　6．休みの日に何をするか
7．学生の時どんなアルバイトをしたか　8．ビールは飲むか

練習（れんしゅう） 5	Special honorific verbs

例　旅行に行ったのはいつか
　　　⇨先生が旅行にいらっしゃったのは，いつでしたか。
　　　　(When did you take a trip, Sensei?)

1．今，言ったことはどういう意味か　　2．来週の授業では何をする予定か
3．今，読んでいる本は何という本か　　4．見ておもしろかった映画は何か
5．毎日食べるのは日本料理か　　　　　6．明日講演をする所はどこか

練習（れんしゅう） 6	Humble verbs

例　先生の家に行った
　　　⇨昨日，先生の家にお邪魔しました。
　　　　(Yesterday, we visited Sensei's house.)

1．先生の新しい本を見た　　　　　　2．先生の奥さんに会った
3．先生の奥さんの料理を食べた　　　4．先生の若い時の写真(photo)を見た
5．また，先生の家に行く　　　　　　6．先生のお母さんに会う

練習（れんしゅう） 7	お＋stem＋する

例　そのかばんを持つ
　　　⇨先生，そのかばんをお持ちしましょうか。
　　　　(Shall I carry that bag, Sensei?)

1．ここで待つ　　2．その本を探す　　　　　　3．そのことを他の学生に伝える
4．高橋さんを呼ぶ　5．その本を図書館に返してくる　6．その仕事を手伝う

Lesson 30

練習(れんしゅう)　8　　　　　Sentence final か in casual conversation

例　この手紙，直してもらえませんか。
　　　⇨この手紙直してもらえない。(Won't you correct this letter?)
　　一緒に行きましょうか。
　　　⇨一緒に行こうか。(Shall we go together?)

1．今，時間がありますか。　　　　2．何を最初にしましょうか。
3．今晩(こんばん)講演を聞きに行きませんか。　4．あそこに立っている人は誰ですか。
5．外は寒いですか。　　　　　　　6．結婚式(けっこんしき)には何を着て行きましょうか。

練習(れんしゅう)　9　　　　　Honorific forms of verbs

例　書く　⇨書かれる

1．読む　2．呼ぶ　3．来る　4．行く　5．する　6．起きる　7．寝る　8．買う

練習(れんしゅう)　10　　　　　Honorific forms of verbs

例　今日の新聞を読む　⇨先生，今日の新聞を読まれましたか。
　　　　　　　　　　　　(Did you read today's paper, Sensei?)

1．もう，論文を書く　　　2．新しい車を買う　　　　3．今日の講演に行く
4．何日に帰って来る　　　5．いつ，その本を出版(しゅっぱん)する　6．宿題を直す

練習(れんしゅう)　11　　　　　～ことは～だ

例　あの先生の授業はおもしろいですか。(大変だ)
　　　⇨ええ，おもしろいことはおもしろいんですが，大変ですよ。
　　　(It certainly is interesting, but it's difficult.)

1．シカゴの冬は厳しいそうですね。　　　　（そんなに大変じゃない）
2．東京の夏は暑いですか。　　　　　　　　（人が死ぬことはない）
3．あのレストランは料理がおいしいですか。（値段(ねだん)が高(たか)い）
4．この問題，終わりましたか。　　　　　　（正しいかどうかわからない）
5．着物，一人(ひとり)で着られますか。　　　（上手(じょうず)に着られない）
6．このケーキはおいしいですねえ。　　　　（作るのに時間がかかる）

練習(れんしゅう)　12	御＋漢語＋ください，お＋stem＋ください

例　指摘してください。⇨御指摘ください。(Please point it out.)
　　休んでください。　⇨お休みください。(Please take a rest.)

1．これを全部読んでください。
2．ここにありますから，安心してください。
3．試験を始めてください。
4．行きますから，準備してください。
5．御両親に相談してください。
6．交番で聞いてください。

練習(れんしゅう)　13	～てくださるとありがたい

例　私の部屋に来て欲しい。
　　⇨私の部屋に来てくださるとありがたいのですが。
　　(I would appreciate it if you would come to my room.)

1．推薦状を書いて欲しい。
2．日本語のテープを貸して欲しい。
3．私の書いた手紙を直して欲しい。
4．この部屋でたばこをすわないで欲しい。
5．時間が空いている時に，仕事を手伝って欲しい。
6．少し，ここにいて欲しい。

三十一課

内容表

文法	Causative		
	To make s.b./s.t do		子供を学校に行かせる。
			きれいな花を咲かせる。
	To allow s.b. to do		子供に行かせる。
	Causative for Permission		読ませてください (Let me do〜)。
	Causative Passive		帰国させられます。
	Long form vs. Short form		行かせる vs. 行かす
	S ため(に)		忘れさせないため(に)
	だって／でも		結婚式だって行かせません。
	〜だけじゃなくて		熱が高いだけじゃなくて
	〜通り		おっしゃる通りにします。
機能	Requesting Clarification	7-9	〜というのは、どういう意味ですか。
	Expressing an Opinion	2-33	多くは…みたいですよ。
	Reason for Action/Non-Action	2-41	なんで
	Justifying	2-52	忘れさせないためでしょう。
			でも…帰国させられますからね。
	Expressing Regret	3-34	いいチャンスなのに、もったいない。
	Requesting Permission	2-22	行かせてください。
			御馳走させてください。
	Expressing Impossibility	2-13	行かせるわけにはいきません。
	Commenting on a Topic	7-11	君、いいですか。
	Making Threat(s)	5-9	死にたくなかったら
	Giving Directions/Commands	5-8	今夜の試合は諦めなさい
	Apologizing	4-1	どうもお待たせしてしまいました。
	Expressing Relief	3-35	やっと終わってほっとしている。
	Expressing Modesty	4-6	大したものじゃありませんが
			お祝いしていただくものじゃない。
	Accepting Invitations	5-7	それじゃ遠慮なく御馳走になります。

Lesson 31

会話 (かいわ)

1

A：アメリカに住んでいる日本人のサラリーマンは，子供を普通の学校に行かせますか。

B：普通の学校というのは，どういう意味ですか。アメリカの学校という意味ですか。［そういう意味です。］多くは，日本人学校に子供を行かせているみたいですよ。

A：なんで，普通の学校で勉強させないんでしょうね。

B：子供に日本語を忘れさせないためでしょう。

A：でも，英語を覚えさせるのにはいいチャンスなのに，もったいないですね。

B：ええ。でも，ほとんどのサラリーマンは二，三年で日本へ帰国させられますからね。

2

A：先生，私，今夜，バスケットボールの試合があるんですが，出られるでしょうか。

B：とんでもない。君の結婚式だって，出席させるわけにはいきませんよ。

A：とっても大事な試合なんで，是非行かせてください，先生。お願いします。

B：君，いいですか。君は，今，熱が高いだけじゃなくて，肺炎になりそうなんですよ。

A：肺炎というのは，先生，英語で何と言うんですか。

B：Pneumoniaです。死にたくなかったら，今夜の試合は諦めなさい。

A：そんなにひどいんですか。仕方がないですね。先生のおっしゃる通りにします。

3

A：山岡さん，どうも，お待たせしました。［いいえ。］大分お待ちになりましたか。

B：いいえ，私も三分程前に来たばかりなんです。

A：それなら，いいんですが。ところで，論文ができあがったそうですね。

B：ええ，おかげさまで。やっと終わって，ほっとしているところなんですよ。

A：大変だったでしょう。［いいえ。］今度，是非一度読ませてくださいね。

1

A : I wonder if the Japanese businessmen living in the States make their children go to an ordinary school?

B : What do you mean by an "ordinary school?" Do you mean an American school? [That's what I mean.] Most of them seem to be sending them to Japanese schools.

A : I don't see why they don't send them to an ordinary school, do you?

B : I suppose they want their children not to forget the Japanese language.

A : It's really a shame, isn't it? Isn't it a good chance to make children study English?

B : That's right. But most of them are made to go back to Japan in a couple of years.

2

A : Doctor, I have a basketball game tonight but can I play?

B : You are kidding! I wouldn't even let you attend your wedding.

A : It's a very, very important game. So please let me go.

B : Listen. You not only have a high fever but you're likely to have *haien*.

A : What is *haien* in English?

B : It's pneumonia. Unless you want to kill yourself, give up tonight's game.

A : Is my condition that bad? I guess I have no choice but to do as you say.

3

A : Yamaoka san, sorry to have kept you waiting. [No, not at all.] Have you been waiting long?

B : I just came here about three minutes ago.

A : In that case, I am relieved. By the way, I heard you completed your thesis.

B : Yes. Thank you. I feel relieved to have finally finished it.

A : It must have been a lot of work. [Not really.] Please let me read it by all means.

Lesson 31

B：ええ，大したものじゃありませんが，一度読んでいただけたら，と思っていました。

·······················(中略)······················

A：今日は私に御馳走させてくださいね，論文ができあがったお祝いに。

B：お祝いしていただくほどのものじゃないんですよ。

A：そんなこと言わないで。私にお祝いさせてください。ずいぶん頑張ったんですから。

B：そうですか。それじゃ遠慮なく御馳走になります。

A：じゃ，すぐ出掛けましょうか。私，いい所，考えておきましたから。[はい。]

単語表 (たんごひょう)

1

普通(ふつう)のN	ordinary, normal
行かせる	☞文法
なんで	どうして
帰国(きこく)する	自分の国に帰る

2

(に)出席(しゅっせき)する	be present at, attend
とっても	☞ことばの使い方
大事(だいじ)だ	important
熱(ねつ)がある	have a fever
肺炎(はいえん)	pneumonia
(を)諦(あきら)める	give up Ⅱ
おっしゃる通(とお)りにする	do exactly as you tell me to

3

ほっとする	breathe a sigh of relief, be a load off one's mind
御馳走(ごちそう)する	treat someone to a meal
(〜が)できあがる	be completed, be ready
〜ほどのものだ	(a thing) as good as to〜
遠慮(えんりょ)なく	without reservation
御馳走(ごちそう)になる	be treated to a meal

B：Well it isn't something I can show off, but I would like you to read it for me.

·· Middle part omitted. ···

A：Let me treat you today to celebrate the completion of your thesis.

B：It's not worth it.

A：Don't be ridiculous. Let me do it. You have really worked hard.

B：Alright, then. I will accept your treat without reservation.

A：Then, let's go right away. I have already thought about a good place. [OK.]

関連語句（かんれんごく）

目(め)が悪(わる)い	have problems with one's eyes, near-sighted
心臓病(しんぞうびょう)	heart failure
糖尿病(とうにょうびょう)	diabetes
心臓(しんぞう)まひ	heart attack
癌(がん)	cancer
結核(けっかく)	tuberculosis
食中毒(しょくちゅうどく)	food poisoning
脳卒中(のうそっちゅう)	stroke

Lesson 31

文法 (ぶんぽう)

● **Causative** （使役——しえき）

An important lesson in grammar that we shall cover in this chapter is how to formulate the causative forms of verbs. The causative phrase means: "make/force someone do something" or "allow someone to do something."

Before we go into detail about the use of the "causative form," let us learn its construction.

| Group I | Pre-ない form ＋ せる |

会う ⇨ 会わせる　　　　書く ⇨ 書かせる
話す ⇨ 話させる　　　　立つ ⇨ 立たせる

| Group II | Pre-ない form ＋ させる |

始める ⇨ 始めさせる　　　いる ⇨ いさせる
疲れる ⇨ 疲れさせる　　　調べる ⇨ 調べさせる

| Group III | する ⇨ させる　　　　来る ⇨ 来させる |

Note 1　Causative verbs conjugate as group II verbs.

Note 2　The short causative form is made by replacing せる with す. Its conjugation, in comparison to the せる form is shown below. The blanks in the list indicate that the forms are not widely acceptable. The short causative form of the Group I verbs (読ます) is more widely used than that of verbs in Group II and III.

〜ない	〜ます	dic. f.	〜ば	vol. f.
読ませ	読ませ	読ませる	読ませれ	読ませよう
読まさ		読ます		
		食べさす		

The causative construction needs two agents: one agent exercises influence over the other. Take the following sentence as an example:

| 両親が | 子供が日本人学校に行く | せる |

In this example, 両親 makes or allows the child to go to a Japanese school, and the child is the agent who goes there.

The sentence above, in reality, would appear as either one of the two below.

1.　両親が子供 { を / に } 日本人学校へ行かせる。
2.

The difference in meaning between the two sentences is: the first sentence indicates that it is the parents' will that their child goes to the Japanese school. In other words, the parents decide to send him/her to school regardless of what the child may want. The second sentence,

410

on the other hand, indicates that the parents take the child's will into consideration.

These sentences can be translated as follows:
1. The parents make their child go to the Japanese school.
2. The parents allow their child to go to the Japanese school.

If the second agent (i.e. the 'child' in the example above) is non-animate, then the second sentence cannot be constructed because the second agent does not have its own will. The sentence below with the asterisk is illogical.

1. 私はきれいな花を咲かせました。
*2. 私はきれいな花に咲かせました。

In the conclusion up to this point, we can say the following:

N1が ｜N2 {を/に} v.i.｜ +(さ)せる ⇨ N1 makes N2 v.i.
⇨ N1 allows N2 v.i.

When the original verb is a transitive verb (see the second example below), or there is another transitive verb included in the causative sentence (see the first example below), it is only に that can be used to mark the second agent.

1. 子供{を/に}行かせる ⇨ 子供｜に｜パンを買いに行かせる。
2. 子供が花に水をやる ⇨ 子供｜に｜花に水をやらせる。

This is due to the fact that in Japanese there is a strict rule that, in most cases, prohibits two object-markers from co-existing in a single sentence. This is why only に can be used in the sentences above.

Note that the sentence below does not violate this rule since the first を is not an object-marker.

雨の中を，歌を歌いながら歩くのが好きです。
(I like to walk while singing in the rain.)

In the causative sentence, it is not clear whether or not the will of the second agent is taken into account. Only the context makes it clear.

● 帰国させられます　　1-7

This is the causative passive form of 帰国する, which is formed in the following way:

帰国する ⇨ (causative) 帰国させる ⇨ 帰国させられる

All the causative verbs with -(さ)せる conjugate as Group II verbs, and the passive suffix that is attached to them is -られる, whereas short causative forms with す conjugate as group I verbs. The short forms of Group I verbs (読ます, 買わす, etc.) are often used to make causative passive forms, but short forms of Group II and III are hardly used in this formation.

The general meaning of the causative passive phrase is "made to do."

書く ⇨ 書かせる／書かす ⇨ 書かせられる／書かされる

● 忘れさせないため　　1-5　☞P.192

The pattern "S1 ため(に) S2" indicates that S1 is the purpose or goal of S2 when S1 ends in the dictionary form of controllable verbs; controllable verbs signify actions that you can do or stop intentionally. See (1) and (2).

S1 indicates a cause if S2 in the same phrase signifies a thing over which you have no control, such as an occurrence in the past or the present state. See (3) to (5).

1. 弁護士(lawyer)になるためには，ロー・スクールを卒業しなければならない。

Lesson 31

(You have to graduate from a law school in order to become a lawyer.)

２．私は真面目に勉強するために，新しい机を買おうと思っています。

(I am thinking of buying a new desk so that I can study diligently.)

３．週に二十時間もアルバイトをしているために，勉強する時間がない。

(As I am working twenty hours a week, I have no time to study.)

４．あの人は論文が書き上げられないために，学者になるのを諦めたそうです。

(I heard that the person gave up the idea of becoming a scholar because he could not complete his thesis.)

５．父はパイロットになりたかったけど，目が悪かったためになれなかった。

(My father wanted to be a pilot but couldn't because of his weak eye-sight.)

● 覚えさせる<u>のに</u>はいいチャンスだ　　1-6

のに in this pattern is not the same as that in "S1 のに S2." This のに is made up of the nominalizer の and に that signifies evaluation or estimation, translated as "for" in the first sentence.　☞P.158「話しにくい」，P.191「私にわかる」

１．この本は小学校の一年生には難しいでしょう。

(This book is difficult for a first-grader.)

２．この本は小学校の一年生が読むのには難しいでしょう。

(This book is difficult for a first-grader to read.)

● 結婚式<u>だって</u>　　2-2　☞P.355「たとえ家の子供が手伝ってくれたって」

● ～だけじゃなくて　　2-4

だけ is a dependent noun used with various kinds of modifiers. It means "only" and, in this pattern, "not only but also."

１．頭が痛いだけじゃなくて，熱も高いんですよ。

(I not only have a headache but also have a high fever.)

２．彼は，勉強が嫌いなだけではなく，仕事も嫌いなんですから，困った人ですよ。

(Not only does he hate to study, he also hates to work. He really is a pain.)

● おっしゃる通りにする　　2-7

通り is a dependent noun used with verbs that indicate such verbal actions as 言う，読む，書く，説明する，教える，聞く，話す, etc. This phrase means "I will do exactly as you say, read, explain, etc."

Another frequently used pattern is the combination of この，その，あの and 通りです. This expression means "It is exactly like this/that etc."

１．言われた通りにやってください。(Please do exactly as you are told.)

２．説明に書いてある通りに作ったと思うんだけど，変なものができちゃった。

(I am sure I made it according to these written directions, but it turned out to be something strange.)

３．A：先生，これはここが間違っていると思うんですが，いかがでしょう。

　　B：そうです。その通りですよ。そこが違うんですよ。

(A：Sensei, I think this is wrong here, but what do you think?)

(B：Right. That's exactly so. That part is wrong!)

● 読ませてください　　3-5

As we have seen in this lesson, one of the implications of the causative form is "to allow someone to do something." This is another way of getting permission from somebody. We have studied ～て(も)いいですか. The difference between this form and the "causative て-form＋ください" is that the latter is a humble way of soliciting permission and, consequently, it is more polite and formal than the form "～て(も)いいですか." Note that the agents are totally different between the pattern with causative verb and that with the ordinary て-form.

　　　この本を読んでください。　(Please read this book.)
　　　この本を読ませてください。(Please allow me to read this book.)

In the second sentence, if you add 私 as an agent of "reading," it has to be 私に as explained on P. 410.

ことばの使い方 (ことばのつかいかた)

● 多く　　1-3　☞P. 80　文法「遠く，近く，多く」

There are some い-adjs. whose く-form is used as a noun. They are 近く, 遠く and 多く. 多く can be used to mean many things including people.

1. 私はこの近くに住んでいます。(I live around here.)
2. 富士山はかなり遠くからでも見えますよ，冬なら。
   (Mt. Fuji can be seen even from a good distance, if it is in the winter time.)
3. この大学の卒業生の多くは大学院に行くようですね。
   (It seems like most of the graduates from this university are going to graduate school.)
4. 私が最近読んだ小説の多くは，つまらないものだったけど，これはおもしろい。
   (Most of the novels I've read recently are boring, but this one is interesting.)

● なんで　　1-4

This interrogative word means "why" or "by what" (で is a particle indicating a "means" or an "instrument.") There may be ambiguity in sentences such as the one below, but the context will determine the correct choice.

　　　なんでデパートに行ったんですか。(Why/How did you go to the department store?)

● とっても　　2-3

This is the emphasized form of とても and should be used only in conversation. It is not suitable for use in writing. When a word or an expression is emphasized, the syllables may be elongated, the word may be pronounced loudly, or the pitch may be heightened. The accent pattern is not affected by the degree of emphasis.

● 大事な試合なんで　　2-3

Just as ～のです is usually pronounced んです, there are occasions when ので is pronounced んで in conversation.

● 君　　2-4　☞P. 206　ことばの使い方「あなた」

This word means "you," but like あなた, its use is restricted. 君 can be used to refer to

Lesson 31

your friend or your inferior in an informal situation. 君 is not suitable for women to use.

● いいですか　　2-4

This expression indicates that the speaker is about to emphasize the important point in a discussion. The phrase may be placed either before or after the point.

1．A：それじゃ，また，明日。
　　B：はい。いいですか。明日，三時に，ここですよ。いいですね。
　　　　（A：Well then, see you tomorrow.）
　　　　（B：Yes. Now remember, here tomorrow at three. Is that clear?）
2．A：奨学金の申請（application）をしたいんですが。
　　B：ええっ。いいですか。締め切りは一月前ですよ。
　　　　（A：I would like to apply for a scholarship.）
　　　　（B：What? Listen! The deadline was a month ago.）

● 肺炎になる　　2-4

The verb used to express catching a cold is ひく. With most other illnesses, however, the verb used is なる. Some illnesses that occur suddenly use (を)起こす. Here is a list of illnesses with the appropriate verbs:

1．With ～になる

癌	cancer
心臓病	heart disease
結核	tuberculosis
糖尿病	diabetes
食中毒	food poisoning

2．With ～を起こす

| 心臓まひ | heart attack |
| 脳卒中 | stroke |

● 論文ができあがる　　3-3

This expression means that a process is completed and that something is now ready. You can substitute this phrase with できる.

1．お父さん，御飯ができあがりましたよ。(Daddy, dinner is finally ready.)
2．A：この橋は何年にできたんですか。
　　B：本によると，1899年にできあがったそうです。
　　　　（A：When was this bridge completed?）
　　　　（B：According to a book, it was completed in 1899.）

● 一度読んでいただけたら，（嬉しい／ありがたい）　　3-6

This is a part of "S1 たら S2." The second portion of the sentence omitted here goes something like "I would be happy" or "I would appreciate it." This interpretation is implied by the use of いただける "I can receive the favor."

● 御馳走　　3-8

The literal meaning of 馳走 is "to run around." 御馳走する supposedly means "run around (to get good materials)." Today, this etymological sense has disappeared and 御馳走 means "feast" or "treat," and 御馳走する means "to treat" or "to serve a feast." From the receiver of the feast, it is 御馳走になる. Many Japanese people say 御馳走さまでした, after a meal, to thank the person who cooked the food. ☞P. 208 ことばの使い方「いただきます」

● お祝いしていただくほどのものじゃない　3-9

We have already seen this ほど in sentences of comparison: シカゴは東京ほど物価は高くない. (The cost of living in Chicago is not as high as that in Tokyo.) ほど indicates the (highest) limit or maximum. The sentence in the dialogue means "My paper is not good enough to celebrate," or "My paper is not worth celebrating."

  A：そのお仕事，大変じゃありません？　手伝いましょうか。
  B：いいえ。大変と言うほどの仕事じゃありませんから，結構ですよ。
   (A：Isn't that a hard job? Shall I help you?)
   (B：No, thank you. You can't call this job hard. I am fine.)

● 遠慮なく　3-11

When a Japanese person is offered or invited to do something in a formal situation, he/she may initially turn it down politely. The person doing the offering insists, and the receiver turns it down a few more times. When this exchange is over, the receiver uses the expression 遠慮なく preceded by such phrases like そうですか, それでは(じゃ)before agreeing to accept whatever he/she is offered. This hesitant manner is called 遠慮 ; having no 遠慮 is considered to be lacking in politeness. The hearer admits that his/her manner (i.e. accepting the offer) is lacking in politeness. This is the full meaning of the expression 遠慮なく.

The offerer can use this expression with 御 to encourage the potential receiver to take the offer without hesitation.

 1．A：どうぞ，召し上がってください。　(Please have some.)
   B：そうですか。それじゃ，遠慮なくいただきます。
    (Well then, I'll eat them without hesitation.)
 2．A：この本，お借りしてもいいですか。(May I borrow this book?)
   B：どうぞ，御遠慮なく。　　　　　(Yes, please go ahead.)

Lesson 31

練習 (れんしゅう)

練習(れんしゅう)　1	Causative forms

例　行く　⇨行かせる (make/allow someone to go)

1．来る　2．する　3．読む　4．買う　5．走る　6．食べる　7．見る　8．歩く

練習(れんしゅう)　2	Make s.b. do

例　子供は学校が嫌いだと言いました。(My child said he hates school.)
　　　⇨でも，私は子供を学校へ行かせました。
　　　(But I made my child go to school.)

1．弟は買い物に行きたくないと言いました。
2．妹は私の家に手伝いに来たくないと言いました。
3．子供は医者になるのはいやだと言いました。
4．小学生たちは図書館で静かにしませんでした。
5．妹は今夜は早く寝たくないと言いました。
6．妹は友達の家に遊びに行かないと言いました。

練習(れんしゅう)　3	Make/allow (to) do

例　妹が切符を買いたいと言いました。
　　(My sister said that she wanted to buy tickets.)
　　　⇨だから，私は，妹に切符を買わせました。
　　　(So, I made/allowed my sister (to) buy tickets.)

1．弟が私の車を運転したいと言いました。　2．妹がピアノを習いたいと言いました。
3．子供が宿題をすると言いました。　　　　4．弟が英語を勉強したいと言いました。
5．家内が友達に電話をかけると言いました。　6．弟が犬を連れて行くと言いました。

練習(れんしゅう)　4	Causative passive

例　帰国する　⇨私は，父に帰国させられました。
　　　　　　　(I was made to return home to my country by my father.)

1．運転を習う　　　　　　2．ピアノの練習をする　　3．英語を覚える
4．父の会社に電話をかける　5．夕食の買い物に行く　　6．料理を作る
7．たばこをやめる　　　　8．おもしろくない本を読む　9．図書館から本を借りて来る

練習(れんしゅう)　5	～というのは，どういう意味ですか

例　子供を普通の学校に行かせます。
　　(I will send my child to an ordinary school.)
　　⇨普通の学校というのは，どういう意味ですか。
　　(What do you mean by an "ordinary school?")

1．君は肺炎ですよ。　　　　　2．今日の試合に出させるわけには行きません。
3．今日の試合は諦めなさい。　4．私，来月帰国します。
5．今夜御馳走しますよ。　　　6．これはとても大事な論文です。

練習(れんしゅう)　6	S1 ために S2

例　日本語を忘れさせない，日本語学校へ行かせる
　　⇨日本語を忘れさせないために，日本語学校へ行かせるんですよ。
　　(They send their children to the Japanese school so that they won't forget the Japanese language.)

1．日本へ行く，アルバイトをしている　　2．宿題をする，図書館に行く
3．日本語を覚える，テレビを見る　　　　4．元気でいる，運動をしている
5．田中さんに御馳走する，買い物に出掛ける　6．旅行で写真を撮る，カメラを買った

練習(れんしゅう)　7	～のに，いい

例　子供が英語を覚える
　　⇨子供に英語を覚えさせるのには，いいチャンスですね。
　　(It's a great opportunity to make children study English, isn't it?)

1．弟が一人で旅行する　　2．主人がたばこをやめる
3．妹がピアノを習う　　　4．家内がワード・プロセッサーの使い方を覚える
5．犬が運動をする　　　　6．あの人が論文を書き終わる

Lesson 31

練習(れんしゅう) 8	だって

例　君の結婚式でも，出席させるわけにはいかない。
　　⇨君の結婚式だって，出席させるわけにはいきませんよ。
　　　(Even if it were your wedding, I wouldn't let you attend it.)

　　薬を飲んでも，治らない。
　　⇨薬を飲んだって，治りませんよ。
　　　(Even if you took the medicine, you wouldn't be cured.)

1．肺炎になっても，出席する。　　2．論文で忙しくても，授業は休まない。
3．死んでも，諦めない。　　　　　4．論文が終わっても，ほっとするわけにはいかない。
5．おもしろくなくても，頑張る。　6．この論文は何回読んでも，わからない。

練習(れんしゅう) 9	～だけじゃなくて～

例　熱が高い，肺炎になりそうだ
　　⇨あの人は，熱が高いだけじゃなくて，肺炎になりそうなんですよ。
　　　(He not only has a high fever but he may also be getting pneumonia.)

1．頭がいい，よく勉強する　　　　2．頭がよくない，全然予習復習をしない
3．テニスが上手だ，走るのも速い　4．授業で静かだ，家でも話をしない
5．よく遊ぶ，よく勉強もする　　　6．よく食べる，よく眠る

練習(れんしゅう) 10	～たら，～といけない

例　死にたくない，試合を諦める
　　⇨死にたくなかったら，試合は諦めないと，いけませんね。
　　　(If you don't want to die, you must give up the game.)

1．わからない，辞書を引く　　　　2．アメリカの学校のことだ，あの人に聞く
3．出席したくない，電話しておく　4．論文が終わる，のんびりする
5．用事がある，すぐ出掛ける　　　6．家に帰る，なるべく早く寝る

練習(れんしゅう) 11	～の通り(に)

例　先生がおっしゃる　⇨先生がおっしゃる通りにやってみます。
　　　(I will try doing exactly as you say.)

1．先生が教えてくださった　　2．先生に教えられた　　3．本に書いてある
4．本で読んだ　　　　　　　　5．父が言う　　　　　　6．母に言われた

練習(れんしゅう) 12	できあがる

例　論文　⇨やっと論文ができあがりました。(My paper is finally completed.)

1．新しい家　　2．御馳走　　3．赤ん坊の写真　　4．結婚式に着る着物
5．世界で一番長い橋　　　6．大変，簡単で便利なコンピューター

練習(れんしゅう) 13	〜ところだ

例　ほっとしているんですよ。　⇨ほっとしているところなんですよ。
　　　　　　　　　　　　　　　　(I am feeling relieved.)
　　今，終わったんですよ。　　⇨今，終わったところなんですよ。
　　　　　　　　　　　　　　　　(It has just finished.)
　　これから，始めるんですよ。⇨これから，始めるところなんですよ。
　　　　　　　　　　　　　　　　(I am just about to start.)

1．家でのんびりしているんですよ。　2．今電話をしようと思っていたんですよ。
3．これから出掛けるんですよ。　　　4．肺炎で病院にいるんですよ。
5．今旅行から帰って来たんですよ。　6．これから医者に行くんですよ。

練習(れんしゅう) 14	Causative て＋ください

例　読む　⇨私に読ませてください。(Please let me read it.)

1．払う　2．言う　3．入る　4．書く　5．話す　6．お祝いする　7．調べる

APPENDICES

Kanji List（漢字表） ········ 422

Japanese-English Glossary（和英索引） ········ 427

Kanji List

漢字表 (Kanji List)

This list presents all of the important *kanji* that have appeared in the textbook. From Lesson Six on, *kanji* are listed according to whether they are *kanji* for writing or for recognition. Please note that the underlined kanji in the kanji for writing have been introduced in the previous lessons.

	書く漢字 (For Writing)	読む漢字 (For Reading)
六課	一 二 三 四 五 六 七 八 九 十 大学院 四年生 私 古い	出身 専門 人類 州 新聞 駅 図書館
七課	何 上 下 中 右 左 色 女 男 人 見て 先生 車 国	お願い 机 黄色い 困った 前 後ろ 彼 彼女 時間 始まります
八課	時間 半 分 月 火 水 木 金 土 日 百 千 今 小さい	お知らせ 来週 曜日 試験 教室 今日 失礼 明日 昨日
九課	休み 行きます 家 帰ります 近く 父 母 兄 弟 姉 妹 家族 来ます	お金 御両親 遠く 集まります 楽しい 悪い 若い 本当に 多く 授業

十課	起きます 毎朝 晩 勉強 昨日 食べます 作ります 読みます 週 何回 明日 早く 昼	御飯 自分 時々 料理 全然 運動 週末 元気 電話 終わります
十一課	才 本 冊 枚 台 個 匹 円 安い 買います 売ります 犬 子 万	誕生日 欲しい 値段 卵 猫 要る 生まれる
十二課	日本語 東京 育つ 住む 両親 南 北 西 漢字 好き 終わる 始まる	学期末 最後 便利 京都 一人 練習 意味 調べる 何度も 少し 東
十三課	待つ 食堂 話す 開ける 閉める 友達 手紙 書く 秋山 雪 雨 本当に 飲む	遅れる 暑い 部屋 窓 紙 飛ぶ 動く 降る 遊ぶ 酒 歩く
十四課	知っている 前 後 授業 遅れる 思う 今夜 映画 出る 電話 会う 買い物	僕 時 宿題 家内 主人 町 食事 出す 遅い
十五課	返す 簡単 直す 習う 困る 持つ 調べる 引き方 聞く 上野	問題 過ぎる 方がいい 覚える 忘れる 誰か 教科書 貸す 運転 教える

十六課	中村 背 高い 低い 長い 短い 着る 楽しみ 北川 質問 以上 多い 若い 太る	髪 結婚式 靴 合う 中年 頭 目 青い 黒い
十七課	止まる 遠い 忙しい 借りる お茶 入れる 新しい 教える 味 白い 青い 黒い	心配 交通事故 この頃 小説 論文 準備 久しぶり 気に入る 実は 緑色
十八課	運動 体 痛い 元気だ 大変だ 疲れる 寝る 天気 頭 図書館 探す	次 非常に お大事に 風邪をひく 祖父 祖母
十九課	失礼 少し 自由に 無理 言う 今度 集まり 音楽 決める 返事	申す 下手 上手 雑誌 生活する 難しい 奨学金 全く 教師 頼む
二十課	切符 悪い 実は 病気 治る 学校 安心 発音 一番 英語 文法 練習	興味 歌 人気 嫌いだ 他の 誘う 初めて 言葉 感心 自然だ 予習 復習
二十一課	貸す 森 試験 問題 全部 目 番号 研究室 連れる 花	お宅 娘 息子 相談する 時計 魚

課	漢字	漢字
二十二課	仕事　経済的　難しい　広い 同じ　夏　春　必要だ 交通	比較　例えば　家賃　物価　野球 通う　払う　安全だ　隣
二十三課	冬　走る　体重　卒業　会社 勤める　部屋　午後　机 使う　寒い　暑い　冷たい	気候　この辺　増える　減る 間違い　就職する　医者　反対 賛成　手伝い
二十四課	誰　急用　頃　家内　伝える 欲しい　初めに　次に　最後に 大田　石原	着く　楽に　留守　明日中　必ず 約束　伝言
二十五課	駅　この辺　道　全然　工事 所　横　信号　曲がる　橋 向こう　目的地　銀行　角	確か　御存じ　通り　渡る こちら側　結構　細かい
二十六課	赤ちゃん　お祝い　相談　直接 授業料　払う　学期　働く 子供　彼　泣く	赤ん坊　喜ぶ　優しい　寄る　声
二十七課	降る　晴れる　曇る　空　夕方 準備　歩く　歌　足　口 世界	大丈夫　今朝　予報　腕　筋肉 冷やす　貧乏だ

二十八課	医者(いしゃ) 心配(しんぱい) 規則(きそく) 正(ただ)しい 生活(せいかつ) 考(かんが)える 時計(とけい) 奥様(おくさま) 眠(ねむ)い 外(そと) 不規則(ふきそく)	厳(きび)しい 間(ま)に合(あ)う 締(し)め切(き)り 気(き)が狂(くる)う 徹夜(てつや) 原稿(げんこう)
二十九課	昔(むかし) 西洋(せいよう) お年寄(としよ)り 台風(たいふう) 呼(よ)ぶ 怒(おこ)る 宿題(しゅくだい) 渡(わた)す 旅行(りょこう) 取(と)る 盗(ぬす)む 建(た)てる	小学校(しょうがっこう) 作曲家(さっきょくか) 竜巻(たつまき) 経験(けいけん) 違反(いはん)
三十課	お宅(たく) 申(もう)す お願(ねが)い 主人(しゅじん) 関西(かんさい) 特別(とくべつ) 僕(ぼく) 予定(よてい) 写真(しゃしん)	恐(おそ)れ入(い)りますが 二日程(ふつかほど) 明晩(みょうばん) 複雑(ふくざつ) 明後日(あさって) 歴史(れきし) 空(あ)いている ご覧(らん)になる 拝見(はいけん)する 承知(しょうち)する
三十一課	普通(ふつう) 意味(いみ) 忘(わす)れる 覚(おぼ)える 出席(しゅっせき) 君(きみ) 熱(ねつ) 死(し)ぬ 結婚式(けっこんしき)	帰国(きこく) 肺炎(はいえん) 諦(あきら)める 仕方(しかた)がない 遠慮(えんりょ)なく

Japanese-English Glossary──和英索引（わえいさくいん）

＊The number following each entry is the page where the word appears.
＊The parenthesized number shows the page where the word is explained.

あ

ああ　oh, ah　37
ああいう　that kind of　(194)
ああ、そうそう　oh, yes／what you've said has reminded me　(113), (146)
ああ、そうですか　Is that so?　(13)
ああです　like that over there, as he/she does　(40)
ああ、よかった　I'm relieved.　(59)
アイスクリーム　ice cream　100
あいだに（間に）　while, during　(314)
あいだで（→～のあいだで）　376
あう（会う）　meet, see　154
あう（合う）　fit　186
あおい（青い）　blue　187, 209
あおき（青木）　[a surname]　248
あかい（赤い）　red　28, 209
あかちゃん（赤ちゃん）　a baby　(340)
あかんぼう（赤ん坊）　a baby　(340)
あき（秋）　fall　78
あきやま（秋山）　[a surname]　138
あきらめる（諦める）　give up　408
あく（開く）　open(v.i.)　138
あく（空く）　be unoccupied, vacant　391
あげられる　can give　262
あける（開ける）　open(v.t.)　138

あげる　give　(265)
あさ（朝）　morning　92
あさごはん（朝御飯）　breakfast　91
あさって（明後日）　the day after tomorrow　(399)
あさひしんぶん（朝日新聞）　the *Asahi*　(51)
あさまでに（朝までに）　by morning　310
あし（足／脚）　foot, leg　351
あじ（味）　taste　203
あした（明日）　tomorrow　37, 67
あしたじゅうに（明日中に）　during tomorrow, within tomorrow　310
あ、そうだ　I've gotten an idea!　(146)
あそこ　over there　(40), 49
あそぶ（遊ぶ）　have fun with　97, (125), 138
あたたかい（暖かい）　warm　(41)
あたま（頭）　brain, head　216, 351
あたまがいい（頭がいい）　smart　187
⇔あたまがわるい（頭が悪い）　dumb　187
あたらしい（新しい）　new　28
あちら　that one over there　280, (328)
あっ　oh [male]　31
あつい（暑い）　hot　38, 138
あっち　that one over there　280, (328)
あつまり（集まり）　gathering, meeting　232
あつまる（集まる）　gather　77
あと　[Numeral] another N　(128), (237)
[Nの]あと（後）　after N　91
[S＋]あと（後）　after S　(156)
あとで（後で）　later　186
あとのこと　things to be done after something is done　(268)
あなた　you　(206)
あに（兄）　elder-brother　78
あね（姉）　elder-sister　78
あのN　that N　(28), (157)

あのう　①Er, excuse me!　(22)
　②fluency and politeness　(393)
アパート　apartment　72, 154
[シャワーを]あびる（浴びる）　take a shower　92
あべ（阿部）　[a surname]　232
あまり…ない　not very　67, (93), (381)
あめ（雨）　rain　139
アメリカ　America, the U.S.A　19
アメリカがっしゅうこく（アメリカ合衆国）　the U.S.A.　266
アメリカ人　American　19
あら　oh [female]　(31)
あらう（洗う）　wash　92
あらたまった（改たまった）　formal　(194)
ありがとうございました　Thank you.　3
ありました　Here it is!　(56)
ありまして　polite て-form　(393)
ありません　[い-adj.＋～]　(29)
ありゃあ　a contracted form of あれは　299
ある　①there is/are　(50)
　②posession　(68), (127)
　③to be held　(128)
　④二キロある　(327)
あるく（歩く）　walk　138
アルバイト　part-time job　(83)
あれ　that, those　(28)
あれだけ　as much as this, to that extent　(356)
あんしんする（安心する）　feel relieved　248
あんぜんだ（安全だ）　safe　279
あんな　that kind of　189

い

いい　good, nice　28
いいえ　no　(11), (392)
いいえ（どういたしまして）　You're welcome.　11, (51)
いいです　It is good.　29
いいですか　Listen!　(414)

427

Japanese-English Glossary

いいですねえ　That's good.　(71)
いいですよ　It's good./Fine.　(29),(59)
いう(言う)　say, call　97
いえ(家)　house(hold)　376
いえいえ　①No, no.　10　②It's O.K.　(51)
〜いか(以下)　lower than 〜 [including 〜]　(194)
いかが(如何)　⇒どう　(399)
いかせる(行かせる)　make s.b. to go　(410)
イギリス　Britain　19
イギリスじん(イギリス人)　British　19
いく(行く)　go　(5),(81),97
いくつ　how many/old　106
いくら　how much　(30),(328)
[Sと]いけない　must　(282)
いけなかったんでしょうね　I guess it was not right.　(355)
いけばな(生け花)　flower arrangement　171
いけません(←いけない)　no good　216
いこう(行こう)　plain volitional form of 行く　(156),(190)
いしい(石井)　[a surname]　57
いしはら(石原)　[a surname]　310
いしゃ(医者)　medical doctor　292,(367)
〜いじょう(以上)　above 〜 [including 〜]　(194)
いす　chair, stool　57
いそがしい(忙しい)　busy　40,187
いたい(痛い)　hurting, painful　216
いたす(致す)　⇒する　395
いただきます　[greeting]　(208)
いただく　①⇒receive, take　202　②⇒polite of もらう　232,(264)
いただけたら　(→〜して)いただけたら　If you could kindly do 〜,　(414)
[〜を]いためる(痛める)　hurt, injure　350
イタリア　Italy　20
いち(一)　one　(69)
いちにち(一日)　one day　(110)
[〜に]いちにちかける(一日かける)　spend a day on 〜　292
いちねんせい(一年生)　freshman　3

いちばん(一番)　-est　(60),(281)
いつ　when?　(79),122
いつか　sometime　(79)
いっか(一課)　Lesson 1　1
いっしょに(一緒に)　together, with　172,(252)
行っていらっしゃい　[greeting]　(269)
行ってきます　[greeting]　(269)
いつでも　all the time　249
いつも　always　(79),(93),(177)
いとう(伊藤)　[a surname]　106
いぬ(犬)　a dog　106,336
いま(今)　now　67
いま(居間)　living room　49
います　be, exist　(50)
いますぐ(今すぐ)　right now　216
いみ(意味)　meaning　122
いもうと(妹)　younger sister　78
いやあ　[exclamatory expression]　(299)
いやですねえ(嫌ですねえ)　I don't like it./It's terrible.　(71)
いやな(嫌な)　unpleasant　37
イヤリング　earring　193
いらして　て-form of いらっしゃる　(147)
いらっしゃる　polite of いる, 来る, 行く　(147),188,234
いる　be　(50)
[Nが]いる(要る)　need N　(111)
いろ(色)　color　57
いろいろ(色々)　in wide variety　106
いろいろありがとう(色々ありがとう)　Thank you for everything.　350
いわれる(言われる)　passive form of 言う　(366)
インド　India　20

う

ううん　[informal word to show disagreement]　(128)
うえ(上)　on, above　(58)
うえき(植木)　(potted)plant　262
うごく(動く)　move　138
うしろ(後ろ)　behind　(58)
うた(歌)　song　248
うたをうたう(歌を歌う)　sing a song　154

うたわれる(歌われる)　be sung　376
うち(家)　(my)house　49,293
うで(腕)　arm　350
うでどけい(腕時計)　wrist watch　364
うまれてはじめて(生まれて初めて)　for the first time in one's life　377
うまれる(生まれる)　be born　106,122
うめだ(梅田)　[a surname]　262
うる(売る)　sell　106
うれしい(嬉しい)　be happy　217,248,338
うん　[informal word to show agreement]　(128)
うんてんする(運転する)　drive a car　171,233
うんどうぐつ(運動靴)　sports shoes　186
うんどうする(運動する)　exercise, sports　91

え

えいが(映画)　movie　133,154
えいがかん(映画館)　movie theater　107,325
えいご(英語)　English　11,19
えいこく(英国)　England　19
えいこくじん(英国人)　British　19
えいよう(栄養)　nutrition　364
ええ　yes　(11)
ええ、そうです　That's right.　(11)
ええっ　[indicator of surprise]　(356)
ええ、まあ　Well, Sort of　(30)
えき(駅)　station　49
えきまえ(駅前)　open space before a station　325
エジプト　Egypt　20
えん(円)　[monetary unit(¥)]　(108)
エンジン　engine　177
エンジンがかかる　engine starts　177
えんどう(遠藤)　[a surname]　310
えんぴつ(鉛筆)　pencil　57,106
えんりょなく(遠慮なく)　without reservation　(415)

お

お [honorific prefix] 13, (20)

お＋stem＋ください(下さい) [request] (234)
お＋stem＋する humble form (172), (393)
お＋stem＋だ 🈁 (394), (395)
お＋stem＋になる 🈁 (394)

おいくら how much (328)
おいしい tasty, delicious 38, 205
おいしそうだ look tasty (205)
おいでだ →いらっしゃる (394)
おいわい(お祝い) gift 336
おえる(終える) finish 216
おおい(多い) many, much (80), 187
おおえ(大江) [a surname] 310
おおき(大木) [a surname] 72
おおきい(大きい) big, large 57
おおく(多く) many (80), (413)
おおくの(多くの) many of, most 78
おおさか(大阪) Osaka 399
おおた(大田) [a surname] 310
おおどおり(大通り) main street 324
おおみや(大宮) [a surname] 278
おおゆき(大雪) heavy snow fall 337
おかあさん(お母さん) mother 78
おかえりなさい(お帰りなさい) Welcome back. (314)
おかげさまで [greeting] (253)
おかしい strange, funny 37
おかね(お金) money 77
おかねがかかる(お金がかかる) cost money 278
おきられる(起きられる) passive/ potential form of 起きる (378)
おきる(起きる) get up, wake up (97)
おく(億) one hundred million (114)
おくさま(奥様) Mrs. ~ (368)
おくさん(奥さん) Mrs. ~ (161)
おくれる(遅れる) get late 138
おこられる(怒られる) be scolded/ chided 376
おこる(怒る) get angry 263
おさけ(お酒) sake, alcoholic drinks・138
おしえられる(教えられる) be taught, can teach 376
おしえる(教える) teach, tell 171
おじゃまする(お邪魔する) visit🈁 (83)
おしらせ(お知らせ) news, notice 67
オーストラリア Australia 20
おそい(遅い) late 171
おそくまで(遅くまで) until late 154
おそれいりますが(恐れ入りますが) 🈁 すみませんが (398)
おだいじに(お大事に) take care (223)
おたく(お宅) ①you (206) ②house🈁 (268), (392)
おっしゃる 🈁say (21), (147), (188)
おっしゃるとおりにする(おっしゃる通りにする) do exactly as you tell me to (412)
おっと(夫) husband (161)
おつり change(to return) 324
おてあらい(お手洗い) toilet, bathroom 49
おてつだいする(お手伝いする) help s.b. do work 293
おとうさん(お父さん) father 78
おとうと(弟) younger brother 78
おとこ(男) man 57
おとしより(お年寄り) elders 376
おととい(一昨日) the day before yesterday 399
おどろく(驚く) be surprised 252
おなか stomach, belly 216, 351
おなかがすく get hungry 216
おなじ(同じ) same (283)
おにいさん(お兄さん) elder brother (30), 78
おねえさん(お姉さん) elder sister (30), 78
おねがい(お願い) request 57
おねがいします(お願いします) please 106, (208)
おねがいする(お願いする) ask, request 170
オーバー overcoat 193
おはようございます(お早うございます) Good morning. (40)
おふろ(お風呂)(→ふろ) bath 92, 98
オーブン oven 203
おぼえている(覚えている) remember (176)
おぼえる(覚える) memorize (176)
おまえ(お前) you (207)
おまちになる(お待ちになる) 🈁待つ (396)
おめでとうございます Happy ~, Congratulations. (113)
おもう(思う) think (81), (155), (190)
おもしろい(面白い) interesting 122
おもちゃや(おもちゃ屋) toy shop 316
おやすみなさい(お休みなさい) Good night. 41
およぐ(泳ぐ) swim 97
おります 🈁います (394)
[を]おりる(降りる) get off 324
おわらせる(終わらせる) have s.t. finished (316)
おわる(終わる) finish 37, 66
Stem＋おわる(終わる) finish ~ing (354)
おんがく(音楽) music 232, 248
おんなのこ(女の子) a girl 336
おんなのひと(女の人) woman 57
おんよみ(音読み) Chinese reading (5)

か

か ①[particle for question] (13), (20)
②[its ommission] (11), (59)
か [exclamatory particle] (13)
か(課) lesson 1, 67
か[N か N] or (174)
が [conjunctive particle] (31), (96)
が [agent-particle] (58)
~かい(回) times (108)
かいぎ(会議) meeting, conference 171
かいけいし(会計士) accountant 293
かいしゃ(会社) company 11, 187

Japanese-English Glossary

かいしゃいん（会社員） office worker 293
かいもの（買い物） shopping (94), 154
かいわ（会話） dialogue, conversation 2
かう（買う） buy 106, 138
〔～を〕かう（飼う） keep animals/pets 336
かえす（返す） return (v.t.) 139
かえる（帰る） return, go back 77
かお（顔） face 176
かおをあらう（顔を洗う） wash one's face 92
かかる take (time, money) 37, 70
かかれる（書かれる） passive form of 書く (378)
かきなおす（書き直す） rewrite 170
かく（書く） write 138
かぐ（家具） furniture 293
がくしゃ（学者） scholar 233
がくせい（学生） (college)student 2
～かげつ（か月） months (108)
〔めがねを〕かける wear (193)
かける（書ける） can write 234
〔いすに〕かける sit on 232
〔水を〕かける sprinkle 263
〔時間を〕かける spent (300)
かじ（火事） fire 203
かしや（菓子屋） cake shop, confectionery (316)
～かしら I wonder ～. (296)
かす（貸す） lend 171
かぜをひく（風邪を引く） catch cold 217
かぞく（家族） family 77
かた（肩） shoulder 351
かた（方） 人■ 186
～かた（方） the way of ～ (173)
かつ（勝） [a surname] 232
～がつ（月） [name of months] (108)
がっかい（学会） (academic) conference 390
がっかりする get disappointed 252
がっき（学期） school term 122
がっき（楽器） musical instrument 232
カード card 106

かとう（加藤） [a surname] 170
～かどうか whether or not (312)
～かな（→かしら） I wonder ～. (296)
かない（家内） my wife (161)
かならず（必ず） surely 310
かなり pretty, relatively 28, 138
かね（金）（→おかね） money 278
かのじょ（彼女） she (60)
かばん bag 28
〔帽子を〕かぶる wear, put on (193)
かみ（紙） paper 107, 138
かみ（髪） hair 186
カメラ camera 129
カメラや（カメラ屋） camera shop (316)
～かもしれない may (281)
かよう（通う） commute 278
かようび（火曜日） Tuesday (71)
から from (70)
～から [conjunctive particle] (79), (157)
からだ（体） body 187
からだじゅう（体中） all over one's body 293
からだをこわす（体をこわす） harm one's health 364
カリフォルニア California 100
かりる（借りる） borrow 202
ガールフレンド girl-friend 30, 56
かれ（彼） he (60)
かわいい cute, lovely 336
かわく get dry 216
かわれる（買われる） passive form of 買う (378)
かん can 296
がん（癌） cancer 409
かんえいじてん（漢英辞典） Chinese-English dictionary 122
かんがえる（考える） think, consider 364
かんこく（韓国） Korea 19
かんこくご（韓国語） Korean 19
かんこくじん（韓国人） Korean 19
かんさい（関西） Kansai area (399)
かんじ（漢字） Chinese character 4, 120
かんしゃさい（感謝祭） Thanksgiving 77
かんしんする（感心する） be impressed (252)
かんたんな（簡単な） simple 37
かんとう（関東） Kanto area (399)
がんばってください（頑張って下さい） Keep at it! (72)
がんばる keep at it 67, 232
かんれんごく（関連語句） related phrases 2

き

きがくるう（気が狂う） become insane 365
きにいる（気に入る） appeals to (208)
きになる（気になる） worry about (299)
きのせい（気のせい） imagination (298)
きをつける（気を付ける） be careful about ～ 138, (269)
きいろい（黄色い） yellow 57, (209)
きかい（器械） machine 27
きく（聞く） hear, listen, ask (177)
きこう（気候） climate, weather 292
〔～が〕きこえる（聞こえる） reach one's ear, can be heard 337
きこくする（帰国する） go back one's own country 408
きそくただしい（規則正しい） orderly, well-regulated 364
きた（北） north (128)
きたない（汚い） dirty, messy 28
きたむら（北村） [a surname] 203
ぎちょう（議長） chairman 236
きっと definitely (82), 278, 336
きっぷ（切符） ticket 248
きのう（機能） function 1
きのう（昨日） yesterday 37, 67
きびしく（厳しく） strictly 364
きみ（君） you (206), (413)
きむら（木村） [a surname] 57
きめる（決める） decide 232
きもち（気持ち） feeling 336
きもの（着物）をきる（着る） wear a kimono 186
きゅう（九） nine (69)

430

和英索引

きゅうよう(急用) urgent business 310
きゅうり cucumber 106
きょう(今日) today 37, 67
～ぎょう(行) lines 263
きょうかしょ(教科書) textbook 171
きょうし(教師) teacher (239)
きょうしつ(教室) classroom 67
きょうだい(兄弟) siblings 78
きょうと(京都) Kyoto (old capital Lit. Capital) 114, 399
きょうみがある(興味がある) have interest in ～ 248
きょねん(去年) last year 67
きらいだ(嫌いだ) hate 173, (251)
きる(着る) wear 171, (193)
きれいな beautiful, clean 57, 67, (299)
キロ kilo (meter, gram) 109
きんぎょ(金魚) gold fish 127
ぎんこう(銀行) bank 324
きんにく(筋肉) muscle 350
きんようび(金曜日) Friday (71)

く

く(九) nine (69)
ぐうぜん(偶然) by chance 268
くすり(薬) medicine 297
くすりや(薬屋) drug store 316
くだけた informal 194
ください(下さい) Please give me ～. (111)
くださる(下さる) ⬆s.b. gives me (264)
くたびれる get exhausted 365
くだものや(果物屋) fruit shop 316
くち(口) mouth 351
くつした(靴下) socks 193
くつや(靴屋) shoe shop 316
くに(国) country 19
くび(首) neck 351
くもる(曇る) get cloudy 139
くらい、ぐらい about, roughly (41), (297)
クリスマス Christmas 78
クリップ clip 104
クリーニングや(クリーニング屋) laundry, cleaners 316
くる(来る) come (81), 97
くるま(車) car 27
くれる s.b. gives me 154, (264)
くろい(黒い) black 187, 209
くわしく in detail 227
くんよみ(訓読み) Japanese reading (5)

け

けいえいがく(経営学) management 3
けいかん(警官) policeman 377
けいけん(経験) experience 377
けいご(敬語) *keigo* (188), (392)
けいざいがく(経済学) economics 3
けいざいてきだ(経済的だ) economical 278
けがをする(怪我をする) get injured 249
ケーキ cake 28, 100
けさ(今朝) this morning 253
けしゴム(消しゴム) eraser 106
けっかく(結核) tuberculosis 409
けっこうだ(結構だ) ①No thank you. (222) ②That's perfect. (284)
けっこん(結婚) marriage 83
けっこんしき(結婚式) wedding 186
げつようび(月曜日) Monday (71)
けど colloquial variant of が (96)
けど though, but (205)
げんかん(玄関) entrance to a building or house 49
げんきいっぱい(元気いっぱい) full of energy 92
げんきがない(元気がない) have no energy 216
げんきだ(元気だ) healthy, well 203
げんきづける(元気づける) cheer up 336
けんきゅう(研究) research 351
けんきゅうしつ(研究室) professor's room 262
けんきゅうする(研究する) do research 233
げんこう(原稿) manuscript 365
げんごがく(言語学) linguistics 3, 49

こ

こ(子) child 106
～こ(個) [counter for small objects] (108)
ご(五) five (69)
ご～(御) [honorific prefix] (20), (78)
～ご(語) language, word 19
ご(御)+漢語+ください(下さい) [polite request] (396)
こういう this kind of 194
こういん(工員) factory worker 293
こうえん(講演) public lecture 154
こうこう(高校) high school 154
こうこうせい(高校生) high school student 337
こうじちゅう(工事中) under construction 324
こうちゃ(紅茶) black tea 202
こうつう(交通) transportation 279
こうつうじこ(交通事故) traffic accident 202
こうです like this, in this way, as I do (40)
こうばん(交番) police-box 324
こうべ(神戸) Kobe (399)
ここ here (40)
ごご(午後) afternoon (84)
ございます ⬅ある (394)
こし(腰) waist, hip 351
ごしんぱいなく(御心配なく) Don't worry. (268)
ごぜん(午前) befor noon (84)
ごぞんじだ(御存じだ) ⬆知る (326)
こたえる(答える) answer 175
ごちそうする(御馳走する) treat someone to (lunch, dinner) (414)
ごちそうになる(御馳走になる) be treated (415)
こちら ①this person, this side 19, (328) ②this one (of the two) (280)
こちらがわ(こちら側) this side 324

Japanese-English Glossary

こちらこそ　It is I who should say so.　(21)
こっち　this one　(280), (328)
コップ　glass, cup　154
こと　[nominalizer]　(158)
[Nの]こと(→Nのことなんですが)　(175)
〜ことがある／ない　[experience]　(191)
〜ことがおおい／すくない(〜ことがおおい／すくない)　[occasion]　(192)
〜ことができる　[possibility]　(251)
〜ことにしている　[habit]　(220), (295)
〜ことにする　[decision]　(220), (294)
〜ことになっている　It is arranged 〜　(295)
〜ことになる　It is arranged 〜　(294)
〜ことは〜ですが　It is certainly 〜 but 〜　(396)
S＋ことはない　There is no need to 〜　(366)
ことし(今年)　this year　67
ことば(言葉)　word, phrase, language　95, 154
こども(子供)　child　154
このN　this N　(28), (94)
このあいだ(この間)　the other day　138
このごろ(この頃)　these days, recently　(207)
このところ(この所)　these days　(297)
このへん(この辺)　this area, around here　292
このまえ(この前)　the other day　170
ごはん(御飯)　meal, rice　92
コーヒー　coffee　38, 92
こまかいの(細かいの)　small note　324
こまった(困った)　got in trouble, having troubles　(59)
こまったこと(困ったこと)　problem　154
こまる(困る)　be in trouble　57
こめや(米屋)　rice shop　316
ごめんください(御免下さい)　Excuse me.　(395)

コーラ　coke　52
こられる(来られる)　①can come (161), (234)　②passive form of 来る　(378)
ごらんください(御覧下さい)　formal request of　見る(🈴)　(234)
ごらんになる(御覧になる)　見る(🈴)　395
こりゃあ　contracted form of これは　299
ゴルフ　golf　221
これ　this　(28)
これから　from now　138
ころ、ごろ(頃)　[time] around　(95)
こわされる(壊される)　be broken, damaged　376
こわれる(壊れる)　get broken　138
こんげつ(今月)　this month　67
こんしゅう(今週)　this week　67
コンタクトレンズ　contact lens　193
こんど(今度)　this/next time　(239)
こんな　this kind of　189
こんにちは　Good afternoon.　41
こんばん(今晩)　this evening　164, 200
こんばんは　Good evening.　41
コンピューター　computer　27
こんや(今夜)　tonight　154

さ

さあ　well, let me see　(60)
〜さい(才)　〜 years old　(108)
さいご(最後)　last　122
さいごに(最後に)　at the end　310
さいふ(財布)　wallet, pocket book　57, 351
さえ　[particle]　339
さがす(探す)　look for　216
さかな(魚)　fish　263
さかなや(魚屋)　fish shop　316
さけ(酒)(→おさけ)　sake, alcoholic drinks　138
さしあげる　give　(265)
さそう(誘う)　invite along　(253)
〜さつ(冊)　[counter for books]　(108)
さっき　a little while ago　69

さっきょくか(作曲家)　composer　376
ざっし(雑誌)　magazine　49
さっそくですが(早速ですが)　[Lit.] It is too abrupt or too soon.　(237)
さとう(砂糖)　sugar　202
さとう(佐藤)　[a surname]　138
さびしい(寂しい)　feel lonely　171, 248
さむい(寒い)　cold　30, 37
さようですか　🈴そうですか　390
さようなら　good-bye　(42)
サラリー　salary　107
サラリーマン　white-collar　292
される　passive form of する　(378)
さん(三)　three　(69)
Nさん　Mr./Mrs./Miss/Ms. N　(21)
さんこうしょ(参考書)　reference books　49
さんせい(三世)　third generation　19
さんせいする(賛成する)　agree　292
サンドイッチ　sandwich　224
さんねんせい(三年生)　junior　3
さんぽ(散歩)　a walk　262

し

し(四)　four　(69)
〜し〜　[conjunctive particle]　(81), (191)
じ(字)　characters, letters　37
〜じ(時)　〜 o'clock　(70)
しあい(試合)　match, game　350
ジェイ・アール(JR)　Japan Railways　325
しお(塩)　salt　112
しかし　but, however　216
しかたありません　There is no alternatives.　(72)
しか…ない　just, only　(128)
しかられる(叱られる)　be scolded　376
じかん(時間)　time　(41)
じかんです(時間です)　It's time!　37
しけん(試験)　test, exam.　67
しごと(仕事)　work, job　11, 83
じしょ(辞書)　dictionary　122
しずかな(静かな)　quiet　154

432

和英索引

しぜんな(自然な) natural 248
した(下) under, below (58)
しち(七) seven (69)
じつは(実は) The fact is ~ (208)
しつもん(質問) question 187
しつれいする(失礼する) ☞goodbye, etc. (22), 37
しつれいですが(失礼ですが) Excuse me, but ~ (12), (31)
してきする(指摘する) point out 391
じてん(辞典) dictionary 122
じてんしゃ(自転車) bicycle 28
じどうしゃ(自動車) automobile 202
しぬ(死ぬ) die (97)
しばい(芝居) drama 217
しばらく for the time being, for a while 293
じぶんで(自分で) by oneself (96)
しめきり(締め切り) deadline 365
しめる(閉める) shut, close (v.t.) 139
じゃ then (41)
じゃ+unfavorable expression (158), (191)
じゃありません not be (20)
~じゃありませんか/ないですか strong assertion (172)
~じゃう colloquial variation of ~でしまう (380)
しゃかいがく(社会学) sociology 3, 11
じゃがいも potato 106
しゃしん(写真) photograph 391
しゃちょう(社長) president 30
じゃ, ちょっと excuse me for a while (51)
シャツ shirt 115
じゃ, また See you again. (42)
シャワー shower 92
しゅう(州) state 2
~しゅう(週) week 92
じゅう(十) ten (69)
じゅういちがつ(十一月) November 69, 106
~しゅうかん(週間) weeks (108)
しゅうしょくする(就職する) have a full-time job 292
しゅうに(週に) per week 91
じゆうに(自由に) freely 232

じゅうにがつ(十二月) December 108
じゅうぶんだ(十分だ) enough, sufficient 350
じゅうぶんに(十分に) fully 232
しゅうまつ(週末) weekend 78
じゅぎょう(授業) class (84)
じゅぎょうにでる(授業に出る) attend class 336
じゅぎょうりょう(授業料) tuition 336
しゅくだい(宿題) homework 37
しゅじん(主人) husband (161)
ジュース juice 208
しゅっしん(出身) native place 2
(~に)しゅっせきする(出席する) present at ~ 408
しゅっぱんしゃ(出版社) publishing co. 310
じゅんび(準備) preparation 202
じゅんびうんどう(準備運動) preparatory exercises 350
じゅんびする(準備する) prepare 350
しょうかい(紹介) introduction 19
しょうかいする(紹介する) introduce 19
しょうがくきん(奨学金) scholarship 171
しょうがっこう(小学校) elementary school 235, 376
しょうがない There is no way of doing ~ (316)
しょうしょう(少々) ☞少し, ちょっと 390
じょうずだ(上手だ) good at ~ 154, 233, 248
しょうせつ(小説) novel 200
しょうちする(承知する) ☞わかる (399)
ジョギング jogging 94
しょくじ(食事) meal, dinner 154
しょくじをする(食事をする) have a meals, dine 364
しょくちゅうどく(食中毒) food-poisoning 409
しょくどう(食堂) dining room/hall 49, 138
しょこ(書庫) book-stack 49
しょさい(書斎) study room 49
じょしがくせい(女子学生) female student 122

しらせ(知らせ) notice, news 67
しらせる(知らせる) inform 79, 216
しらべる(調べる) investigate 122, 139
しろい(白い) white 209
~じん(人) people of ~ (19)
しんごう(信号) traffic signal 324
じんこう(人口) population 107
ジーンズ jeans 193
じんせい(人生) life 233
しんせき(親戚) relatives 77
しんぞうびょう(心臓病) heart failure 409
しんぞうまひ(心臓まひ) heart attack 409
しんちょう(身長) height of body 325
しんぱいする(心配する) be worried, concerned about 202
しんぶん(新聞) newspaper 49
じんるいがく(人類学) anthropology 2

す

スイス Switzerland 20
すいせんじょう(推薦状) recommendation 278
ずいぶん(随分) extremely 27, (113)
すいようび(水曜日) Wednesday (71)
すう smoke, inhale 139
スカート skirt 193
スキー skiing 87
~すぎ past (70)
すきだ(好きだ) like, be fond of 122
すきな(好きな) favorite 122
~すぎる(過ぎる) too ~ (173)
すく become empty 216
すぐ right away 91
すくなくても(少なくても) at least (238)
すこし(少し) a little 37, 122
少しも…ない not at all (129)
すし *sushi* 100, 279
すずしい cool (41)
ずっと all the time, all through the way 202, (253)
ずっと far, much (282)

433

Japanese-English Glossary

スティーブン・フォスター Stephen Collins Foster 376
ステレオ stereo 62
〜ずに without 〜ing （268）
スーパーマーケット supermarket 49
すばらしい（素晴らしい） wonderful 249
スピードいはん（スピード違反） speeding violation 377
スペイン Spain 20
すみません I am sorry. 66
すみませんが Excuse me, but 〜 （42），（51）
すむ（住む） live （125），（238）
する ①do （83），97，（236） ②appearance （193） ③wear （193）
すんでいる（住んでいる） be living 122

せ

せ(せい)がたかい／ひくい（背が高い／低い） tall／short （189）
せいかくな（正確な） accurate, exact 248
せいかつする（生活する） live （238）
せいかつをする（生活をする） lead a life 364
せいじがく（政治学） political science 3, 11
せいぶ（西武） Seibu ［name of a department store］ 324
せいよう（西洋） West 376
せかい（世界） world 351
せき（席） seat 28
〜せずに without doing 〜 （268）
セーター sweater 171
せつめい（説明） explanation 187
ぜひ（是非） by all means （207）
せびろ（背広） suits 186
せん（千） thousand （70）
せんがっき（先学期） last term, previous term 336
せんげつ（先月） last month 67
せんしゅ（選手） player 194
せんしゅう（先週） last week 67
せんせい（先生） Prof. 〜, Mr./Ms. 〜 （30），（367）
ぜんぜん（全然）…ない not at all 93, （129）

せんたくする（洗濯する） wash 299
センチ centimeter 138
ぜんぶ（全部） all (of things) （266）
ぜんぶで（全部で） all （266），（356）
せんもん（専門） major, speciality 2

そ

そういう that kind of 194
そうかもしれない it may be so 278
そうじする（掃除する） clean （rooms） 171
〜そうだ looks 〜 （205），（353）
そうだんする（相談する） consult 262, 336
そうです ①That's right. （11） ②in that way, as you do （40）
〜そうです ［hearsay patterns］ （338）
そうですねえ Well, let me see. （95）
そこ there, that part （40）
そして and （223）
そだつ（育つ） grow （125）
そちら that one （280）
そつぎょうする（卒業する） graduate 154
そっち that one （280），（328）
そと（外） outside, foreign 365
そのN that N （28），（94）
そのとおりだ（その通りだ） That's exactly so. 248
そば buck-wheat noodles 208
そばや（そば屋） noodle shop 316
そふ（祖父） grandfather 217
ソフトボール softball （83）
そら（空） sky 350
そりゃあ contracted form of それは （299）
それ that one （28）
それ vs あれ referring to the third party （157）
それから and, after that 67, 106, （114）
それが Well, 〜 （207）
それで because of that （207），292
それでは then （395）

それと in addition 262
それとも or （208）
それに and, besides 187
それはいけませんね That's too bad. （223）
それまで until then （157）
そろそろしつれいする（そろそろ失礼する） I'd better be on my way. 367
ぞんじています（存じています） ⇩ 知っています （326）
そんな that kind of 189
そんなことありません It can't be. （82）
そんなに as you think 28

た

タイ Thailand 20
タイご（タイ語） Thai 19
タイじん（タイ人） Thai 19
〜たい ［desiderative］ （250）
〜だい（台） ［counter for machinery］ 106
ダイエット diet 210
だいがく（大学） college, univ. 11, 38
だいがくいん（大学院） graduate school 2
だいきらいな（大嫌いな） hate very much 248
たいくつな（退屈な） boring 122
だいじだ（大事だ） important 408
たいしたことはない（大したことはない） It's nothing to speak. （399）
たいじゅう（体重） weight (of body) 292, 325
だいじょうぶ（大丈夫） all right 350
だいすきだ（大好きだ） like very much 251
だいたい（大体） roughly （93）
だいどころ（台所） kitchen 49
だいぶ（大分） かなり, quite 292, 350
たいふう（台風） typhoon 376
タイプライター（タイプ） typewriter （31）
たいへん（大変） very （127）
たいへんな（大変な） (need) a lot of work 37, 66

434

和英索引

たかい(高い) ①[背が]tall 187
　②[ねだん(値段)が]expensive 27, 187, 278
たかはし(高橋) [a surname] 292
だから　therefore (96)
たくさん　a great deal 106
タクシー　taxi 165, 324
だけ　to this extent, as much as this (356)
～だけ　only ～ (266), (367)
たけい(竹井) [a surname] 154
だけじゃなくて　not only but also (412)
たしか(確か)　I may be wrong but ～ 324
だす(出す)　hand in, mail 154
ただ　but (176)
ただしい(正しい)　correct, right 37
ただのN　mere, simple (367)
たつ(立つ)　stand (125)
たって　but (355)
たつまき(竜巻)　tornado 376
たてもの(建物)　building 49
たてる(建てる)　construct, build 377
たとえ～ても／たって　even if ～ (355)
たとえば(例えば)　for example (282)
たなか(田中) [a surname] 19
たのしい(楽しい)　enjoyable 77, 122
たのしみにする(楽しみにする)　look forward to (194)
たのむ(頼む)　ask s.b. to do (239)
たばこ　cigarette 57, 107, 139
たぶん(多分)　probably 49
たべさせる(食べさせる)　make s.b. eat 263
たべもの(食べ物)　food 216
たべられる(食べられる)　passive form of 食べる (378)
たべる(食べる)　eat 91
たまご(卵)　egg 106
だめだ(駄目だ)　no good (239)
S1ため(に)S2　S1 is the purpose or goal of S2 (411)
～ために　in order to ～ (192)
CL1たらS2　→CL1たら(CL2) (414)

CL1たらCL2　if CL1, then CL2 (219), (252)
～たりする　do ～ and the like (379)
たりない(足りない)　be lacking 350
だれ(誰)　who 28, 57, 79
だれか(誰か)　somebody (79)
だれの(誰の)　whose 28
だれも(誰も)…ない　nobody (79)
～だろう　Pl. form of でしょう (155)
たんごひょう(単語表)　word list 2
だんしがくせい(男子学生)　male student 122
たんじょうび(誕生日)　birthday 106

ち

ちいさい(小さい)　small 67
ちかい(近い)　near (80)
ちかいうちに(近いうちに)　in the near future 364
ちがいます(違います)　It isn't right. / s. t. is different. 11, (95)
ちがう(違う)　be different, differ 56, 91
ちかく(近く)　near ～ (80)
[～に]ちかづく(近付く)　come close to 324
ちかみち(近道)　short-cut 154
チーズ　cheese 114
チーズケーキ　cheese cake 33, 52
ちち(父)　(my)father 78
ちっとも…ない　not at all (129)
ちゃ　contracted form of ては (297)
ちゃいろ(茶色)　brown 209
～ちゃう　contracted form of ～てしまう (176), (380)
ちゃんと　in the way it should be (223)
～ちゅう(中)　in(the middle of)～ (327)
～ちゅうに(中に)　(sometime) in ～ (315)
ちゅうがっこう(中学校)　junior high school 239
ちゅうかりょうり(中華料理)　Chinese cooking 252
ちゅうごく(中国)　China 19

ちゅうごくご(中国語)　Chinese 19
ちゅうごくじん(中国人)　Chinese 19
ちゅうねん(中年)　middle-age(d) 187
ちょう(兆)　trillion (114)
ちょうしがいい／わるい(調子がいい／悪い)　one's physical condition is good/bad (298)
ちょうどいい　just right 391
ちょくせつ(直接)　directly 336
ちょっと　①a little 28, 122
　②for a moment 37, (51)

つ

ついたち(一日)　first day 110
ついて(→～について) (298)
つかう(使う)　use 116, (125), 158
つかれる(疲れる)　get tired 91, 216
～つき(月)　months 92
つぎ(次)　next 216
つきあたり(突き当たり)　dead end 325
つぎに(次に)　next 310
つぎの(次の)　next (328)
[電気が]つく　be switched on 139
[～に]つく(着く)　arrived at 310
つくえ(机)　desk 57
つくる(作る)　make (97)
[名前を]つける(付ける)　to name 337
つたえる(伝える)　pass words to, relay a message 310
～って　①called (82) ②I hear (221), (338)
～って→というのは (238)
[～に]つとめる(勤める)　work for 292
つま(妻)　wife (161)
つまらない　boring 122
つめたい　cold(tangible) 293
つもりだ　frame of mind (157)
つもる(積もる)　accumulate 138
つれて[いく／くる](連れて)　take／bring (268)

Japanese-English Glossary

て

て→～って (82)
て(手) hand 351
〔何〕て colloquial variation of quatational と (367)

～て [causal] (251)
～て＋VP and (40),(143)
～てある [state] (174)
～て〔も〕いい It's all right to do ～ (141)
～ている [progressive／state] (142),(174),(189)
～ておく do ～ in advance (172)
～てから after ～ing (159)
～てください(て下さい) please ～ (142)
～てください(て下さい) [Causative] let/allow(to) do ～ (413)
～てくる continuation up to the present (295),(313)
～てくる indicating the direction (313)
～てくれませんか please ～ 59
～てしまう do ～ completely, do ～ regretfully (172)
～てすみません sorry for ～ (142)
～てみる try and see (172)
～てもらう receive a favor (205),(236)
～てもらえる can receive a favor (236)

で て-form of です (4),(39)
Nで(車で) by means of ～ (13)
で [cause](病気で学校を休みました) (94)
で [place of action](東京で生まれた) (71),(93)
で [within](一時間で行きます) (147)
で [unit of the numbers](三本で百円) (266)
で＋favorable statement (191)

～でございます 🅟です (394)
～でしょうか more humble way of asking questions (175),(392)

ていこくホテル(帝国ホテル) Imperial Hotel 218
でかける(出掛ける) go out, set out 78,(268),310
てがみ(手紙) a letter 138,154
〔～に〕てがみをだす(手紙を出す) send a letter(to) 154,310
〔～が〕できあがる be completed, be ready (414)
できたら if possible (283)
できる ①can do ～ (221),(234) ②something has come into being (313) ③be good at, be smart, be bright (340)
できれば if possible (283)
でした perfect form of です (38)
でしょう presumptive of です (30),(60),(144),(155)
です [copula] (3),(11),(38),(50),(110)
ですか です＋か (11)
ですね [interjection] (326)
てちょう(手帳) memo-book 262
てつがく(哲学) philosophy 3
てつだう(手伝う) ①help, assist 350 ②help s.b. do ～ 263
てつやする(徹夜する) stay up all night 365
テニス tennis 83
では＋unfavorable statement (191)
デパート department store 94, 253
てまえ(手前) this side 324
～ても [indicating limits] (238)
でも [conjunctive] 77,170, (356)
Nでも things like ～ (95),(207)
〔誰／何／…〕でも whoever, anybody, whatever, anything (313)
てらやま(寺山) [a surname] 278
でる(出る) get out 154
〔Nに〕でる(出る) attend 78
テレビ television 61,78
てんき(天気) weather (41)

でんき(電気) light, electricity 139
でんきや(電気屋) home appliance shop 316,325
てんきよほう(天気予報) weather forcast 177,350
でんごん(伝言) message 310
でんしゃ(電車) electric train 154,279
でんしレンジ(電子レンジ) microwave oven 218
てんぷら tempura 100
でんわ(電話) telephone, call 57, 154
　電話する phone, call 91
でんわばんごう(電話番号) telephone number (267)
〔～から〕電話がある there is a call from ～ 311
〔～と〕電話ではなす(話す) talk to ～ over the telephone 311
〔～に〕電話をかける／する call 311
〔～が〕電話をきる(切る) ～ hang up the phone 311
〔～が〕電話をくれる ～ call 311
〔～が〕電話をしてくる ～ call 311
〔～に／から〕電話をもらう receive a call from ～ 311

と

と [quotational](～と言う／思う) (155),(190)
と [conjunctive](春になると) (218)
と [mutuality](田中さんと会う) (283)
と (はっきりと) (283)
と (NとN) N and N (94)
と (S1とS2) [cause and effect] (218),(327)

Sとありがたい(Sと有り難い) [polite way of asking something] (397)
Sといいですね wish, desire, advice (340)
Nといいます named ～ (4)
という(と言う) [quoting a person] (312)

N1 という N2　N2 called N1　(51),(128)
N というのは　what is called N　(238)
〜というはなしだ(〜という話だ)　The story is 〜　(338)
〜とおもいます(〜と思います)　I think 〜　(81),(155)
S ときいた(S と聞いた)　I heard S, it is said that S.　(338)
〜とのことです(との事です)　[quoting s.b.]　(315)

〜ど(度)　times　(108)
ドイツ　Germany　20
どう　what, how　(60),(175)
どういう　what kind of 〜　(194)
とうきゅうデパート(東急デパート)　[name of the department store]　324
とうきょう(東京)　Tokyo [Lit. Eastern Capital]　2,(399)
どうして　why　(30)
どうしても　by any means　(177)
どうしました　What's the matter?　(59)
どうします　What will you do?　(81)
どうぞ　please　(146),(175),(268)
どうぞごしんぱいなく(御心配なく)　Leave it to me without worrying.　(268)
どうぞよろしく　How do you do?　(21)
どうでしたか　How was 〜?　(41)
どうでしょう　Well, I don't know.　(60)
どうですか　like what/how　(40)
とうにょうびょう(糖尿病)　dibetes　409
どうぶつえん(動物園)　zoo　263
どうも　[indicator of negative sentence following]　(114)
どうやって　how　(223)
とおい(遠い)　far　(80),202
とおか(十日)　ten day, tenth day　(69)
とおく(遠く)　far [place]　(80)
とおり(通り)　street　324
とおる(通る)　take a way　154
〜とか〜とか　like 〜 or 〜　(381)

〜とき(時)　time(when), When 〜　(156)
ときどき(時々)　sometimes　(93)
とくべつだ(特別だ)　special　390
とけい(時計)　watch, clock　178, 263
どこ　where　11,(40),(79),(339)
どこか　somewhere　(79)
どこも…ない　nowhere　(79)
ところ(所)　place　37,(51),122
〜ところだ　(174)
ところで　by the way　(41)
としょかん(図書館)　library　49
とちゅう(途中)　on the way　202
どちら　which of the two　(22),(280),(328)
どっち　which of the two　(280),(328)
とっても　colloquial variation of とても　(413)
とても　very　(127),170
とても〜ない　(seemingly)impossible to 〜　(356)
どなた　who　(254)
となり(隣)　next　279
となりのうち(隣の家)　the house next to 〜　279,337
どの N　which N　(28),(94)
どのへん(どの辺)　where, around where　324
とぶ(飛ぶ)　fly　(125),138
トマト　tomato　115
とまる(止まる)　stop　202
とまる(泊まる)　stay over-night at 〜　218
[〜を]とめる(止める)　stop, halt　324
ともだち(友達)　friend　138
ともだちができる(友達ができる)　make friends　310
[〜と]ともだちになる(友達になる)　become friends(with)　310
どようび(土曜日)　Saturday　(71)
とられる(取られる)　be collected, be taken, be stolen　377
とる(取る)　take off　193
ドル　dollars　109
どれ　which one　(28)
とんでもない　Not at all.　(381)
どんな　what kind of　(189)

な

なあ　[sentence final particle]　(59),(177)
〜ないで　[negative て-form] without 〜ing　(236)
〜ないでください(〜ないで下さい)　Please don't 〜　(143)
〜ないといけない　must 〜　(282),(366)
ないよう(内容)　contents　1
なおす(直す)　correct　390
〜なおす(直す)　do 〜 again　(176)
なおる(治る)　recover　248
なか(中)　in, inside　(58)
ながい(長い)　long　67,186
ながい(長井)　[a surname]　248
なかがわ(中川)　[a surname]　310
ながされる(流される)　be washed away　376
なかなか…ない　not easily　(267)
なかむら(中村)　[a surname]　91,184
〜ながら　while 〜　(144)
なきごえ(泣き声)　cry, sobbing　337
なくす　lose　377
なくちゃ　contracted form of なくては　(297)
なくて　[て-form of ない] and, but　(355)
〜なければならない　must　(204),(366)
〜なさい　[imperative]　(314)
なさる　する　(234),(356),395
なつ(夏)　summer　78
なつやすみ(夏休み)　summer vacation　78
なな(七)　seven　(69)
ななめまえ(斜め前)　diagonal　325
なに(何)　what　27,79
なにいろ(何色)　what color　57
なにか(何か)　something　(79)
なにしろ(何しろ)　above all　248
なにも…ない(何も)　nothing　(79)
なにようび(何曜日)　what day of the week　(71)
なまえ(名前)　name　11
なら(奈良)　Nara(old capital)　122,(399)
〜なら　if, when 〜　(221),(235),(352)

Japanese-English Glossary

ならう(習う)　learn　(176)
なる　become, get　(218), (236), (294), (414)
なるべく　as ～ as possible　232
なん(何)(→なに)　27
なんか(何課)　which lesson　67
N なんか　things like N　(254)
なんかい(何回)　how many times　92, (129)
なんがつ(何月)　what month　(113)
なんさい(何才)　how old　106
なんじ(何時)　what time　(70)
なんだか(何だか)　somehow, for some reason　(297)
なんで(何で)　Why, By what　(413)
なんですか(何ですか)　What is ～?　11, 29
なんといいますか(何といいますか)　What do you call ～?　11
なんというN(何というN)　What's the name or title?　(51)
なんども(何度も)　more than a few times　(129)
なんにち(何日)　how many days, what day of the month　(113)
なんにんも(何人も)　not a few people　(129)
なんねん(何年)　what year　(113)
なんぷん(何分)　how many minutes　67
なんページ(何ページ)　which page, how many pages　67
なんまいも(何枚も)　not a few sheets　(129)

に

に　[locative particle]　(50)
に　[temporal particle]　(68), (93)
に　[destination, goal, purpose]　(80), (94), (144)
に　[per](週に一度)　(96)
に　[causal](漢字に困る)　(177)
に　[criterion](私には難しい)　(191)
～について　concerning, about　(298)
～にまにあう(間に合う)　be in time for　365

N によって　depending on N　(95)
N によると　according to ～　(352)
～によろしく　Say hello to ～, Give my regards to ～　364
に(二)　two, second　(69)
にぎやかな(賑やかな)　lively　77, 292
～にくい　difficult to ～　(158)
にし(西)　west　(128)
にしかわ(西川)　[a surname]　202
にじかん(二時間)　two hours　(41)
にち(日)→ひ(日)
にちようび(日曜日)　Sunday　(71)
にっけいアメリカじん(日系アメリカ人)　Japanese American　19
にっぽん(日本)→にほん
にねんせい(二年生)　sophomore　2
にほん(日本)　Japan　19
にほんご(日本語)　Japanese language　11, 19, 27
にほんじん(日本人)　Japanese people　19
にほんじんがっこう(日本人学校)　Japanese school　410
ニュージーランド　New Zealand　20
～にん(人)　[counter for people]　(108)
にんきがある(人気がある)　popular　248

ぬ

ぬぐ(脱ぐ)　take off　(193)
ぬすまれる(盗まれる)　be stolen　377

ね

ね　①[sentence final particle]　(21), (41), (159)
　　②[interjection]　(326)
ねえ　[sentence final particle]　(177)
ネクタイをする　wear a tie　186
ねこ(猫)　cat　106
ねこのこ(猫の子)　kitten　106
ねだん(値段)　price　106

ねつがある(熱がある)　have a fever　408
ねぼうする(寝坊する)　oversleep　249
ねむい(眠い)　sleepy　365
ねむくなる(眠くなる)　become sleepy　217
ねむれる(眠れる)　can sleep　217
ねる(寝る)　sleep, go to bed, lie　91
～ねん(年)　year　92, (108)
～ねんかん(年間)　years　(108)

の

の　[possessive]　(3)
の　[deletion of a noun]　(31), (126), (380)
の　[nominalizer]　(127), (380)
の　[appositive]　(317)
～のあいだで(～の間で)　among ～　376
のうそっちゅう(脳卒中)　stroke　409
N のことなんですが　(175)
～ので　since, as　(158)
～のです　[explanatory sentence]　(146)
ノート　notebook　28, 57
のど　throat　216
のどがかわく　get thirsty　(222)
～のに　although　(206), (296), (315)
のみもの(飲み物)　drinks　107
のむ(飲む)　drink　92
のりもの(乗り物)　transportation　122, 279
のる(乗る)　get on, ride　154
のんびりする　get relaxed　187

は

は　[topic-marker]　(3)
は　[contrastive は]　(50), (58), (93)
は(歯)　teeth　351
は(歯)をみがく　brush teeth　92
バー　bar　85
～ば　[ば-form]　(220)
～ばいいんです　All you have to do is ～　(221)
はい　yes(that's right.)　(11), (392)

438

はい Here you are. (175)
はい yes(I am listening.) (51)
〜はい(杯) [counter for things in cups or bowls] (108)
はいいろ(灰色) gray 209
はいえん(肺炎) pneumonia 408
はいけんする(拝見する) ☞見る (399)
はいざら(灰皿) ash-tray 57
ハイヒールをはく wear high-heels 186
はいる(入る) enter 98
〔泥棒が〕はいる(入る) (thief)enter, rob, steal 377
〜ばかりだ have just done 〜 (218), 377
〔くつを〕はく put on (193)
〜はこ(箱) [counter for boxes] (108)
はし(箸) chop sticks (5), 154
はし(橋) bridge (5), 324, 376
はし(端) a tip, edge (5)
はじまる(始まる) begin(v.i.) 57
はじめて(初めて) for the first time 249
はじめに(初めに) at first 310
はじめまして How do you do? (21)
はじめる(始める) begin(v.t.) 37, 67, 97
V. stem＋はじめる(始める) start 〜ing (354)
はしる(走る) run 98
バス bus 279
バスのていりゅうじょ(バスの停留所) bus stop 325
バスケットボール basketball 194
〔めがねを〕はずす take off (193)
〜はずだ [conjecture] (265)
〜はずはない there is no possibility of 〜 266, 339
パスポート passport 111
パーセント percent (108)
パーソナル・コンピューター(パソコン) personal computer (31)
〔〜で〕はたらく(働く) work at 〜 336
はち(八) eight (69)
はっ Pardon? (13)
はつおん(発音) pronunciation 82, 248
はっきり clearly (175)
ばっきん(罰金) fine 377

パーティー party 71
パトカー police car 127
はな(鼻) nouse 351
はな(花) flowers, blooms 262
はなされる(話される) passive form of 話す (378)
はなす(話す) speak 97, (125), 138
はなせる(話せる) potential of 話す 232
バナナ banana 100
はなや(花屋) florist 316
はは(母) (my)mother 78
はやい(早い) fast, quick (94)
はやし(林) [a surname] 5
〔ひげを〕はやす(生やす) grow 186
〔〜が〕はやる prevail, be popular 337
はら(腹) stomach, belly 351
はらがたつ(腹が立つ) get angry 252
はらう(払う) pay 279
はらえる(払える) can pay 336
ハリケーン hurricane 376
はる(春) spring 78
はれる(晴れる) clear up 139
〔〜が〕はれる(腫れる) get swollen 350
〜はん(半) half (70)
ばん(晩) evening 91
〜ばん(番) [counter for order] (108)
パン bread 302
ばんごはん(晩御飯) dinner 92
はんたいがわ(反対側) opposite side 325
〔〜に〕はんたいする(反対する) oppose 〜 292
バンド band 193
ハンバーガー hamburger 50
パンや(パン屋) bakery 295, 316

ひ

ひ(日) day 37, 92, 122
ひによって(日によって) it depends on the day (95)
ひかく(比較) comparison 278
ひがし(東) east (128)
ひがしアジアけんきゅう(東アジア研究) East Asian Studies 3

ひがしやま(東山) [a surname] 186
〜ひき(匹) [counter for small animals, fish] (108)
ひきうける(引き受ける) take responsibilities 262
ひきだし drawers 57
〔辞書を〕ひく(引く) consult (125)
〔風邪を〕ひく(引く) catch cold 218
〔楽器を〕ひく(弾く) play (238)
ひげ moustache, beard, whisker 186
ひざ(膝) knee 351
ピザ pizza 115
ひさしぶり(久し振り) first time in a long while 202
ひじ(肘) elbow 351
ビジネス・スクール business school 3
びじゅつし(美術史) art history 3
ひじょうに(非常に) very 216, 336
ひだり(左) left (58)
びっくりする get surprised 252
ひつような(必要な) necessary 278, 336
S＋必要はない There is no need to S. (366)
ひと(人) person 49
ひどい terrible, cruel 28, 377
ひどく terribly 127
ひとつ(一つ) one (108), (110)
ひとつきほど(一月ほど) just about a month ＝一か月くらい 292
ひとり(一人) one person 122
ひとりで(一人で) alone, without any help 292
ひゃく(百) one hundred (70)
〔〜を〕ひやす(冷やす) to cool, chilly, refrigerate 350
ひょう(表) list 1
びょういん(病院) hospital 203
びょうき(病気) illness 156, 171
病気はしたくない I don't want to get sick(due to my carelessness). (254)
ひる(昼) noon, daytime 92
ビール beer 93
ひるごはん(昼御飯) lunch 92

Japanese-English Glossary

ひろい(広い) ①spacious 278, 293 ②wide, broad 324
びんぼうだ(貧乏だ) poor 351
ピンポン pingpong 81

ふ

ふうとう(封筒) envelope 57
ふうん [exclamatory expression] (356)
ふえる(増える) increase 292
ふきそくだ(不規則だ) irregular, unregulated 365
ふく(服) clothes 171
ふく play(wind instruments) (238)
〔風が〕ふく(吹く) blow 296
ふくざつだ(複雑だ) complicated 390
ふくしゅうする(復習する) review 249
ふじさん(富士山) Mt. Fuji 325
ふたつ(二つ) two items (108), (110)
ふたつみっつ(二つ三つ) a couple of 177
ふたはこ(二箱) two boxes 106
ふたり(二人) two persons 122
ふだん(普段) usually 187
ふつう(普通) usually (93)
ふつうのN(普通のN) ordinary, normal 408
ぶっか(物価) prices 278
ふとった(太った) fat 187
ふとる(太る) gain weight 187
ふとん(布団) futon 293
ふとんや(布団屋) futon-shop 316
ふゆ(冬) winter 78
ブラウス blouse 299
ふられる(降られる) suffering passive (379)
フランス France 20
ふりがな furigana (4)
ふりそうだ(降りそうだ) It is likely to rain. (353)
プリンター printer 27
ふる(降る) fall 138
ふるい(古い) old 27
ふるほんや(古本屋) second-hand book store 268
ふろ(風呂) bath 92
  ふろにはいる(風呂に入る) take a bath 92
プロ professional 302
ふろや(風呂屋) public bath 316
ふん／ぶん(分) minutes (70)
ぶんがく(文学) literature 3
ぶんぽう(文法) grammar 1
ぶんぽうぐ(文房具) stationery items 106
ぶんぽうぐや(文房具屋) stationery shop 106, 316

へ

へ [particle for direction] (80)
べいこく(米国) U.S. of America 19
米国人 American 19
ページ page 67, (109)
へただ(下手だ) poor in/at (237)
ベッド bed 164
ベトナム Vietnam 20
へや(部屋) room 138
へる(減る) decrease 292
ベルト belt 193
べんきょうする(勉強する) study (83), 91
べんごし(弁護士) lawyer 293
へんじ(返事) reply, answer 232
へんな(変な) strange, absurd, funny 154
べんりな(便利な) convenient (123), 279

ほ

〔～の〕ほう(方) comparing two things (280), (340)
〔～の〕ほう(方) one of the two 268
～ほうがいい(方がいい) should do ～ (173)
ほうりつがく(法律学) law 3
ほかの(他の) other ～ 248
ぼく(僕) I[male] 138, (160), (393)
ポケット pocket 61
ほしい(欲しい) ①Nが欲しい I want N. (111) ②N2に＋て-form＋欲しい N1 would like N2 to do ～ (313)
ほっとする [breathe a sigh of relief]be a load of one's mind 408
ほど [approximate quantity] (297)
～ほど(程) ⓟくらい (399)
～ほど…ない not as … as ～ (282)
ほどのものだ as good as to ～ (415)
ほとんど(殆ど) almost all, hardly any (93)
ボールペン ball-point pen 57
ほん(本) book 28
～ほん(本) [counter for narrow long things] (108)
ほんとうに(本当に) really 28, 77 cf. 本当は～＝The fact is ～
ほんや(本屋) book store 316

ま

まあ well (237)
まあ sort of 27
まい(毎)[＋日，月，年 etc.] every (day, month, year, etc.) 92
まいにち(毎日) everyday 92
～まい(枚) [counter for flat things] (108)
まいにちしんぶん(毎日新聞) the Mainichi (51)
まいります(参ります) ⓟ行く，来る 395
〔～に〕まいる(参る) tired out, be exhausted, have hard times with ～ (299), 362
マイル mile 109
まえ(前) before (58)
〔～の〕まえに(前に) [conjunctive] before (58), (156), 170
まがりかど(曲がり角) corner 325
〔～を〕曲がる turn, curve 324
まくら(枕) pillow 293
まさこ(正子) [a female given name] 390
まじめだ(真面目だ) serious, diligent (254)
マージャン(麻雀) mahjong 351
～ましょう [volitional] 36, (156)
まず first of all (316)
まずい [for food]terrible, tasteless 38
まずしい(貧しい) poor 294

440

ませ imperative form of 〜ます（316）
また again 37
まだ still, not yet （146）
まだ…ない not yet 170
またせる（待たせる） keep s.b. waiting （206）
まち（町） town 154
まちがい（間違い） mistake 365
まちがいなく（間違いなく） without a mistake （298）
まつ（待つ） wait 97, 138, 206
〜まつ（末） end of 〜 122
まつかわ（松川） [a surname] 262
まっすぐ（真っ直ぐ） straight 324
まつだ（松田） [a surname] 154
まったく（全く） completely 232, 248
マッチ match 62
まつばら（松原） [a surname] 336
まで till （70）,（160）
までに by （315）
まど（窓） window 138
まにあう（→〜にまにあう） 365
まるで〜みたいだ just like 〜 （297）
まん（万） ten thousand （114）

み

みえる（見える） come into sight （340）,（354）
[歯を]みがく brush 92
みぎ（右） right （58）
みじかい（短い） short 67, 187
みず（水） water 154, 262
みずいろ（水色） light blue 209
〜みたい It seems that S （145）
〜みたい like 〜 （295）,（352）
みち（道） road, street, way 324
みっか（三日） three days, third day （110）
みつかる（見つかる） be found （267）, 336
みつける（見つける） find 249
みっつ（三つ） three （110）
みてください（見て下さい） Please look at 〜 37
みどりいろ（緑色） green 209
みなさん everybody （71）
みなみ（南） south （128）
みみ（耳） ear 351

みょうばん（明晩） ⇒明日の晩 （399）
みる（見る） see 57
ミルク milk 202
みんな everyone, all 77
みんよう（民謡） traditional folk songs 376

む

むかし（昔） long time ago, in the past 376
むこうがわ（向こう側） the other side 324
むずかしい（難しい） difficult 37
むすこ（息子） son （269）
むすめ（娘） daughter （269）
むね（胸） chest, breast 351
むらさきいろ（紫色） purple 209
むりだ（無理だ） hardly possible （238）

め

め（目） eye 187, 351, 409
〜め（目） 〜th （267）
めがね（眼鏡） glasses 189
めざましどけい（目覚まし時計） alarm clock 365
めしあがる（召し上がる） eat, drink ⬆ （208）, 234, 395
めをとおす（目を通す） take a quick look 365

も

も too, either （59）
も as many(much)as （112）
も even （192）
N1 も N2 も both N1 and N2, neither N1 nor N2 80
もう already, still 37,（146）
もう [with numerals]another 〜 （266）
もうします（申します） ⬇言う 232,（393）
もうすこし（もう少し） a little more 217
もくてきち（目的地） destination 324
もくようび（木曜日） Thursday （71）
もし if, suppose 216

もしもし hello[telephone] （59）, 138
もしもし Excuse me. （59）
もし, よかったら if you don't mind （299）
もちろん（勿論） of course, needless to say 77, 184
もつ（持つ） hold, carry 171
もったいない waste 216
もっていく（持っていく） take 138
もっと more 216
ももいろ（桃色） pink 209
もらう receive （205）,（250）,（264）
もらえる can receive 336
もり（森） ①[a surname] 138 ②forest
もんだい（問題） question, problem 170

や

〜や（屋） [suffix showing the kind of store, shops] 106,（316）
N1 や N2 N1 and N2 and the like, things like N1 and N2 （80）,（94）
やあ [casual greeting among men] （253）
やおや（八百屋） green grocer 316
やきゅう（野球） baseball 233
[〜と]やくそくする（約束する） promise s.b. 310
やさしい easy 38
やさしい（優しい） kind, considerate 336
やすい（安い） inexpensive 28
V. stem＋やすい easy to 〜 （158）
やすく（安く） inexpensively 106
やすみ（休み） day-off, holiday, vacation 77
やすむ（休む） take a rest （84）
授業を休む skip class （84）
やせた slim 186
やせる lose weight 186
やちん（家賃） rent 278
やっと finally （254）
やはり as expected （381）
やまだ（山田） [a surname] 37
やむ stop[rain, snow] 139
やめる（辞める） resign, quit 187

Japanese-English Glossary

やる ＝する 154
やる give⬇ （265）

ゆ

ゆうがた(夕方)　time of sunset, dusk　350
ゆうべ　last night　365
ゆき(雪)　snow　138
ゆび(指)　finger　351

よ

よ　[sentence final particle]　(30),(159)
〜よう　Pl. vol. of Group II verbs and 来る　(156),(173)
ようじ(用事)　errand, bussiness　91
S＋ようだ　It seems S. （352）
S＋ように＋と言う／頼む　tell／ask to do S　(380)
〜ようになる　start to 〜　(235)
よかった　I am relieved!　(59)
よかったら　If it is OK, If you don't mind　(299)
よく　often, well　27,(93)
よくない　plain form of よくありません　(68)
よくわかりませんが　I'm not sure but 〜　(29)
よこ(横)　by, beside　324
よこい(横井)　[a surname]　232
よごす(汚す)　soil, make dirty　377
よこはま(横浜)　Yokohama [place name]　122
よしだ(吉田)　[a surname]　77
よしゅうする(予習する)　prepare for class　249
よって(→N によって)　(95)
よてい(予定)　schedule, plan　390
よねんせい(四年生)　senior　3
よばれる(呼ばれる)　be called, summoned　376
よふかしをする(夜更かしをする)　be around until late at night　364
よみうりしんぶん(読売新聞)　the Yomiuri　(51)
よみかた(読み方)　how to read　170
よむ(読む)　read　97

よめる(読める)　potential of 読む　232
よる(夜)　night　207
[〜に]よる(寄る)　drop in 〜　336
よる(→N によると)　(352)
よろこぶ(喜ぶ)　look happy, be pleased　338
よろしい　formal equivalent of い い　(284),(398),391
よろしく　in favorable way　(268)
よろしく(→〜によろしく)　364
よん(四)　four　(69)
よんまんえん(四万円)　forty thousand yen　(114)

ら行

らいげつ(来月)　next month　(42),67
らいしゅう(来週)　next week　(42),67
らいねん(来年)　next year　67
らくに(楽に)　with ease　310
S＋らしい　It seems S　(352)
リポート　paper, report　170
りょう(寮)　dormitory　248
りょうしん(両親)　parents　77
りょうりする(料理する)　cook　91
りょくちゃ(緑茶)　green tea　202
りょこう(旅行)　travel　83,377
りんご　apple　107
るす(留守)　being away from home　310
れい(例)　example　49
れいぞうこ(冷蔵庫)　refrigerator　325
れきし(歴史)　history　390
れきしがく(歴史学)　history　3
レストラン　restaurant　101
レモン　lemon　115
れんしゅう(練習)　practice, drills　2,122
ろく(六)　six　(69)
ロシア　Russia　19
ロシアご(ロシア語)　Russian　19
ロシアじん(ロシア人)　Russian　19
ロースクール　law-school　2
ろんぶん(論文)　thesis　202,233

わ行

わ　[sentense-final particle]　(112),(117),(159)
ワイン　wine　93
わかい(若い)　young　77
わかりました　I understand.　3
わかりません　I don't know. I can't understand.　27
わかる　understand, know　28
わけ　reason, cause　251
〜わけじゃない　do not mean 〜　(251),(355)
〜わけにはいかない　can not 〜 for social reason　(236)
わすれる(忘れる)　forget, leave behind　26,139
わたくし(私)　I　(393)
わたし(私)　I　2,(160),(393)
わたしの(私の)　mine　28
わたす(渡す)　pass　217
わたなべ(渡辺)　[a surname]　350
わたる(渡る)　cross　324
ワード・プロセッサー(ワープロ)　word-processor　(31)
わりあい(割合)　relatively　232
わるい(悪い)　causing trouble, bad　77
わるいですよ(悪いですよ)　I am causing inconvenience for you.　(82)
を　[object-marker]　(58)
を　from, through　(157)

ん

〜んじゃないですか　I guess 〜　(193)
〜んでしょう　[well-founded conjecture]　(283)
S＋んでしょうか　I wonder if S　(339)
〜んです　[explanatory sentence]　(143)

CPSIA information can be obtained at www.ICGtesting.com
Printed in the USA
BVOW061411300911

272476BV00002B/1/P

9 781934 269244